THE LEGACY OF
EGYPT

Panorama of Egypt, from the frontispiece to the first edition of the
Déscription de l'Égypte

THE LEGACY OF

EGYPT

SECOND EDITION

EDITED BY

J. R. HARRIS

OXFORD

AT THE CLARENDON PRESS

1971

Oxford University Press, Ely House, London W. 1

GLASGOW NEW YORK TORONTO MELBOURNE WELLINGTON
CAPE TOWN IBADAN NAIROBI DAR ES SALAAM LUSAKA ADDIS ABABA
DELHI BOMBAY CALCUTTA MADRAS KARACHI LAHORE DACCA
KUALA LUMPUR SINGAPORE HONG KONG TOKYO

PRINTED IN GREAT BRITAIN
AT THE UNIVERSITY PRESS, OXFORD
BY VIVIAN RIDLER
PRINTER TO THE UNIVERSITY

CONTENTS

EDITORIAL NOTE

THE transcription of hieroglyphs in the present volume follows the usage of A. H. Gardiner's *Egyptian Grammar* (3rd ed., Oxford, 1957), from which the table overleaf has been adapted.

The titles of the following periodicals have been abbreviated throughout.

ASAE   *Annales du Service des antiquités de l'Égypte* (Cairo)
BIFAO   *Bulletin de l'Institut français d'archéologie orientale du Caire* (Cairo)
JEA   *The Journal of Egyptian Archaeology* (London)
ZÄS   *Zeitschrift für ägyptische Sprache und Altertumskunde* (Leipzig)

THE 'ALPHABET'

SIGN	TRANS-LITERATION	APPROXIMATE SOUND-VALUE
	ꜣ	the glottal stop heard at the commencement of German words beginning with a vowel, ex. *der Adler*.
	i	usually consonantal *y*; at the beginning of words sometimes identical with ꜣ.
(1) (2) \\	y	*y*
	ꜥ	a guttural sound unknown to English
	w	*w*
	b	*b*
	p	*p*
	f	*f*
	m	*m*
	n	*n*
	r	*r*
	h	*h* as in English
	$ḥ$	emphatic *h*
	$ḫ$	like *ch* in Scottish *loch*
	$ẖ$	perhaps like *ch* in German *ich*
(1) (2)	s	*s*
	$š$	*sh*
	$ḳ$	backward *k*; rather like our *q* in *queen*
	k	*k*
	g	hard *g*
	t	*t*
	$ṯ$	originally *tsh* (*č* or *tj*)
	d	*d*
	$ḏ$	originally *dj* and also a dull emphatic *s* (Hebrew צ)

LIST OF PLATES

The frontispiece to the first edition of the *Déscription de l'Égypte*, from the copy in the Peet Memorial Library, The Queen's College, Oxford. By courtesy of the Provost and Fellows *Frontispiece*

At end

1. The Egyptian Hall, Piccadilly. From a print of 1828

2. Canina's Egyptian portico in the gardens of the Villa Borghese. Photograph by courtesy of E. Harris

3. The so-called metrological relief. By courtesy of the Department of Antiquities, Ashmolean Museum, Oxford

4. *a*. Dyad of Menkaurē. By courtesy of the Museum of Fine Arts, Boston
   b. Statue of Antinous from Hadrian's villa. Photograph by Anderson

5. *a*. An Egyptian lion of Nectanebo I. Photograph by Anderson
   b. A Cosmati adaptation in the portal of SS. Apostoli, Rome. Photograph by Mlle A. H. M. Roullet, Paris

6. Pedestal in imperial porphyry in the form of a sistrum handle. Photograph by Gabinetto Fotografico Nazionale, Rome

ERRATA

List of Plates (p. ix)

   5 *b. Read* Photograph by courtesy of Mlle A. H. M. Roullet. . .

List of Text Figures (p. xi)

   6. *Read* The alchemical apparatus of 'Cleopatra' (*sic*). From *Journal of Hellenic Studies, l* . . .

LIST OF TEXT FIGURES

INTRODUCTION

To everyone who tours the Nile, or pauses in a museum, or turns the pages of a book on Egyptian art or culture, some portion of the varied heritage of ancient Egypt may be said to have been communicated. Yet, in the main, this is a superficial and ephemeral legacy which can become real only when the recipient is capable of giving his personal insight meaningful expression. There is, in other words, a fundamental difference in the abuse of Egyptian paraphernalia by a suburban 'witch' and, for example, Cocteau's intellectual fascination with the potential symbolism of the inlaid eye. The true heritage of Egypt is, indeed, that which down the centuries has become woven almost imperceptibly into the never ending web of man's experience. And if particular emphasis is laid upon the Western European tradition this is to some extent inevitable since it is chiefly here that the transmission is documented—though, even so, the Egyptian influence is by no means comparable to that of Greece and Rome.

Like Caesar's Gaul, the mainstream of this heritage may be divided into three: the legacy to the three millennia of the ancient world, that to the long and crucial period from late antiquity through to the eighteenth century, and that to the years from the rediscovery of Egypt up to the present. Such a division appears to ignore historical perspective, but is in fact consistent with the recognition of two important turning-points—the elaboration of the *interpretatio romana* in the Imperial period, which lasted down beyond the Renaissance in the West (and had a bearing on the transmission of ideas in the Arab Orient and, via Meroë, to Africa), and the emergence of an academic interest in Egyptian antiquities during the eighteenth century, on which the seal was set by the discovery of the essential key to the hieroglyphs.

A major problem in dealing with any aspect of legacy is that of distinguishing between coincidence and continuity. (The fact that mesh and fishnet are again attributes of velvet fashion is scarcely to be interpreted as a direct consequence of Snofru's evident predilection.) The difficulty is most acute in the case of the ancient world, for, while it is reasonable to suppose a degree of Egyptian influence in certain fields, notably medicine and socio-legal institutions, the fact is often impossible to establish simply because no documents exist for comparison with the Egyptian sources, and even where there are definite parallels, as in tech-nology, the available indications may not substantiate a real connection. The absence of any tangible evidence for the dis-semination of popular literature is especially tantalizing, since it is probable that many a well-known theme originated in Egypt and that, through the Mediterranean world and Ionia, Egyptian story-telling had an important bearing on the development of the Hellenistic novel. Moreover, existing analogies in Hebrew (see Chapter 10) would suggest that, just as quotations from the Bible or from Shakespeare have now become common parlance, so sundry Egyptian phrases may have passed into general usage. '*Exegi monumentum aere perennius*' will not be the only line to echo a pharaonic commonplace. The same uncertainty exists in the realm of folk belief, though without doubt there are numerous survivals in modern Egypt and Africa. More problematic is the tracing back of various widespread superstitions—the esoteric significance of numbers (in particular seven), the mystique of interpreting dreams, the conventions of image magic, or the recognition of a Satanic/Sethian colour in individuals. The one substantial legacy to the ancient world is that of Egyptian architec-tural and artistic elements, freely adapted to the point of parody in Phoenicia and the Levant, and spreading thence throughout the Mediterranean and to mainland Greece.[1] Features such as the

[1] See in general F. W. von Bissing, *Der Anteil der ägyptischen Kunst am Kunstleben der Völker*, München, 1912, and W. S. Smith, *Inter-connections in the Ancient Near East*, New Haven–London, 1965. Particular

torus moulding and cavetto cornice (often with the winged solar
disk) were widely imitated, and even the broad idea of columned
halls and dromoi lined with statues may have been taken over,
while in the industrial arts Egyptianizing figures and decorative
motifs were used extensively. Pieces of Middle Kingdom jewellery
were reproduced at Byblos in the second millennium B.C., the
ivories from Megiddo and the later groups from Nimrud and
other sites incorporate a range of Egyptian details, the Cypro–
Phoenician metal bowls of the eighth and seventh centuries B.C.
are markedly pharaonic in inspiration, the archaic Greek *kouroi*
seem to reflect the Egyptian canon (see Chapter 3), the Phoenician
anthropoid coffins of the fifth to fourth centuries are based upon
Saite mummiform sarcophagi, and there is a wealth of Nilotic
influence in the design and ornament of trivia such as seals and
amulets, personal trinkets, and cosmetic accessories. In all, however, it is merely the outward semblance of Egyptian art that is
imitated, without, apparently, any appreciation of its principles—
and this is equally true in later ages.

The attitude of the Graeco–Roman world to things Egyptian
had a decisive influence on subsequent tradition. At the simplest
level, the choice of learning handed down to the Middle Ages and
Renaissance was largely governed by what was interesting to
classical and Byzantine scholarship, as may be seen in the case of
medicine (Chapter 5), while, more importantly, the late antique
impression of Egypt as the repository of hermetic wisdom conditioned both academic and popular ideas down to the eighteenth
century, as exemplified by the arcane interpretation of the hieroglyphs (Chapter 7) and the prestige attached to pseudo–Egyptian
magic (Chapter 6). The point may aptly be illustrated from the
broad field of art and iconography, not only in the conversion to

instances of the derivation of motifs from Egyptian art are also noticed
in H. Frankfort, *The Art and Architecture of the Ancient Orient*, Harmondsworth, 1954, and D. B. Harden, *The Phoenicians*, London, 1962—and,
for the Greek world, in J. Boardman, *The Greeks Overseas*, Harmondsworth, 1964.

Christian purposes of Egyptian deities and religious symbolism, but in the Imperial Roman vogue for Nilotic antiquities, so many of which survived through the Dark Ages to be rediscovered and imitated by Italian artists from the twelfth century onwards.

The tracing of pagan elements in Christianity is always controversial,[1] but in certain areas there is undoubted continuity. Whether or not the figure of Isis suckling Horus (Pl. 19*b*) was the actual prototype of the Blessed Virgin, the portrayal of Christ triumphant over noxious beasts is evidently derived from that of Horus upon the crocodiles (Pl. 9), while Horus *Imperator* was the antecedent of St. George and the Roman Anubis of the once dog-headed Christopher. The persistence of Isiac memories may well account for the distribution of '*Vierges noires*' in central and southern France, together with some ancient dedications to the *Virgo paritura*, and figures of Isis are known to have been preserved and worshipped in a number of places, for example, at Metz and Ranville (Orne) and in the abbey church of St.-Germain-des-Prés, where the image (clearly a pharaonic statue) was destroyed in 1514. Indeed, the very festival of the *navigium Isidis*, still celebrated at Rome at the close of the fourth century, has been perpetuated, as at Les-Saintes-Maries-de-la-Mer and the little chapel of Notre Dame de Bequerel in the Morbihan—and there are other less obvious survivals. Even the presence of the *ankh* sign on some medieval tombstones in the Balkans may have an Isiac connotation, since in antiquity it was there associated with a Mother Goddess, probably of Egyptian origin.

Roman devotion to Isis and Serapis in the first three centuries of the present era had a significant influence on later ideas of Egyptian art in Western Europe, for, apart from the earliest secular use of obelisks (Pl. 14*a*), it was largely to create atmosphere

The matter is further complicated when it touches upon folk legend, but one may note the suggestion that the actual object once preserved as the Arthurian Holy Grail was in fact an imperial porphyry altar table of the *gradale* type.

in Isiac shrines and to decorate Imperial villas and pleasances in the fashionable Nilotic manner that pharaonic antiquities were imported and later reproduced.[1] The many sculptures that periodically have been unearthed in Rome, elsewhere in Italy, and throughout the Empire (even as far afield as York), and notably those recovered from the site of the great *Iseum Campense* and from Hadrian's villa, are of considerable interest—not least in relation to their eventual impact. Of the imported Egyptian pieces a high proportion date from the later dynasties (Twenty-sixth to Thirtieth) and from the Ptolemaic period, being to that extent unrepresentative of pharaonic art, while of the reproductions one or two are actual copies made to pair with known antiquities, but the majority either original creations in the Egyptian style or misconceived pastiches verging on travesty. The preponderance of late sculpture may not be wholly accidental, the objects having perhaps been chosen for their association with a specific site or a particular pharaoh—chiefly the two kings Nectanebo (Nekhtnebef and Nekhtharhebe) whose attachment to Isis seems to have been remembered—and some of the Roman imitations also argue antiquarian learning and an appreciation of the external forms of Egyptian art. The obelisk of Domitian (Pl. 14*b*), for example, shows both a knowledge of hieroglyphs and a certain acquaintance with the traditional manner of dedication,[2] the inscription of the prenomen of Nectanebo I on an inept Canopic figure now in the Vatican was in all likelihood deliberate, and, on the artistic side, the porphyry Bes from Portus (Pl. 6) is so competent that, but for the Hathor mask and the choice of material, it might easily

[1] This does not, of course, apply to the many smaller antiquities such as bronzes, shawabti figures, and scarabs, of which the majority will have been either objects of personal piety or mere curiosities.

[2] The same is true of the obelisk set up by Hadrian and the smaller pairs from Beneventum and Praeneste. That which now stands before SS. Trinità dei Monti is, on the other hand, a pure imitation, probably dating from the late first or the early second century A.D., the period of the Egyptianizing 'folly' in the *Horti Sallustiani* of which it was part.

pass for a late dynastic piece. It is, however, probable that such examples are a reflection of the individual expertise and manual skill of expatriate Egyptians, and the ordinary extent of Roman familiarity may be more accurately mirrored in the mistaken reconstruction of a well-known Isiac statue from two unrelated fragments, or the precaution taken in 'labelling' a naophorous figure in Greek and Latin. Certainly there was no clear realization that Egyptian objects might be of widely different date, nor any inkling of the sculptor's principles and aims, and it is even doubtful how far genuine pieces were distinguished from obvious and improbable imitations or from the various hybrid Hellenistic types.

From the close of antiquity until the seventeenth century, when the collection of curios from Egypt was again resumed, Egyptian art and architecture were very largely represented by the antiquities preserved among the ruins of Rome and from time to time aroused from their 'strange animal slumber' underground.[1] The earliest European travellers rarely went beyond Alexandria and Grand Cairo, where they admired the pyramids, and even so the common impression of these was based on the steeply angled monument of Cestius (the *'Meta Remi'*) and its apparently more imposing counterpart the *'Meta Romuli'*. The latter was one of several important landmarks that escaped destruction until the

[1] The Roman ambience has not been adequately studied. The later European tradition, including some nineteenth-century aspects, is variously approached in the following: F. W. von Bissing, op. cit. (above p. 2, n. 1); K. H. Dannenfeldt, 'Egypt and Egyptian Antiquities in the Renaissance', *Studies in the Renaissance*, vi (1959), 7–27; R. Enking, *Der Apis–Altar Johann Melchior Dinglingers*, Glückstadt–Hamburg–New York, 1939; L. Greener, *The Discovery of Egypt*, London, 1966; E. Iversen, *The Myth of Egypt and its Hieroglyphs in European Tradition*, Copenhagen, 1961; E. Iversen, *Obelisks in Exile*, I: *The Obelisks of Rome*, Copenhagen, 1968; S. Morenz, *Die Begegnung Europas mit Ägypten*, Leipzig, 1968; S. Morenz, *Die Zauberflöte*, Münster–Köln, 1952; N. Pevsner and S. Lang, 'The Egyptian Revival', *The Architectural Review*, cxix (1956), 242–54: reprinted, with additions, in N. Pevsner, *Studies in Art, Architecture and Design*, i, London, 1968, pp. 212–35, 245–8; L. Volkmann, *Ägypten-Romantik in der europäischen Kunst*, in the press.

Renaissance, another being the ancient entrance to the *Iseum Campense*, the so-called *Arco di Camigliano*, and there is evidence that many Egyptian objects were then known which have since disappeared. Of extant pieces, some, such as the larger obelisks, would appear to have survived above ground through the Dark Ages, while others were rediscovered at an early date. The famous lions of Nectanebo I (Pl. 5*a*) were first recorded in the twelfth century, and the ape of San Stefano del Cacco can be traced back to the mid fourteenth century, some thirty years before the recovery of an obelisk and other fragments from the area of the Iseum. There are also contemporary instances of the copying of Egyptian sculptures, the oldest being two porphyry lion masks of Norman Sicilian origin, while to the thirteenth century belong the lions and sphinxes of the 'Cosmati' workshops (Pl. 5*b*), the models used for the rather characteristic sphinxes being as yet unidentified. The Quattrocento saw the discovery both of the *Hieroglyphica* of Horapollo, the fundamental source book for the hieroglyphic tradition, and of the two telamones from Hadrian's villa, the first exemplars of the much imitated Antinous type, but it was not until the sixteenth century that Egyptian antiquities became more widely known. Chance finds and excavations both in Rome and at Tivoli produced new material, including the (?) Claudian '*Mensa Isiaca*' (Pl. 15), most influential of all Egyptianizing pieces, pharaonic sculptures passed into collections like that of the Cesi family and were also sketched by artists such as van Heemskerck and Ligorio, the greatest of the surviving obelisks were re-erected by Fontana under Sixtus V, and derivative motifs were employed by architects and artists not only in Italy but, notably, in France. Several important books were published, among them that of Mercati on the obelisks, and the number of these increased in the seventeenth century with the accounts of travellers such as Sandys and serious treatises like Greaves's *Pyramidographia*—not to mention the several works of Athanasius Kircher. However misguided his approach, the learned Jesuit had an enormous influence on

Egyptian studies and was in no small degree responsible for the more academic attitude of the succeeding century, a tendency further encouraged by a fresh wave of interesting discoveries from Rome itself and in excavations at Tivoli, which added further to the list of Egyptian and Egyptianizing monuments recovered from the Imperial past. The now quite numerous European collections were also enriched by an increasing flow of objects brought direct from Egypt, and the quality of contemporary scholarship is exemplified in the careful and comprehensive publication of Montfaucon (1719–24) and that of the albeit less erudite Caylus (1752–64), while the compendious *De origine et usu obeliscorum* of Zoega (1797) is on any reckoning an outstanding work—and still remains to be superseded. The plates of antiquities in volumes like the two first mentioned were an abundant source of inspiration to artists in many fields, as may be seen, for example, in the exuberant decoration of the so-called Apis-altar of Johann Melchior Dinglinger (1731), one of the most remarkable pieces in the Egyptianizing taste, or in the motifs incorporated in the designs of Piranesi. On a different plane, selections from the growing corpus of illustrations were also reproduced quite indiscriminately in unintelligent compilations in which the old exotic-esoteric view of Egyptian relics was mindlessly perpetuated. A classic example of this is the *Monumens égyptiens* published by Bouchard and Gravier in 1791 (within the same decade as Zoega's masterpiece!), in which are mingled cuts of Egyptian objects from the works of Kircher, Montfaucon, and Caylus, and the description of the villa Alticchiero (1787), drawings from earlier publications such as those of Boissard, Hoerwarth von Hohenburg, and Sandrart, purely fanciful creations taken from Fischer von Erlach and even Piranesi, and a wild assortment of other curios—figures of Aion-Ahriman, odd Indian pieces and the like—the whole collection presented as 'Egyptian', in much the same way as in the nineteenth century the monuments of unfamiliar mystery cults were lumped together on the principle *omne ignotum pro mithriaco*.

The discovery of the Rosetta Stone and the publication of the monumental *Déscription de l'Égypte* (Frontispiece) and other works inspired a popular enthusiasm for things Egyptian, though the succeeding legacy has in the main been transient and subject to the vagaries of fashion. The early nineteenth-century vogue for Egyptianizing furniture and interior decor has its counterpart in the design of some modern furnishing fabrics and other domestic items, while 'Cleopatra' dress materials, costume jewellery, and cosmetics are paralleled by the enamelled brooches made for the Paris exhibition of 1867 and Mme Rachel's notorious 'Egyptian Kohl'.[1] In architecture too it has intermittently been fashionable to imitate the Egyptian style, though many of these buildings have not survived, including, alas, the Egyptian Hall in Piccadilly (Pl. 1), where Belzoni exhibited his 'curious remains of antiquity'. The mood of nineteenth-century pharaonic was generally sombre —granitic cemetery portals, masonic lodges, lawcourts, prisons, customs houses, stations, even a dark satanic mill based on the temple of Edfu—a notable exception being Canina's charming portico in the Borghese Gardens (Pl. 2), which is quite Hadrianic in spirit but was in fact designed by Asprucci after a view of Luxor in Norden's *Voyage*. The twentieth-century approach has been more varied, with a preference for the creation of a clean Egyptian shape without the exotic detail, though in a lighter vein it has produced some colourful extravaganzas in a genre which might fairly be dubbed 'Gents Gyppy', among the most spectacular being the movie palaces such as Grauman's Hollywood *Egyptian*, the Streatham *Astoria*, or the old *Odeon*, Islington. The cinema has also advertised the heritage of Egypt on a grander scale through innumerable soap operas centred on Cleopatra, Moses, or the Amarna episode, as well as those which have starred

[1] It may come as something of a surprise to Egyptologists to learn that one may now purchase *kyphi* incense recreated 'by means of a careful study and comparison of rare papyri' and 'by following the sacred hieroglyphic instructions.'

The Mummy ('beware the beat of the bandaged feet'), a never failing hieroglyph for instant horror. By contrast, the influence of Egypt in the field of literature has been less interesting, despite the varied use that has been made of Egyptian background, often, as with Sax Rohmer, as an appropriate setting for the occult. Best known, perhaps, are two rather different works of the late nineteenth century, the playful *Caesar and Cleopatra* and Rider Haggard's *She*, the latter acknowledged as an influence by Henry Miller and still today reprinted as a paperback. Most lasting, however, of all the post-Napoleonic legacy has been *Aïda*, written to mark the opening of the Suez Canal and with original scenery designed by Mariette, as opera less sophisticated than the *Magic Flute* and without its intellectual pedigree, but undeniably more evocative of Egyptian splendour.

A remarkable feature of the tradition in the West is the extent to which pharaonic Egypt has been symbolized by things in no way typical or representative. The cranes, pygmies, and negroes of Greek art were doubtless meant to belittle in the same sense as the terms 'pyramid' and 'obelisk', but the various Roman images were more seriously intended. The Nile landscape with its quasi-heraldic animals, reproduced in mosaic and mural decoration (Pl. 22), the sacral-idyllic genre with Egyptian elements, the stone crocodiles in gardens and in temple precincts, the favourite figure of Osiris Canopus and the other hybrid deities were none of them truly pharaonic, even in spirit, but yet were scarcely differentiated from the genuine sphinxes, lions, and other sculptures brought to Rome. So too in the Renaissance it was antique interpretations and pastiches that came to represent the essential Egypt—the *Hieroglyphica* of Horapollo, the '*Mensa Isiaca*', the atlantes and Antinous statues found at Tivoli (Pl. 4*b*), and other analogous items—to the exclusion, strangely, of the obelisks, which, though they were the pattern for the ubiquitous *guglia*, were not specifically associated with Egypt, any more than may have been the lion-and sphinxes. And even since the Napoleonic rediscovery and the emergence of Egyptology as a discipline this curious tendency has been maintained. Egyptianizing buildings of the nineteenth century were largely modelled on Ptolemaic temples, with exaggerated cornices and mouldings and a variety of composite capitals, while imitations of reliefs have generally reproduced the rounded plumpness characteristic of Graeco–Roman work. Moreover, in the popular view of Egypt at the present day, the quite untypical Amarna period with its fatal blend of sexual and religious intrigue has become paramount (if not MGM), the famous head of Nefertiti ranking as the twentieth-century symbol of Egyptian art and Tutankhamūn's tomb as the epitome of pharaonic glory. To the same category belongs the figure of Cleopatra, the 'lass unparallel'd', dramatic heroine out of Plutarch through Jodelle and the neo-Senecans to Shakespeare, Fletcher, Dryden, Shaw, and latterly the cinema and the adventures of Astérix. An Alexandrian queen who, but for her suicide, might have lived into the Christian era, she has become a timeless image of most ancient Egypt, whose 'needles' stand in London and New York, to whom antiquity attributed the composition of cosmetic recipes, and who was later associated both with gynaecology and the long tradition of pseudo-Egyptian alchemy and magic, embracing on the one hand Hermes Trismegistus and the Medieval Nectanebo and on the other charlatans like Cagliostro and Aleister Crowley.[1]

The essential irrelevance of such symbols underlines the basic incomprehension that has always been an obstacle to the fuller appreciation of Egypt's legacy. The borrowings of succeeding ages have in a sense been incidental, for, although the varied manifestations of the Egyptian genius have inspired an almost superstitious awe, little if anything of its intellectual background

---

[1] Crowley first encountered the astral light in the King's Chamber of the Great Pyramid, and became a servitor of Ra-Hoor-Khuit [*sic*] on seeing the deity represented on a Cairo stela with the apocalyptic number 666, that of the Great Beast with whom he identified himself.

has been understood, still less assimilated. The point is nicely illustrated by former attitudes to Egyptian art, which Piranesi was the first to defend as having a character of its own, though only during the last half century has it become more generally accepted. This wider recognition is in great measure owed to the work of scholars like Heinrich Schäfer who have made clear the underlying concepts of pharaonic representation, but is also a reflection of the abandonment of standards sanctified by classical and later Western European tradition—a change which has found expression not only in the various modern movements but in the greater interest shown in the more abstruse creations of artists such as Bosch. It may be that eventual liberation from the last tyranny of Greece and from the inhibitions of Judaeo–Christian thought and prejudice will lead to a better understanding of other aspects of the Egyptian heritage and ultimately to a truer assessment of the universal debt to pharaonic culture. But there are influences more consciously inimical by which such an objective view may yet be denied—among them that insensate nationalism which disclaims the past, lest to admit its contribution should belie the apocalypse of socialist 'progress'. 'The battle for truth', as Kingsley Amis has remarked in another context, 'is never done'.

J. R. HARRIS

1

THE CALENDARS AND CHRONOLOGY

ACCORDING to ancient tradition, when in 45 B.C. Julius Caesar decided to reform the unwieldly lunar-based calendar of Rome, he took advice from an Alexandrian astronomer, Sosigenes, who applied his calendarial experience to the problem. The result, with Augustus' correction a few years later, became the Julian calendar, used by all Christendom until the time of Pope Gregory, when it was further reformed into our present calendar. Though the length of the year as $365\frac{1}{4}$ days had been common knowledge for some centuries before Sosigenes, the Egyptians were surely the earliest people to have arrived at that figure and, as well, to have devised a calendar divorced from the awkward lunar month. These remain two of the most significant of all their legacies to us, and how they arrived at them may well serve as an introduction to the catalogue of their accomplishments.

Primitive man was, of course, far from the realization that the year had a constant length. In his gradually developing sense of time he would first be aware only of the alternation of day and night, with the passage of the sun across the sky in the one and the passage of the stars in the other. The waxing and waning of the second great celestial body, the moon, would lead him to the longer time measure of the lunar month, and when he had learned to count he would be able to reckon that from one disappearance of the crescent moon to the next—or from one new crescent to the next, or from one full moon to the next—would be around twenty-nine or thirty days.[1] Finally, the rhythm of the seasons,

[1] Quite unlike the majority of ancient peoples the Egyptians began their lunar month when the *old* crescent of the moon could no longer be

especially when primitive man abandoned food-gathering and turned to food-producing, would become of paramount interest and would come to be reckoned in terms of lunar months.

In Egypt primitive man, settled in the valley of the river Nile or wandering near it, had in the river itself a giant seasonal clock which swelled with its annual flood, overran its banks, and then gradually withdrew to its bed, getting lower and lower until the next flood began the cycle over again. As an agriculturalist and food-producer, he would adjust to this rhythm, building his home on high ground, waiting for the several lunar months while the river grew and the flood lay over the land, tilling the soil and planting seed when the land was exposed again, cultivating and watering his field as the river sank lower and lower through several more lunar months, and finally harvesting and waiting again through the months of low water for the flood to recur. Gradually he would thus come to associate some four lunar months with the season of flood, four with the season of planting and growth, and four with the season of harvest and low water.

How long this process of calendar approximation went on and when finally it was systematized we have no idea, but we do know that the first calendar-maker in Egypt took the broad concepts outlined above and by adding one very important observation formulated a calendar, which we can detect in the written records, at least by protodynastic times and probably earlier. The new element was derived from observation of the behaviour of the brightest star in the sky, the dog-star Sirius. Like all except the circumpolar stars, Sirius would apparently change its place in the sky at night as the earth moved around the sun and so shifted the point of observation. Eventually earth, sun, and star would be so nearly in a line that the light of the star would be swallowed

seen just before dawn, i.e. with cresent invisibility as opposed to new crescent visibility. As a consequence, their days ran from dawn to dawn instead of from sunset to sunset. See R. A. Parker, *The Calendars of Ancient Egypt*, Chicago, 1950, pp. 9 ff.

up in the sun's brightness and the star be invisible for a period
later recognized by the Egyptians as of seventy days. At the end
of this period there would be a night when, just before dawn, the
star would again become visible, if but momentarily, in the eastern
horizon, an astronomical event known as its heliacal rising. The
Egyptians saw Sirius as a goddess, Sopdet (Sothis), and, as it
happened, the heliacal rising of the goddess would usually occur
just about the time when the period of low water was coming to
an end. As a result, the rising of Sothis came to be regarded as
the herald of the inundation, and it provided a most satisfactory
peg on which to hang a true calendar.

As we may formulate it, the calendar year consisted of three
seasons, each of four lunar months. The months had names,
taken from important festivals occurring in them, and the seasons
were called *akhet*, 'flood' or 'inundation', *peret*, 'emergence', and
shomu, 'low water' or 'harvest'. The great feast of the rising of
Sothis, called *wep renpet*, 'opener of the year', by the Egyptians,
gave its name to the fourth month of the third season, i.e. the
last month of the year. Unlike the other month festivals, which
were in each case assigned to various days of the lunar month
such as the first day, first quarter-day, full-moon day, etc., the
rising of Sothis was a stellar event with no relation whatever to
the moon, and it was necessary therefore to arrange a calendar
which would keep this event properly within the month which it
named. Experience led to a very simple rule. Since twelve lunar
months total on the average 354 days—some eleven days shorter
than the natural year—whenever the rising of Sothis took place
in the last eleven days of the month *wep renpet*, the following
month was not taken as the first of the year, but as an intercalary
or extra month, and the next year became a 'great' year of thirteen
months, some 384 days, which would keep the rising of Sothis
safely in its month.

To make this more clear, let us assume that one year Sothis
rose heliacally on the sixteenth of the month *wep renpet*: the next

year it would fall on the twenty-seventh, eleven days later. Were nothing done, the next year it could be another eleven days later, and out of its month entirely. But an intercalary month of twenty-nine or thirty days would save it and place the next rising of Sothis early in *wep renpet*, on perhaps the seventh or eighth day.

Such then was Egypt's first calendar on record—a normal year of three seasons, each of four lunar months, with an extra month every three, or more rarely two, years, and kept in place in the natural year by being tied to the heliacal rising of Sirius/Sothis, and so a luni–stellar calendar. For the predynastic and proto-dynastic Egyptian such a year would have been completely adequate, and the small oscillation about the rising of Sothis inherent in it would have been of no concern.

In time, however, Egypt became a well-organized kingdom, and such a fluctuating calendar, with now twelve months and now thirteen, and all beginning by observation, must have become an administrative handicap. To be sure, other peoples in the ancient Near East used lunar months and lunar years throughout their history and made do, despite the awkwardness. It was the genius of the Egyptians to be the first to break the bonds imposed by the lunar month and to devise a more workable calendar. What they did was to create a schematic or averaged lunar year, and there are two ways in which this might have been done. The less likely would have been to keep a record of the total days in each year, whether of twelve or thirteen months, and average them: after eleven years this would have given a figure of 365·09 days, after twenty-two years of 365·04, and after twenty-five of 364·96,[1] inevitably the figure of 365 would have been selected.

An easier way, and perhaps the more probable one, would have been to count the days between successive heliacal risings of Sothis, since that star was the peg upon which the present calendar

[1] For the above figures see Parker, *Calendars*, p. 53. The Egyptians themselves would have used unit fractions.

was hung. With allowance for errors in observation and poor observational conditions, a few years would be all that was necessary to decide on 365 as the correct number of days. The new calendar year, which we may call the 'civil' year, consisted, like its predecessor, of three seasons of four months each. The great advance was, however, to fix all the months at thirty days each; the extra five days were called the 'days upon the year' (by the Greeks, the 'epagomenal' days) and were in essence an intercalary period, similar to the thirteenth lunar month. The resulting achievement was the calendar which has been aptly termed 'the only intelligent calendar which ever existed in human history'.[1]

It should be remarked that the new thirty-day months were divided into 'weeks' of ten days each. While the lunar month divides naturally into quarters, these are uneven—for the Egyptians they were of seven, eight, seven, and seven or eight days each to the lunar month.[2] Since such irregularity was precisely what they were trying to avoid, as evidenced by the rounding-off of all the months to thirty days, for the new months they abandoned quarters and instead settled on thirds. This had a most far-reaching and quite unforseen effect, in that the ten-day week led directly to another of our legacies from Egypt—the division of the day into twenty-four hours. Precisely how this came about will be discussed elsewhere.[3]

Though the length of the civil year was probably determined by Sothis, it is important to note that it was never tied to its rising as was the lunar year. Presumably after it was installed—

[1] O. Neugebauer, *The Exact Sciences in Antiquity*, Providence, 1957, p. 81. Its lack of intercalation made it an ideal instrument for astronomical calculations. This was recognized by Hellenistic astronomers and by their successors through the Middle Ages to Copernicus, whose lunar and planetary tables still used the Egyptian civil calendar.

[2] The days of the lunar month were named. The seventh day was called 'part day' as was also the twenty-third. The fifteenth day was 'half-month day' (see Parker, *Calendars*, p. 11).

[3] See below, p. 52.

and we can place this between about 2937 and 2821 B.C.—,[1] though
running concurrently with the lunar year, it was restricted to
administrative and economic purposes, while the original lunar
year continued to determine the dates of temple service and
religious festivals, just as our own liturgical year is fixed. The two
years, civil and religious, will have complemented one another
excellently, and because of the vacillation of the lunar year it will
for a long time have remained unnoticed that the civil year was
not remaining in place with it but, because there was never a
leap-year with a sixth extra day, was slowly moving forward in
the natural year at the rate of one day every four years. Eventually
it cannot have escaped attention that no month of the civil year
ever coincided even for a day with its lunar counterpart and that
the dual character of the year was being nullified. Instead of
adjusting the situation by adding a number of days to a particular
civil year, so forcing it back into agreement with the lunar year,
and then keeping it in place by a sixth extra day every four years
(since by now, through Sothic risings, the year was surely known
to have $365\frac{1}{4}$ days), a rather astounding solution was imposed.
The civil year, having proved its worth to officialdom for a
century or more, was left untouched to continue its creeping
progress through the natural year, but since it was after all an
artificial creation, a schematic year, it was given a lunar counterpart to provide the same sort of dual year that existed at first.
This second lunar year was not tied to Sothis but rather to the
civil year, so that its months would coincide generally with their
civil counterparts. From this time (perhaps about 2500 B.C.)
Egypt had three years, one civil and two lunar, all of which continued in use to the very end of pagan Egypt. The civil year and
its lunar counterpart moved forward through the seasons, while

[1] On the reasonable assumption that the first day of both civil and
lunar years coincided, with the latter being as close as twelve days to the
heliacal rising of Sirius or as far away as forty-one days. In about 2773
B.C. the first day of the civil year came to coincide with the rising.

the original lunar calendar, since it remained in place, continued to provide an agricultural and festival year.[1]

In the last centuries B.C., the second lunar year, while still preserving its lunar character, divorced itself from observation for determining the beginning of its months, and adopted instead a twenty-five-year-cycle scheme based on the civil year.[2] Henceforth, lunar months began on predetermined dates which repeated themselves every twenty-five years. At its inception (about 357 B.C.) the cycle scheme, though relatively simple, had a rather high degree of agreement with observation.[3] Over the centuries, however, since twenty-five civil years have 9,125 days, and 309 lunar months (sixteen years of twelve months and nine years of thirteen months) have only 9,124·95231 days, this good agreement began to lessen, and by the time of the Carlsberg demotic papyrus itself (A.D. 144) it had disappeared and reflected instead a situation in which new-crescent visibility would seem to have been the underlying basis of the cycle. Nevertheless, just as earlier with the civil year, no adjustment or correction was made.

It is, of course, the civil year of 365 days which is so well known to students of Egyptian history, and it must again be emphasized that we have no evidence of any adjustment of or tampering with

---

[1] It needs to be emphasized, in view of the vast amount of sheer speculation and undemonstrable hypotheses about Egyptian calendation, that these three are the only calendars for which there is any solid evidence. Particularly attractive to earlier chronologers has been the idea of a fixed or Sothic year, one whose first day always coincided with the rising of Sothis by having a leap-year of 366 days every four years. There is no evidence for such a year, and the postulated need for it (so that natural feasts such as that of the harvest might be celebrated at their proper times) was fully met by the original lunar calendar.

[2] Discovered in Carlsberg demotic papyrus No. 9 by O. Neugebauer and A. Volten and published by them in *Quellen und Studien zur Geschichte der Mathematik*, Abt. B, Bd. 4, Berlin, 1938, pp. 383–406. See also Parker, *Calendars*, pp. 13 ff.

[3] Calculated dates for two years of lunar months, twenty-five in all, show agreement with derived cycle dates in eighteen cases, an accuracy of 72 per cent (Parker, *Calendars*, p. 25).

this year from the time of its installation in the early third millennium B.C. until 238 B.C., when Ptolemy III made an unsuccessful effort to keep it in place by the device of a sixth epagomenal day every four years.

It is upon this unchanging civil year that Egyptian chronology has been built, for any event which can be fixed precisely in the astronomical year will, as we have remarked, fall on the same day of the Egyptian civil year for four years, on the day after for the next four years, and so on until the civil year has made a complete circuit through the seasons in some 1,460 years (365×4). This is the period that because of the prominence of the heliacal rising of Sirius/Sothis in Egyptian chronology has been called the 'Sothic cycle'. Now Censorinus informs us that in A.D. 139 the first day of the civil year and the heliacal rising of Sirius coincided, and we might then expect a similar coincidence 1,460 years earlier in 1322 B.C., and again in 2782 B.C. In point of fact, since the star Sirius is itself moving, the coincidences must be calculated by astronomical tables and are set as more probable in 1317 and 2773 B.C. respectively. Earlier historians, knowing that the civil calendar was in use before 2773 B.C. and assuming that it must have been established in a year when the heliacal rising of Sirius fell on its first day (since later texts name the first day of the civil year *wep renpet*, 'opener of the year', which is also, as we have noted, a name for the rising of Sothis), thought it necessary to place the establishment of the civil year another cycle earlier, and 4241 B.C. became, e.g. for Breasted, 'the earliest fixed date in the history of the world'.[1] We have seen above, however, that the civil year was not tied to Sothis at its installation but developed from the lunar calendar, and we are thus no longer forced back to the fifth millennium but may set the first civil year in the century or so before 2773 B.C. There are a few texts scattered throughout Egyptian history which give dates for a heliacal rising of

---

[1] J. H. Breasted, *A History of Egypt*, 2nd ed., London, 1909 and following, p. 14.

Sothis in terms of the civil year, and their prime importance for dating purposes will readily be appreciated, but before we examine them some general remarks on Egyptian chronology may be appropriate.

Following the pattern set by Manetho, an Egyptian historian and priest who lived under the first Ptolemies, the rulers of Egypt are divided into dynasties, thirty-one in all, beginning with Menes, who, as first king of the First Dynasty, unified the Two Lands (the upper valley of the Nile and its lower delta), and continuing down to the conquest of Alexander the Great. The dynasties, which broadly speaking consist of related kings (a change of ruling house was the principle of Manetho's division), are now for historical purposes grouped into periods—the Old, Middle, and New Kingdoms, the intermediate periods, and the various distinct phases of Egypt's later history (for which, see the summary table at the end of the chapter). The situation of the kingdoms and periods, the dynasties and their kings, in time is the first task of the historian, and here only written records are of use, though these are all too frequently lacking or of dubious value.

After the earliest dynasties, when a year was named after an important event occurring in it or by a numbered repetition of a biennial cattle count, the kings numbered the years of their individual reigns, though not all according to the same system,[1] Had we contemporary records of every king it would indeed be a simple matter to work by dead reckoning, but in only a few dynasties can this be done, and other indications are required to assign them to specific years B.C. King lists have in fact been preserved which help to establish the sequence of dynasties and kings but provide no other information. Manetho gives lengths

---

[1] The regnal years of the kings of the Twelfth Dynasty, for example, agreed with the civil year, and every New Year's Day began a new regnal year. In the Eighteenth Dynasty, however, regnal years began with the king's accession, and so usually contained part of one civil year and part of the following one. See A. H. Gardiner, 'Regnal Years and Civil Calendar in Pharaonic Egypt', *JEA* xxxi (1945), 11–28.

of reigns and dynastic totals, but what we now have is not his own work but extracts from it by later historians, and in many cases either he or they have made demonstrable errors. Of much greater value are two more contemporary sources, the fragments of a tablet (or tablets) from the Fifth Dynasty, the largest known as the Palermo Stone, which recorded the reigns of previous kings, each year in a separate field, and a papyrus known as the Turin Canon which listed the kings of Egypt from the earliest dynasties down to the end of the Hyksos period, that is just prior to the New Kingdom, and gave the length of reign for each. Were these documents complete, most of our problems would disappear, but unhappily they are both fragmentary. Much useful information can, nevertheless, be gained from them when combined with other data.

In the fluid state of Egyptian chronology as it may appear from the foregoing remarks, the few records of the heliacal rising of Sothis stand out as strong anchors. The first and most important of them predicts, some days before the event, a heliacal rising on the sixteenth day of the fourth month of the second season in the seventh year of King Senwosret III of the Twelfth Dynasty. It is easily possible to calculate that this must have been in the neighbourhood of 1870 B.C.,[1] and certain lunar dates for the same king in his third and twenty-ninth years enable us to fix the exact year as 1872 B.C. Since we are well informed on the Twelfth Dynasty, and on the Eleventh also, it is possible to date the beginning of the former to 1991 B.C. and of the latter to 2134 B.C. From contemporary sources historians are moreover convinced that the Tenth Dynasty and the Eleventh were concurrent and that the Ninth was of but short duration and also partially contemporary with the Eleventh.

---

[1] A full Sothic cycle earlier can be ruled out because of synchronisms with Western Asiatic history. The possible years are set by Edgerton (*Journ. Near Eastern Studies*, i (1942), 307–14) from 1875 to 1865 B.C. because of the range of the *arcus visionis* (the height of the star above the sun) from 9·5° to 8·4° and also the possibility that the sighting was finally made at either Heliopolis (lat. 30·1°) or el-Lāhūn (lat. 29·2°).

It is here that the Turin Canon supplies a most useful figure, a total of 955 years and some days for the first eight dynasties. Since this figure is supported by reconstructions of the royal annals of the First and Second Dynasties and by other indications, there is small reason to question its accuracy, and if we add it to 2134 B.C., the date for the Eleventh Dynasty, we arrive at 3089 B.C. To this we must further add whatever length we wish to give to the Ninth Dynasty when it ruled alone, so that, as a round figure, 3110 B.C. may be taken to mark the beginning of Egypt's dynastic history.

With the Twelfth Dynasty firmly fixed in time, the dynasties which follow, some of which were contemporary with others, are more easily placed, with possible errors of a number of years but no longer of centuries. Moreover, other Sothic dates help to achieve accuracy. An important one is given as the ninth day of the third month of the third season, in the ninth year of Amenhotpe I, the second king of the Eighteenth Dynasty. If the star was sighted at Heliopolis the possible years for this would be 1544 to 1537 B.C.; if it was sighted at Thebes they would be 1526 to 1519 B.C.[1] In any circumstances the reign of Amenhotpe I is thus fixed within a twenty-six-year range, and other considerations will surely narrow the choice.

Enough has been said to show how the chronologer, with the help of all his source material—Sothic dates, lunar dates, genealogies of long-lived officials who served successive kings, king lists, historical records, business documents, temple calendars, records of the lives of sacred animals, synchronisms with other peoples, and other miscellaneous data—is able to build a fairly

---

[1] This is a possibility which, though pointed out by Edgerton, *American Journ. of Semitic Lang. and Lit.* liii (1937), 193, was not generally taken into account by chronologers until the appearance in 1964 of Hornung's study (see bibliography). It should be recalled that the Ebers medical papyrus, which has the Sothic date as a calendar notation on it, was actually found at Thebes, which was surely the working capital of the country under Amenhotpe I.

solid structure of dates.[1] For the benefit of the reader a skeleton chronology may now be given against which the political and cultural history of ancient Egypt may be viewed and its accomplishments assessed.

RICHARD A. PARKER

PROTODYNASTIC PERIOD: 3110–2665 B.C.
Dynasty I: 3110–2884
Dynasty II: 2883–2665

OLD KINGDOM: 2664–2155 B.C.
Dynasty III: 2664–2615
Dynasty IV: 2614–2502
Dynasty V: 2501–2342
Dynasty VI: 2341–2181
Dynasty VII: Interregnum
Dynasty VIII: 2174–2155

FIRST INTERMEDIATE PERIOD: 2154–2052 B.C.
Dynasty IX: 2154–*c.* 2100
Dynasty X: *c.* 2100–2052
Dynasty XI: 2134–1999

MIDDLE KINGDOM: 2052–1786 B.C.
Dynasty XII: 1991–1786

[1] The reader may wonder why no mention has been made of the dating results derived from the use of Carbon 14. This is because, for dynastic Egypt, we are in most cases already well within the range of accuracy of the method. For the periods of predynastic Egypt, into which I have not gone, Carbon-14 dating has considerable value, and eliminates quite decisively the 'long' chronologies favoured by some older scholars, which would place the First Dynasty and Menes in the fifth and sixth millennia B.C. For the early Carbon-14 dates, see W. F. Libby, *Radiocarbon Dating*, 2nd ed., Chicago, 1955, and for more recent series, together with comment upon refinements in the method, the annual volumes of *Radiocarbon Supplement*, later *Radiocarbon*, New Haven, 1959 and following.

SECOND INTERMEDIATE PERIOD: 1785–1554 B.C.
>   Dynasties XIII–XVI: 1785–1550
>   Dynasty XIV: *c.* 1715–*c.* 1650
>   Dynasty XV: 1652–1544
>   Dynasty XVII: *c.* 1600–1554

>   NEW KINGDOM: 1554–1075 B.C.
>   Dynasty XVIII: 1554–1304
>   Dynasty XIX: 1304–1192
>   Dynasty XX: 1192–1075

>   LATE PERIOD: 1075–664 B.C.
>   Dynasty XXI: 1075–940
>   Dynasty XXII: 940–730
>   Dynasty XXIII: *c.* 761–715
>   Dynasty XXIV: 725–710
>   Dynasty XXV: 736–657

>   SAITE PERIOD: 664–525 B.C.
>   Dynasty XXVI: 664–525

>   FIRST PERSIAN PERIOD: 525–404 B.C.
>   Dynasty XXVII: 525–404

>   LAST EGYPTIAN KINGDOM: 404–341 B.C.
>   Dynasty XXVIII: 404–398
>   Dynasty XXIX: 398–378
>   Dynasty XXX: 378–341

>   SECOND PERSIAN PERIOD: 341–332 B.C.
>   Dynasty XXXI: 341–333

>   GREEK PERIOD: 332–30 B.C.

>   ROMAN PERIOD: 30 B.C.–A.D. 395

BYZANTINE OR COPTIC PERIOD; A.D. 395–A.D. 640

BIBLIOGRAPHY

The Calendars

R. A. PARKER, *The calendars of ancient Egypt*, Chicago, 1950 (with references to all earlier studies).

Chronology

W. C. HAYES, in *The Cambridge ancient history*[2], i, Ch. VI, Cambridge, 1962 (with full bibliography).

E. HORNUNG, *Untersuchungen zur Chronologie und Geschichte des Neuen Reiches* (Ägyptologische Abhandlungen xi), Wiesbaden, 1964.

A. H. GARDINER, *Egypt of the pharaohs*, Oxford, 1961; *The royal canon of Turin*, Oxford, 1959.

H. W. HELCK, *Untersuchungen zu Manetho und den ägyptischen Königslisten* (Untersuchungen xviii), Berlin, 1956.

L. BORCHARDT, *Die Mittel zur zeitlichen Festlegung von Punkten der ägyptischen Geschichte und ihre Anwendung*, Cairo, 1935.

2

MATHEMATICS AND ASTRONOMY

1. *Mathematics*

OUR knowledge of Egyptian mathematics depends largely on two documents from the Middle Kingdom, the Moscow papyrus and the Rhind papyrus (the latter a copy from the Hyksos period of a Twelfth Dynasty original). Both are collections of problems with the answers worked out. There are a number of shorter documents from the same period or later, in hieratic, demotic, Coptic, and Greek, one as late as the sixth century A.D. These supplement the picture we form from the two major pieces of evidence, but do not essentially change it. There is nothing of an earlier date of a specifically mathematical nature; but we know that mathematics was the province of the scribe, and that he exercised it for purely practical ends—the calculation of areas of land, volumes of masonry, distribution of rations, and so on. So we can be sure that the techniques displayed in the two great mathematical papyri were developed long before. Thus it is impossible to give any account of the historical development of Egyptian mathematics. What follows is a brief description of its essential features at the stage where we find it in those two papyri —a stage from which it made no significant progress.

The Egyptian numeral system is decimal, with separate signs for 1, 10, 100, and so on (see Inset 1). In the writing of a number each sign is repeated as many times as is necessary.[1] Thus 142,357 is written:

$$\text{\reflectbox{N}} \quad \text{||||} \quad \text{ᔆᔆ} \quad \text{ᖆᖆ} \quad \begin{matrix} \cap\cap\cap \\ \cap\cap \end{matrix} \quad \begin{matrix} \text{||||} \\ \text{|||} \end{matrix}$$

[1] Multiples of 100,000 and 10,000 were sometimes denoted by writing the sign with the multiplier beneath it; thus $\begin{matrix} \text{\reflectbox{N}} \\ \cap \text{ ||||} \\ \cap \text{ ||||} \end{matrix}$ = 2,800,000.

INSET 1

1	ǀ
10	∩
100	⌒
1,000	⚱
10,000	⌡
100,000	⟅
1,000,000	𓀂

The last two signs fell out of use in the course of time.

The only kind of fractions used are unit fractions (those whose numerator is 1). These were denoted by writing the sign ⌒ above the ordinary numeral.[1] To reproduce this system we denote a half by $\overline{2}$, a third by $\overline{3}$, and so on. The only fraction found in the mathematical texts which is not a unit fraction is $\frac{2}{3}$,[2] which we denote by $\overline{\overline{3}}$. It is clear that for the Egyptians this was a natural fraction, familiar from everyday life, like a half or a quarter. Other proper fractions are expressed by the combination of unit fractions, so that for instance $\frac{3}{4}$ is represented by $\overline{2}\ \overline{4}$, and $\frac{5}{6}$ by $\overline{2}\ \overline{3}$.

Egyptian mathematics is characterized by its additive procedures. Addition and subtraction we may take for granted; but multiplication and division, as performed by the Egyptian scribe, involved no new principle. As an example of a multiplication let us take 13·17:

[1] There were special signs for $\frac{1}{2}$, $\frac{2}{3}$, $\frac{3}{4}$ (very rare), and, in hieratic, for $\frac{1}{3}$ and $\frac{1}{4}$.

[2] This statement must now be qualified. Professor R. A. Parker has pointed out to me in some unpublished demotic mathematical papyri expressions for proper fractions. $\frac{6}{11}$, for instance, is written in a way which we could express by $\underline{6}$ 11. It seems probable to me that this is derived from Greek usage.

$$
\begin{array}{rr}
\backslash 1 & 17 \\
2 & 34 \\
\backslash 4 & 68 \\
\backslash 8 & 136 \\
\text{Total} & 221 \\
\end{array}
$$

Here the multiplicand is successively doubled (and doubling is nothing more than the addition of a number to itself); the multipliers which add up to 13 are ticked off, and the numbers corresponding to them added together. Direct multiplication by 10 is also found (this is simple in the Egyptian numeral system, as all it involves is changing each unit into the next higher one). So a multiplication of 17 by 12 would run:

$$
\begin{array}{rr}
1 & 17 \\
\backslash 10 & 170 \\
\backslash 2 & 34 \\
\text{Total} & 204 \\
\end{array}
$$

Division is effected by a process similar to multiplication. So, for instance, division of 221 by 17 would look exactly the same as the above example of the multiplication of 17 by 13. The difference is that the scribe would first discover which products add up to 221 and then sum the corresponding multipliers to find the answer 13. The operation is well characterized by an expression applied to it in the texts: 'Count with 17 to find 221.' More often than not, however, the result of division will not be a whole number. Then the technique must be extended. Let us first take a simple example, $17 \div 8$:

$$
\begin{array}{rr}
1 & 8 \\
\backslash 2 & 16 \\
\overline{2} & 4 \\
\overline{4} & 2 \\
\backslash \overline{8} & 1 \\
\text{Result:} & 2\ \overline{8} \\
\end{array}
$$

The scribe doubles until he reaches 16, less than the required result by 1; then he successively halves until he reaches 1. Another example will illustrate the main alternative technique to halving, $19 \div 3$:

$$
\begin{array}{rr}
1 & 3 \\
\backslash 2 & 6 \\
\backslash 4 & 12 \\
\overline{3} & 2 \\
\backslash \overline{3} & 1 \\
\text{Result:} & 6\ \overline{3}
\end{array}
$$

Perverse as it seems to us, finding a third of a number by first finding two-thirds and then halving is standard practice in the Egyptian mathematical texts. These two series, $\overline{2}, \overline{4}, \overline{8}, \ldots$, and $\overline{3}, \overline{3}, \overline{6}, \ldots$, play a major role in Egyptian arithmetical techniques.

In our exposition of division we have had to introduce operations with fractions; thus we come to the central problem of Egyptian mathematics. The two basic requirements, (1) the exclusive use of unit fractions and (2) the additive system of multiplication, lead necessarily to a third: to express twice any unit fraction as the sum of other unit fractions. Suppose we have to multiply $1\ \overline{9}$ by 7. The calculation goes:

$$
\begin{array}{rl}
\backslash 1 & 1\ \overline{9} \\
\backslash 2 & 2\ \overline{6}\ \overline{18} \\
\backslash 4 & 4\ \overline{3}\ \overline{9} \\
\text{Total} & 7\ \overline{3}\ \overline{9}
\end{array}
$$

The transition from line 2 to line 3 is clear enough: doubling a unit fraction is effected by halving the denominator; but how does one get from line 1 to line 2 or from line 3 to line 4? Both transitions involve knowing that $2 \cdot \overline{9} = \overline{6} + \overline{18}$. It might be asked why one could not proceed:

$$
\begin{array}{rl}
1 & 1\ \overline{9} \\
2 & 2\ \overline{9}\ \overline{9}
\end{array}
$$

—and so on. The answer lies in psychology rather than mathematics. Perhaps the Egyptian scribe who was asked to multiply $\bar{9}$ by 2 would feel, if he wrote down $\bar{9}\ \bar{9}$, that he had not given an answer, but merely restated the problem.[1] A formulation in terms of unit fractions all differing from each other was felt to be essential. It was therefore necessary to know a resolution into unit fractions of the double of every unit fraction with odd denominator, or at least of all such unit fractions as one needed to operate with. And, indeed, at the beginning of the Rhind papyrus we find what is in effect a table of resolutions of $2\bar{n}$ for every odd value of n from 3 to 101. It begins:

> 'Divide 2 by 3
> 2 is $\bar{3}$
> Divide 2 by 5
> $1\ \bar{\bar{3}}$ is $\bar{3}$, $\bar{3}$ is $\overline{15}$
> Divide 2 by 7
> $1\ \bar{2}\ \bar{4}$ is $\bar{4}$, $\bar{4}$ is $\overline{28}$',

i.e.
$$\frac{2}{3} = \bar{\bar{3}}$$
$$\frac{2}{5} = \bar{3}+\overline{15}$$
$$\frac{2}{7} = \bar{4}+\overline{28}$$

—and so on.

The problem of breaking up $2\bar{n}$ into unit fractions has an infinite number of solutions for any value of n, and, even if one restricts it by specifying that the number of constituent unit fractions be as small as possible, there is often more than one solution. For instance, $2\cdot\overline{15}$ can be resolved into $\overline{10}+\overline{30}$ or $\bar{9}+\overline{45}$ or $\overline{12}+\overline{20}$. However, in general just those resolutions which are given by the Rhind papyrus table are found in Egyptian mathematical texts. Consequently much effort has been devoted to finding out

---

[1] A. H. Gardiner (*Egyptian Grammar*[3], p. 196) makes the interesting suggestion that the reason why expressions like $\bar{7}\ \bar{7}$ were impossible for the Egyptian is that $\bar{7}$ meant *the* seventh part, i.e. 'the part which occupied the seventh place in the row of seven equal parts laid out for inspection', so there could never be more than *one* 'seventh'.

on what basis these particular resolutions were reached. All that need be said here is that the greater part of the table could certainly have been calculated by the known methods of Egyptian mathematics and the operation of a simple principle;[1] that for a few of the resolutions the method of calculation is an open question; and that in any case the resolutions given by the Rhind papyrus are not quite so 'canonical' as was once thought: in later texts

INSET 2

A quantity whose two-thirds, half, and seventh are added to it becomes 37.

$$
\begin{array}{lrllll}
1 & 1 & \overline{\overline{3}} & \overline{2} & \overline{7} \\
2 & 4 & \overline{3} & \overline{4} & \overline{28} \\
4 & 9 & \overline{6} & & \overline{14} \\
8 & 18 & \overline{3} & & \overline{7} \\
\backslash 16 & 36 & \overline{\overline{3}} & \overline{4} & \overline{28} \\
& & 28\ 10\ \overline{2}\ 1\ \overline{2}
\end{array}
$$

$$
\begin{array}{ll}
1 & 42 \\
\backslash\overline{\overline{3}} & 28 \\
\overline{2} & 21 \\
\backslash\overline{4} & 10\ \overline{2} \\
\backslash\overline{28} & 1\ \overline{2}
\end{array}
$$

Total 40, remainder 2

$$
\begin{array}{ll}
1 & 42 \\
\overline{3} & 28 \\
\overline{2} & 21 \\
\overline{7} & 6
\end{array}
$$

Total 97

$$
\begin{array}{lll}
& \overline{97} & \overline{42} & 1 \\
\backslash\overline{56}\ \overline{670}\ \overline{776} & \overline{21} & 2
\end{array}
$$

Total 37

---

[1] For details see O. Neugebauer, *Vorlesungen*, pp. 147–65, or *Exact Sciences*, pp. 74–7 and 92, where further bibliography is given.

other resolutions are found, some poorer (for instance, $\overline{6}\ \overline{14}\ \overline{21}$ instead of $\overline{4}\ \overline{28}$ for 2·$\overline{7}$), at least one better ($\overline{7}\ \overline{91}$ instead of $\overline{8}\ \overline{52}$ $\overline{104}$ for 2·$\overline{13}$).

As an example of how the Egyptian scribe worked with fractions let us take problem no. 33 of the Rhind papyrus[1] (see Inset 2). This is one of a number of problems which we should express by a linear equation in x (here $x+\frac{2}{3}x+\frac{1}{2}x+\frac{1}{7}x = 37$). These have been misleadingly referred to as 'Egyptian algebra'. In fact, as will be clear from this example, they are problems in simple arithmetic. Here 37 is divided by the compound fraction $\overline{1}\ \overline{3}\ \overline{2}\ \overline{7}$. The latter is successively doubled in the usual way; notice the use of the 2·$\bar{n}$ table in the substitution of $\overline{4}\ \overline{28}$ for 2·$\overline{7}$ in the second line. With the multiplier 16 a point has been reached where we are near the required number 17, and further doubling would take us beyond it. We now have to determine what fraction is left to make up 37, and that is done in the next section. In order to find out what the sum of the fractions $\overline{3}\ \overline{4}\ \overline{28}$ comes to (which is not obvious) the sub-fraction $\overline{42}$ is introduced, and the above fractions expressed in terms of that. 1 contains 42·$\overline{42}$, so $\overline{3}$ contains 28·$\overline{42}$, $\overline{4}$ contains $10\frac{1}{2}$·$\overline{42}$ and $\overline{28}$ contains $1\frac{1}{2}$·$\overline{42}$, making 40·$\overline{42}$ in all, which leaves 2·$\overline{42}$ to make up 37. Or, in other words, what do we have to multiply $1\ \overline{3}\ \overline{2}\ \overline{7}$ by to make 2·$\overline{42}$? We find out how many $\overline{42}$s there are in $1\ \overline{3}\ \overline{2}\ \overline{7}$: this is done in the next section, and the answer is 97. So $1\ \overline{3}\ \overline{2}\ \overline{7}$ must be multiplied by 2·$\overline{97}$ to make 2·$\overline{42}$, and this is stated in the final section, where the expression for 2·$\overline{97}$ is taken from the 2·$\bar{n}$ table. Thus the answer to the problem is $16\ \overline{56}\ \overline{679}\ \overline{776}$. The introduction of auxiliary sub-fractions where the relationships of the existing fractions are not immediately obvious is standard practice. The numbers of these sub-fractions are often written below the fractions to which they refer (as in the sixth line here, where they are printed in heavy type, to represent the red ink which is used for them in the Rhind papyrus and usually elsewhere). This practice has been erroneously described as

---

[1] Corrected in places.

D

the introduction of a lowest common multiple. That this is not so here will become clear from the following considerations: firstly, 42 is the L.C.M. not of 3, 4, and 28, but of 3, 2, and 7, the denominators of the first line. The auxiliary numbers are thought of as being carried through from the beginning, though they are written (and, as the subsidiary working shows, calculated) only where they are really necessary. This procedure, like many others in the texts, appears absurd until one realizes that practical convenience, and not mathematical considerations, are behind it: it was practical to have a simple rule of thumb for choosing the sub-fraction; the scribe was not at all bothered that this often led (as here) to fractions of the sub-fraction. For by the nature of the calculation such fractions were usually of the sort that he could easily add in his head (i.e. in the sequences $\bar{2}, \bar{4}, \bar{8}$ or $\bar{3}, \bar{3}, \bar{6}$). Secondly, if the scribe had really introduced the L.C.M. 42, he would have formulated the problem in a way which we may express as:

$$\frac{97}{42}x = 37$$

—and then solved it by multiplying 37 by 42 and dividing by 97. Instead he divides 37 by 1 $\bar{3}$ $\bar{2}$ $\bar{7}$ and introduces the auxiliary $\overline{42}$ only in order to find out how much he still falls short of the desired total of 37. Other problems too employ auxiliary numbers in a way which would be absurd if they had been chosen as common multiples in the modern sense, but which serves the purpose of checking and aiding computation in the Egyptian manner perfectly satisfactorily.

We have described one type of problem which is found in the mathematical texts. Another common one is the '*pesu* calculation'. *pesu* is a technical term used in the making of bread and beer, and is conventionally translated 'strength'. A loaf of bread is said to be of strength 10 when ten loaves of that size can be made out of one *hekat*[1] of corn. Similarly, beer is of strength 10 when ten standard

[1] A measure of capacity, rather more than a gallon.

measures of that type of beer can be made out of one *hekat* of corn.[1] Thus the term creates a convenient standard for the exchange of loaves of different sizes or of bread for beer (such a standard would be an important thing in a non-monetary economy). A number of problems in the Rhind and Moscow papyri are concerned with just such exchanges. Examples:

Rhind papyrus no. 76

'A thousand loaves of strength 10 exchanged for a number of loaves of strength 20 and 30.' (Here it turns out that the number of loaves of strength 20 is to be the same as that of strength 30.)

Rhind papyrus no. 78

'Example of exchanging bread for beer. If it is said to you, a hundred loaves of strength 10 exchanged for a quantity of beer of strength 2 . . .'

The solution of these problems is a matter of simple proportion, and involves no new principle. But the type of problem illustrates very well the strictly practical nature of Egyptian mathematics. The term *pesu* is found in many different types of document and was clearly a familiar concept to anyone dealing with the assignment of rations, for instance. (Another type of problem frequent in the mathematical texts is the distribution of loaves among workers in equal or unequal proportions.)

This impression of the nature of Egyptian mathematics is strengthened when we look at those problems which are labelled 'Egyptian geometry'. In fact they are nothing of the kind[2] (except in the etymological sense of 'land measurement'). They are concerned with the determination of areas of land and volumes (cubic

---

[1] The difference is that loaves of different *pesu* vary in size, beer of different *pesu* in specific gravity.

[2] That the distinction between 'geometry' and 'arithmetic' did not exist in Egypt is clearly shown by the arrangement in the Rhind papyrus. The 'geometrical' problems do indeed come in the same part: first those concerned with volume (nos. 41–6), then those concerned with area (nos. 48–55). But they are separated by no. 47, which is concerned with

content) of bodies, and incidentally make use of formulas (never even explicitly stated, much less proved) which we should call 'geometrical'. These include the formulas for the area of a rectangle, a triangle, and a trapezium. The area of a circle is found in a way which we may represent by:

$$A = \left(\frac{8}{9}d\right)^2$$

(where A is the area, d the diameter). This would give $\pi \approx 3 \cdot 16$, a good approximation, much better for instance then the value 3 ordinarily used in Babylonian mathematical tablets.[1] However, this accuracy is not mathematically significant, since we can be sure that it was not reached by any process of mathematical reasoning.[2] At best it is an indication of the carefulness of Egyptian measuring. Much the same may be said of the famous calculation of the volume of a truncated pyramid found in the Moscow papyrus. The working implies the correct formula:

$$V = \frac{h}{3}(a^2 + ab + b^2)$$

(where h is the height and a and b the sides of the base and top). A correct mathematical derivation of this (or of the volume of the whole pyramid) would imply the use of an infinitesimal calculus, which is a world away from the level of the rest of Egyptian mathematics. But it is not surprising that long experience in the construction of the pyramid should have led to the empirical

expressing the fractions of a hundred quadruple-*hekat*, and is a purely arithmetical problem. It has been grouped with nos. 41–6 because all involve measures of capacity, i.e. the unit of measurement, and not the type of mathematics, is the basis for arrangement.

[1] This is also found in some Egyptian texts written in demotic and Greek.

[2] For an example of how this was in fact done, and the degree of mathematical subtlety required, see Archimedes, *Measurement of a Circle*, Proposition 3 (T. L. Heath, *The Works of Archimedes*, Cambridge, 1897, pp. 93–8).

discovery of the way to calculate the volume of the whole and parts of it.[1]

The above is far from an exhaustive description of Egyptian mathematics. One could add much more from the published texts, and recent discoveries have brought a number of previously unknown things to light. (In particular one might mention a method[2] for extracting the square root of 10 which is identical with one given by Heron of Alexandria (first century A.D.). The concept of the square root is known from the older mathematical texts, but there is no example in them of finding the square root of a number which is not a perfect square. Whether this part of the new text should be attributed to Greek influence is impossible to say in our present state of ignorance about the origins and growth of the 'Heronic' methods of calculation.) However, enough has been said to indicate what kind of mathematics this was.

We have been using the term 'mathematical texts' because it is a convenient one; but it is misleading if it makes us think of a specific class of texts concerned with the science of mathematics, to be compared with the works of Euclid or Archimedes. The Rhind and Moscow papyri are handbooks for the scribe, giving model examples of how to do things which were a part of his everyday tasks. This is confirmed, if confirmation were needed, by a papyrus in the form of a satirical letter (Pap. Anastasi i),[3] in which a scribe ridicules a colleague for his inability to do his job, and cites among other examples of his failures calculations of the rations of soldiers and of the number of bricks required for building a ramp of given dimensions. A further indication of the

---

[1] For a suggestion how the formulas for the complete and truncated pyramid might have been arrived at empirically, see O. Neugebauer, *Vorlesungen*, pp. 127–9.

[2] In one of the demotic papyri to be published by Professor Parker.

[3] A. H. Gardiner, *Egyptian Hieratic Texts*, i, Leipzig, 1911, pp. 16 f.; A. Erman, *The Literature of the Ancient Egyptians* (tr. A. M. Blackman), London, 1927 (reprinted New York, 1966), pp. 223 f., quoted by O. Neugebauer, *Exact Sciences*, p. 79.

origin of these texts is the kind of expression used to introduce problems, for instance: 'If a scribe says to you ..., let him hear ...' The texts are in one respect similar to the Babylonian mathematical texts, in that these too are in the form not of treatises but of specific problems with solutions. But there the similarity ends: the cuneiform texts have a claim to be called mathematical in a fully scientific sense. The problems are only formally about the measurement of areas, determination of lengths, etc. Many of them are not of a kind which could conceivably ever occur in actual mensuration, and the whole point of them is the algebraic procedure involved. They are really 'pure' mathematics. However, this difference from the Egyptian texts is not the important one; mathematics can be applied to practical ends without losing any of its scientific quality. What really distinguishes Babylonian mathematics is the systematic development of intricate algebraic techniques which we can deduce from the working of the problems.[1] These techniques could never have been created by mere empiricism, and we must posit an order of mathematical reasoning of which there is no trace in the Egyptian sources.

To illustrate the elementary and practical nature of Egyptian mathematics, we set out in full problem no. 42 of the Rhind papyrus[2] (see Inset 3).

The problem is to determine the cubic content of a cylinder of diameter (D) 10 cubits and height (h) 10 cubits. This is complicated by the fact that for the Egyptian cubic content means how much it will hold of some specific thing, so an answer in cubic cubits is not satisfactory. It is therefore necessary to convert to hundreds of quadruple-*hekat* of corn by way of the equivalences:

1 cubic cubit $= 1\frac{1}{2}$ *khar*.
1 *khar* $= 20$ hundreds of quadruple-*hekat*.

[1] This working can be understood only by one who has mastered the underlying techniques. The texts as we have them can be no more than written helps to what must have been essentially an oral tradition.
[2] Slightly emended.

Inset 3

1. A circular container of 10 by 10.

2. You are to subtract a ninth of 10, namely 1 $\overline{9}$: remainder 8 $\overline{\overline{3}}$ $\overline{6}$ $\overline{18}$.

3. You are to multiply 8 $\overline{\overline{3}}$ $\overline{6}$ $\overline{18}$ by 8 $\overline{\overline{3}}$ $\overline{6}$ $\overline{18}$: result 79 $\overline{108}$ $\overline{324}$.

4. You are to multiply 79 $\overline{108}$ $\overline{324}$ by 10, it becomes 790 $\overline{18}$ $\overline{27}$ $\overline{54}$ $\overline{81}$.

5. Add its half to it, it becomes 1185.

6. Multiply 1185 by $\overline{20}$, giving 59 $\overline{4}$. This is the amount that will go into it in quadruple-*hekat*, namely, 59 $\overline{4}$ hundreds of quadruple-*hekat* of corn.

7. Form of its working:

1	8 $\overline{\overline{3}}$ $\overline{6}$ $\overline{18}$
2	17 $\overline{\overline{3}}$ $\overline{9}$
4	35 $\overline{2}$ $\overline{18}$
\8	71 $\overline{9}$
\$\overline{\overline{3}}$	5 $\overline{3}$ $\overline{6}$ $\overline{18}$ $\overline{27}$
$\overline{3}$	2 $\overline{\overline{3}}$ $\overline{6}$ $\overline{12}$ $\overline{36}$ $\overline{54}$
\$\overline{6}$	1 $\overline{3}$ $\overline{12}$ $\overline{24}$ $\overline{72}$ $\overline{108}$
\$\overline{18}$	$\overline{3}$ $\overline{9}$ $\overline{27}$ $\overline{108}$ $\overline{324}$
Total	79 $\overline{108}$ $\overline{324}$

8.

1	79 $\overline{108}$ $\overline{324}$
10	790 $\overline{18}$ $\overline{27}$ $\overline{54}$ $\overline{81}$
$\overline{2}$	395 $\overline{36}$ $\overline{54}$ $\overline{108}$ $\overline{162}$
Total	1185

9.

$\overline{10}$	118 $\overline{2}$
\$\overline{20}$	59 $\overline{4}$

The working is:

1–2 $\dfrac{8}{9}D$

3   $\left(\dfrac{8}{9}D\right)^2$ (The working for this is in section 7.)

4    $h.\left(\dfrac{8}{9}D\right)^2 = C$

5    $1\frac{1}{2}C^1$ (The working for sections 4 and 5 is in section 8.)

6    $\dfrac{1}{20}.1\frac{1}{2}C$ (The working is in section 9.)

In the working, some of the steps, which would require the use of auxiliary fractions, have certainly been omitted. But what is set down is enough to show that the real difficulty for the Egyptian scribe was the mastering of elementary arithmetical calculations; we can see how hemmed in he was by his numerical system, his crude methods, and his concrete mode of thought.

In contrast let us take two other examples, the first from a Greek mathematical work. Everyone is familiar with Euclid, if not in the original, at least from the traditional school textbook of elementary geometry, since all are modelled on him. Nothing could be further removed from the Egyptian texts than the construction of an interconnected body of theorems by rigid deduction from the minimum number of postulates. This is certainly a Greek invention, and has nothing to do with the mathematics of earlier civilizations.[2] Instead let us take something which has at least the same external form of a solved problem: Diophantus, Book IV, no. 15[3] (see Inset 4). In this elegant example of the use of a false hypothesis to solve a set of quadratic equations in three unknowns, the method adopted is crystal clear. Any explanation necessary is provided by the text. Though the solution is given for particular numbers, the problem is posed as a general one, and the general method of solution is easily grasped. (The same can hardly be said of the Egyptian example, where it is easy to get bogged down in the mere numerical computation.) Above all, there is a facility

---

[1] Here the terminal fraction is dropped.

[2] This is not to deny that some of the results of Euclid may have been derived from elsewhere. But the method is Greek only.

[3] Cf. T. L. Heath, *Diophantus*, Cambridge, 1910, p. 175.

in dealing with abstract concepts, with magnitudes as such, which is nowhere to be found in Egyptian mathematics.[1]

INSET 4

To find three numbers, X_1, X_2, X_3, such that the sum of any two multiplied by the third is a given number.

Let $(X_1+X_2).X_3 = 35$, $(X_2+X_3).X_1 = 27$,
$(X_3+X_1).X_2 = 32$.

Let X_3 be x.
Then $(X_1+X_2) = 35/x$
Assume $X_1 = 10/x$, and $X_2 = 25/x$,
then $(X_2+X_3).X_1 = 27$ and $(X_3+X_1).X_2 = 32$.
But $(X_2+X_3).X_1 = 10+250/x^2$, so $10+250/x^2 = 27$,
and $(X_3+X_1).X_2 = 25+250/x^2 = 32$.

The difference between the two above numbers is 5, so if

$$\left(25+\frac{250}{x^2}\right)-\left(10+\frac{250}{x^2}\right)$$

were equal to 5, the equations would be correct. But 25 is the coefficient in X_2, 10 the coefficient in X_1; we want the difference between these coefficients to be 5. They are not taken at random, since their sum is 35: so we have to split 35 into two numbers such that their difference is 5: they are 15 and 20. So we put

$$X_1 = 15/x, X_2 = 20/x.$$
Then $(X_2+X_3).X_1$ gives $15+300/x^2 = 27$,
and $(X_3+X_1).X_2$ gives $20+300/x^2 = 32$,
so $x = 5$,
and $X_1 = 3$, $X_2 = 4$, $X_3 = 5$.

(The notation here used is an adaptation of the Greek, which is equally algebraic in form.)

---

[1] The ultimate source of much of Diophantus' work is certainly Mesopotamian. But it is the method of exposition that is important here.

Our second example is taken from a Babylonian mathematical tablet[1] (see Inset 5). It requires considerable explanation because, as already stated, the texts were written only as a supplement of examples to oral instruction. The working has therefore been expressed in modern algebraic notation in a parallel column to the translation of the original text.

x is the length, y the breadth, z the depth

Various relations are stated between these three quantities, namely:

$$\mu x = Az, \quad xy + xyz = B, \quad \alpha x = y$$

(in this example $B = 1;10$,[2] $\alpha = 0;40$, $A = 1$, $\mu = 12^3$).

This leads to the cubic equation

$$\frac{\alpha \mu x^3}{A} + \alpha x^2 = B$$

or

$$\frac{\mu x^3}{A} + x^2 = \frac{B}{\alpha}.$$

The text (line 10) forms the expression $\dfrac{B}{\alpha}\left(\dfrac{\mu}{A}\right)^2$.

So in other words line 10 is equivalent to $\left(\dfrac{\mu x}{A}\right)^3 + \left(\dfrac{\mu x}{A}\right)^2 = 4,12$.

The solution $\dfrac{\mu x}{A} = 6$ is just stated. This would be completely mysterious if we did not know that there existed tables giving $n^3 + n^2$ for many different values of n. (The reciprocals of lines 5 and 9 were similarly found direct from tables.)

[1] *Mathematische Keilschrift-Texte* (ed. O. Neugebauer, Berlin, 1935), Tl. 1, iii. 5, p. 200 (adapted) with the commentary on p. 210.

[2] The numerals are written sexagesimally, so that, e.g.,

$$1,2,3;4,5 = 1 \cdot 60^2 + 2 \cdot 60 + 3 + 4 \cdot \tfrac{1}{60} + 5 \cdot \tfrac{1}{60^2}.$$

[3] It is stated in line 1 that the depth is the same as the length; but since the length is always measured in GAR and the depth in ells, and 1 GAR = 12 ells, this ratio has to be taken into account.

Inset 5

1. Length, breadth. The depth is the same as the length	$\mu x = Az$
2. Sum of area and volume: 1;10	$xy + xyz = B$
3. 0;40 is the coefficient of the breadth	$\alpha x = y$
4. What is the length and the breadth?	
5. Form the reciprocal of 12, the coefficient of the depth: 0;5	$\dfrac{1}{\mu}$
6. Multiply by 1: 0;5	$\dfrac{A}{\mu}$
7. Multiply by 0;40: 0;3,20	$\alpha \cdot \dfrac{A}{\mu}$
8. Multiply 0;3,20 by 0;5: 0;0,16,40	$\alpha \cdot \dfrac{A}{\mu} \cdot \dfrac{A}{\mu} = \alpha\left(\dfrac{A}{\mu}\right)^2$
9. Form the reciprocal of 0;0,16,40: 3,36	$\dfrac{1}{\alpha}\left(\dfrac{\mu}{A}\right)^2$
10. Multiply 3,36 by 1;10: 4,12	$\dfrac{B}{\alpha}\left(\dfrac{\mu}{A}\right)^2 = \left(\dfrac{\mu x}{A}\right)^3 + \left(\dfrac{\mu x}{A}\right)^2$
11. 6 is the side	$\dfrac{\mu x}{A}$
12. Multiply 6 by 0;5: 0;30	$\dfrac{\mu x}{A} \cdot \dfrac{A}{\mu} = x$
13. Multiply 6 by 0;3,20: 0;20 is the breadth	$\dfrac{\mu x}{A} \cdot \dfrac{\alpha A}{\mu} = \alpha x = y$
14. Multiply 6 by 1: 6 is the depth	$\dfrac{\mu x}{A} \cdot A = \mu x = Az = z$
15. That is the procedure	

Here, though the method is quite mysterious until one has been given the clue, there is revealed a high degree of mathematical competence. Despite the absence of symbols, the algebraic technique is handled in a way which shows complete insight and familiarity. The problem of dealing with fractions, which so hamstrung Egyptian mathematics in its infancy, has been overcome by the construction of tables on a large scale. There are not only multiplication tables, but also tables of reciprocals, so that division is effected by finding the reciprocal and multiplying (cf. lines 5–6). Such reciprocal tables are practicable only when one has a place-value numeral system, and the development of the latter (which allows one to express fractions in the only really convenient way) was of great importance for the progress of Babylonian mathematics.

Egyptian mathematics has had some influence on later civilization. The use of unit fractions was very common in the Graeco–Roman world and on into the Middle Ages, and we can hardly doubt that the origin of these is in Egypt,[1] though the continuing use after the knowledge of proper and sexagesimal fractions became widespread must be explained by psychological factors common to all men. Whatever the explanation, the tradition was a bad one. A whole science of 'logistic' (the art of calculation) was erected on this foundation. (Some of the traditional problems of this may well be Egyptian in origin. Problem no. 79 of the Rhind papyrus poses the sum $7+7^2+7^3+7^4+7^5$; each term in the sum is associated with a thing, the first with houses, the second with cats, the third with mice, and so on. Clearly the problem was once formulated: 'There are seven houses, in each are seven cats, each cat catches seven mice. . . .' There is a similar problem in Leonardo of Pisa's work on calculation (thirteenth century), and the rhyme 'As I was going to St. Ives' is an undoubted modern descendant.) It is only a few hundred years since the subject became one that is exhausted in the first three years of school.

[1] The Greek symbol for $\frac{1}{2}$ is probably related to the demotic.

Though the Egyptian system of multiplication was certainly known to some Greeks, there is no trace of its being seriously used outside Egypt. Similar systems found in Europe in the Middle Ages and later are probably to be explained as independent developments—the concept is not a difficult one.

The stories current in antiquity about Thales and other Greeks learning geometry from the Egyptians are beyond any doubt false. The most that the Egyptians could have given is some empirically derived formulae for the exact or approximate calculations of areas and volumes. It is quite possible that some such material may have passed from Egypt into the 'Heronic' tradition, or even have been made known to Thales and others, though we do not have the evidence to affirm this. But that has nothing to do with geometry as understood by the Greeks and by us.

The truth is that Egyptian mathematics remained at much too low a level to be able to contribute anything of value. The sheer difficulties of calculation with such a crude numeral system and primitive methods effectively prevented any advance or interest in developing the science for its own sake. It served the needs of everyday life (it is only a relatively advanced technology, such as was never achieved in the ancient world, which demands more than the most elementary mathematics), and that was enough. Its interest for us lies in its primitive character, and in what it reveals about the minds of its creators and users, rather than in its historical influence.

11. *Astronomy*

With mathematics remaining at such a low level, it was impossible for the Egyptians to develop theoretical astronomy to a significant stage. The mathematical descriptions of the movement of the heavenly bodies which were developed in the Greek world by Apollonius, Hipparchus, and Ptolemy, and by the Babylonian astronomers under the Seleucids, though very different from each other, both require a mathematical apparatus far beyond anything the Egyptians had. So it is no accident that there is no trace of any such thing in the Egyptian texts. Nor are there any records of observations of eclipses or other heavenly phenomena. The Egyptians had recognized the planets as wandering bodies, and had named stars and constellations (very few of which can be identified now); but the only products of theirs which can be dignified by the name of 'astronomy' are some crude devices for measuring time at night by the stars. These are of considerable historical interest, but their scientific content is very small.

The first is the system of the so-called decans. This is a kind of star-clock which has been found on coffin lids from the Ninth to the Twelfth Dynasty. It is probable that these are adaptations for ordinary people of astronomical ceilings in royal tombs.[1] Though nominally intended for practical use (so that the dead may tell the time), they are essentially ritualistic, and very carelessly executed. Fortunately, the system is such a simple one for the most part that its reconstruction is certain.

The decans are thirty-six groups of stars (constellations or sub-divisions of constellations). Each of these in turn marks the end of night by its rising. The period for which each is supposed to serve as a marker is the Egyptian calendaric unit known as the 'decad', a third of a month or ten days: hence the number thirty-six. Let us suppose that Decan I marks the end of night for ten days, and is then replaced by Decan II: Decan I will now rise some time before dawn, in full darkness. We can consider its rising to mark the end of the 'hour' of the night next to the last. When Decan II is replaced as marker ten days later by Decan III, Decan II will mark the next to last 'hour', and Decan I the last 'hour' but two. This process can be continued, and thus we have a means of subdividing the night by means of the rising of the decans. It can be shown that in summer, at the latitude of Egypt, only twelve decans could be seen rising in darkness. This fact

[1] A fragment of a similar star-clock is in the much later cenotaph of Sety I (beginning of the Nineteenth Dynasty).

led to the division of the night into twelve 'hours'. Consequently the star-clocks consist essentially of thirty-six columns with twelve lines (see Inset 6), giving for each decad and each hour of night the decan whose rising marks the end of that hour. Each decan moves diagonally upwards in regular fashion from one decad to the next.

INSET 6

								Hours
36	35	34	Decads	4	3	2	1	
XXXVI	XXXV	XXXIV	....	IV	III	II	I	1
....	XXXVI	XXXV	....	V	IV	III	II	2
		XXXVI	....	VI	V	IV	III	3
				VII	VI	V	IV	4
				VIII	VII	VI	V	5
				IX	VIII	VII	VI	6
				X	IX	VIII	VII	7
				XI	X	IX	VIII	8
				XII	XI	X	IX	9
				XIII	XII	XI	X	10
				XIV	XIII	XII	XI	11
				XV	XIV	XIII	XII	12

Unfortunately this simple scheme is complicated by the fact that the Egyptian year contains not 360 but 365 days. In order to reckon time at night during the five epagomenal days which were added to the twelve regular months another twelve intermediate decans were introduced. However, by the time the coffin star-clocks were made this element of the scheme was hopelessly out of step with the remainder: at best it may represent a corrupt fossilization of a system which would have worked several centuries before. The fact that the Egyptian year contained only 365 days, instead of about $365\frac{1}{4}$, meant that it fell a complete decad behind every forty years: this would entail frequent revision of the relation of decans to hours and decads in the star-clocks, and there is in fact some evidence of such revision in the texts. But whether the system was still usable for time-measurement even at the period of the earliest extant texts seems to me doubtful.

Additional information about the decans is given in a cosmological text found in the cenotaph of Sety I (Nineteenth Dynasty)
and the tomb of Ramesses IV (Twentieth Dynasty), together with
the commentary on this text contained in a demotic papyrus. In
the latter it is stated that, like Sothis (Sirius), each decan spends
seventy days in the *Duat* (underworld), i.e. the decans were
selected so as to have the same period of invisibility as Sirius.
This would seem to afford a means of identification of the decans
(no identifications are certain except Sirius and a constellation
roughly corresponding to Orion). But we cannot assume that
seventy days is more than a round number, and the brightness of
a star affects its visibility period considerably. So the most that
can be established is that the decans lie in a belt roughly following
the line of the ecliptic, and lying slightly south of it.[1]

The cosmological texts also tell us that the decans now mark
the hours not by their rising but by their culmination (reaching
of the highest point on their course, in other words meridian
transit). This modification may have been introduced to rectify
the cumulative error due to the 365-day year mentioned above.
It involved considerable changes in the decans used, for two stars
which cross the horizon an hour apart may cross the meridian
at a much greater or smaller interval if they have different declina-
tions, which will usually be the case. The results of the change
can be seen in the decan lists of the two later tombs, which show
omissions and insertions as compared with earlier monuments.
However, it is not credible that the decans were still being employed for time measurement in the Nineteenth and Twentieth
Dynasties. We must regard them rather as traditional iconographic
elements; in this role they were destined for a long life.

In the New Kingdom another method for telling time by the
stars was devised. Examples of it are found in the tombs of
Ramesses VI, VII, and IX (whose reigns belong to the latter half

[1] For a demonstration of this, see *Egyptian Astronomical Texts*, i,
pp. 97–100.

of the twelfth century B.C.). It consists of twenty-four tables, one for each half-month interval. With each table there is a representation of a seated figure (see Inset 7).[1] Above him is a grid of nine vertical lines intersected by fourteen horizontal lines. The inner

INSET 7

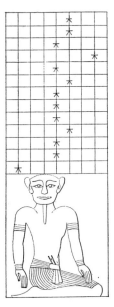

Head of the giant	Beginning of night
his neck	1st hour
his hip	2nd hour
his shank	3rd hour
his pedestal	4th hour
ꜥryt	5th hour
Head of the bird	6th hour
its rump	7th hour
Star of the thousands	8th hour
Star of sꜥr	9th hour
Predecessor of Orion	10th hour
Star of Orion	11th hour
Star of Sothis	12th hour

seven vertical lines are associated, from left to right, with the figure's left[2] shoulder, left ear, left eye, heart, right eye, right ear, and right shoulder respectively. For the beginning of night, and for the end of each hour up to the twelfth, a star is named, and described as being 'opposite the heart', 'on the left eye', or

[1] This is a schematic version not corresponding exactly to any single table. For instance, the description of the location of the stars has been omitted, because this is indicated on the chart. But the stars shown are those of *Egyptian Astronomical Texts*, ii, table 2, and the figure and chart have been taken from C. R. Lepsius, *Denkmäler*, iii. 227a.

[2] That is 'left' as seen by the observer.

in one of the other positions listed above. It is also marked on the grid in the appropriate place.

What we have here is clearly a list of transits. We may assume that the central line 'opposite the heart' represents the meridian, and the other lines altitude circles to east and west as seen by an observer seated opposite the figure and facing south. Whether the figure represents a dummy fixed on a particular spot, or just another man who takes up a position to the south of the observer, we have no means of deciding. In either case the device is a very crude one, as a small shift in the position of the observer's eye could make a comparatively large time difference. The reason for the use of the seven altitude circles instead of the single meridian is that only a limited number of stars, belonging to a few constellations (and hence easily recognizable), were employed to mark time throughout the year. The hours must have originally been measured by some mechanical device (the only one known to have been used in Egypt at the time is the water-clock), and the transits marking the ends of the hours observed and recorded, or, if none of the marker stars was crossing the meridian at the end of an hour, one which was close to the meridian was chosen, and its distance to east or west fixed by association with the figure as described above.

The system is obviously inspired by the decanal transit scheme. But the substitution of fifteen- for ten-day intervals brings awkward consequences with it. Clearly any particular star can no longer move back one hour from table to table as the decans do (cf. Inset 6). The reason is that the twelve hour division is a natural result of the thirty-six-division of the year. A twenty-four-division of the year leads naturally to a division of the night into a smaller number of 'hours'. The combination of the twenty-four-division of the year with the twelve-hour division of the night means that any star has to skip two or three hours in passing from marking the twelfth hour to marking the beginning of night; so more stars have to be introduced. To keep these to a minimum, the device of the additional lines to right and left was invented. But this is highly unsatisfactory from an observational point of view. Moreover, the decanal system guarantees equal division of hours. The other system has inherent in it errors caused by the inaccuracy of the water-clock, the compromises necessitated by the use of only a few marker stars, and the crudeness of observation implied by 'on the right eye', etc.[1] It must have resulted in considerable variation in the length of the hours of any one night. Such variation can in fact be deduced from the tables alone.

However, the system would work after a fashion. But by the time of the monuments where it appears it was long out of date. It can be shown from the date and time of the culmination of Sirius in the tables that they were composed about 1500 B.C. Without revision they would have been perfectly useless after about a hundred years. So here again the representations have become traditional iconographic features, and we need not suppose that the system was still in use for measuring time.

There are a number of later Egyptian astronomical texts, but their contents are entirely Greek in origin,[2] and do not concern us here. The texts we have described show that the Egyptians never really began to construct a theoretical astronomy. The systems presuppose knowledge of the uniform rotation of the heavens, and the annual cycle of phenomena connected with the rising of stars, and nothing more. The decanal system worked reasonably well because the length of night does not vary greatly in Egypt (in more northerly latitudes it would be very inadequate for dividing the period of darkness into twelve). But both this and the second system became obsolete because of the inability of the Egyptians to take proper account of the difference between

[1] These considerations, together with our ignorance of what distances from the meridian are indicated by such expressions as 'on the right eye', make identification of the stars on the basis of these texts impossible.

[2] The one exception (Carlsberg demotic papyrus No. 9) is calendarical rather than astronomical. See above, p. 19.

calendaric and tropical year. It is not surprising that Egyptian astronomy as such had absolutely no effect on later astronomy.

What is surprising is the persistence of the tradition in the Greek world that the Egyptians were both theoretical and observational astronomers. We can say with certainty that the first adjective is false; of the second all that can be said is that there is no trace of astronomical observation (beyond what has been described above) in all the immense mass of documents from Egypt, and that the Greek astronomer Ptolemy, who lived in Egypt and used all the observational material available to him, including Babylonian records, does not quote a single Egyptian observation in all his voluminous work.

However, Greek astronomy did take something from the Egyptians: the 365-day year was adopted for astronomical time-reckoning so that dates could be expressed in an unambiguous way and the intervals between them easily computed (which was not possible with the complicated Greek calendars). A year of unvarying length was particularly useful in the construction of astronomical tables.

Furthermore, the division of the day into twenty-four hours was first developed in Egypt.[1] We have seen how the night came to be divided into twelve hours as a result of the use of ten-day intervals between the decans marking the end of night. The day was divided into ten hours, and one hour reckoned at either end for twilight, giving a total of twenty-four hours of unequal length. By 1300 B.C. at the latest the concept of twenty-four equal hours had been developed, and this is the unit used by the Greek astronomers, which has since been universally adopted. (In the Graeco–Roman world, however, the civil hours were one-twelfth of the day and night respectively, and so varied in length seasonally. The seasonal hour too probably originated in Egypt, but its history there is obscure.)

[1] For a detailed discussion of the whole subject see *Egyptian Astronomical Texts*, i, pp. 116 f.

Finally, we have to mention the later development of the decans. When the zodiac was introduced into Egypt by the Greeks, the decans were associated with it, each of the thirty-six being assimilated to a third of a zodiacal sign. (This can be seen on the famous zodiac of Dendera, and several other Egyptian monuments.) Thus they ceased to have even a nominal connection with groups of stars (as we have seen, the original decans all lay south of the ecliptic), and became merely pictures with an added astrological significance. In this guise they enjoyed popularity wherever astrology flourished, and can be traced all over Europe and the lands of Islam through antiquity and the Middle Ages into the Renaissance. It is appropriate to the Egyptian genius that the elegant pictorial element survived while the crude astronomical one vanished. G. J. TOOMER

BIBLIOGRAPHY

Mathematics

The main texts to be consulted are *The Rhind mathematical papyrus*, edited by T. E. Peet, Liverpool University Press, 1923, and the Moscow papyrus (*Mathematischer Papyrus des Staatlichen Museums der Schönen Künste in Moskau*, herausgegeben von W. W. Struve, *Quellen und Studien zur Geschichte der Mathematik*, Abt. A, Bd. 1, Berlin, 1930), both with translation and commentary. There is another edition of the Rhind papyrus by A. B. Chace (2 vols., Oberlin, 1927 and 1929), chiefly remarkable for the reproductions of the papyrus and for the bibliography of Egyptian mathematics by R. C. Archibald. By far the best account of Egyptian mathematics is that by O. Neugebauer in *Vorlesungen über Geschichte der antiken mathematischen Wissenschaften: Vorgriechische Mathematik*, Berlin, 1934. This book deals with both Babylonian and Egyptian mathematics, but should be read as a whole for the illuminating comparison. Shorter accounts in English are those by T. E. Peet in the *Bulletin of the John Rylands Library*, xv (1931), and by O. Neugebauer in Chapter IV of his book *The exact sciences in antiquity*, 2nd ed., Brown University Press, 1957, reprinted Harper Torchbooks (New York, 1962). Rather more detailed is Kurt Vogel's *Vorgriechische Mathematik* Tl. 1, Zweiter Teil, *Mathematische Studienhefte*, Heft 1, Hannover und Paderborn, 1958.

Astronomy

All the extant texts and monuments dealing with decans, star-clocks, zodiacs, and planets have been published with photographs, translations, and commentaries by O. Neugebauer and R. A. Parker as *Egyptian astronomical texts*, in three volumes (Brown University Press, 1960, 1964, 1969). (I wish to thank Messrs. Parker and Neugebauer for allowing me access to vols. ii and iii before publication.) A brief account of Egyptian astronomy can be found in Chapter IV of Neugebauer's *Exact sciences*. For the history of the water-clock and the problems of Egyptian time-measurement in general, see L. Borchardt's *Die Altägyptische Zeitmessung*, Bd. 1, Lieferung B of *Die Geschichte der Zeitmessung und der Uhren*, herausgegeben von Ernst von Bassermann–Jordan, Berlin und Leipzig, 1920. For the later history of the decans the standard work is W. Gundel, *Dekane und Dekansternbilder*, Studien der Bibliothek Warburg xix, Hamburg, 1936.

3

THE CANONICAL TRADITION

THE various canons or systems of proportion which from Egypt to the Renaissance were used as tabulations of the mutual relations of the different parts of the body in its artistic representation constitute a distinct and continuous tradition in Western art, but in recent times, ever since they lost their artistic and technical significance during the mannerism of the sixteenth century, they have been strangely ignored and forgotten, or considered as technicalities of no particular interest or importance.[1]

From an artistic standpoint they were soon reduced to simple technical devices, or completely abandoned, by artists who felt their formal claims incompatible with the new demands for artistic liberty and unrestrained freedom of expression, and they became suspect even as historical phenomena, partly because their speculative and metaphysical overtones made them distasteful to historians of art who were unmetaphysical and rationalistic by nature, conviction, or principle, and partly because their technical and mathematical implications made them repellent to influential schools of aestheticists confessing to 'the romantic interpretation of a work of art as something utterly irrational',[2] to the understanding of which it was considered philistine as well as sacrilegious to adduce factual evidence based on formal considerations, reason, or commonsense.

In recent years a reaction has set in against this unhistorical attitude towards the problem, and Panofsky in particular has demonstrated how, irrespective of any changes in the underlying

[1] E. Panofsky, 'The History of the Theory of Human Proportions as a Reflection of the History of Styles', in *Meaning in the Visual Arts*, New York, 1955, pp. 55 f. (no. 2). [2] Ibid.

conceptions of art and the canons, the various canonical systems of Egypt, Greece, Rome, Byzantium, and the Renaissance were simple mathematical projections of the styles they reflect. By tabulating the formal pattern and the stylistic characteristics of the different periods and epochs in concrete numerical terms they express their *Kunstwollen*, that is, their basic conception of the nature, aim, and appearance of art, 'in a clearer or, at least, more definable fashion than art itself'.[1]

Thus considered, the stylistic problems are transferred from the abstract sphere of aesthetics to the concrete realm of what the ancients themselves termed 'geometry', and the systems of proportion acquire a new art-historical and archaeological significance, because 'the history of the canons *eo ipso* becomes a reflection of the history of style'.

It is obvious, though, that in order to turn this theoretical attitude to practical advantage and interpret the stylistic message of the canons we must necessarily be able to define them as systematic entities, explain the principles of their construction, and express in simple numerical terms the ratios determining the mutual relations of their units. Strangely enough, this elementary analysis has proved the stumbling-block which more than any other difficulty has barred the way to a satisfactory solution of the canonical problem.

In the following pages we shall adopt a historical approach, in an effort to demonstrate the origin and development of such ideas in Egypt, where a proper theory of human proportions was first advanced and developed into an artistic canon determining the ratios of the various parts of the body. Curiously enough, the theory was originally advanced to serve not artistic but metrological purposes. It was based on the empirical observation, made long before the Egyptians had inaugurated their artistic tradition, of the well-established physiological fact that the mutual relations of the various parts of the human body are constant and immutable

[1] E. Panofsky, loc. cit.

in all individuals irrespective of any differences in size and dimensions. That the Egyptians had indeed made this observation in predynastic or protodynastic times and already established a correct standardization of the ratios involved is proved by the fact that they used them as the basis of their ordinary measure of length, the so-called small cubit.

Like all linear measurements before the introduction of the decimal system, the Egyptian measure was composed of units corresponding to the various parts of the body, which as metrological units retained the mutual relations of their natural proportions. The basic unit was the cubital armlength from the elbow to the tip of the thumb, which also in Egyptian was known as 'the forearm'. In accordance with the natural proportions it was divided into 6 palms or handbreadths measured on the back of the hand across the knuckles, and each handbreadth represented 4 fingers. As in all pre-metrical measures the thumb (*pollux*, *uncia*, inch) represented $1\frac{1}{3}$ ordinary fingers, and the full handbreadth or fist of 4 fingers plus the thumb was consequently $5\frac{1}{3}$ fingers or $1\frac{1}{3}$ ordinary handbreadths. The distance from the elbow to the wrist corresponded to 4 handbreadths or $\frac{2}{3}$ cubits. In Egypt this unit was known as the two-thirds measure, but in the otherwise identical systems of linear measurement of the Mediterranean world, including Greece and Rome, it was called the foot (πούς).

Four cubits constituted one fathom, originally identified with the distance from thumb to thumb measured along the stretched arms across the chest, but also, according to the explicit statement of Herodotus in his account of Egyptian metrology, with the height of a standing man, measured, as we shall see, from the feet to the hairline of the forehead. The so-called royal cubit, also in later times known as πῆχυς βασιλικός, was identified with the armlength from the elbow to the tip of the medius. It was consequently 4 fingers or 1 handbreadth longer than the small cubit, that is 7 handbreadths. It was originally introduced for fiscal reasons as a *Bauelle*.

For ease of consultation we may tabulate the units and the ratios involved in the following manner:

Finger	1					
Inch or thumb	1⅓	1				
Handbreadth	4	3	1			
Full handbreadth:[1] four fingers plus thumb	5⅓	4	1⅓	1		
Two-thirds measure: arm-length from elbow to wrist	16	12	4	3	1	
Cubit: armlength from elbow to thumb tip	24	18	6	4½	⅔	1
Fathom: height	96	72	24	18	6	4	1
Royal cubit: armlength from elbow to tip of medius	28	21	7	5¼	..	..	..

As a standardization of the natural proportions of the body these ratios constitute in themselves a system of human proportions, an elementary canon, which was fully established at the beginning of dynastic times when the artistic traditions of Egypt were inaugurated.

When faced with what has everywhere and at all times been the basic canonical problem, namely, how to scale the various parts of the body in artistic representation, the Egyptians chose what to them was the only natural solution: to use the anthropometric description of the linear measurements as their artistic canon of proportions. From a practical point of view this ingenious solution

[1] The modular full handbreadth of 4 fingers plus 1 thumb or inch of 1⅓ fingers is sculpturally expressed in the characteristic clenched hand or fist, and represents a standardization of its natural anatomical proportions, that is 5⅓ fingers or 1⅓ handbreadths. In the metrological systems, where the modulus was 1 handbreadth of 4 fingers, there was no specific unit corresponding to 1⅓ handbreadths, simply because this was always resolved into 1 handbreadth plus 1 inch. On the cubit rods and in metrological texts the hieroglyphic signs, ⌒, ⌒, and ⌒ are therefore used to signify 4, 5, and 6 fingers respectively. This is a practical metrological convention derived from finger-counting, and has nothing to do with the anatomical and proportional relationships of the parts concerned.

had the great advantage that the individual representations could be made to agree with the theory of proportions simply by letting their members retain the numerical relations of the corresponding units of the linear measurement. In this way they would always conform with the canon and each other, irrespective of their varying dimensions, and they would always reflect the natural proportions of the body.

In order to ensure the correct proportioning of the individual representations in practice, the Egyptians invented a method of great efficacy by the introduction of the so-called grids, a system of squares representing a geometrical projection of the canon (Fig. 1). On the rectangular blocks intended for sculpture in-the-round, the squares were drawn or incised on at least two sides, and on the plane surfaces prepared for two-dimensional representations they were either ruled with a straight-edge or marked by means of strings dipped in red ochre.

The connection between the body and the grids was established along the frontal axis of the figures, which in sculpture in-the-round ran between the eyes, along the ridge of the nose, and through the navel to a point between the feet, dividing the entire body into identical halves. In two-dimensional representations, i.e. reliefs and paintings, of which Fig. 1 is a typical example still inscribed in its original grid, the axis ran through the ear, the neck, and the chest from a to Z. Apart from the chest between 14h and 16d, which is seen from the front and divided into two halves of which the front for obscure reasons is always one quarter of a square broader than the back, the various parts of the figure are turned around the axis in such a way that what is seen in front of it represents the forepart of the body, and what lies behind it is the back. The latter is always seen in profile, but the front is partly in profile (the nipple) and partly in '*Schrägansicht*' (the navel).[1]

---

[1] The navel is not indicated in Fig. 1. Comparisons show that it should be placed in square no. 12, immediately to the left of the vertical line through α, and above the horizontal line through 11l.

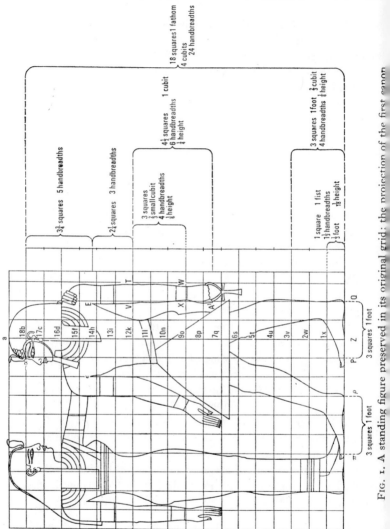

FIG. 1. A standing figure preserved in its original grid: the projection of the first canon.

It will be seen that by turning the various parts *until they regain their natural positions in relation to the line a–Z*, the figure is made to resume its normal appearance in a frontal aspect, and the line itself assumes its original position as the three-dimensional frontal axis. The realization of this function of the axis is of great importance for the understanding of the difference between two- and three-dimensional renderings of the human body in Egyptian art. It demonstrates with great clarity the constructional principles involved, and proves that the former are merely geometrical projections of the latter, leaving no essential part of the body unaccounted for. They represent the Egyptian solution of the eternal problem of how to confine a three-dimensional body in a two-dimensional plane, and, as no optical, visual, or mental problems are involved, they cannot possibly be used in support of theories of a particular Egyptian attitude towards visual phenomena.

The technical problem about the construction of the grids and their theoretical relation to the system of proportion has also been the subject of much discussion and many controversies, but seen against the background of the metrological origin of the latter it finds a simple and natural solution.

We have seen that the canonical height from feet to hairline corresponds to the metrological unit of one fathom. As it is always divided into 18 squares by the grids, the sidelength of one individual square must necessarily represent a metrological unit which is an eighteenth part of the fathom. The table on page 58 shows that the eighteenth part of the fathom is the full handbreadth of 4 fingers plus thumb (1 fathom = 24 handbreadths; $\frac{1}{18}$th fathom = $1\frac{1}{3}$ handbreadths; $1\frac{1}{3}$ handbreadths = $5\frac{1}{3}$ fingers = 4 ordinary fingers plus 1 inch or thumb), and Fig. 1, as well as all other inscribed figures, shows that the only anatomical part which always corresponds exactly to the sidelength of the modular square is in fact the full handbreadth of the clenched or extended hand, which is therefore the anatomical modulus used for the construction of the grids. Against this background the relation between drawing and grid such as is seen in Fig. 1 becomes clear and understandable. The 18 squares of the height from a to Z represent the 24 handbreadths of one metrological fathom ($18 \times 1\frac{1}{3} = 24$). The $4\frac{1}{2}$ squares of the cubital armlength from elbow to thumb (V to A^1) become the 6 handbreadths of the cubit ($4\frac{1}{2} \times 1\frac{1}{3} = 6$), and retain the correct metrological relationship to the fathom height of four to one ($18 (24): 4\frac{1}{2}(6) = 4$). The distance from elbow to wrist (3 squares) is $\frac{2}{3}$ of the cubital armlength ($4\frac{1}{2} \times \frac{2}{3} = 3$), and therefore represents correctly the 4 handbreadths of the two-thirds measure ($3 \times 1\frac{1}{2} = 4$) and $\frac{1}{6}$ of the height. In accordance with their natural proportions, the feet (π–ρ and P–Q) are of uneven length ($3\frac{1}{4}$ and $3\frac{1}{2}$ squares respectively) and longer than the canonical 3 squares. This is a notation frequently used for kings and persons of exalted rank, the ordinary canonical length being 3 squares (4 handbreadths) corresponding to the armlength from elbow to wrist (the two-thirds measure).

All other parts of the body are accordingly fixed in the grids at their 'natural' positions when measured in modular squares of $1\frac{1}{3}$ handbreadths or simple fractions thereof, generally $\frac{1}{4}$, $\frac{1}{2}$, or $\frac{3}{4}$. In its entirety, therefore, any canonical figure represents a complete anthropometric description of the body, based on the anatomical units and the established ratios of the linear measurement.

The mutual relations between anatomy, metrology, and grids may be tabulated in the following manner:

Anatomical parts	Metrological values	Number of squares
Full handbreadth, four fingers plus thumb	$1\frac{1}{3}$ handbreadths	1 square
Armlength from elbow to wrist, foot	Two-thirds measure: 4 handbreadths	3 squares
Armlength from elbow to thumb-tip	Cubit: 6 handbreadths	$4\frac{1}{2}$ squares

Anatomical parts	Metrological values	Number of squares
Armlength from elbow to tip of medius	Royal cubit: 7 handbreadths	5¼ squares
Height from feet to hairline, distance from thumb to thumb	Fathom: 4 cubits: 24 handbreadths	18 squares

A comparison with the table on page 58 makes it clear that the significant anatomical parts of the canon are those corresponding to the basic units of the linear measurement, and that the former have the same mutual relations as the latter. We are therefore able to define the Egyptian canon as *a system of proportions representing an anthropometric description of the body based on the standardization of its natural proportions expressed in the ratios of the Egyptian measure of length.* At the same time the grid may be defined as *a geometrical projection of the canon, in which the sidelength of the modular square represents the anatomical unit of one full handbreadth (four fingers plus thumb) with the proportional value of* 1⅛ *metrological handbreadths.*

Throughout the history of Egyptian art the standing male figure remained the canonical archetype of all other types of representation, and the methods employed to make these comply with the original canonical pattern are clearly illustrated by Fig. 2, a typical representation of a seated figure preserved in its original grid. To understand its relation to the standing figure it is necessary once more to draw attention to the basic importance of the axis a–Z, for the canonical structure of the seated figure can be understood only when it is realized that the canonical divisions follow the bends of the body from the heel to the knee (square no. 6), along the upper part of the leg *until the axis*, and from here along the torso across the chest seen *en face*, to the ear. Thus considered, each separate part of the body is placed in its correct anatomical and canonical position in exactly the same

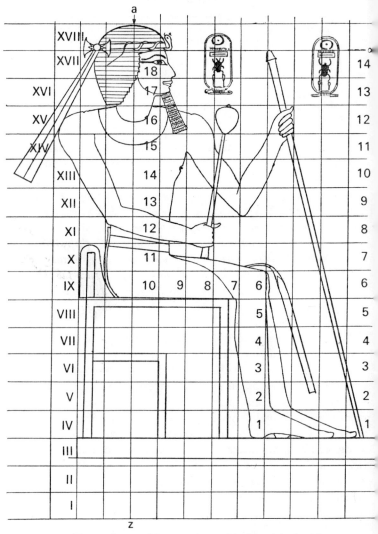

Fig. 2. A seated figure preserved in its original grid

squares as on Fig. 1 when counted from the feet or the head. If therefore the entire figure is straightened out along the a–Z axis, so that its feet are made to rest on the bottom line of the grid, its hairline is immediately transferred to the top line of the eighteenth square, and it is automatically transformed into a correct representation of a standing figure, while its proportions remain unaffected and in every way conform with the canon.

Exactly the same method was used to construct any other type of figure, and to make every single gesture, movement, and position, however stylized or complex, conform with the system of proportions, with the result that the canonical material developed into an enormous code comprising the entire formal pattern of Egyptian art. Essentially stable and unalterable, but forever changing in detail owing to subtle modifications in style and fashion, it permitted the development of stylistic periods and epochs almost as distinct as our own, while yet remaining dependent upon the same artistic intentions and the same unbroken tradition.

The registration of these contrapuntal variations of the canonical theme has hardly been begun; but an analysis of their geometrical reflections in the grids—which with our present knowledge of the canon we are able to reconstruct for any canonical figure—would provide entirely new possibilities for the identification, reconstruction, dating, and localization of monuments, and an unparalleled opportunity to follow the stylistic evolution of the oldest and longest continuous tradition in the history of art. Nothing demonstrates with greater clarity the inner stability and balance of Egyptian culture than the fact that for more than two millennia Egyptian artists were able to find complete harmonious expression within a single tradition, without once changing its principles and ideas—with the sole exception of the Amarna age, which cannot be considered here. If, therefore, one of the eternal differences between classical and romantic art may be defined in the ability of the former to fulfil itself within the framework of an established form, which the latter must of necessity destroy in

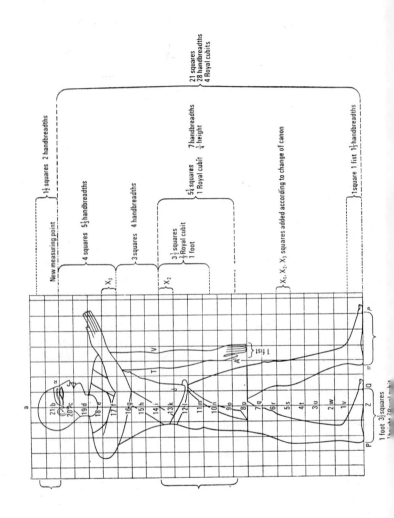

New measuring point

1½ squares 2 handbreadths

4 squares 5⅓ handbreadths

3 squares 4 handbreadths

X_3

X_2

3½ squares
⅔ Royal cubit
1 foot

5¼ squares
1 Royal cubit

7 handbreadths
¼ height

21 squares
28 handbreadths
4 Royal cubits

X_1, X_2, X_3 squares added according to change of canon

1 square 1 fist 1⅓ handbreadths

1 foot 3⅔ squares
1 height 20 royal cubits

1 fist 1

21 b
20 c
19 d
18 e
17 f
16 g
15 h
14 i
13 k
12 l
11 m
10 n
9 o
8 p
7 q
6 r
5 s
4 t
3 u
2 w
1 v

a
α
T
V
A
P
Z
Π
P

order to find expression, then Egyptian art was truly classical throughout its history. Even the canonical reform of the Twenty-sixth Dynasty, known as the Saite canon, did not represent a deliberate break with the old traditions, brought about by artistic necessity or an irresistible urge to find new formal expression for changes in intention or attitude, but was in every respect merely a technical effort to adapt the old principles to new conditions.

Our present understanding of the Saite canon, of which a typical example is seen in Fig. 3, is unfortunately still imperfect, and the scope of the present study does not permit discussion of the highly technical metrological problems involved. The following observations are therefore of necessity hypothetical as well as preliminary.

Considering the origin and general character of the system of proportions as such, it is significant that the canonical change coincided with a metrological reform by which the original small cubit was abandoned as an ordinary measure of length in favour of the royal cubit, and there are strong indications that the Saite canon and the new projection of the grids were merely technical efforts to adjust the ancient canon to the new conditions arising from the exchange of the two units also in the system of proportions.

In this respect it is highly important to realize the changed metrological functions and divisions of the royal cubit after the reform. In the ancient system it was merely an extension of the small cubit by 1 handbreadth, corresponding to the natural relation between the armlength from the elbow to the thumb-tip (6 handbreadths) and the armlength from the elbow to the tip of the medius (7 handbreadths). In the reformed system the royal cubit was still identified with the full armlength, but was henceforward divided into 6 new 'royal' handbreadths, which from a metrological viewpoint were larger than the old ones, but, by dividing the armlength into 6 instead of $5\frac{1}{4}$ parts, represented a finer division, that is, a division undertaken with a smaller modulus than that of the full handbreadth of the old grids.[1] The new projection of the grid characteristic of the Saite canon will be seen in Fig. 3. The full armlength from elbow to medius is here 6 squares and the old cubital armlength to the thumb-tip is $5\frac{1}{4}$ squares, which was the old division of the full armlength (the royal cubit) in the old grids. It is still $\frac{1}{4}$ of the height, which is now measured to a new line through the eye and the root of the nose and divided into 21 squares instead of 18, but the distance from elbow to wrist is now 4 squares like the feet, which means that these are no longer $\frac{2}{3}$ of the armlength to the thumb, but of the new cubital armlength to the medius ($6 \times \frac{2}{3} = 4$).[2]

Since the proportional value of the modulus has become diminished it must necessarily also have changed its anatomical identity, and a comparison of the relatively few representations still preserved in original grids does show that the full handbreadth of Saite representations is always broader than the sidelength of the new modular square, which seems to correspond to 1 ordinary handbreadth of 4 fingers.[3] This is a strong corroboration of the assumption that the armlength to the thumb-tip was no longer considered the cubital modulus of the system in spite of its unchanged relation to the height, and that it had been replaced by the full armlength, that is the royal cubit, of which the two-thirds measure and the feet were now therefore considered $\frac{2}{3}$. The constructional modulus of the new grid was consequently no longer the original full handbreadth of $5\frac{1}{3}$ fingers but the ordinary handbreadth of 4, which henceforward was considered $\frac{1}{6}$th of the new cubital armlength. This would represent a simplification of

[1] This was pointed out by R. Hanke in an important contribution in *ZÄS* lxxxiv (1959), 113–19.

[2] Through influence from the old canon the feet frequently retain their old division into 3 squares representing $\frac{1}{7}$th of the canonical height; cf. below, p. 75.

[3] This cannot be seen directly in Fig. 3, the hands of which are seen in a side view. This shortens their notation from $1\frac{1}{3}$ squares to 1; but cf. for instance the hands of the figure represented in *JEA* iv (1917), pl. xviii, no. 3.

the system, and it would explain the nature of the diminished modulus as well as the theoretical reasons for its introduction. But until the change of the measuring-point has been explained, and the relations between the old and the new notations have been accounted for in all their details, the problem of the Saite canon and its projection remains essentially unresolved, and must await a final solution. That it did not represent an artistic, but merely a technical reform seems evident, and this is confirmed by the monuments, which did not change their basic style and formal appearance.

When, nevertheless, its introduction did in fact effect a fateful and decisive break in the tradition it was because, by abandoning the empirical approach to the problem of human proportions in favour of a theorizing one, it broke the rigorous logic of the old system and its basic law that the canon should in every respect reflect the natural proportions of the body. This led to a hitherto unknown inconsistency in the application of the canonical principles such as we have seen in the proportioning of the feet,[1] and contributed eventually to the dissolution of the sublime interplay of craftsmanship and art which had always characterized Egyptian art with its perfect balance of form and content, of artistic intentions and technical possibilities. For, against the attitude of other periods towards artistic freedom, it is curious to observe that the self-imposed restrictions of the canon had never hampered the creativeness of Egyptian artists or lowered the standard of their work. Rather the opposite would seem to have been the case, for the most rigorously canonical representations in Egyptian art are also as a rule those of the highest artistic perfection.

The important question as to what extent the canonical principles influenced the appearance of Egyptian art in other respects than proportioning is an art-historical problem which cannot be considered here, but it is worth remembering that the technical procedure associated with their application resulted in the dependence

[1] See above, p. 68, n. 2.

of the finished works of art upon the cubic or rectangular shape of the original block of stone. They were also at the bottom of the entire typological development of Egyptian representational art, and its dependence on standardized and conventional types and gestures, and were directly responsible for its characteristic geometrical anatomy. The practice of making the dimensions of the subordinate figures and decorative elements of each episodic representation directly dependent on those of the main figure by inscribing them in grids representing simple fractions of those used for the latter created a 'concord of dimensions' contributing essentially, as a strong centripetal force, to the harmonious interplay of the otherwise often isolated and unreconciled elements of Egyptian episodic art, with its loose and schematic construction.

However, for the true understanding of the significance of the canonical principles it would be a grave mistake to let their technical nature and functions overshadow the cult reasons for their introduction and employment. Mobilized as one of the principal instruments in the heroic and continuous struggle against death and destruction which was the *leit-motiv* of the religious culture of Egypt throughout its history, the ultimate aim and purpose of Egyptian art was always magico-religious—to guarantee the eternal bodily survival of its representations in the hereafter. The human body was therefore always its principal object, and the formal appearance of monuments on which depended the eternal existence of the models became necessarily a problem fraught with fateful import and consequence. Only by making it subordinate to the inviolable rules of an immutable canon, equally independent of the temporal appearance of the model and of the conception of the artist, was it possible to obtain the characteristic stylized naturalism in which the objects were seen as it were *sub specie aeterni*, irrespective of their appearance in time and space. Such representation was considered essential for the fulfilment of their cult purpose and only against this background can the immutability and ritual observance ot the canonical rules be understood.

In addition to its technical and cult functions the canon served one more essential purpose, as the principle upon which were based the aesthetic conceptions of the Egyptians as well as their entire evaluation of art and beauty. There is no evidence of the existence of a literary theory of art in Egypt, and it is probable that the Egyptians never felt the urge or the inclination to reduce to words what they had given such sublime expression in art. On the other hand, it is obvious that they must have had certain standards and principles for their appraisal and appreciation of art. Considered against the background of what has already been said it seems evident—to the author at least—that, like the Greeks and the Romans, the Egyptians considered the harmonious proportions of the *homo bene figuratus* a standard of beauty in itself, and that their conception of formal beauty is perfectly defined in Galen's introduction to his account of the canon of Polycleitus, where it is stated that 'beauty does not consist in the elements but in the harmonious proportion of the parts'.[1]

This represents the Stoic attitude towards art,[2] and corresponds with the conception of Egyptian art generally expressed by Greek authors such as Diodorus, who stresses its geometrical and symmetrical nature and makes the keen observation that in Egypt 'the symmetrical proportions of the statues are not fixed in accordance with the appearance they present to the artist's eye, as is done among the Greeks',[3] and Plato, who praises its immutability and stable regularity.[4] More than a half millennium later, when the death knell of Egyptian art and culture had been rung, the Stoic conception of art was elaborated by a native Egyptian, the 'divine'

[1] See below, p. 76, n. 2.

[2] See Bréhier's remarks in his edition of the *Ennéades* of Plotinus, Paris, 1924, i. 96.

[3] *Bibliotheca*, i. 98. 7. The translation is that of C. H. Oldfather, Loeb Classical Library.

[4] *Laws*, ii. 656 D. E.

Plotinus (A.D. 205–70), whose definition of beauty expresses the essential characteristics of Egyptian art even more clearly than that of Galen: 'the symmetry of the parts towards each other and towards a whole . . . constitutes beauty', and 'to be beautiful is to be symmetrical and fashioned after a certain measure'.[1] In its lapidary conciseness this definition of beauty constitutes a canonical aesthetic valid from Egypt through Greece to the Italian and German Renaissance, irrespective of all the inevitable changes in the underlying conception of art.

For the appreciation of the Egyptian contribution to the subsequent canonical tradition the establishment of this accord between the praxis of the Egyptians and the theory of the Greeks is of no mean importance. Before approaching this controversial problem it should be made clear that, as the supreme and quintessential manifestation of the Egyptian genius, Egyptian art was, generally speaking, too subtle an exponent of indigenous cultural conditions to permit its successful transplantation to other cultural climates. Nevertheless, its intrinsic values, its artistic, aesthetic, and technical qualities, were always appreciated and admired abroad, and throughout antiquity genuine Egyptian works of art were imported and treasured all over the Mediterranean world.

Certain architectural features such as the column, the cornice decorated with the winged disk of the sun, and possibly also the masonry vault may have been directly borrowed from Egypt, but otherwise the Egyptian influence on foreign arts outside Crete, Nubia, and Greece was almost exclusively restricted to decorative motifs and ornamental patterns, minor *objets d'art*, and the articles and utensils of applied art. Efforts, in ancient as well as in modern times, to imitate Egyptian sculpture have always been fatal, and resulted in barbarous travesties representing the Egyptian prototypes seen as it were in a distorting mirror (Pl. 4*b*), quite simply because the autochthonous spirit of Egyptian art could not

[1] Plotinus, *Enneads*, i. 6. The translation is from S. MacKenna, *Plotinus On the Beautiful*, Stratford on Avon, 1908.

manifest itself abroad, and its stylistic characteristics could not be caught and reproduced without an intimate knowledge of the canonical principles and rules, which were complicated and difficult to apprehend, could only be taught in Egypt, and were probably carefully guarded as professional if not esoteric secrets.

As a model and example of craftsmanship and technical skill Egyptian art undoubtedly exerted a widespread, though not easily traceable, influence on the ancient world, but not until the latest periods of its own development was it to become an active element in a new and fertile tradition through its encounter with the early art of Greece.

Owing to the difficulty of finding a mutual and profitable basis for comparison, the problem of the Egyptian influence on archaic Greek art has always been approached with diffidence and reluctance, especially by the classicists of former generations, most of whom were dogmatic believers in the spontaneous generation of everything Greek, convinced that all Greek mice had sprung miraculously from Greek rags in Greek lofts, and considered tactless and distasteful any talk about an influence on Greek art from what they considered a barbarous and inferior culture.

Not until recent years has the unmistakable stylistic resemblance between the *kouroi* and the corresponding Egyptian representations been acknowledged, and by authorities such as Panofsky and Miss Richter declared the result of an Egyptian influence or inspiration. In corroboration of the more abstract and theoretical evidence based on *Stilgefühl* and aesthetics, we shall here consider the problem in its canonical aspect. In this respect the curious evidence provided by Diodorus is highly important. We are told in the *Bibliotheca*[1] how two well-known artists from the sixth century, Telekles and Theodorus,[2] were commissioned by the

[1] *Bibliotheca*, i. 98. 5. Diodorus' statement is based on Hecataeus, See Pauly–Wissowa, *Realencyclopädie*, vii. 2 (1912), 2750, no. 4.

[2] Theodorus was the son of Telekles, not his brother as Diodorus has it; he lived about 550 B.C. See Pauly–Wissowa, V.A. 2 (1934), 1917, no. 195.

people of Samos with the execution of a statue of the Pythian Apollo, and that they made it in the Egyptian fashion by 'dividing the structure of the entire body into twenty-one parts and one fourth [τέταρτος] in addition'. That the 'twenty-one parts' correspond to the 21 squares into which the Saite grids divide the canonical height (from Z to 21b in Fig. 3) was already pointed out by Lepsius, but the 'one-fourth', which must necessarily refer to the supra-canonical distance from the canonical measuring-point to the crown of the head (the $1\frac{1}{2}$ squares above 21b in Fig. 3), has been considered erroneous owing to a misinterpretation of the term τέταρτος.

In metrological contexts this word is used exactly as the corresponding English term 'quarter' to designate the fourth part or quarter of each of the principal units of the current measures of weight, capacity, and length.[1] When referring to a linear measure τέταρτος is therefore the fourth part of the cubit, which in the Saite canon we have seen to be identified with the armlength from the elbow to the tip of the medius, and divided into 6 squares by the grids (cf. Fig. 3). We have also seen that the anatomical identification of τέταρτος must be the distance from the canonical measuring point at the root of the nose to the crown of the head. On ordinary figures without ceremonial head-dress this part represents $1\frac{1}{2}$ squares in the grids (Fig. 3), and $1\frac{1}{2}$ squares is exactly one-fourth of the 6 squares of the cubital armlength. The passage should therefore be translated 'twenty-one parts plus [the metrological unit of] one quarter'. Thus understood it becomes both perfectly clear and absolutely correct.

Whether the report as such represents a historical or an anecdotal truth is entirely irrelevant, since the indisputable fact remains that, at the time of Hecataeus at any rate, Greek scholars were correctly informed as to the basic principles of the Saite canon, frankly admitted their Egyptian origin, and had a

---

[1] Liddell and Scott, *Greek–English Lexicon*, s.v. τέταρτος ii. 2; iii. 2.

historical tradition relating to their first introduction and employment by Greek artists.

That we are not faced with an isolated phenomenon seems evident from Michaelis's analysis of the so-called metrological relief in the Ashmolean Museum, Oxford, dating from a period anterior to 439 B.C., and curiously enough, like the above-mentioned statue of the Pythian Apollo, supposedly of Samian origin.[1] It represents the upper part of the figure of a man with both arms extended, and with the outline of a foot inserted separately above the right arm (Pl. 3). Michaelis has demonstrated how the relations between the various parts of the figure, the armlength from the elbow to the tip of the medius, the foot, and the full extension of the body measured from the tip of one medius to the other, equal those of the corresponding units of the Greek measure of length with one significant variant, that the foot is $\frac{1}{7}$th of the fathom instead of $\frac{1}{6}$th. Owing to the above-mentioned conformity between the linear measurements of Egypt and Greece the ratios correspond to those known from the Egyptian canon, and even the proportioning of the foot has a direct parallel in the Saite canon, where the foot of 3 squares ($\frac{1}{7}$th fathom) is frequently used instead of the 'normal' one of $3\frac{1}{2}$ squares, owing to influence from the old canon.[2] The whole monument shows, therefore, the same characteristic interplay between anatomy and metrology as the late Egyptian system of proportion, has the same units, and operates with thes ame ratios and proportions, a conformity which can hardly be fortuitous.

The crucial question of whether the *kouroi* and the corresponding representations of Saite art are linked by a similar canonical conformity is more difficult to answer. Except for Caskey's efforts to demonstrate the dependence of archaic sculpture on established principles of proportion,[3] the canonical problems of the

[1] A. Michaelis, 'The Metrological Relief at Oxford', *Journ. Hellenic Studies*, iv (1883), 335–50.   [2] Cf. above, p. 68, n. 2.

[3] L. D. Caskey, 'The Proportions of the Apollo of Tenea', *American Journ. of Archaeology*, xxviii (1924), 358–67.

kouroi have never been systematically investigated, and we are therefore left without adequate material for comparison. However, from an Egyptological point of view it is not without interest to observe the rather curious results of a canonical analysis of the *kouros* in the Metropolitan Museum, New York. Miss Richter's original publication is provided with a geometrical projection of the statue based on the measurements of the original, and if, by way of experiment, we inscribe this projection in a grid constructed according to the rules of the Saite canon, dividing the canonical height from the feet to a line through the root of the nose into 21 squares (Fig. 4), a comparison with Fig. 3 shows that the two grids intersect the two figures at identical places. They must therefore necessarily reflect identical systems of proportion—must, that is, represent identical canons.[1]

Until the other *kouroi* have been subjected to a similar analysis their canonical relationship to the one from New York remains obscure, but Caskey's demonstration of their dependence on an established system of proportion is corroborated by the information that an already established canon was reformed by Polycleitus as early as the fifth century. This reformed canon is briefly described by Galen,[2] who states that 'beauty does not consist in the elements but in the harmonious proportion of the parts, the proportion of one finger to the other, of all fingers to the full extent of the hand from the wrist,[3] of these to the forearm, of the forearm to the whole arm, in fine, of all parts to all others, as described in

[1] Owing to the difference in head-dress the supra-canonical distance to the crown of the head from the measuring point is 1¾ squares in Fig. 4 as against 1½ in Fig. 3. The modulus of the grid is in each case the ordinary handbreadth of 4 fingers representing ⅙ of the cubital arm-length.

[2] *De Placitis Hippocratis et Platonis*, ed. I. Mueller, Leipzig, 1874, v. 449 (p. 426).

[3] The parallel passage from Vitruvius has 'the palm of the hand from the wrist to the top of the medius', which tends to show that μετακάρπιον here means the full extent of the hand from the wrist. The translation is otherwise that of Panofsky (above, p. 55, n. 1).

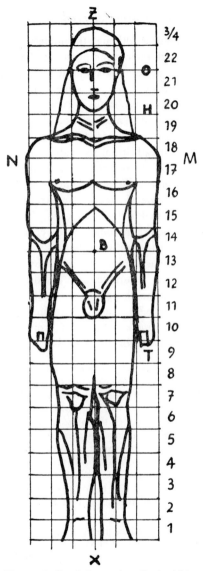

FIG. 4. A Greek *kouros* inscribed within
a reconstructed Saite grid

the canon of Polycleitus'.[1] Although the numerical relations of the parts are not indicated, their anthropometric origin is quite clear. They operate with the same anatomical units as the Egyptian canon and are dependent on the same principles. Even the sequence of the units is the same in each case, and the entire passage might just as well be a description of the Egyptian as of a Greek canon, with the important difference that the latter was obviously deduced directly from the natural proportions of the body, and not based on the metrological standardizations of them. Owing to their common origin this did not change the proportions, but gave greater anatomical accuracy in details, a circumstance which eventually resulted in the disappearance of the geometrical anatomy of the finished representations, by creating a new direct contact between the artist and his subject.

Even more instructive in this respect is Vitruvius' description of what he considered the 'natural' canon. The description is found as an introduction to the chapter on the building of temples in his book on architecture,[2] because in Vitruvius' view the human body constituted a paragon of natural proportions on which architecture also should be based. It runs:

For Nature has so planned the human body that the face from the chin to the top of the forehead and the roots of the hair is a tenth part; also the palm of the hand from the wrist to the top of the middle finger is as much; the head from the chin to the crown, an eighth part; from the top of the breast with the bottom of the neck to the roots of the hair, a sixth part; from the middle of the breast to the crown, a fourth part; a third part of the height of the face is from the bottom of the chin to the bottom of the nostrils; the nose from the bottom of the nostrils to the line between the brows, as much; from that line to the roots of the hair, the forehead is given as the third part. The foot is a sixth of the height

---

[1] The various efforts to deduce the canon from different copies of the Diadumenos cannot be considered here.

[2] *De Architectura*, iii. 1. 2. The translation is that of F. Granger, Loeb Classical Library.

of the body; the cubit a quarter, the breast also a quarter. The other limbs also have their own proportional measurements.

The passage displays several textual corruptions of which we are able to correct some by reference to the Egyptian canon with which they conform in almost every respect.[1] Their anthropometrical nature is indisputable and they operate with the same units and ratios, but like the canon of Polycleitus they are obviously derived directly from the body without any metrological medium.

The dependence of all these accounts, dating from different periods, on one continuous tradition seems indisputable, and no unbiased observer can deny that the material provides overwhelming evidence for the direct connection of the Greek with the Egyptian canon, or that the records of Hecataeus and Diodorus reflect a historical truth. This can hardly be thought surprising, for not only does it provide a simple and natural explanation of the unmistakable resemblance between the *kouroi* and their Egyptian prototypes, but it accords in every respect with the historical, political, and cultural conditions of the seventh and sixth centuries B.C., the embryonic and receptive period of Greek culture. In fact, it is difficult to imagine where it would have been more natural for the Greeks to turn for artistic guidance and inspiration, as well as technical instruction, than to Egypt, where they had already established their trading posts and served as mercenaries against the common enemy, where their philosophers and statesmen had travelled and become acquainted with an age-old culture which had struck them with awe and admiration, and where they had encountered a fully developed artistic tradition which was not only the oldest in the world, but unsurpassed in artistic perfection and technical skill.

However, in order to appreciate the true relationship between

[1] The measurement from the pit of the throat, for instance, should probably be $\frac{1}{9}$ instead of $\frac{1}{6}$, and the distance from the pit of the throat to the crown of the head $\frac{1}{6}$ instead of $\frac{1}{7}$.

the Egyptian and the Greek traditions, it is essential not merely to register what unites them, but also to realize their basic difference. In this respect it is highly significant that the outward resemblance between Egyptian and Greek representations was restricted to archaic sculpture dating from a period when Greek artists were still grappling with artistic and technical problems in the raw. From an artistic standpoint the canon was at that time still an unabsorbed technical instrument which the Greeks had not yet imbued with a spirit of their own, and which therefore revealed its foreign origin as a natural result of the eternal interplay of form and content, matter and idea. After the decisive crisis of the fifth century this was changed. The resemblance with Egyptian figures disappeared, effaced by the emergence of a new original style imbued with a new spirit, a new ethos, and a new theoretical purpose of its own.

The canonical principles continued to play a significant part in the development, but were from now on completely absorbed and incorporated as organic elements in a new conception of art, based on new values and new ideas. The basic problem remained unchanged—to establish a 'true' description of the human body— but its purpose was no longer to serve the ancient demands of cult magic, but to manifest the new ideas of *symmetreia* (*proportio*) and *eurhythmia* in their new aesthetic definitions. This fundamental change in attitude became responsible for the new visual approach to artistic objects, which were no longer represented as they were *an sich* or *sub specie aeterni*, but as they appeared to the artist's eye in time and space. It opened the way for the introduction of foreshortenings and shifts of perspective, which reduced the canon from an inflexible rule, enforced in its full rigour upon each individual representation, to a more theoretical standard against which the perspective deviations could be measured. Even the numerical tabulations of the parts became subjects of discussion, and from a universal code to which all artists had to submit unconditionally it became almost an individual problem to which each of them had to find his own solution in accordance with his personal conception of art and aesthetics.

The rigid canon of the Egyptians had been superseded by a more subtle and flexible one within which there was room for what Panofsky has called 'the irrationale of artistic freedom', and as such it retained its importance and influence throughout the history of Greek and Roman art.[1] Revived in its classical form by the artists of the Renaissance it became once more a distinct feature in Western art, but the Egyptians were the first to define it as a principle, to observe the fixed natural relations between the various parts of the body, and to tabulate them into a system of proportions, and also the first to use them in practice as a sculptural canon, certain ratios of which were still unchanged in the canons of Leonardo and Dürer.

In the history of Western art the canonical tradition is indeed the only real and direct Egyptian inheritance—the true legacy of Egypt.   ERIK IVERSEN

[1] The canonical principles of Byzantine and Gothic art fall outside the authority of the author. They are considered in Panofsky's article mentioned above (p. 55, n. 1).

BIBLIOGRAPHY

M. BAUD, *Les Dessins ébauchés de la nécropole thébaine*, Le Caire, 1935 (Mém. IFAO lxiii).

C. C. EDGAR, 'Remarks on Egyptian "Sculptors' Models"', *Recueil de Travaux*, xxvii (1905), 137–50.

—— *Sculptors' studies and unfinished works*, Le Caire, 1906 (Cat. gén. Museé du Caire).

R. HANKE, 'Beiträge zum Kanonproblem', *ZÄS* lxxxiv (1959), 113–19.

E. IVERSEN, *Canon and proportions in Egyptian art*, London, 1955.

—— 'A canonical master-drawing in the British Museum', *JEA* xlvi (1960), 71–9.

—— 'Diodorus' account of the Egyptian canon', *JEA*. liv (1968), 215–18.

—— 'The Egyptian origin of the archaic Greek canon', *Mitteilungen des deutsch. arch. Instituts Abt. Kairo*, xv (1957), 134–47.

C. R. LEPSIUS, *Die Längenmasse der Alten*, Berlin, 1884.

C. R. LEPSIUS, 'Proportionen im Grabe des ⏋↟✕⏝ (Sakkara No. 17)', in *Denkmäler aus Aegypten und Aethiopien*, Textband I (ed. E. Naville), Leipzig, 1897.

E. MACKAY, 'Proportion squares on tomb walls in the Theban necropolis', *JEA* iv (1917), 74–85.

E. PANOFSKY, 'The history of the theory of human proportions as a reflection of the history of styles', in *Meaning in the visual arts*, New York, 1955, pp. 55–107 (no. 2).

4

TECHNOLOGY AND MATERIALS

In order to demonstrate 'legacy' in the field of technology and applied science it is necessary to show first that specific discoveries may be traced to a particular culture—with the rider that they are unlikely to have been made independently at a later date—and second that their development has had real influence, even if indirectly, upon the continuous technical tradition from the ancient world to the present. In dealing with Egypt there is some need to emphasize this simple truism, if only because in the past the early sophistication of Egyptian material civilization, typified in the *'grandiose absurdité'* of the pyramids, has in itself been taken to indicate an extraordinary contribution to the heritage of the West. In that Edwardian heyday when the ancient Orient seemed in retrospect to have centred upon the Nile valley—a nice reflection of the pharaonic viewpoint—it was naturally assumed that the several crafts so nearly perfected in the course of Egyptian history, some of them already practised with high competence as far back as the dawn of the dynastic period, had in fact been evolved there, the Egyptians being generally acknowledged as a most inventive and inquiring people. Indeed, belief in Egyptian ingenuity has known few bounds, and it is no exaggeration to say that the antique conception of Egypt as a storied wonderland of learning, the *fons et origo* of all wisdom, has in some measure persisted in the attitude towards their achievements in the applied arts and in engineering. Scholars, and notably Egyptologists, have blindly intimated the existence of the most bizarre techniques, and the public, ever eager to believe the incredible, has accepted that, for example, both tools of steel and saws and borers set with diamonds were used in working stone, that copper was tempered by some 'lost art', that glass-blowing was practised in the New Kingdom, that unknown pigments were used in wall decoration, and that the wheels of chariots were fitted with rubber tyres.

Sober research and scientific method have done much to reveal the fantasy inherent in such ideas, though yet unable to still their occasional iteration in print, and half a century of excavation in the Near East, abetted in recent years by the dispassionate witness of new dating methods, has utterly transformed the pattern of culture before the third millennium, depriving Egypt of its fancied claim to primacy. Though gaps in the evidence remain, the principal areas from which technological advancement filtered south and west to Egypt both in predynastic and later times may now be defined, and the previous knowledge of certain processes by other peoples established beyond question. It is clear, moreover, that apart from the periodic introduction of new discoveries from abroad there was but little progress in the majority of crafts, the Egyptians being no more prone to innovation in this respect than in any other. That which had been 'since the antiquity of the land', 'the time of the god', was in a manner sacrosanct, though often, in fact, susceptible of improvement, and it is interesting to note that in several cases the fundamental step forward seems almost to have been avoided. To take a single example, the Egyptians do not appear to have grasped the principle of the lathe until about the end of the fourth century B.C., when the inspiration will have come from the Greek world, and this in spite of the fact that the bow-drill had been in common use from the early dynastic period and work suspended between points for ease of handling at least from the New Kingdom, if not before.

The innate conservatism of the Egyptian craftsman was doubtless accentuated by the circumstances in which he was trained to work, for in historical times the ordinary artisan was a mere executant who laboured accordingly to instructions. To judge from the scenes in which workshops are represented, there would seem to have been some specialization in particular media (the making of statues in wood and metal was, for instance, the province of the carpenter and smith), but the worker was generally one of a team and might be responsible for only a part of the manufacture. Such was evidently the case with sculpture and painting, the decoration of a wall or the carving of a stone statue being executed in stages and presumably by different hands, so that the finished product was as a rule the outcome of collective endeavour. Under these conditions of almost industrial labour, improvements in technique were less likely to occur than if individuals had worked alone, and although there were certainly overseers, some of whom may themselves have been master craftsmen, it is not clear to what extent they became involved in the actual work. Many were probably no more than 'managers' responsible for the general organization of a project, others may personally have superintended the work in hand, and some, particularly those charged with major architectural and engineering enterprises, will surely have had real technical expertise. In fact, it is evident that in the New Kingdom a certain knowledge of constructional and mechanical methods and experience in the deployment of manpower were deemed an essential part of the equipment of a military scribe, army contingents being often used as a convenient labour force.

It should further be borne in mind that few of the pressures and incentives which today lead to the betterment of manufacturing processes were at all relevant in the social and economic climate of Egypt. Apart from the ordinary peasant who furnished his own and perhaps his neighbour's needs in humble chattels such as pots and baskets, most artisans, particularly those engaged in more sophisticated crafts, were attached to royal, state, or temple workshops or those of larger estates, where there was little stimulus to better production, nor any reason to operate more efficiently or to lower costs. As has often been pointed out, the Egyptian genius lay in the successful marshalling of large numbers toiling long hours, and though this is chiefly true of operations such as mining, quarrying, and building construction, it is also applicable to other work in so far as, the need arising, skilled labour could be concentrated on a specific task.

The apparent reluctance of the Egyptians to learn from others—perhaps in some degree reflecting their chauvinism—will in the main have been conditioned by extraneous factors: how far in fact there was opportunity for the transmission of specialist knowledge, save through the migration of craftsmen, and the extent to which, in any case, ideas were guarded jealously as craft secrets. It is often assumed, loosely, that certain developments reached Egypt through trade or, during the New Kingdom, with the armies returning victorious from Syria, but, while it is true that strange materials and exotic artefacts were brought by merchants and as booty, the similar transfer of outstanding skills is scarcely probable. Communication of expertise requires understanding on both sides and perhaps some actual demonstration, and neither traders nor fighting men are likely to have been competent in technical matters. The Egyptian soldier was no Roman legionary, though clearly he might be expected to repair equipment and construct siege works, implying some cognizance of simple smithing and of military engineering. Moreover, there is reason to think that those who discovered new methods or materials were often loath to lose control of them, as the slow dissemination of even the most useful inventions would suggest. Thus, although the production of true bronze was known in Byblos towards the end of the third millennium B.C., the Egyptians, who had close contacts with the port from the Old Kingdom, did not receive the technique until about the middle of the second millennium. Bowl-bellows too were apparently used in Mesopotamia some thousand years before their appearance in Egypt, and the Hittites retained a virtual monopoly of practical iron-working for several centuries. Again, at an earlier period, the gradual diffusion of faience from northern Mesopotamia to neighbouring lands seems to have spanned a period of up to fifteen hundred years. The value of such developments cannot have been ignored—faience, glazing, bronze, and iron were all known in Egypt before the means of their production were understood—and the fact that as late as the second millennium B.C. the spread of even major advances in metallurgy was restricted must surely indicate that, for one reason or another, commerce and the razzias of armies played no great part in the propagation of technical discoveries.

The transfer of craft instruction through the movement of the workers themselves would be more intelligible, for a migrant (or captive) craftsman would have no problem in communicating his skill at first hand, as well as, perhaps, less inducement to secrecy, and, indeed, it is clear that in many cases knowledge did actually travel in this way. Egypt may be said to have experienced two major industrial revolutions prior to the New Kingdom, each of which coincided with the settlement of groups of immigrants from the Near East, the obvious inference being that the authors of such unwonted change were from among the newcomers. The first of these occasions was during the later predynastic period, when successive waves of intruders, their Western Asiatic connections underlined by their use of lapis lazuli and silver, completely transformed the material culture of the Nile valley.[1] The former bifacial flint industry was replaced by a developed blade technique, in pottery the common use of Nile mud was bettered by the exploiting of a special kind of clay such as is still the basis of the modern Qena and Ballas wares, and crude mud bricks were made for the first time, More important, the manufacture of faience was introduced (the few stray pieces of earlier date being evident imports), and glazing too will have been contemporary, though previous occurrences of glazed steatite beads are perhaps less easily dismissed as of foreign origin. The use of metal became

[1] The first groups of Naqada II (Gerzean) settlers were apparently either of Near East origin or of African stock with strong Near Eastern connections, while the later (Semainean) invaders, who became the first dynastic rulers, were undoubtedly from the Near East.

more common, and the sudden appearance of practical copper tools and weapons is suggestive of some fundamental advance, reliance upon native metal having perhaps been superseded by the smelting of ore—which cannot, however, be proved. No doubt in connection with the making of satisfactory tools, carpentry came into being as a craft, and to the years immediately preceding the dynastic period may also be ascribed the fixing of the Egyptian system of linear measurement and, tentatively, of the related canon applied to the representation of the human figure.

The second era of change was ushered in by the infiltration of Asiatics into the eastern delta at the end of the Middle Kingdom and the subsequent rise to power of their tribal rulers, who, as the 'Hyksos' kings of the Fifteenth and Sixteenth Dynasties, brought Egypt into closer contact with Palestine and Western Asia than ever before. The extent of the 'Hyksos' contribution to Egyptian civilization has been a matter of some dispute, particularly with regard to developments in the military field, but there can be no doubt that many of the technical innovations attested only from the beginning of the New Kingdom were in fact initiated under their rule.[1] Apart from the chariot (and with it the spoked wheel)[2] the fighting-equipment owed to the Asiatics included the strong composite bow and metal arrow-heads, improved types of daggers, swords, and battle-axes, and probably also body armour and the helmet, the employment of bronze for such weapons being generally accepted, albeit without analytical confirmation. It is, however, a fair inference that the knowledge of making bronze by melting and mixing the component metals and of bowl-bellows as a more effective means of forcing the essential fire was actually acquired from the 'Hyksos', for both advances were already familiar to the Egyptians in the early part

[1] Cf. H. E. Winlock, *The Rise and Fall of the Middle Kingdom at Thebes*, New York, 1947, pp. 150–70.

[2] The only wheel known previously was a solid one turning with the axle, and even this (depicted on a scaling-ladder and a siege tower) may not have been adapted to vehicles.

of the Eighteenth Dynasty. It follows that the independent working of tin should have a similar origin, which is indeed consistent
with its first appearance in the fifteenth century B.C., while the
substance akin to niello, of which the earliest instance in Egypt
is almost contemporary with the last 'Hyksos' kings, is clearly of
Asiatic origin and was known in Syria during the Middle Kingdom. At a more mundane level, there were changes in textile
techniques, notably through the introduction of the upright loom,
and agriculture too may have benefited by the domestication of
an alien breed of humped cattle and the adoption of the *shadūf*,
a device whose usefulness has stood the test of time.

No less significant than the immediate contribution to technology was the long-term bearing of the 'Hyksos' episode upon
the Egyptians' attitude to the world around them. Secure no
longer in superior isolation they now looked towards the lands
which had bred the scourge—for so the 'Hyksos' came to be
regarded—and through this new consciousness maintained the
flow of ideas from the north-east. The one outstanding discovery
to reach Egypt during the New Kingdom was the process of glass
manufacture, which seems to have originated in Mesopotamia and
may have been further developed in Syria, though of this there
is as yet no evidence. The appearance of glassware in the Eighteenth Dynasty is indeed quite sudden and seems to coincide with
the Asiatic conquests of Thutmose III, and this fact, together
with the initial sophistication of the craft and its very rapid expansion, would strongly suggest the importation of experienced workmen. That Thutmose was interested to secure specimens of the
flora and fauna of Syria is known from the pictorial record preserved in his festival temple at Karnak, and it may well be that
his curiosity also prompted the inclusion of glass technicians
among the captives brought back to Egypt from his several campaigns. The particular question of glass apart, it is clear that
occasional foreign bondmen laboured in the craft workshops of
the New Kingdom, and the number was probably greater than

can now be determined—just as during the first millennium whole teams of Egyptian artisans were transported both to Babylon and, later, to Susa, to work with others on Darius' palace. Again, in the sixth century B.C., it was Greek smiths settled at Naucratis and Defenneh who introduced iron-working into Egypt, though the technique may have reached Nubia at a slightly earlier date and the metal itself had been known from the end of the Eighteenth Dynasty.

Although the Marxist-inspired doctrine of a parallel and separate evolution of cultures is in essence no more acceptable than the earlier extremes of diffusionist belief that it contradicts, it is none the less idle to speculate upon the origins and initial development of the more homely crafts. Pottery, the dressing of hides and skins, spinning and weaving, the making of basketry, matting and cordage, and the elementary working of wood and stone have each arisen independently in more than one cultural context (their existence in pre-Hispanic America is indicative) and even within the confines of the ancient Orient there is no clear evidence of dissemination from a single source. Apparent priority in any of these fields is therefore of doubtful consequence, the more so in that the relative chronology of the Near East before the end of the fourth millennium is anything but assured, with, in the case of Egypt, the added complication that certain allegedly 'neolithic' sites are probably of much later date.[1] It is, in other words, unreasonable to infer a definite legacy to civilization from the mere occurrence in a given area at an early period of one of the 'domestic' crafts, though notable advances in their technology, especially if involving new or refined appliances, may fairly be assumed to have diffused from a unique discovery.

In the case of Egyptian pottery, which in some respects was never more accomplished than in the Badarian period, the

---

[1] Cf. E. J. Baumgartel, *The Cultures of Prehistoric Egypt*, i (2nd ed.), Oxford, 1954, pp. 120–2; *Journ. American Oriental Soc.* lxxxv (1965), 502–11; in *The Cambridge Ancient History*², i, Ch. IX(a).

significant developments, apart from the employment of calcareous clay in preference to Nile mud, were the introduction of the kiln and of the potter's wheel. Both were undoubtedly in use in the Near East some centuries before they first appeared in Egypt, where neither can be shown to antedate the third millennium. A rudimentary form of turntable—a mat or such rotated on the ground—may indeed have been known earlier, in the predynastic period, but not until the Old Kingdom is there definite evidence for the use of a simple form of wheel, a disc turned by hand upon a pivot. Some time before the middle of the Eighteenth Dynasty this was bettered by the introduction of a compound wheel maintained in motion with the foot or by an assistant, and eventually, at a much later date, by the adoption of the swiftly spinning wheel with free momentum.

Similarly, the essential processes of textile manufacture seem to have been familiar in Badarian times and even before, and to have suffered little fundamental change until the dawn of the New Kingdom. The fibre commonly employed was flax, though fabrics of grass and hemp have been identified; until the Roman period wool was comparatively rare, and silk and cotton virtually unknown. The Egyptians spun in the S direction (i.e. to the left), either by hand or with a spindle, held whorl uppermost as it may be seen in Egypt at the present day. Three different methods, all of which survive, are documented in the Middle Kingdom, the spindle being grasped and rotated in the hand, rolled on the thigh, or suspended to turn freely, while from the Eighteenth Dynasty, when an improved spindle was in use, two or more might be suspended independently, perhaps an innovation of the 'Hyksos'. To the same period may be ascribed the only major improvement in the art of weaving; until the close of the Middle Kingdom the work was done on a horizontal ground loom, but by the Eighteenth Dynasty this had been superseded by the vertical form. There is no indication that the reed was used before the Roman era, and the weave of pharaonic textiles, though often of extreme fineness, is characteristically irregular. Fabrics were mostly plain down to the Middle Kingdom, when there are instances of pile and loop techniques, but again it was not until the Eighteenth Dynasty that more complicated pattern weaves were introduced, perhaps from Syria. These included different warp weaves and tapestry weave, and it was then too that the first examples of embroidery appeared. Dyeing with vegetable substances was practised from before the First Dynasty.

The various techniques of basketry and matting are akin to those of weaving, and should logically have been developed at an earlier date, though as yet there is no evidence in Egypt—or elsewhere—of a stage at which basketry alone was known. The principal materials used were palm fibres, halfa and other grasses, rushes, flax, and reeds, the last mostly in matting work, and these, with the addition of papyrus, were employed also in making ropes and other cordage—including nets, of which some specimens are identical with those made by modern Egyptian peasants. Matting was woven on a ground loom, as it is even today in country districts, or was made by joining fibres with a wrapping strip or intertwining strands, and twined work was also used for bags and hamper-like receptacles. Wickerwork proper, the familiar form of basketry, was unknown, and all Egyptian baskets were constructed by the coil technique, a core of fibres like an untwisted rope being built up spirally and wrapped and stitched together with a sewing strip. In Roman times a plaited strand replaced the covered coil, and baskets of this kind have remained in common use in Egypt. Innovations during the pharaonic period were few, but one that may be noted is the introduction of the four-cross centre, apparently evolved in Nubia in the early Middle Kingdom.

Papyrus, most famous of Egyptian fibres, was virtually unknown in basketry, though it was sometimes used in matting and had many other applications. Light skiffs such as are yet found on the Upper Nile were made from bundles of the plant, and from the outer rind sandals, thick ropes, and articles of furniture, mostly small stools and stands. But it was as a writing-ground that it was chiefly valued, and from as early as the First Dynasty thin sheets of whitish 'paper' were produced by laying strips of the inner pith side by side, with others crosswise, and beating them together, the natural juice acting as the adhesive. These sheets, of varying size but rarely more than 17 inches square, were then gummed into rolls, of which the longest known extends to 45 yards.

Like basketry, leather-working was developed at an early date, the basic operations being known already in the fourth millennium B.C. The simplest methods of preparing hides and skins— by drying, smoking, salting, treating with ochreous earths, or softening with fat, brain substance, or excreta—were probably of great antiquity, and there are indications that both salt and ochres were in fact used in the predynastic period. Oil-tannage also will have been familiar at this stage, and was indeed common throughout dynastic times, often, it seems, in combination with a tawing process. Tawing with alum was in turn known from the predynastic period onwards, and so too were the elements of tanning proper, for which the Egyptians used principally acacia pods. On predynastic leather also, pigments and vegetable dyes, chiefly red, green, and yellow, have been noted. It is, however, from the New Kingdom that the most interesting leather items have survived. These include some with embossed, punched, and and appliqué decoration, one woven fragment, and a few network 'loincloths' cut from a single skin with rows of small slits breaking joint with one another—a technique recently revived, unconsciously, by footwear manufacturers. The use of leather as a writing-ground was not uncommon, and a crude form of parchment, found as a covering for sounding-boxes, may, if very occasionally, have been employed. Parchment proper was not produced until the third century B.C.

Though wood was roughly worked from the earliest times, there was no carpentry as such until the late predynastic period, when serviceable copper tools came into use. Fine wooden fragments from royal tombs of the First Dynasty suggest, indeed, that joinery was introduced as a developed craft, but once established it assumed an individual character. Since there were no conifers in Egypt, and native trees such as acacia, sycamore fig, and tamarisk could not provide planks and panels of any size, a curious technique of 'patchwork' was evolved. Small and irregular pieces were joined with flat dowels, cramps, and pegs, by lacing, and occasionally by tongue and groove. Mortise-and-tenon joints and dovetailing were common, and several varieties of mitre were employed as early as the Old Kingdom, mitred angles, like butt joints, being generally pegged and lashed. Flaws were made good with plugs and patches, and poor surfaces were often finished with gesso and painted, sometimes in imitation of more costly woods. Veneer, inlay, and marquetry, especially of ebony and ivory, were also used to mask inferior timber or as mere decoration, the thicker pieces pegged, the smaller slips glued into place. No use was made of nails and pins in joinery until the Eighteenth Dynasty, though they were earlier employed to fasten metal to wood, nor does the metal hinge appear to have been known before this time. The tools of the Egyptian carpenter were simple, namely, adzes, axes, the bow-drill, two kinds of chisel, mallets, sandstone rubbers, and pull-saws, the cutting blades of copper and later bronze. The plane was quite unknown until the Roman period, and the lathe was not introduced until the fourth century B.C. The Egyptian contribution to the development of the joiner's craft is difficult to assess, for certain expertise may well have been acquired from foreign workers, particularly in the New Kingdom. That chariot construction, using principally imported timber, was of Asiatic origin is clear, and a degree of outside influence is suspect in the sophisticated furniture and other luxury items of the Eighteenth Dynasty. Jointing devices, on the other hand, were an essential feature of pharaonic woodwork from an early date, and in so far as their diversity was due to the specific need to make the best use of available material it is quite likely that the Egyptians were the first to test a number of familiar methods. Moreover, the peculiar 'patchwork' form has itself survived with little alteration in the building of small Nile boats, and the ancient adze is still employed by village carpenters in Egypt.

The material known as Egyptian faience, which is not a true faience (as *maiolica* or delftware) but a glazed quartz frit, was known in the Near East many centuries before its appearance in the Nile valley, where it was first manufactured in the late pre-dynastic period. Egypt, however, soon became pre-eminent in its production, and in dynastic times faience was widely used not only as a substitute for semi-precious stones in making beads, amulets, and inlay, but also for larger pieces such as bowls, chalices, and other vessels, statuettes—especially shawabti figures, tiles, and other elements of architectural decoration. The powdered quartz was made into a paste, perhaps by adding natron, and was shaped either by hand, by pottery methods, or in moulds. The characteristic glaze, applied also to steatite and solid quartz, was alkaline, and this too seems to have been discovered in northern Mesopotamia. A glaze containing lead was introduced about the Twenty-second Dynasty but did not supersede the older one, which even in the Roman period remained more common. A form of faience with an alkaline glaze was still being made in Egypt in the fourteenth century A.D. The type of frit familiar as a pigment appears likewise to have originated in the Near East, the earliest known specimens from Egypt being of the Fourth Dynasty. From the same period unglazed blue frit was also fashioned into beads and similar small objects, though on a relatively small scale until the Eighteenth Dynasty, when it was used more frequently and for larger pieces such as statuettes and vessels.

Glass was presumably discovered in connection with the use of glaze, and there is evidence that it again was employed in Mesopotamia some time before its first intentional manufacture by the

Egyptians. The scattered instances of 'glass'—beads and small amulets—that definitely antedate the Second Intermediate Period were almost certainly prepared as faience but turned vitreous through accidental overfiring, and, though from about this time occasional glass objects seem to have been made in Egypt, the rise of the industry as such dates from the mid Eighteenth Dynasty. The inference is that, while some elementary knowledge may have been acquired from, perhaps, the 'Hyksos', real understanding of the processes of manufacture followed the Asiatic conquests of Thutmose III. The vogue for glass lasted throughout the New Kingdom, but thereafter it declined in popularity until the fourth century B.C.—its disuse to some extent coinciding with the development of a new material, 'glassy faience', whose composition was somewhere between faience and glass. Egyptian glass was generally opaque and coloured, though a few examples of transparent glass are known. It was used principally for beads and inlay and for vases (many with multicoloured decoration), as well as, less frequently, for bowls, small figurines, and other purposes. Moulding and various manual methods were employed in shaping objects from molten glass, the vases being built up on a core by dipping, and glass was also worked cold. Blown glass was not known until the beginning of the Roman period. Despite the fact that these materials were developed previously in Western Asia, the later and more widespread use of both faience and glass, notably in the first millennium B.C., may well owe something to Egyptian influence. But beyond this no legacy is traceable, the evolution of vitreous materials since late antiquity being quite independent.

It seems that the origins of copper metallurgy are to be sought in the regions of north-east Persia and the Caucasus, and, whether the few small objects from Badarian and early predynastic Egyptian contexts were fashioned from native metal worked cold or were the outcome of crude smelting, it is evident that the systematic extraction of copper for the manufacture of practical tools and weapons dates from late predynastic times. Bronze too was known in the Near East some centuries before its appearance in Egypt, where although it came into use in the Middle Kingdom—presumably through the importation of ingots or the smelting of mixed ores—it was not produced by melting together copper and tin until after the period of the 'Hyksos' domination. Brass, the other significant alloy of copper, was first made intentionally in Roman times. The date at which the Egyptians learned how to smelt and work iron is uncertain, though it is clear that Egypt was the last country in the Near East to enter the Iron Age. The very few instances of the use of minute amounts of iron before the New Kingdom are no indication that the metal was recognized as such, and, although examples are somewhat more numerous from the end of the Eighteenth Dynasty onwards, it would appear that even in the Twenty-second Dynasty the metallurgy of iron, already mastered by the Hittites some five hundred years before, was still at a primitive level in Egypt. Not until the sixth century B.C. was iron production instituted on any scale, while in Nubia the industry may have been half a century older.

Of the noble metals, gold was no doubt the first to be discovered, though as yet only one occurrence is to be dated before the later predynastic period. The earliest gold was in all probability alluvial, but it is likely that the metal was being mined by proto-dynastic times, when electrum also was used. Thereafter, both gold and electrum, obtained principally from the eastern desert south from the Wadi Hammamat into Nubia, were employed in increasing quantity, and while during the New Kingdom natural alloys of various grades were distinguished, refining does not appear to have been practised until about the Persian period. The earliest silver objects are of late predynastic date, but until the end of the Middle Kingdom the metal was rare and of greater value than gold, remaining scarce down to the Eighteenth Dynasty. Neither silver nor silver ores proper are known to occur in Egypt, and, although among gold alloys mined anciently there may have been some with an exceptional silver content, it is doubtful whether this can have been as high as the percentage found in the analysis of certain early pieces. Moreover, the separation of silver from gold was a late (post-pharaonic) discovery, nor can it be shown that the Egyptians extracted it from lead ores—especially during the third millennium B.C.—the inference being that much of the early silver was imported from Western Asia, as was later the case with the Tōd treasure, and during the New Kingdom.

In that the basic metallurgy of copper and bronze was evidently of foreign origin, it is probable that many of the essential procedures employed by Egyptian metalworkers were introduced initially from outside—though the possibility that some at least were original discoveries cannot be excluded. Indeed, it is often claimed that the *cire perdue* method of casting was itself developed in Egypt, albeit no evidence can be found to substantiate this. Independent advances are in fact most likely to have been made in connection with goldsmithing, the principal techniques of which were already sophisticated by the end of the Middle Kingdom, and many of them well known at a much earlier date. Thus the art of granulation, later adopted by Etruscan and Greek jewellers and finally lost at the close of antiquity, was almost certainly of Egyptian origin, and so too may have been that of engraving metal, while cloisonné, although a Sumerian invention, appears to have been perfected in Egypt, whose mines yielded a variety of stones suitable for inlay.[1] There are, on the other hand, processes once thought to be Egyptian which it is now clear were not, among them the preparation of alloys akin to niello, which was evidently an Anatolian development, and also true fire-gilding which, if known at all, was learned from the Persians during the Twenty-seventh Dynasty.

---

[1] Those chiefly used were lapis lazuli, turquoise, felspar, jasper, carnelian, garnet, and amethyst, of which only lapis lazuli, the most prized, was not found in Egypt. The true precious stones, such as diamond, ruby, sapphire, emerald, and opal, were not known.

The fact that, until the coming of iron, the Egyptians lacked metal tools of sufficient temper to carve rocks such as granite had an essential bearing on their stone-working techniques.[1] Apart from the flint industry and the crude shaping of the first palettes, the earliest exploitation of the stones of the Nile valley and the eastern desert was in the manufacture of vessels, which flourished already in the later predynastic period and may be said to have reached its peak by the Third Dynasty. Initially, when only stone implements were available, vases and bowls of even the toughest materials were worked laboriously with grinders held in the hand, or possibly in some cases fixed to a primitive boring device. Tubular drills of copper used with abrasives were known from the First Dynasty, but were applied chiefly to softer substances like alabaster, and in dynastic times the principal tool employed in hollowing out the interior of vessels was a heavily weighted crank drill with a range of hard stone cutting heads, while for the exterior, hand-dressing was still usual.

In the case of statuary, the method of executing which was evolved in the early dynastic period, the harder rocks were again worked mainly by pounding and chipping with stone mauls and picks, and sometimes cut with metal saws and drills fed with an abrasive (probably quartz sand), while for carving limestone and the like both chisels and adzes with blades of copper, and later bronze, were also in common use. The basic procedure was, however, the same, amounting in effect to the working together of profile and frontal aspects of the intended sculpture. Sketches were made on at least two sides of a cuboid block, which was then reduced systematically by jarring and pecking off successive layers of stone all round, so that throughout the statue had a certain form, though not until the final stages was it modelled in detail. The possible influence of Egyptian methods is hard to assess, since comparable techniques of working stone without

[1] Cf. A. Zuber, 'Techniques du travail des pierres dures dans l'ancienne Égypte', *Techniques et civilisations*, v (1956), 161–80, 195–215.

effective metal tools are known to have been developed quite independently in other cultural contexts. The dressing of some archaic Greek statuary seems, none the less, to have been derived from Egypt, and the heroic *kouroi* of the late seventh and sixth centuries B.C. retain the proportions and the typical stance of an Egyptian figure. Indeed, in so far as the characteristic 'cubism' and rigid symmetry of Egyptian sculpture were influenced by the manner of its execution and the strict application of the canon, this may be seen as a continuing legacy to art—although in the event most Roman and Renaissance imitations, while superficially 'pharaonic' in style, do not conform in these essentials (Pls. 4*b*, 5*b*).

A similar garbled legacy to art may be claimed for Egyptian relief and painting, but the conventional drafting of two-dimensional compositions and the almost diagrammatic reconstruction of individual objects, notably the canonical human figure (above, Chapter 3), were not, as with statuary, conditioned by technical procedures. In either case, the ground was simply prepared to a smooth surface, and on this the representation was sketched out in detail, filling the space available. For a relief the sculptor merely cut round the outlines and then modelled the resulting flat shapes, while the painter, whether working directly or upon a relief, first washed in the background and then coloured the separate items, which were finally picked out in line. Neither low nor sunk relief was ever conceived as three-dimensional, but was treated almost as a form of reinforced drawing, and the technique employed was thus of very limited application. Nor had the Egyptian method of painting a vital influence, it being essentially a type of distemper or gouache, with water or dilute gum as the vehicle, and so irrelevant to the tradition of true fresco. Moreover, with the exception of frit (below, p. 108), the basic pigments were substances of common occurrence, principally minerals, whose very colour will have ensured their independent exploitation.

The abundance of good building stone in the Nile valley was an important factor in the development of Egyptian architecture.

Reeds and rushes (reinforced with mud) and baulks of wood were the first materials used, and bricks were introduced in late pre-dynastic times, but from the early dynastic period occasional dressed slabs were incorporated in brick and timber construction, while to the Third Dynasty belongs the oldest known structure built entirely of stone—the step-pyramid complex at Saqqara. Thereafter, stone was regularly employed in monumental architecture, the use of brick (exclusively sun-dried until the Roman period) being virtually confined to domestic and secular buildings which were not destined for eternity—whereas in Mesopotamia kiln-baked bricks were universally used. Thus, while the ancient method of making bricks has survived almost unchanged in Egypt down to the present day, pharaonic brick construction was of little importance, nor did it have a significant influence on architecture in stone. Even as essential a principle as that of the true arch, though known in brickwork from the Third Dynasty, was not applied in monumental masonry until late, corbelled and false arches being the only forms employed down to the Twenty-fifth Dynasty, when a type of semi-corbelled arch with keystone was introduced. Keyed arches with joggled voussoirs were constructed from the Ptolemaic period, but no arch of modern type with the voussoirs mutually supported by friction has as yet been noted.

The initial use of reed and similar materials had, on the other hand, a marked influence on pharaonic architecture, as may be seen, for example, in the various motifs reproduced in the step-pyramid complex and in the common types of column which imitate plant forms. Indeed, several of the most characteristic elements of Egyptian masonry are merely translations into stone of features belonging to more primitive construction, and, in that certain of these, such as the torus moulding and cavetto cornice, have been widely copied, there is here a degree of technical—as well as artistic—legacy. More generally, the use made by the Egyptians of columnar supports may have provided the broad inspiration for the Greek orders, though this is not to say that the

Doric column was derived from the kind of polygonal pillar known in Egypt, which has no proper capital, a straight or only slightly tapered shaft, and, frequently, flat facets rather than flutings.[1]

Although there can be little doubt that the general concept of large-scale building in stone originated in Egypt and passed thence, via the Levant, to the rest of the ancient world, the true extent of the Egyptian contribution in terms of architectural practice is debatable. Because most pharaonic masonry was held together by its sheer mass, sound principles of construction were much neglected until about the Twenty-fifth Dynasty. Attention was concentrated on the external appearance of a monument, and the treatment of elements which would not be noticed, such as foundations, core masonry, and roofing, was often dangerously inadequate. It is thus probable that the true importance of these and other structural features was first realized elsewhere than in Egypt—possibly in Phoenicia—and it may be also that devices like the false arch and corbelled vault were evolved anew rather than copied. Nor is it clear that the relieving arch as such was of Egyptian origin, for, although in pyramid building steps were taken to reduce the pressure upon internal chambers, the principle was not extended to other forms of construction and was completely forgotten after the Middle Kingdom, until its reintroduction at the end of the Thirtieth Dynasty. Similarly, the appearance at Mycenae and elsewhere in mainland Greece of large block masonry analogous to that common in Egypt from the Old Kingdom onwards may be incidental. The use of irregularly sized blocks in the same course, often with oblique rising joints between and with re-entrant corners cut out to accommodate blocks of the course above, can be paralleled in Inca work, notably at Cuzco and Sacsahuamán, as well as from a few Maya and Toltec monuments, and the Vinapu *ahu* on Easter Island. The object of the

---

[1] One may also doubt the suggested derivation of the East Greek palm capital from Egypt, since the type was by no means common until the Ptolemaic period.

technique was doubtless to minimize the labour of stone-cutting by using blocks approximately as they were quarried, and dressing them only to fit rather than to a standard size, and such an advantage may indeed have suggested itself wherever hard stone had to be worked with simple tools.

Through trial and error the Egyptians learned the limitations of different building stones—for instance, that limestone slabs would span a maximum of 3 yards whereas sandstone would bridge gaps of 8 or more, or that the ratio between the length of a granite obelisk and the width of its base could not exceed 10 or 11 to 1 without the risk that it might fracture in course of erection.[1] The method of quarrying varied with different types of stone. In extracting the softer varieties (limestone, sandstone, and alabaster) vertical cuts were made and the blocks detached from below by wedging, while in the case of the harder rocks (granite, quartzite, basalt, etc.) blocks were split off by means of wedges—presumably of wood expanded by wetting—the slots for which were cut with stone hand-picks, or were separated by pounding out channels with stone mauls.

In the absence of winches or pulley systems with tongs or lewises for handling blocks, the Egyptians relied almost entirely on direct manpower aided by simple wooden levers—though in that the tourniquet principle was known it is possible that the 'Spanish windlass' was also applied. The extent to which rollers may have been used is questionable, and there is little to justify the common idea that transport sleds were normally run on them.[2] That blocks

[1] This is not to say that such was the ratio recognized by the Egyptians. In all probability they reckoned the shaft and pyramidion separately and made some allowance for the degree of taper.

[2] The use of rollers presents certain problems, which are greatly accentuated when the load is very heavy; cf. F. Niel, *Dolmens et menhirs*, Paris, 1961, pp. 53–4; R. J. C. Atkinson, *Stonehenge*, Harmondsworth (Penguin Books), 1960, pp. 115, 120. For some idea of what may be accomplished without rollers cf. Atkinson, op. cit., pp. 114–15; T. Heyerdahl, *Aku-Aku*, Harmondsworth (Penguin Books), 1960, pp. 139–40.

of middling size were manœuvred with rollers is not unlikely, and rollers and sleepers were perhaps employed in moving moderate loads mounted upon small sleds. Larger and heavier burdens, such as obelisks or colossal statues will, on the other hand, have been transported without the use of either rollers or track baulks—though wooden beams may have served occasionally as sand trays—for not only do all the extant representations illustrate sleds in direct contact with the ground, but no Egyptian tree could have furnished rollers of the size and strength required, while imported coniferous timbers were too valuable for such a purpose. Similar reservations apply also to the wooden cradles or 'rockers' known from foundation deposits, whose function remains in doubt, although it seems clear that they were neither a form of sled nor a device for raising blocks.

On site, ramps and embankments were constructed of brick and earth, and simple scaffolding was perhaps erected, but no other appliances than those mentioned already were employed in the actual work of building. The laying of large blocks was, however, assisted by a thin layer of gypsum mortar acting essentially as a lubricant (lime cement being unknown before Graeco–Roman times), and there is evidence that in positioning huge monoliths the Egyptians adopted variants of the sand-box principle, used according to Pliny (xxxvi. 21. 96) in building the temple of Ephesus, and, for example, in launching warships even as late as the present century. The erection of a monument by this technique is indeed referred to in a papyrus of the Nineteenth Dynasty, in which are formulated problems relating to the construction of a ramp, the movement of an obelisk, and the emptying of sand from the compartments of a magazine underneath it.[1]

In short, the genius of the Egyptians lay not in sophisticated

---

[1] A. H. Gardiner, *Egyptian Hieratic Texts*, i, Leipzig, 1911, pp. 16* f., with discussion on pp. 31* f. The nature of the problems and their essential unity is more clearly appreciated by F. M. Barber, 'An Ancient Egyptian Mechanical Problem', *The Open Court*, Dec. 1912.

engineering science, but in the skilful application of the most elementary aids and the efficient deployment and control of unlimited manpower. Routine also played an important part in their achievements, for any departure from established practice, whether through accident or otherwise, was ever liable to create a problem which, with no theoretical knowledge of mechanics, they could not solve. But this is not to imply that for each given task there was a single recognized procedure which was rigidly followed, and it is safe to assume that work was as a rule accomplished by the simplest means appropriate to the particular circumstances. Thus, where a gang of men could handle blocks without the assistance of levers, sleds, or embankments, they will surely have done so, and although the combination of ramp and sand-box was the most satisfactory system for the erection of a large obelisk or colossus,[1] it was not necessarily so in the case of smaller obelisks or monolithic columns, which were probably raised by a technique akin to that used, apparently, for the Easter Island statues, or (in 1805) for the Seringapatam memorial, the shaft being levered up gradually from the horizontal and packed beneath with earth or rubble.[2] Lastly, it may be noted that Egyptian methods were in a measure influenced by local conditions—the lack of adequate timber for large baulks or rollers, the ready availability, on the other hand, of mud brick for ramps, and the omnipresence of endless quantities of dry, free-running sand whose movement might conveniently be harnessed. And in this respect, as by the failure to develop force-multiplying machines, the possible contribution of Egypt to ancient engineering was somewhat limited.

[1] Cf. R. Engelbach, *The Aswân Obelisk, with Some Remarks on the Ancient Engineering*, Cairo, 1922, pp. 35–43; *The Problem of the Obelisks*, London, 1923, pp. 66–84; H. Chevrier, *ASAE* lii (1954), 309–13.

[2] Cf., in particular, F. M. Barber, *The Mechanical Triumphs of the Ancient Egyptians*, London, 1900, pp. 115–17: L. Borchardt, 'Zur Baugeschichte des Amonstempels von Karnak', in K. Sethe, *Untersuchungen zur Geschichte und Altertumskunde Aegyptens*, v (1912), 15–17; M. Pillet, *Chronique d'Égypte*, vi (1931), 294–305.

The tendency of this brief survey has been to contradict the popular estimate of Egypt's contribution in the field of industrial arts, and rather to vindicate Winlock's considered judgement that the Egyptian was never an inventive genius.[1] Not only does it emerge quite clearly that almost all important technical advances came from without, but many of the methods effectively exploited by the Egyptians are seen to have been such as were, inevitably, superseded. Herodotus himself remarked upon the quaint perversity of Egyptian usages, so very different from those of other peoples, and even five centuries later technology remained eccentric in many respects, to be transformed eventually under the aegis of Imperial Rome.[2]

But if the legacy of Egyptian craft techniques as such was of small account, the indirect influence of the applied arts was none the less considerable. The very fact that for many centuries—from the rise of the Old Kingdom, roughly, until the end of the New—Egyptian craftsmen were catering to the most affluent and materially sophisticated society of the ancient Near East was in itself significant, for nowhere else at this time was there the same impetus towards an almost industrial scale of production with all that it entailed. A growing demand for raw materials, some not obtainable at all or in sufficient quantity within the bounds of Egypt, and the consequent need to explore external sources of supply were major factors in promoting trade and territorial expansion. The first incursions into Nubia were doubtless prompted by a desire to gain control of the gold-bearing regions and to have closer contact with the supply of ebony and ivory from the south, no ivory having been obtained from Western Asia before the New Kingdom. For Egyptian presence in Syria following the expulsion of the 'Hyksos' there were more immediate reasons, but ready access to natural resources, above all metals and the

[1] H. E. Winlock, op. cit. (above p. 88, n. 1), p. 150.
[2] Cf. H. E. Winlock and W. E. Crum, *The Monastery of Epiphanius at Thebes*, i, New York, 1926, pp. 96–7.

coniferous timber of the Lebanon, was of obvious economic advantage—as underlined by the experience of the wretched Wenamūn, sent to fetch wood from Byblos at the close of the Twentieth Dynasty when Egyptian influence was no more. During the New Kingdom also, the products of foreign craftsmen were received in increasing quantity, and therewith the decorative motifs of Western Asia and the Aegean reached Egypt, to be absorbed, piecemeal, into the repertoire of pharaonic ornament. Conversely, and more important, objects manufactured in Egyptian workshops had begun to find their way to neighbouring lands at least as early as the Old Kingdom, and subsequently were carried throughout the ancient world by trade and settlement, and (notably during the Roman period) in the wake of Egyptian cults. The wide dispersal of such 'exports' from the New Kindgom onwards was of no little significance in the diffusion of Egyptian art forms, the copying and adaptation of these over many centuries being a further aspect of Egypt's legacy.

Whether handled as ingots or in the form of artefacts, the gold for which Asiatic rulers clamoured in the Amarna letters was clearly intended as bullion, like the imported silver and lapis lazuli of the Tōd treasure, and gold was, indeed, one of the comparatively few materials that Egypt exported before the Roman period. Chief among others were linen and papyrus, both traded during the New Kingdom, while Egyptian alum is mentioned in Neo-Babylonian texts of the sixth century B.C., when it is also said to have been shipped to Greece. That Egypt was the granary of Rome is a commonplace, and the importance of her papyrus as the Empire's most useful writing material is equally known. But these were not the only resources exploited at this period, and among the semi-precious stones and other minerals described by Pliny are several found principally or solely in Egypt. Thus the mines of the Sikait–Zabara region of the Red Sea hills, first worked under the Ptolemies, were certainly the major source of beryl and 'emerald' in classical times, and probably the only one, and imperial porphyry too was obtained exclusively from Gebel Dokhan (*Mons Porphyrites*) in the eastern desert—the occurrence in Karelia which supplied the material for Napoleon's sarcophagus being then unknown. Red granite, the *syenites* of Pliny, was extracted from the ancient quarries at Aswan, and fresh workings in the Wadi Fawakhir may have been opened up, while from Gebel Fatiri (*Mons Claudianus*) in the eastern desert the Romans procured a characteristic black-and-white variety. Both imperial porphyry and the hornblende granite of *Mons Claudianus* enjoyed a certain vogue during the second and third centuries A.D. (Pls. 6, 20, 24), particularly under Hadrian and (in the case of the former) Diocletian. Chiefly in evidence in Rome itself, they have, with other Egyptian stones, been noted elsewhere in Italy and in the Empire, the porphyry as far afield as Constantinople and Baalbek and even in Britain, at Silchester, Colchester, and Canterbury. Each too has been found reused in later work, principally in the decoration of medieval and early Renaissance churches in Rome and central Italy, but also, for example, in the great mosque of Sultan Ḥasan.[1]

One other material, an artificial substance, should also be mentioned in this context, namely, the well-known 'Egyptian' or 'Vestorian' blue much used in antiquity and described by Theophrastus as a species of κύανος and by Vitruvius and Pliny under the heading of *caeruleum*. Although the frit itself seems to have originated in Mesopotamia rather than in Egypt as the classical tradition assumes, it may be that the Egyptians were in fact the first to realize its value as a pigment, the earliest identified examples of which date from the Fourth Dynasty. How far its subsequent diffusion is then attributable to Egyptian influence, and whether in specific instances its occurrence implies knowledge of manufacture

[1] For the use of imperial porphyry cf. R. Delbrueck, *Antike Porphyrwerke*, Berlin–Leipzig, 1932, for the granite of *Mons Claudianus* T. Kraus and J. Röder, *Mitteilungen des deutsch. arch. Instituts Abt. Kairo*, xviii (1962), 80–120 (particularly pp. 117–20), and for other stones D. Meredith, *JEA* xxxix (1953), 105, n. 7; J. Couyat, *BIFAO* vii (1910), 67–70.

or merely that the made-up material was traded can scarcely be gauged, but there is little reason to assume that the pigment was not produced outside Egypt 'until a comparatively late date'. Indeed, there are clear indications to the contrary. Not only is there recurring evidence of 'local' fabrication of frit objects in the Near East, but from the middle of the second millennium B.C. the process of fritting must have been widely known in connection with the making of glass, and it would therefore be curious had the blue not been prepared also for use in painting and as an inlay. Theophrastus does not specify whether in his day frit was manufactured in Greece, as would seem likely, though his account suggests that it was formerly a product of Phoenicia and elsewhere. Nor is it certain at what date it was introduced into Italy. According to Vitruvius, the making of *caeruleum* was instituted at Puteoli by Vestorius, the contemporary of Cicero, but Pliny states that what Vestorius developed was a specific preparation of the pigment, called *lomentum*, and the reproduction of the original Egyptian blue may thus have been established earlier. However this may be, frit was the principal blue pigment of the Roman world during the early centuries A.D., and specimens have been identified throughout the Empire, including both Gaul and Britain. It seems in fact to have survived in use until about the fifth or sixth century A.D., and thereafter to have disappeared, presumably because the technique of its manufacture was forgotten.

The full extent of the Egyptian contribution to ancient knowledge of raw materials is impossible to assess, though it is not unlikely that the properties and applications of many substances were first realized in Egypt. From the beginning of the dynastic period, the rich resources of the Nile valley, the adjacent deserts, and some neighbouring lands were shrewdly exploited, and a wide range of natural products utilized, not only in industry and the applied arts, but, notably, in medicine and in connection with embalming. How many of these were clearly identified and distinguished one from another is evident from the diversity of Egyptian mineralogical and botanical terms, and it is, moreover, significant that in certain cases actual connections appear to have been observed and something approaching a rational classification developed.[1] But, while the Egyptians may well have been the earliest to recognize and make intelligent use of various materials, it does not follow that elsewhere knowledge of them was ultimately derived from Egypt. On the contrary, it may be presumed that trial was made independently of many substances, particularly those striking in appearance or of common occurrence, and that in consequence their real value was established more than once. That such was indeed the case is partially confirmed by the slender influence of Egyptian terminology upon that of other Near Eastern peoples. Not only have comparatively few Egyptian names for mineral and other products passed into Semitic languages (and fewer still into Greek and Latin), but, where, as in the case of Assyrian vocabulary, there is comparable or even greater precision in nomenclature, the underlying concepts are seen to have been somewhat different. And yet in spite of this it is clear that antiquity was in fact indebted to Egypt for much received learning, both practical and esoteric, as to the specific uses of a variety of substances. A few isolated examples have already been noticed in relation to technical processes, and there are others. The virtues of natron will, for instance, have been realized largely through its exploitation in Egypt (as the very origin of its name suggests), and so too may the properties of different resins. Nor can there be any doubt that the more sophisticated Egyptian cosmetic preparations and perfumes were studiously imitated in the Mediterranean world, the tradition being subsequently handed down through Alexandria to Rome and late antiquity. Of importance, however, is the diverse knowledge communicated through the medium of medical literature, a subject to be discussed elsewhere (below, Chapter 5). The sheer range of the Egyptian

[1] Cf. in general J. R. Harris, *Lexicographical Studies in Ancient Egyptian Minerals*, Berlin, 1961.

pharmacopoeia was extraordinary, including numerous products of real therapeutic virtue and others of which the qualities were wholly imagined. Many of these passed into classical and later medicine, among them serviceable materials whose use as drugs was incidental. What is significant in the present context is that in some cases cognizance of the materials as such may thus have been spread abroad.   J. R. HARRIS

BIBLIOGRAPHY

A. LUCAS, *Ancient Egyptian materials and industries*, 4th ed. (J. R. Harris), London, 1962.

S. CLARKE and R. ENGELBACH, *Ancient Egyptian masonry: the building craft*, London, 1930.

A. F. SHORE, 'Arts and Crafts', in *A general introductory guide to the Egyptian collections in the British Museum*, London, 1964, pp. 172–221 (Ch. 7).

C. SINGER, E. J. HOLMYARD, and A. R. HALL (ed.), *A history of technology*, vols. i–ii, Oxford, 1954–6.

5

MEDICINE

ACCORDING to Manetho, Athothis, the second king of the First Dynasty, practised medicine and wrote anatomical works which were still extant in the third century B.C., and by tradition the sage Imhotep, the vizier and architect of Djoser in the Third Dynasty, was also a skilled physician, in later times deified and likened to Asklepios. Whatever the historical truth of these beliefs, it is clear from the number of doctors whose names are known that by the Old Kingdom medicine was a flourishing science in Egypt, and several of the extant medical papyri—the earliest of Middle Kingdom date—may in fact stem from older compilations of this period. From the New Kingdom there is already evidence of the reputation of Egyptian medicine abroad in the treatment of a Syrian prince by a court physician under Amenhotpe II, and in the sending first of a medical expert and then of a healing statue of the god Khons to a princess of Bakhtan, allegedly during the reign of Ramesses II. The fabled sophistication of Egyptian drugs and medical knowledge is also alluded to by Homer—it was in Egypt that Helen learned to doctor drinks—and several of the early Greek natural philosophers were reputed to have been influenced by Egyptian thinking. Thales of Miletus, the supposed founder of the Ionian school of medicine, was said to have been taught by Egyptian priests, Pythagoras to have studied at Heliopolis, and his younger contemporary Alcmaeon of Croton to have derived his pneumatist doctrine from Egypt. Such was the fame of Egyptian physicians in the sixth century B.C. that Cyrus of Persia preferred to employ them, and Darius too had Egyptians about him, though Herodotus has it that when his ankle was dislocated their ministrations were ineffective. However that may be, it is clear that Darius valued the Egyptian tradition of medicine, for as overlord of Egypt he commanded Udjahorresne to restore the medical school of Sais. During the fifth and fourth centuries B.C. there was steadily increasing contact between Egypt and the Greek world, and there is definite evidence of the influence of Egyptian medical ideas in Ionia, particularly in the theories of the Cnidian school, but also to some extent in those of the school of Cos. It is, however, in the period following the conquests of Alexander, when Greek schools existed in Egypt, that the interchanges of ideas will have been greatest, with Alexandria the gateway through which the ancient lore of the Egyptian physicians passed to the West.

The prestige of Egyptian medicine in the latter half of the first millennium was no doubt fostered in part by the existence of skilled specialists, remarked by Herodotus, and of a written code which, according to Diodorus, determined the course of treatment. The nature of this medical corpus may be gathered from Clement of Alexandria, who states that of the forty-two 'hermetic books' of the Egyptians six were devoted to specific aspects of medicine, the first dealing with anatomy, the second with illnesses, the third with surgical instruments, the fourth with drugs, the fifth with eye ailments, and the sixth and last with gynaecology. Whether such comprehensive works existed at an earlier date is a matter of speculation, since none of the extant texts is of this form nor can it be shown that any is wholly or in part derived directly from such a source. The Edwin Smith surgical papyrus and several of the shorter fragments dealing with gynaecological problems, diseases of the anus, and muscular complaints[1] are, however, systematic compositions with a single theme and may be copied from monographs on these subjects, while certain sections of the more miscellaneous manuscripts,

[1] Namely, Pap. Carlsberg viii and Pap. Kahun; Pap. Chester Beatty vi; Pap. Ramesseum v.

notably those in the Ebers papyrus dealing with eye ailments, stomach conditions, various kinds of swelling, and the properties of the castor-oil plant, would appear to have a similar origin. But it is evident that the style of these monographs varied, some being more clearly defined than others which were mere collections of remedies, nor do the topics covered appear to be consistent with the basic classification alleged by Clement. Yet it may be that they in turn owed something to more fundamental books, the sketch of the castor-oil plant, for example, being perhaps an excerpt from some greater herbal,[1] or the different gynaecological fragments scattered extracts from a compendium.

The character of the existing material and its relative insufficiency must be borne in mind in any assessment of Egyptian medicine. Opinions have, indeed, varied considerably in the ninety years since the publication of the Ebers papyrus, each new discovery inviting a reappraisal, but it is now generally acknowledged that the empirico-rational element was far greater than has hitherto been admitted.[2] True, the Egyptians often confused the cause or symptoms of a disease with the disease itself, and prescribed accordingly, as well as making frequent use of incantations, but their therapy was never wholly dependent upon a belief in the equation of sin, possession, and disease such as vitiated the medical methods of Babylonia and Assyria. This may have been because a certain distinction was maintained between empirical, sacerdotal, and magical medicine, recourse being had to prayers and spells chiefly in cases where the physician's art was deemed ineffectual.[3] The presence of magical elements in several of the better-known papyri is thus explained, since these were evidently working-manuals compiled for ordinary practitioners

[1] W. R. Dawson, *Aegyptus*, x (1929), 47–72.

[2] Cf. G. Mérei, *Az Országos Orvostörténeti Könyvtár Közleményei*, x–xi (1958), 173–256.

[3] Cf. P. Ghalioungui, *Cahiers d'Alexandrie*, July 1965, 17–34, where the essential difference between the sacerdotal and the magical is underlined.

whose approach might vary according to the circumstances. Not, indeed, that the mere use of spells should necessarily be condemned, for, as Sigerist has observed, 'you can cure or improve a great many internal diseases with incantations, that is, with religious or magic means you can place the patient in a frame of mind that will activate the natural healing forces of the organism'. But, if there is clear evidence of rationality and system, there is as yet no indication of a purely scientific interest in medicine, and the fact that, for example, the Edwin Smith papyrus describes cases regarded as untreatable cannot be used to support such an assertion. In a manual of this kind it was just as important to define clearly what should not be touched as to indicate appropriate treatment, and it is significant that, according to Horapollo, the Egyptian physicians possessed a book called *ambrēs*, from which they were able to predetermine the outcome of an illness.

A feature of Egyptian medical literature is the richness of the pharmacopoeia, which includes several well-known drugs in their earliest recorded applications.[1] Parallel uses suggestive of direct borrowing have been noted in Hebrew, Syriac, Persian, and Arabic texts, and, more important, in the works of many classical writers such as Theophrastus, Celsus, Pliny, Dioscorides, and Galen, and even in the Hippocratic collection—not to mention the compilations of various late-Imperial and Byzantine authorities. It was largely from these sources that physicians of the Middle Ages, like those of the Salerno school, drew their knowledge of *materia medica*, and from them also that much of the plant lore embodied in the popular medical compendiums of the Renaissance and later was ultimately derived. Among simples first exploited by the Egyptians were colocynth, coriander, cummin, dill, and galingale, as well as figs, onions, and pomegranate—used characteristically as an astringent and vermifuge. The virtues of castor oil,

---

[1] Various instances have been noted by W. R. Dawson in *The American Druggist* and elsewhere. References to a number of these articles are to be found in W. R. Dawson, *Magician and Leech*, London, 1929, pp. 135–49.

honey, and certain resins were also recognized, and hartshorn and tortoise-shell were among prescriptions of animal origin. Alum too was employed, together with other astringent salts, and Iversen, in an important lexicographical study,[1] has shown that the medicinal properties of a number of mineral pigments are similar to those ascribed to them in classical contexts. The list might easily be extended, and it is probable that yet other examples would be revealed if the identity of the many unknown substances mentioned in the Egyptian papyri could be established.

The fact that a common drug known to the Egyptians may be traced in later medical works or in folk remedies as part of the stock-in-trade of the travelling quack or Cunning Man is not in itself conclusive proof of direct transmission. If the plant or mineral is readily available and of real efficacy its value may be realized independently, and the recurrence of fanciful medicaments is thus of greater significance in establishing a continuous tradition. The use of calcined hedgehog's spines for alopecia or of bat's blood as a depilatory are examples of this, and the application of fried lizard to cause baldness, as recommended in a sixteenth-century Arabic manuscript, may be compared to a recipe in the Ebers papyrus where fried worm is the agent. Fried mouse also occurs in the Egyptian papyri, and there is evidence from the predynastic period to suggest that children *in extremis* were made to swallow skinned mice as a last resort, the use of mice in popular medicine, and particularly as a cure for infantile ailments, being known from classical, medieval, and more recent times.[2] Bile too, and urine, are prescribed in both Egyptian and later texts, and 'the milk of a woman who has borne a male child' (which in Babylonia and Assyria was thought noxious) is found in innumerable sources. Cited more than twenty times in the medical papyri,

---

[1] E. Iversen, *Some Ancient Egyptian Paints and Pigments: A Lexicographical Study*, Copenhagen, 1955 (*Det Kgl. Danske Videnskabernes Selskab, Historisk-filologiske Meddelelser*, xxxiv, no. 4).

[2] W. R. Dawson, *JEA* x (1924), 83–6.

it occurs in Coptic medicine—whence it has passed to the Arabs—in Pliny, Dioscorides, Galen, and other classical authors, including the Hippocratic collection, in the writings of Constantinus Africanus and the Salerno school, in early German *Arzneibücher*, in English medical compositions of the fourteenth century as, for example, 'mylke of a woman that berythe a knaue child', and in many other European works from the Middle Ages to the eighteenth century.[1] There are, on the other hand, occasional instances of the complete reversal of such popular beliefs, as in the case of lettuce, which the Egyptians regarded as an aphrodisiac, but which in classical and later tradition had precisely the opposite reputation, one seventeenth-century writer noting that it is 'commended for Monkes, Nunnes and the like sort of People to eate'.

Specifically Egyptian drugs are also mentioned by later writers —for example, Dioscorides, who even gives the names of some, though these are largely unrecognizable—one of the best known being Theban opium, for which, however, there is no certain evidence before the Ptolemaic period. Occasionally, the names of medicaments are closely related to Egyptian terms and seem to be direct translations, as νίτρον ἐρυθρόν, quoted by Alexander Trallianus, from Egyptian *ḥsmn dšr*, 'red natron', or the *lingua marina* of Constantinus Africanus, recalling Coptic ⲗⲁⲥ ⲛ̄ⲉⲓⲟⲙ, lit. 'sea-tongue', which seems to refer to cuttle-fish bone and has been tentatively equated with the Egyptian *ns-š*, lit. 'pond-tongue'. Nor are such cases confined to *materia medica*, for the word migraine may likewise be of Egyptian origin, the Greek ἡμικρανία (Latin *hemicrania*) being derived almost certainly from *gs-tp*, lit. 'half-head', while cataract (Latin *suffusio*, Greek ὑπόχυσις) seems to go back to Egyptian *ꜥḫt nt mw*, lit. 'gathering of water'. Moreover, the pupil of the eye is called in a medical context *twt n irt*, 'the image of the eye', and elsewhere *ḥwnt imyt irt*, 'the maid in

---

[1] W. R. Dawson, *Aegyptus*, xii (1932), 12–15.

the eye', which corresponds to the Greek κόρη and Latin *pupilla*, the classical Arabic 'the human being in the eye', and the Spanish *niña de los ojos*—though these designations may be of independent origin, as James Bond's powers of observation would perhaps suggest.

The casting of prescriptions in the characteristic Egyptian mould is a further indication of direct borrowing. In the medical papyri remedies are headed by a note of the ailment to be cured, or in the case of alternatives by 'another remedy' or simply 'another', a form which is common to classical, medieval, and later texts, and are often terminated by an assurance of their efficacy, which is echoed in the *probatum* or 'tried and found perfect' of subsequent compilations. Again, it is several times directed that a concoction be exposed to the dew, and this recommendation is found also in the Hippocratic writings and in those of the school of Salerno, and so in the German *Arzneibücher*, while the incantations with which Egyptian prescriptions are sometimes interspersed have later, Christian, parallels. Lastly, it has been observed that the aphoristic style of portions of the Hippocratic collection is typically Egyptian, and that Egyptian feeling is apparent in the general spirit of the corpus and notably in the disinclination to attempt treatment of the incurable.

Egyptian influence on Greek medicine in particular may be detected in the widespread resort to incubation as a means of irrational therapy from the fifth century B.C. onwards, the practice having been known in Egypt at least as early as the New Kingdom and being very common in the Ptolemaic period, when the deified Imhotep was identified with Asklepios. To Egypt also may be ascribed certain curious beliefs current in antiquity, for example, that human bites were extremely dangerous, an idea found in the Ebers and Hearst papyri, in Pliny, and in the works of Oribasius, where such bites merit a whole section, and so persisting down to the Middle Ages to be revived by Avicenna (Ibn Sīnā) and other writers. Moreover, as pointed out by

Saunders, the Greek tradition of poison and cosmetic literature seems to have emanated from Egypt, through Apollodorus of Alexandria and Nicander of Colophon, though only the cosmetic side can actually be traced in pharaonic texts, and there is little doubt that in the realms of ophthalmology and gynaecology the debt of the classical world and the Orient to Egypt was considerable. It is, indeed, interesting that Galen, Aetius, and Paulus Aegineta ascribe cosmetic recipes to 'Cleopatra' and that 'Cleopatra' is also named as an authority in some Renaissance compilations of gynaecology.

In the case of ophthalmology precise documentation of such legacy is less easy, but there is nevertheless clear evidence of Egyptian influence in Pliny and Dioscorides, in Alexander Trallianus' section on the treatment of the eyes, in a Coptic medical papyrus of the ninth or tenth century A.D., and in the collections of the school of Salerno. With gynaecology, on the other hand, the various stages in the transmission of Egyptian ideas down to the Renaissance, and even to the present day, may be neatly demonstrated through specific examples.[1] Thus the Ebers papyrus includes a group of related remedies for uterine prolapse—a condition noted in Egyptian mummies—elements from which are found in Dioscorides and Constantinus Africanus and subsequently in the influential handbooks of the sixteenth century and in later compilations such as the *Dreck-Apotheke* of Paullini, as well as in Anatolian folk medicine. Extraordinary contraceptive methods too are traceable to Egypt,[2] a device advocated by Qusṭā ibn Lūqā in the ninth century A.D., and later by Ibn Sīnā, Constantinus Africanus, and Ibn al-Baiṭār, being evidently inspired by two recipes in the Kahun medical papyrus, one of which is matched in a roughly contemporary text from the Ramesseum.

---

[1] G. Ebers, *ZÄS* xxxiii (1895), 1–18; W. R. Dawson, *The Caledonian Medical Journal*, xiii (1927), 296–302.

[2] N. E. Himes, *Medical History of Contraception*, Baltimore, 1936, pp. 59–63.

As might perhaps be expected, the strongest tradition is, however, in the literature concerned with childbirth,[1] that fundamental activity protected by the mother Hathor and the grotesque household godlings Bes (Pl. 6) and Taweret, of which omnipotent Isis with her son Horus was the very apotheosis (Pl. 19*b*), and which in the magic aura of late antiquity was hedged about with mighty amulets (Pl. 11 *a–b*).

The various excerpts from the Egyptian papyri in fact comprise three related notions, the determination of fertility, the diagnosis of pregnancy, and the ascertainment of the sex of the unborn child, but in that these ends are not always clearly distinguished, particularly in later tradition, it is convenient to treat of them together. The simplest prognoses are those which depend upon the inspection of external features, pulsation, the cast of the eyes, and the colour and consistency of the skin and breasts, and, although no exact parallels appear to be known, tests based on similar observations are not uncommon. Cases of pregnancy gauged from the appearance of the eyes and breasts and of sex-determination from the colour of the eyes and skin are found in the Hippocratic corpus and other sources (the Greek $\chi\rho\tilde{\omega}\mu\alpha$ being used exactly as the Egyptian *inm/iwn*), and changes in the breasts are also noted in Renaissance works, while in the present century a green tinge was still considered an indication of pregnancy in Scotland. But these beliefs, which appear in somewhat similar form in Akkadian texts of the first millennium B.C., have a certain justification, at least in so far as pigmentation of the skin and engorgement of the mammary veins may actually occur, and the likelihood of a single continuous tradition is to be judged accordingly.

More characteristic are, however, prognoses involving the oral administration of specifics, the introduction of pessaries and

---

[1] H. L. E. Lüring, *Die über die medicinischen Kenntnisse der alten Ägypter berichtenden Papyri*, Leipzig, 1888, pp. 133–42; H. P. Bayon, *Proc. Royal Soc. of Medicine*, xxxii (1939), 1527–38; T. R. Forbes, *The Yale Journ. of Biology and Medicine*, xxx (1957), 16–29.

fumigations into the vagina, and observation of the effects of pregnancy urine on the germination of grain and other substances. Examples of these have caught the attention of several scholars, and those occurring in Papyrus Carlsberg VIII have been carefully studied by Iversen[1] with reference to the other Egyptian parallels, notably from the Berlin medical papyrus, and ample documentation of their recurrence in later sources. The first, fragmentary, case of the Carlsberg group, and the sixth, based on the colour of the eyes, require no comment. The second, also fragmentary, which turns on the appearance of animalicules in a woman's urine, seems to have no classical derivative, but occurs in variant forms in the Salernitan treatise ascribed to 'Trotula', in the works of Albertus Magnus and Antonio Guainerio, in those of Walther Ryff and Jacob Rueff, in the *Dreck-Apotheke* of Paullini, and in editions of the pseudo-Aristotle (see below), the simple pregnancy test being further adapted as a means of determining which of a woman and her husband is sterile. The fourth and fifth, depending on the use of an onion pessary and on fumigation of the vagina with excrement are obviously related, and both are found in Hippocrates, the latter in a variant. Vaginal fumigations and garlic pessaries are also recommended in compilations of the sixteenth century, including those of Guainerio, Ryff, Rueff, and Savonarola, and their use in later folk medicine both in Europe and—even now—in Anatolia and Egypt has been recorded. The seventh case, in which the woman drinks a sweet potion, appears somewhat differently in the Berlin medical papyrus, where the mixture, also used as a douche, has as its base 'the milk of a woman who has borne a male child', and this version again finds an exact parallel in Hippocrates, whose hydromel test too is of similar principle.

[1] E. Iversen, *Papyrus Carlsberg No. VIII, With Some Remarks on the Egyptian Origin of Some Popular Birth Prognoses*, Copenhagen, 1939 (*Det Kgl. Danske Videnskabernes Selskab, Historisk-filologiske Meddelelser*, xxvi, no. 5).

But the most interesting is the third of the Carlsberg prognoses, one more fully preserved in the Berlin papyrus, where a woman is required to urinate upon barley and wheat (emmer), for this may be traced, with numerous variations, through a succession of popular works. Prior to Iversen's discoveries, the gap between the Egyptian papyri and the handbooks of the Renaissance could not satisfactorily be bridged, though a variant form of the test was to be found in Constantinus Africanus. Now, however, it is clear that this method of prediction was known in Greek medical literature, versions occurring in a work attributed to Galen, but actually of much later (Byzantine) date, in fragments of another, roughly contemporary, manuscript, and in an excerpt of a work under the name of 'Moschion', i.e. the Byzantine Muscio. Much of the text of 'Moschion', though not apparently this item (which is elsewhere ascribed to Priscianus), was adapted from the gynaecological treatise of Soranus, and the book was very influential in the Renaissance, particularly through the medium of Eucharius Roesslin's *Rosengarten*, first published in German in 1512 or 1513 and subsequently translated, with sundry additions, into Latin, English, French, Italian, Spanish, and Dutch. Curiously enough, the test in question does not in fact appear in Roesslin's original edition, though versions are found in Raynalde's *Birth of Mankinde* and the *Rosengarten* of Walther Ryff ('Rivius'), both of which are largely derived from it,[1] as well as in the *Trostbüchle* of Jacob Rueff, the *Vademecum* of the sixteenth-century Florentine Petrus Bayrus, the *Dreck-Apotheke* of Paullini, and the popular compilation variously called *Aristotle's (Last) Legacy*, his *Masterpiece*, or the *Compleat and Experienc'd Midwife*, editions of which

[1] The additions to 'Raynalde' were evidently made by Richard Jonas; cf. J. W. Ballantyne, *The 'Byrth of Mankynde': Its Author, Editions, and Contents*, London, n.d. (reprinted from *Journ. of Obstetrics and Gynaecology of the British Empire*, Oct. 1906, Sept. 1907, Oct. 1907). Both Jonas and Ryff may have found their 'addenda' in the *De Secretis Mulierum* attributed to Albertus Magnus, the earliest editions of which date from the last quarter of the fifteenth century.

continued to be sold until recently under the fatuous title of *The Works of Aristotle, the Famous Philosopher*.[1] A variant is also given in a sixteenth–century Cairene book of erotology, and the method is still applied in Anatolia,[2] the several occurrences varying to the extent that the same basic procedure may be used to show whether a woman will bear a male or female child, or simply whether she is fertile, or further, if she is childless, whether she or the husband is sterile.

As a pendant to his paper, Iversen discusses yet another prognosis, included in the great demotic magical papyrus and closely related to the foregoing, in which the withering effect of a woman's urine upon a given plant is the indication. This again, though not as yet traced in a classical source, is found in Ibn Sīnā, in the sixteenth-century Cairene text just mentioned, and in many books of the Renaissance and later, including those of Guainerio, Ryff, and Rueff, Conrad Kuhnradt's *Medulla*, Culpeper's translation of Riverius, his *Last Legacy*, and versions of the spurious 'Aristotle'. As before, the purpose is variable, what was in origin a simple pregnancy diagnosis being used also to distinguish whether woman or man is barren.

Iversen's study is of great interest for the light it throws upon the channels through which one section of Egyptian medical lore reached Europe, and in particular in indicating the part played by Greek tradition. The old hypothesis of dissemination chiefly through lost Coptic and Arabic texts based on Egyptian sources can, it is clear, no longer be maintained, though this is not to say that there was no such continuity—still less to minimize the importance of the Salerno school in any network of transmission.

---

[1] The several redactions all stem from the pseudonymous *Problemata*, first published in the latter part of the fifteenth century, the later translations being greatly altered and enlarged through the continued incorporation of new material.

[2] A. Bayoumi, *Revue de l'Égypte ancienne*, iii (1931), 110–16; T. R. Kazancigil, in *XVIIᵉ Congrès international d'histoire de la médecine*, i (*Communications*), Athens–Cos, 1960, pp. 79–84.

The several prognoses based on the outcome of the oral or vaginal administration of different substances, sometimes without distinction, seem to reflect a conviction that in fertile women there was communication between the uterus and the abdomen, a theory which would also account for the Egyptian belief in the possibility of oral conception. As to those involving the action of urine upon seeds and plants, it is feasible that they stem from observation (though not, of course, understanding) of hormonal effects, attempts to verify which have in fact been made in the laboratory, for example, by J. Manger and W. Hoffmann. But the idea that the germination of barley and wheat (emmer) thus watered might indicate the sex of an unborn child was probably associated with the different gender of these two staple grains in Egyptian,[1] *it*, 'barley', being masculine—and a homonymn of the word for father—and *bdt*/*bty*, 'emmer', feminine, and it is interesting that in all subsequent versions of the test the roles are reversed, presumably because in Greek barley ($\kappa\rho\iota\theta\dot{\eta}$) is feminine and wheat ($\pi\upsilon\rho\dot{o}s$, $\sigma\hat{\iota}\tau os$) masculine.

The notion, common to certain African tribes, that the bones of a child come from the father's sperm and its flesh from the mother seems also to have originated in Egypt, as does the concept that sperm is generated from the marrow of the spine.[2] Both opinions were held by the philosopher Hippon and are referred to by Plutarch, while the latter was accepted even by Hippocrates and Plato and is found in the *Hieroglyphica* of Horapollo. The origin of these beliefs is obscure, though it is clear that in later times the Egyptians connected the penis with the backbone, and Yoyotte has adduced a possible explanation of the spinal theory in the debilitating effects of undue sexual indulgence as described by a modern Arab. It is, however, significant that in other cultural

---

[1] H. L. E. Lüring, op. cit. (above, p. 120, n. 1), pp. 140–1; S. Sauneron, *BIFAO* lx (1960), 29–30.

[2] S. Sauneron, *BIFAO* lx (1960), 19–27; J. Yoyotte, *BIFAO* lxi (1962), 139–46.

contexts the head, and specifically the brain, have been regarded as a source of fertility, and this may perhaps suggest that speculation as to the source of semen was variously prompted by chance acquaintance with the cerebrospinal fluid.

That such ideas imply no great cognizance of anatomy is evident, though it should be remembered that the importance of understanding the structure of the human body was not generally recognized until the Renaissance. The Egyptians certainly distinguished a great many parts of the body, including the principal internal organs, and as regards gross anatomy their terminology was fairly adequate, their custom of itemizing the body *a capite ad calcem* having perhaps originated the form which was later to become traditional. They did not, however, recognize the significance of certain of the organs they named, such as the brain, and failed entirely to comprehend the muscular and nervous systems, still less the circulation of the blood as is sometimes claimed, a single word, *mt*, being used indifferently of sinews, veins, arteries, and other vessels. This is, indeed, hardly surprising in that, to quote Sigerist, 'the chief sources of anatomical knowledge were the kitchen and the cult', a fact confirmed by the derivation of all hieroglyphs for internal organs from those of animals, principally cattle. Contrary to common belief, the process of mummification will have afforded little opportunity for the study of internal anatomy, the viscera being roughly drawn out of the abdominal and thoracic cavities through a ventral incision with no concern for finesse, nor is there any evidence to show that dissection was practised before the Ptolemaic period. Moreover, Egyptian surgeons did not perform any major operations, and there is no foundation for statements that, for example, limbs were amputated, the skull trepanned, or eye surgery attempted, the earliest operative treatment of cataract in Egypt dating from the second century A.D.

There is, indeed, little operative surgery even in the Edwin Smith papyrus, which consists largely of a monograph on wounds, perhaps intended as a manual of war injuries. Among the treatments described are several relating to fractures and dislocations, including the method of reducing a dislocated mandible and that for dealing with a fracture of the clavicle. In both cases means closely similar are advocated by Hippocrates, and this has been taken to indicate direct borrowing, but there is in fact no other way of coping with a dislocated jaw, and the treatment for a fractured clavicle cannot be bettered, so that either method may well have been discovered independently on more than one occasion.

From the standpoint of legacy, the opening section of the papyrus, dealing with wounds in the head, is, however, of much greater interest and significance, as Iversen has shown.[1] Apart from two which are simple flesh wounds, the injuries fall into three categories, involving *sd*, 'smashing', *pšn*, 'splitting', and *thm*, 'piercing', of the skull respectively, the terms 'being used to signify the three characteristic forms of bone lesion, of which all other lesions are considered to be variants'. The definition of *thm* and *pšn* is clear enough; *sd*, 'smashing', refers to 'actual and complicated fractures in which the cranium is splintered and the injured portion has sunk in'. The procedure in each instance is stereotyped, and the treatment, if any, simple, with no recourse to even the most elementary surgical operation. In the comparable Hippocratic work on wounds in the head, a synthetic account based on a number of typical cases, there are again three basic types of injury, ῥῆγμα, φλάσις, and ἕδρα, and these may be shown to correspond closely to the Egyptian classification. The 'actual fracture of the skull' or 'contusion', φλάσις, is thus the equivalent of *sd*, the 'fissure fracture', ῥῆγμα, of *pšn*, and the 'hole', ἕδρα, of *thm*, while an additional case, the modern *contrecoup*, may be compared to the last of the 'smashes' described in the Egyptian

[1] E. Iversen, 'Wounds in the Head in Egyptian and Hippocratic Medicine', in *Studia Orientalia Ioanni Pedersen . . . dicata*, Copenhagen, 1953, pp. 163–71.

text, which seems to refer to a fracture occurring away from the point at which the blow was delivered, the lesion in both instances being concealed beneath the scalp. The various symptoms described are essentially similar to those adduced in the Edwin Smith papyrus, but the diagnosis includes surgical procedures not found in the Egyptian, and—the only fundamental difference—the treatment too is varied by the introduction in some instances of a surgical operation, trepanning. This distinction apart, there is extraordinary conformity between the Egyptian and Greek views of these lesions, not only in the basic division into three categories, and the evident recognition of *contrecoup*, but in the diagnoses and therapeutic treatment, the latter characterized on both sides by the prohibition of bandaging. In other words, the Hippocratic corpus may here be seen to follow closely Egyptian medical tradition, departing from it only in the particular use of a new surgical method.

A stray example of operative surgery which seems to have originated in Egypt is circumcision, though it must be admitted that the rite was not widespread and that its nature and purpose are far from clear. Herodotus, however, states that the Egyptians were the first to circumcise, and it is to be assumed that the Hebrews, who, in the opinion of Yahuda, 'had a wide and perfect knowledge of Egyptian medicine, of its methods and practices', acquired the custom from them. It is further alleged by Strabo that the operation was also performed on girls, and although this has never been the Jewish habit, it is still common among the poorer classes in Egypt at the present time.

An outstanding characteristic of Egyptian medicine, of great importance in the historical tradition, is the endeavour to treat material systematically. It thus remains to consider whether there were in consequence evolved any general doctrines relating to the nature of disease, and whether, if so, these may be shown to have had any influence on subsequent medical thought. According to both Herodotus and Diodorus, it was considered that diseases arose from superfluous ingested food, with the result that quite excessive reliance was placed upon emetics, purges, and enemas, and a precise statement about the generation of putrefactive residues is actually attributed to an Egyptian, Ninyas, in Papyrus Anonymus Londinensis. That a similar belief may in fact be traced in Egyptian texts has been demonstrated by Steuer,[1] showing that the term *wḥdw* refers to a pyogenic principle or *materia peccans* derived from the corruption of the bowel content and adherent to the faeces, which, being absorbed, was thought to cause coagulation and destruction of the blood and so give rise to suppurative conditions or to the eventual putrefaction of the body.

This concept of corrupt nutriment residues, not evacuated, as a major aetiological factor in sickness is also found in Greek medicine, notably in the teachings of Euryphron of Cnidus and others of his school, as summarized by Anonymus Londinensis, and will undoubtedly have been elaborated in the lost 'Cnidian Sentences'. It occurs, too, in Aristotle, where the residue ($\pi\epsilon\rho\ell\tau\tau\omega\mu\alpha$) is associated with putrefaction ($\sigma\hat{\eta}\psi\iota\varsigma$) attendant upon the second stage of digestion and has four related components, sperm, faeces, phlegm, and bile, as well as in the works of Aristotle's pupil Menon, upon which the Anonymus text is based. There is, indeed, no reference to $\pi\epsilon\rho\ell\tau\tau\omega\mu\alpha$ in the Hippocratic corpus— though the concepts of $\pi\lambda\hat{\eta}\theta\varsigma$ and $\pi\lambda\eta\sigma\mu\nu\nu\acute{\eta}$ (surfeit) occur, which seem to have an Egyptian analogue—but, as Steuer has pointed out, the idea 'is not completely disregarded, because there is ample evidence that great importance was attached to manifestations of putrefaction . . . as the cause of suppuration'. Moreover, although the Cnidian view of putrefaction as an aetiological principle was

[1] R. O. Steuer, *wḥdw: Aetiological Principle of Pyaemia in Ancient Egyptian Medicine*, Baltimore, 1948 (*Supplement to the Bulletin of the History of Medicine*, no. 10); R. O. Steuer and J. B. de C. M. Saunders, *Ancient Egyptian and Cnidian Medicine*, Berkeley–Los Angeles, 1959. See also J. B. de C. M. Saunders, *The Transitions from Ancient Egyptian to Greek Medicine*, Lawrence, Kansas, 1963, pp. 20–23.

largely superseded by the humoral doctrine of Cos, it remained influential, and in a modified form was absorbed into later theories. Thus, for instance, Galen combines elaboration of the theory of humours with extensive comments on the older concept of περίτ-τωμα and its connection with σῆψις.

Other comparisons may also be drawn between Egyptian and Greek ideas as to the causes of disease, though there are serious problems of terminology. Whether the Egyptian *stt* and *ʿrwt* in fact refer to phlegm and bile respectively, as Ebbell has suggested, remains uncertain, but it is clear that they are both fluid substances which circulate in the body and are subject to corruption. The word *tsw*, lit. 'risings', is also used of excremental products, including urine, which find their way into the body, the notion of the rising of noxious agents having an obvious counterpart in the Greek 'flux'. Indeed, *wḥdw* 'rises', as does the περίσσωμα of the Cnidian school; *wḥdw* also coagulates the blood and converts it into pus (*ryt*), the idea that the blood thickens or putrefies finding similar expression in Aristotle. The elimination of pus, like the eradication of superfluous residues, was, moreover, essential, and wounds were therefore made to suppurate, suggesting the existence of a concept akin to that of 'laudable pus'.

That there is nothing in the medical papyri which might be taken to herald the Hippocratic doctrine of humours cannot detract from the importance of Egyptian speculation on the aetiology of disease. The true extent of its influence can hardly be gauged, though it would seem that the idea of putrefaction as the prime cause of illness and the principles it involved had a definite impact on Greek medical thinking. The possibility of a wider bearing upon opinions as to the nature of odours and so upon 'views of the particulate nature of matter on the one hand, and the nature of contagion on the other' has been indicated by Saunders, who also points out that the Egyptian belief in the generation of pestilence by the exhalations of decomposing corpses is comparable to the theory of miasmas, 'a theory which was to exist almost to our own day'.

It has been suggested that the Egyptians regarded pathological suppuration and the decomposition of corpses as parallel processes, and that it was through the practice of mummification that they came to associate putrefaction with the large intestine. If so, the bearing of this realization upon the development of the *wḥdw* thesis would represent a legacy of the embalmer to native medicine and so indirectly to medicine at large. How far embalming may have influenced the Egyptians' appreciation of the properties of various substances and in particular of certain *materia medica* it is difficult to assess, though the wide range of products from time to time employed in attempts to preserve the body[1]—and the use of resins long before mummification proper was developed—would suggest the possibility of such a contribution. The elaboration of wrappings, which seems to have led to the creation of a class of specialists,[2] must, however, have resulted in improvements in the field of medicine, and a specific treatise on bandaging is, indeed, mentioned in the Edwin Smith papyrus. Lastly, although the process of eviscerating the dead can have added little to Egyptian knowledge of anatomy, the mere fact that bodies were daily being handled will surely have encouraged an atmosphere in which research could flourish when the ban on dissection was lifted under the Ptolemies.

The technique of embalming itself has left no great legacy, and, although the practice of preserving the dead by means akin to mummification has been more widespread than is generally realized,[3] there is nothing to suggest that even the most elaborate methods—those of pre-Conquest Peru and the Canary Islands—owe anything to Egypt. The embalming of Poppaea, mentioned

[1] A. Lucas, *Ancient Egyptian Materials and Industries*, 4th ed. (J. R. Harris), London, 1962, pp. 270–326. On mummification in general, see R. Engelbach and D. E. Derry, *ASAE* xli (1942), 235–65; G. Elliot Smith and W. R. Dawson, *Egyptian Mummies*, London, 1924.

[2] F. Jonckheere, *Chronique d'Égypte*, xxviii (1953), 60–76.

[3] L. Dérobert and H. Reichlen, *Les Momies: le culte des morts dans le monde sauvage et civilisé*, Paris, n.d.

by Tacitus, was clearly exotic, and the female bodies found on the Appian Way and at Albano during the Renaissance and in Rome itself early in 1964 may well have been mummified in Egypt or, more probably, by Egyptian priests attached to the Isiac cult at Rome (Pl. 7). A similar connection will account for those mummies discovered in Pannonia, and perhaps also for the famous Gallo-Roman mummy of a child found at Martres-d'Artier near Riom in the Puy-de-Dôme in 1756, a curiosity whose preservation was apparently due as much to the nature of the ground as to the smearing of the body and bandages with a resinous substance. The *Chanson de Roland*, indeed, refers to the treatment of the bodies of Roland and Olivier with balsams and wine, and several royal persons of the Middle Ages are known to have been variously boiled in wine or salt water and steeped in aromatic substances, but this '*boucherie macabre*', far removed from Egyptian practice, was only rarely effective.

Interest in mummification revived in the sixteenth century, no doubt in connection with the trade in dead Egyptians for medicinal purposes, and in 1553 Pierre Belon published a treatise on embalming generally, devoting considerable attention to Egyptian methods and listing the best preservative materials. From the beginning of the seventeenth century attempts were made to apply techniques such as those advocated by Philibert Guybert in his work *Le Médecin charitable*, and by Louis de Bils, a Flemish anatomist of distinction, while Louis Penicher, writing in 1699, details the laborious process employed by Riqueur in embalming the Dauphine. No less complex was that used by Dionis to preserve the body of Louis XIV, which survived intact until the Revolution together with those of Henri IV and Turenne, though others similarly treated had decomposed. Such sophisticated techniques, intended to surpass the art of the Egyptian embalmers, were, however, extraordinary, and although experiments in mummification became increasingly common during the late eighteenth and early nineteenth centuries, the methods devised were often eccentric and devoid of any Egyptian inspiration. A notable exception was the embalming of Alexander, tenth Duke of Hamilton, in 1852, a ceremony carried out after the Egyptian fashion, with T. J. Pettigrew, first Professor of Anatomy at Charing Cross Hospital, as embalmer and Chief Ritualist, the body being laid to rest in an Egyptian sarcophagus 'at one time destined for the British Museum'. Of more recent refinements only the process developed by Barnes is in any way reminiscent of Egyptian usage, the perfection achieved by Hochstetter, the now common practice of injecting formalin into the bloodstream, and the more grotesque ministrations of the Joyboys, adepts of the 'Beautiful Memory Picture', being wholly the product of our time.

Of greater significance is the curious tradition of 'mummy' as a medicament,[1] the origins of which may be traced, albeit indirectly, to the recommended use of bitumen in later antiquity. From classical writers the drug passed into Arab medicine, under the name *mūmīa*, the Persian kind being specially prized as a panacea, and it was then further accepted that the pitch-like substances to be found in embalmed bodies were of similar virtue.[2] The earliest references to this type of *mūmīa* occur at the turn of the ninth and tenth centuries, in the works of Isaachus Judaeus and al-Rāzī, and in the somewhat later writings of Ibn Sīnā (the great Avicenna), who died in 1037. The historian ʿAbd al-Laṭīf in the twelfth century speaks of seeing the matter taken out of the skulls and stomachs of mummies, and Ibn al-Baiṭār, the celebrated thirteenth-century physician, also alludes to the *mūmīa* of the tombs. But already in the eleventh century certain Arab authorities, such as Ibn Riḍwān, had begun to ascribe the

---

[1] A. Wiedemann, *Zeitschrift des Vereins für rheinische und westfälische Volkskunde*, iii. 1 (1906), 1–38; T. J. Pettigrew, *History of Egyptian Mummies*, London, 1834, pp. 7–12.

[2] Generally thought to be true bitumen, though much of it will in fact have been a resinous compound.

therapeutic values of *mūmīa* to the actual flesh of the embalmed, and it was chiefly in this latter sense that 'mummy' was to be understood in Europe.

According to a story handed down by Guyon in his *Leçons*, an Alexandrian Jew named 'Elmagar' treated Crusaders and their Muslim adversaries with 'mummy' and so was responsible for spreading the knowledge of its properties. In fact, the Salerno school of the eleventh century may have played an important part in this, for certainly Constantinus Africanus was familiar with the bituminous *mūmīa* derived from ancient corpses. The use of the cadaverous flesh itself is cited in a work written in 1363 by Guy de Chavillac, surgeon to Pope Clemens VI—the earliest English reference being in a manuscript of about 1400—and by the beginning of the sixteenth century it was so highly regarded, notably in France, that François I himself was accustomed, says Belon, to carry a little packet containing 'mummy' mixed with powdered rhubarb, in case of accident. During the sixteenth and seventeenth centuries, 'mummy' was, indeed, one of the drugs included in the ordinary repertoire of European apothecaries—'Mummy is become merchandise, Mizraim cures wounds, and Pharaoh is sold for balsams', wrote Sir Thomas Browne, and allusions to it are frequent in Elizabethan and Jacobean drama, often with transferred meaning, as of dead flesh, a pulpy substance, or a sovereign remedy. It was considered most efficacious for bruises and wounds, but was also taken internally in various forms, and different qualities were recognized. The best was generally considered to be that which was hard but easily pulverized, dark brown to black in colour, with a bitter taste and a strong smell, while Roquefort alleges that the French found '*fille vierge*' particularly desirable.

But, however loathsome the idea of a 'salvatory of greene mummey', the materials used in the embalming may actually have retained medicinal properties, and contemporary scientific opinion was in fact divided. Endorsed in the influential works of

Avicenna, now in Latin, and by the great Paracelsus, 'mummy' was recommended as a useful medicine by such notable figures as J. C. Scaliger, Sir Francis Bacon, Olaus Wormius, and Robert Boyle, and included in several prescriptions of the *Pharmacopoeia Schroedero–Hoffmanniana*. Among its first opponents were Leonhardt Fuchs and Hakluyt, who was unimpressed by 'these dead bodies . . . the Mummie which the Phisitians and Apothecaries doe against our willes make us to swallow', while the renowned Ambroise Paré roundly condemned the use of 'this wicked kind of drugge', as the English version of his works describes it, adding that it 'inferres many troublesome symptomes'. Another who warned against placing trust in 'old gums' was Nehemiah Grew, the sagacious cataloguer of the rarities of the Royal Society, and there were many more who had misgivings and were careful to insist, as Lemery, that only the *'veritable mumie d'Égypte'* should be employed.

Such caution stemmed from the disconcerting knowledge that not all 'mummy' enjoyed the dubious distinction of having come from a deceased Egyptian. As early as 1564, Guy de la Fontaine, physician to the King of Navarre, had discovered on a visit to Alexandria that the Jews who trafficked in mummies were wont to eke out their supply with the bodies of executed criminals and the dead from hospitals, hastily prepared by stuffing with asphalt and then dried in the sun to ensure a suitably antique appearance. Nor was this gruesome increment peculiar to Egypt, for, just as under the Terror *la graisse de guillotiné* was counterfeited by Parisian butchers, so false mummies were confected in Europe with bodies snatched from gibbets under a waning moon to be dried and macerated in resin. Not, however, that all new 'mummy' was unacceptable. The so-called 'white' variety, made from the remains of travellers overwhelmed by desert sandstorms or cast up drowned upon Egyptian shores, was in some demand, and that prepared from the corpse of a red-headed person or a witch was thought to be of unusual potency. Well might the poet

Shirley write, 'Make mummy of my flesh and sell me to the apothecaries.'

In spite of controversy, the vogue for 'mummy' survived to the end of the eighteenth century, with instances of its use recorded as late as the mid nineteenth in south Germany and Austria, and even more recently in the folk medicine of the Middle East. It appears, too, that it had other than therapeutic applications, being used both as a condition powder for falcons and as a bait for fish, while in a well-known Shakespearian context it is referred to as a dye. 'That handkerchief', says Othello, 'did an Egyptian to my mother give . . . The worms were hallow'd that did breed the silk, and it was dy'd in mummy which the skilful conserv'd of maidens' hearts.' Whether or not this may be taken as evidence of a current practice, it is on record that finely powdered 'mummy' was sometimes added to oil paints, a single corpse sufficing to supply one colourman's customers for twenty years. That 'mummy' should ever have been fancied as a condiment or garnishing seems scarcely credible, and yet such is the purport of Caspar Hofmann's allegation[1] that in Lower Saxony in the seventeenth century no banquet was complete *'sine mummie'*— just as the Indians *'olim sine lasere* [the resinous juice of silphium], *et hodie . . . sine asa foetida nihil comedunt'*.

It would perhaps be cynical to suggest that the public demonstrations of Pettigrew and his contemporaries upon Egyptian mummies were a chapter in the history of entertainment,[2] though the eager curiosity of the often distinguished audiences and of the 'antiquarians tastefully arranged' upon the platform will not have been wholly scientific. It is, however, from such performances and from the more sober examinations of Elliot Smith and Derry

---

[1] C. Hofmann, *De medicamentis officinalibus*, Leiden, 1738, p. 642 (p. 9 of the appended *Paraleipomena officinalia*). But according to Wiedemann (op. cit., p. 33), *'Der biedere Professor hat hier das Braunschweiger Bier Mumme mit den alten Mumien verwechselt'*!

[2] W. R. Dawson, *JEA* xx (1934), 170–82.

that scholarship has reaped a tangible legacy in terms of medical and other knowledge. For the Egyptologist there have been useful gleanings from the mummies of royalty—indications of family relationships, of the age at which individuals died, and even of the manner of their death—and problems too. Why, for example, did a royal youth of the Eighteenth Dynasty die in apparent anguish, to be then hastily embalmed, or what was the domestic drama that led to a young girl of the Saite period being cruelly beaten to death in the sixth month of pregnancy? Much has been learned also of the methods and material used by the Egyptians in embalming their dead and in treating the bodies of animals, the mummies of the latter in turn providing abundant material for the zoologist. But the richest harvest has been in the field of palaeopathology,[1] where the study of mummies has provided valid witness of the incidence of diseases and conditions which cannot satisfactorily be obtained either from the medical papyri or from representations in art, the interpretation of which is notoriously unreliable.[2] A mere list of the congenital and inflammatory lesions, new growths and deteriorations that have been observed would be of little interest to any but the specialist, and perhaps even misleading, in so far as certain conditions are attested only in single instances or from bodies of Coptic or Byzantine date, while in other cases diagnosis remains in doubt. It may be noted, however, that as yet cancer has not been found in a mummy of the pharaonic period, nor any evidence of rickets, or, more important, of syphilis,

[1] M. A. Ruffer, *Studies in the Palaeopathology of Egypt*, Chicago, 1921; G. Elliot Smith and W. R. Dawson, *Egyptian Mummies*, London, 1924, pp. 154–62; W. R. Dawson, *Magician and Leech*, London, 1929, pp. 103–8; H. E. Sigerist, *A History of Medicine*, i, New York, 1941, pp. 37–101; J. T. Rowling, *Proc. Royal Soc. of Medicine*, liv (1961), 409–15.

[2] See in general, S. Tolstoï, *Étude des représentations pathologiques dans l'art égyptien*, Paris, 1939; R. Watermann, *Bilder aus dem Lande des Ptah und Imhotep*, Köln, 1958. A classic instance is the recurrent discussion of Akhenaten's alleged deformity, of which a bibliography alone would run to several pages.

a fact which tends to confirm that this particular scourge is one of the doubtful benefits conferred upon the Old World by the New. Also worth mentioning, if only as an oddity, is the unique example of an anencephalic monstrosity examined by Geoffroy Saint-Hilaire, a portent so disturbing that it was apparently regarded as bestial and so embalmed and buried in the manner of a sacred ape.

J. R. HARRIS

BIBLIOGRAPHY

The outstanding work on Egyptian medicine, which includes a systematic republication of the medical texts in transcription, together with translation and commentary, is:

H. GRAPOW and others, *Grundriss der Medizin der alten Ägypter*, Berlin, 1954 and following.

Other valuable general studies are:

H. E. SIGERIST, *A history of medicine*, i, New York, 1951, pp. 217–373.
G. LEFEBVRE, *Essai sur la médecine égyptienne de l'époque pharaonique*, Paris, 1956.
P. GHALIOUNGUI, *Magic and medical science in ancient Egypt*, London, 1963.

Apart from the various important articles cited in footnotes, the following deal specifically with the question of 'legacy':

J. B. DE C. M. SAUNDERS, *The transitions from ancient Egyptian to Greek medicine*, Lawrence, Kansas, 1963.
P. GHALIOUNGUI, 'Dès papyrus égyptiens à la médecine grecque', in *XVIIᵉ Congrès international d'histoire de la médecine*, i (*Communications*), Athens–Cos, 1960, pp. 296–307.
W. R. DAWSON, *Magician and leech*, London, 1929, pp. 135–49.
G. EBERS, 'Wie Altägyptisches in die europäische Volksmedicin gelangte', *ZÄS* xxxiii (1895), 1–18.

6

MYSTERY, MYTH, AND MAGIC

THE final victory of Christianity under the Roman Emperor Theodosius led unavoidably to the extinction of the pagan Egyptian priests. However much their social and spiritual level had gradually been lowered through centuries of occupation by Persians, Greeks, and—longest of all—Romans, they still held the keys to the scriptural heritage of three millennia of the world's oldest sophisticated civilization; for even if in Mesopotamia urban society may be traced back further in time, it cannot in cultural terms compare with the Egyptian achievement. Significantly, the last hieroglyphic inscription we know about was engraved under that same Emperor Theodosius on the island of Philae in the year 394. If some precarious hieroglyphic knowledge survived, it must have been finally lost when, two and a half centuries after Theodosius, Egypt fell under Islamic rule.

At some time during this period, probably nearer to its beginning, an otherwise unknown Philippus wrote what he announces to be the Greek translation of a treatise on the hieroglyphs, written originally in the Egyptian language by an equally unknown Horapollo[1] (a typically Graeco-Egyptian name combining the Egyptian god Horus with his Greek equivalent Apollo). Although it is clear today that there are distinct traces of authentic knowledge about the original meaning of some of the hieroglyphic signs in Horapollo's *Hieroglyphica*, the whole is a mistaken interpretation of nearly 200 (existent as well as alleged but non-

---

[1] Cf. *The Hieroglyphics of Horapollo*, tr. George Boas, New York, 1950 (Bollingen Series, xxiii).

existent) hieroglyphs as allegorical figures and symbols of ancient wisdom. When a manuscript of this work was found in the early fifteenth century it was uncritically absorbed at its face value. Printed as one of the first books after the invention of this art, it fascinated and profoundly influenced scholars, writers, and artists of the Renaissance and all the following centuries.

Any visitor to the British Museum who has stopped before one of its greatest treasures, the 'Rosetta Stone', knows, of course, how at the beginning of the nineteenth century the discovery of this bilingual inscription of the year 196 B.C.[1] enabled European scholars for the first time to read the immense legacy of ancient Egyptian texts. However, reading was followed by understanding and translating only up to a point. Certainly, scholars have since provided dictionaries and grammars of the ancient Egyptian language, but that is not enough to grasp the Egyptian way of thinking, so utterly different from our Western 'logical' mind. There is first of all what has been called the 'multiplicity of approaches':[2] statements (and answers to problems) which to us would seem absolutely contradictory appear side by side and did not in the least disturb the Egyptian; on the contrary, our own logical abstractions would probably have appeared to the Egyptian mind as an impoverishment and falsification of the fullness of significant truth. Thus the god Thoth could be a baboon or an ibis or the moon; Amūn and Rē could be identified and still be different gods, and there are even trinities of gods which are at one and the same time three distinct persons—a concept which for the logic of Western Christianity is still an inaccessible, if accepted, mystery. Actually, we find in Egyptian religious texts, besides the confusing number of more or less local or fashionable

---

[1] The inscription is written in Egyptian and Greek, the Egyptian text appearing both in hieroglyphic and in demotic (a cursive script developed from hieratic and used for ordinary documents during the Graeco-Roman period).

[2] H. Frankfort, *Ancient Egyptian Religion*, pp. 4 and 19 f.

divinities, expressions which definitely sound monotheistic. Then there is the importance of the single word, not just an abstraction but a reality of a kind for the Egyptian, to whom what we would call puns appeared as mythological facts. All this would lead—as a modern scholar has put it[1]—to 'the impossibility of translating Egyptian thoughts into modern language, for the distinctions we cannot avoid making did not exist for the Egyptians'. However, realization of these facts has now gone some way towards promoting understanding and interpretation in modern Egyptology.

The Greek and Roman authors who dealt with the history and religion of the Egyptians never bothered to learn their strange writing and language. For them it was a system of curious and mysterious symbolic signs and they were satisfied to report shreds of information received from native clerics and tourist guides who were probably, more often than not, only half-educated—information, moreover, which, according to their personal bias, they would either find absurd or translate with suitable awe into their own Hellenistic philosophy or theosophy. What the average educated man of late antiquity thought he knew we might perhaps best summarize by quoting from the fourth-century Roman historian Ammianus Marcellinus:

If one wishes to investigate with attentive mind the many publications on the knowledge of the divine and the origin of divination, he will find that learning of this kind has spread abroad from Egypt through the whole world. There, for the first time, long before other men, they discovered the cradles, so to speak, of the various religions, and now carefully guard the first beginnings of worship, stored up in secret writings. Trained in this wisdom, Pythagoras, secretly honouring the gods, made whatever he said or believed recognized authority. . . . From here Anaxagoras foretold a rain of stones. . . . Solon too, aided by the opinions of the Egyptian priests, passed laws in accordance with the measure of justice. . . . On this source Plato drew and, after visiting Egypt,

[1] H. Frankfort, *Ancient Egyptian Religion*, p. 54.

traversed higher regions of thought . . . gloriously serving in the field of wisdom.[1]

On another occasion, mentioning the extant obelisks, he writes:

Now the infinite carvings of characters called hieroglyphics . . . have been made known by an ancient authority of primaeval wisdom. For by engraving many kinds of birds and beasts, even of another world, in order that the memory of their achievements might the more widely reach generations of a subsequent age, they registered the vows of kings, either promised or performed. For not as nowadays, when a fixed and easy series of letters expresses whatever the mind of man may conceive, did the ancient Egyptians also write; but individual characters stood for individual nouns and verbs; and sometimes they meant whole phrases.

And Ammianus gives two examples:

By a vulture they represent the word 'nature', because, as natural history records, no males can be found among these birds; and under the figure of a bee making honey they designate 'a king', showing by this imagery that in a ruler sweetness should be combined with a sting as well.[2]

Such was the basic common opinion on which scholars as well as cranks and occultists elaborated through the Middle Ages, Renaissance, and 'Enlightenment' according to their gifts and intentions, until Napoleon's campaign in Egypt, which, combining as it did military aims with antiquarian interest (he was accompanied by a corps of scholars), brought the final breakthrough. Based on the Rosetta Stone found by Napoleon's soldiers, J. F. Champollion published in Paris in 1822 his famous *Lettre à M. Dacier secrétaire perpetuel de l'Académie royale des Inscriptions et Belles-Lettres, relative à l'alphabet des hiéroglyphes phonétiques*.[3] Modern Egyptology was born.

---

[1] Ammianus, xxii. 16. 20 ff. The translation is that of J. C. Rolfe, Loeb Classical Library, vol. ii, pp. 306 f.

[2] Ibid. xvii. 4. 8 ff.: Loeb ed., vol. i, pp. 321 f.

[3] J. F. Champollion, *Lettre à M. Dacier* . . ., Paris, 1822: Facsimile reprint mit Nachwort von H. W. Müller, Aalen, 1962 (Milliaria. Facsimiledrucke zur Dokumentation der Geistesentwicklung ii).

But ancient speculation on the occult was not dead, nor were the fraudulent exploiters of the superstitious silenced. In the very same year, 1822, John McGowan in London published a book under the title: *The Book of Fate, formerly in the possession of Napoleon, late Emperor of France, and now first rendered into English, from a German Translation, of an Ancient Egyptian Manuscript, found in the year 1801, by M. Sonnini, in one of the Royal Tombs, near Mount Libycus, in Upper Egypt. By H. Kirchenhoffer, Fellow of the University of Pavia; Knight Grand Cross of the Annunciade of Sardinia; and Chevalier of the Legion of Honour.* From the publishers' point of view Kirchenhoffer's book was most certainly a success far above Champollion's publication: 1826 saw already the fourteenth edition, 1835 the twenty-second, unaltered from the first one, except for the addition of some pretty woodcuts and a short 'Part II. Zodiaology [*sic!*]'. A Spanish translation published in 1849 in Paris was reprinted at least eight times by 1907, and shortened editions were printed and reprinted in England at various places at least until 1925. What Kirchenhoffer's book contained was in fact the centuries-old tables of astrologically embellished geomancy (*Punktierkunst*) of the kind which lovelorn kitchen maids or ambitious stable-men bought on third-class book-stands to explore their destinies. This art was admittedly very old, known from Arabic sources and adapted in medieval manuscripts, revived in the fifteenth century in the *Libro delle Sorti* by Lorenzo Spirito and similar concoctions in all European languages. The better-educated classes used these books rather more as a kind of parlour game—to which was added an element of excitement by the possibility that 'there could be something in it after all'—just as they read nowadays the columns of 'what the stars foretell' in newspapers and magazines. Whether this method of foretelling the future, together with the similarly used tarot (or taroc) playing-cards, really goes back to ancient-Egyptian esoteric knowledge, as is persistently being reiterated by all kinds of occultists (see, for instance, the notorious Aleister

Crowley's *The Book of Thoth. A short essay on the Tarot of the Egyptians*, London, 1944) seems, at the very least, rather doubtful. The only (and not particularly convincing) argument for such a derivation might be found in a fortune-telling table of Graeco-Roman times from Pergamum, which, alongside Greek letters, shows signs which resemble Egyptian hieroglyphs (Fig. 1).[1]

More interesting than the stale and insipid tables in Kirchenhoffer's book is the introduction. Here the alleged translator, who has the effrontery to dedicate his book 'to her Imperial Highness Maria Louise, ex-Empress of France', spins a remarkably elaborate yarn about how a certain M. Sonnini, one of the scholars accompanying Napoleon on his expedition, found on the breast of a mummy in one of the royal tombs a long roll of papyrus with hieroglyphic writing, which he took to Bonaparte; how the latter 'sent for a learned Copt' who succeeded in deciphering the characters and dictated the contents 'to Napoleon's secretary, who in order to preserve the matter secret, translated and wrote it down in the German language'; how Napoleon consulted this treasure often with great advantage; how it was lost in the battle of Leipzig of 1813, in which battle, Kirchenhoffer fears, the fragile papyrus original was also lost and might have disintegrated; how, passing through many hands, the manuscript was at last conveyed to the Empress, who in vain tried to send it to her husband in St. Helena, etc., etc.

The actual text, after an excursus about the 'Ancient Oracles' of Egypt, Greece, and Rome, begins with a letter purported to have been written by a certain Balaspis on the dictation of 'his great master HERMES TRISMEGISTUS' to the priests of Thebais, and containing, among many other instructions, an explanation of how to consult this 'oracle' and an order that copies of this book should be 'transmitted unto the priests of the other temples

[1] S. Agrell, 'Die pergamenische Zauberscheibe und das Tarockspiel', *K. Humanist. Vetenskapssamfundets i Lund. Årsberättelse*, 1935–6, 62–190.

FIG. 1. The equipment of a Pergamene fortune-teller.

throughout the earth' and also be deposited in the tombs of the kings and the high priests.

Certainly Mr. Kirchenhoffer made skilful use of all the available, time-honoured, devices for his job. There is first of all the connection of the spurious wisdom with a popular historical personality. (It is significant that in the same year 1822 the astrologers Robert C. Smith ('Raphael') and G. W. Graham also published in London a geomantic fortune-telling pamphlet *The Philosophical Merlin*, which pretended to be 'the translation of a valuable manuscript, formerly in the possession of Napoleon Bonaparte'.) Scores of such fakes were already current in Roman Imperial times, where some fictitious king of the Egyptians, Arabs, or Persians, some Babylonian or Egyptian priest, or some famous physician was alleged to have sent a precious book of his magic secrets to someone like King Mithridates, Ptolemy, or the Roman Emperors Augustus, Claudius, or Hadrian. The fortune-telling or geomantic circles, like the one of Pergamum mentioned above, appear in medieval manuscripts under the name of some Greek philosopher, Christian saint, or the Egyptian priest Petosiris as their originators. The 'Egyptian secrets' (*Egyptischen Geheimnisse*),[1] which could be bought in the nineteenth century at the annual village fairs in Germany (reprinted again and again by a publisher in Reutlingen), claimed as author no less a person than the learned medieval bishop Saint Albertus Magnus; they contain the same silly conglomeration of incantations, charms, and magic recipes which from the eighteenth century until today have been sold as *Le grand Albert* and *Le petit Albert* by the *bouquinistes* on the banks of the Seine.

The priest Balaspis appears as a worthy colleague of the Sarastro of the *Magic Flute*, and the reader of Kirchenhoffer's book might well have imagined how, after having written down the portentous

---

[1] W.-E. Peuckert, 'Die egyptischen Geheimnisse', *Arv. Journal of Scandinavian Folklore*, x (1954), 40–96.

message of 'Hermes the interpreter of the will of Osiris', Balaspis
went back to the temple to intone Mozart's enchanting song: 'O
Isis und Osiris'. With Hermes Trismegistus we seem to get somewhat nearer to genuine ancient Egypt. For the Egyptians the god
Thoth was the inventor of all science, the guardian of the secrets
of past and future, not least the master of the magic arts. Plato
already wrote about him (*Phaedrus*, 274C f.; *Philebus*, 18B f.) as
the 'father of letters', transcribing his name as 'Theuth'. Thoth
was also the helper of the dead. All this suggested to the Greeks
(and the Romans) an identification with their Hermes (or
Mercurius). Later speculation made him one of several of this
name, the 'thrice greatest' Hermes (a clumsy translation of an
actual Egyptian attribute) who in some treatises was introduced
as writing to his son 'Tat' (obviously = Thoth). Numerous books
went under his name; the late Neoplatonic philosopher Iamblichus
mentions in his work on the Egyptian mysteries (viii. 1) astronomical numbers (20,000, 36,525) alleged to have been written
by him. There may really have been Egyptian books claiming
this authorship, but the Hermetica which were handed down to
us obviously originated in Roman Imperial times, most probably
between A.D. 150 and 300. Details of an astrological, alchemical,
or magical nature which they contain might be derived from
ancient Egyptian tradition. But their main body of mystic-
theosophical philosophy seems pure late-Hellenistic, anti-
rationalistic syncretism typical of late antiquity, although set in
Egyptian scenery and presented by pseudo-Egyptian personalities.
One might almost draw a parallel with the *Magic Flute*, where
contemporary Freemasonry similarly paraded its pretended
antiquity in an old-Egyptian setting. However, like Horapollo's
Hieroglyphica, the *Corpus Hermeticum* also was taken at its face
value (already by the Latin Fathers of the Church) and Hermes
Trismegistus was accepted as the great prophet of remote
antiquity, slightly younger, if not even older, than Moses, and at
any rate much older than Pythagoras, Orpheus, or Plato, who all

learned from him (Pl. 13). When Greek manuscripts began to arrive in Renaissance Florence of the fifteenth century, the *Hermetica* were given precedence in being hurriedly translated into Latin while the works of Plato took only second place. The combination of pious religiosity and 'Egyptian' magic in these writings (first printed in 1471 and reprinted again and again) made what was seen as a reformed and learned magic (that is, the spiritual as distinct from the condemned demonic or black magic) respectable among serious scholars for centuries.[1] Naturally, these secrets were for the truly learned and noble spirits only, 'hermetically' sealed against the man in the street, who, on the other hand, would be duly impressed by getting a taste of them in quotations by such occultists as H. P. Blavatsky or Rudolf Steiner in our times, if not on a still much lower level by impostors like Mr. Kirchenhoffer. With the alleged order of Hermes Trismegistus to Balaspis to deposit copies of the secret scroll of fate 'in the tombs of the kings and the high priests' Kirchenhoffer obviously plays his trump card against any potential sceptics. Was it not common knowledge that such papyrus scrolls had been actually found with ancient Egyptian mummies? It was indeed— only these scrolls were not 'Books of Fate' but, as we now know, 'Books of the Dead', guide-books, if we may say so, or passports into life eternal.

In contrast to Mesopotamian and also early Greek conceptions of death, where the shadowy and miserable existence of the dead hardly deserved the name of after-life, life after death was not only an absolute and fundamental reality for the Egyptian; it was to be a higher, happier, and eternal life. Admittedly, the average Egyptian would not have been human had he not valued life on earth to the full and feared death as an 'enemy'.[2] We even find

[1] D. P. Walker, *Spiritual and Demonic Magic from Ficino to Campanella*, London, 1958 (Studies of the Warburg Institute xxii); Frances A. Yates, *Giordano Bruno and the Hermetic Tradition*, London, 1964.

[2] J. Zandee, *Death as an Enemy according to Ancient Egyptian Conceptions*, Leiden, 1960.

expressions of doubt about the conditions pertaining in the after-life. However, the prevailing attitude remained optimistic, convinced of a life of eternal bliss for the justified, or at least bravely intent to conquer death. Perhaps here too we might find that illogical 'multiplicity of approach' mentioned above. Egyptian thinking has been classified as 'before philosophy'[1]—that is, philosophy as Western civilization accepted and developed it from the Greeks, while at the same time the same eminent scholar suggested that 'the peculiar character of Egyptian religion appears to derive precisely from an implicit assumption that only the *changeless* is ultimately significant'.[2] But, if the Roman Church of today (well versed in philosophy from Aristotle and Plato to Thomas Aquinas) pronounced quite recently that 'man himself, and indeed all creation, has no meaning without reference to eternity and a final destiny beyond life' (Vatican Council, Proemium to Schema 13), then one might wonder whether this does not express fairly exactly what Egyptian theology and *Weltanschauung* fundamentally stood for. That meant that everybody had to provide with great care for his after-life and to take every precaution against the admitted dangers which threatened the journey into and the happiness in eternity. As image and word were identical with the real object in Egyptian thinking in a way we can only try to understand, they had to serve as the essential factors in guaranteeing blessed eternity. We find a veritable treasure of myths, and of incantations and prayers imagined as being pronounced by the dead, in the pictures and inscriptions chiselled into pyramids and stone sarcophagi or painted inside wooden coffins.[3] At a later period, having been more or less codified and illuminated, these appear on the scrolls which were

[1] H. Frankfort (*et al.*), *Before Philosophy: The Intellectual Adventure of Ancient Man*, Harmondsworth (Penguin Books), 1949.

[2] H. Frankfort, *Ancient Egyptian Religion*, p. viii.

[3] S. A. B. Mercer, *The Pyramid Texts in Translation and Commentary*, London, etc., 1952; A. de Buck and A. H. Gardiner, *The Egyptian Coffin Texts*, Chicago, 1935 and following.

entombed with the mummies right down into Roman times.[1] This unique custom obviously influenced those early Greek religious sects associated with the names of Orpheus and Pythagoras which promised their followers 'salvation' from that gloomy fate after death, as pictured, for instance, in Homeric religion. We find in early tombs, especially in southern Italy, thin golden sheets inscribed with Greek verses pretending to be spoken by the dead person (just as in the Egyptian texts) asking for deliverance and permission to join the gods: '. . . for I too vaunt to be of your blessed kin, but Fate subdued me . . .'[2] However, as we find in architecture and sculpture as well as in the earliest 'Ionian' philosophy,[3] the Greeks developed what they accepted from the venerable, 3,000-years-old, Egyptian culture in a quite distinctive manner. But if some classical scholars question the Egyptian derivation of these 'Orphic' gold leaves, one might for instance, point to one of the tomb amulets found in Sardinia (Fig. 2)[4] which, instead of the Greek verses, shows a purely Egyptian scene of the Judgement of the Dead: its container is decorated with lion head, solar disc, and uraeus serpent. Thus it seems not unlikely that the Greek idea of a court where judges decided the fate of the dead (their characteristic names occur first in Plato) might be derived from Egypt—perhaps via the Minoan culture of Crete. The gold leaves surviving were, of course, only the most expensive form of such nether-world passports; other such amuletic capsules

---

[1] T. G. Allen, *The Egyptian Book of the Dead*, Chicago, 1960 (Oriental Institute Publications lxxxii).

[2] A. Olivieri, *Lamellae aureae orphicae*, Bonn, 1915 (Kleine Texte cxxxiii).

[3] J. Pirenne, 'L'Influence égyptienne sur la philosophie ionienne', *Annuaire de l'Institut de phil. et d'hist. orientales et slaves* (Bruxelles), xv (1958–60), 75–82.

[4] G. Pesce, *Sardegna punica*, Cagliari, 1961, p. 115 and figs. 132–3. For similar amulets cf. D. B. Harden, *The Phoenicians*, London, 1962, pls. 90 and 95 (and p. 212); J. Vercoutter, *Les Objets égyptiens et égyptisants du mobilier funéraire carthaginois*, Paris, 1945, pp. 317 f., pl. xxix; P. Gauckler, *Nécropoles puniques de Carthage*, Paris, 1915, ii, pp. 446 f.

Fig. 2. Two gold *lamellae* from Tharros, Sardinia and a gold container from Carthage, with (below) part of a comparable strip of papyrus from Egypt. *Not to scale.*

from Sardinia contained leaves of silver, parchment, or papyrus which tended to disintegrate. But papyrus scrolls with Greek inscriptions have recently been found in tombs in Macedonia as well as in Scythia; although only partly preserved, the names of the goddesses 'Mother Earth' (*Gē Mētēr*) and Hestia are clearly distinguishable on one of them and it has been suggested that, instead of classifying these gold leaves as 'Orphic' or 'Pythagorean', they should rather be regarded as having some sort of connection with the mystery cult of Eleusis.[1]

The fundamental human yearning for a happy after-life found no sort of outlet in the 'established' classical religion which—according to Herodotus, the 'father of history', who wrote in the fifth century B.C.—was fashioned by Homer and Hesiod less than four centuries before his own times (as he thinks). But the mystery cults, such as that of Eleusis, promised to the initiated delivery from the gloomy nether world and eternal bliss with the gods— the very things which Egyptian rituals, amulets, and the 'Book of the Dead' were believed to attain. Herodotus observed that a certain prohibition was common to the Egyptians and to those initiated into Orphic, Bacchic, or Pythagorean doctrine. He also had heard that the pre-Hellenic Pelasgians owed their oracular shrines (especially the venerably old one of Dodona) as well as most of their mystery cults and divinities to Egypt, later handing them down to the Greeks. In fact Herodotus travelled extensively and purposefully in Egypt and was eager to report not only what he had seen but also what he had been told. Considering the overwhelming archaeological evidence for the cultural connection between Egypt and the much more primitive pre-Hellenic Aegean world[2]—not only Crete—as well as the whole Mediterranean,

---

[1] Cf. Ch. Picard, *Revue archéologique*, 1963 (i), 179–94; S. G. Kapsōmenos, 'The Orphic Papyrus Roll of Thessalonica', *Bull. American Soc. of Papyrologists*, ii (1964), 3–14; 'Ὁ ὀρφικὸς πάπυρος τῆς Θεσσαλονίκης (Πίν. 12–15)', *Ἀρχαιολογικὸν Δελτίον*, xix (1964), pt. 1, 17–25.

[2] J. Vercoutter, *Essai sur les relations entre égyptiens et préhellènes*, Paris, 1954 (L'Orient ancien illustré vi).

there is nothing intrinsically improbable about that, even when Phoenicians or Libyans acted as transmitters. True, when Herodotus asserts that 'practically all the names of the [Greek] gods came to Hellas from Egypt', that is obviously wrong and must be due to the fact that his interpreters when dealing with the confusing multitude of the more or less local Egyptian divinities constantly used already standardized Greek versions for the benefit of Greek tourists and sightseers. But there were two gods who, he realized, were worshipped by all the Egyptians and of whom he gives the Egyptian names: Isis and Osiris—persistently confirming their identity with Demeter and Dionysus. These two were in fact the figure-heads of the two most popular Greek mystery cults, that of Eleusis and the Bacchanalia. He mentions the nightly enacting of the story (viz. of Osiris' death, disappearance, finding, and reviving through Isis) which the Egyptians call 'the mysteries', and he adds that he knows more about these things but refuses to tell it, just as he refuses to give details of the Athenian rite of Demeter. However, six centuries later Plutarch wrote the Egyptian *mythos* down in Hellenistic philosophical interpretation,[1] and today we can read and translate the ritual as it is preserved in hieroglyphic inscriptions. But again and again in his book about Egypt we find Herodotus telling us that he knows such-and-such a sacred name or story but finds it against his religious conscience to write it down, thus leaving the impression that he was favoured in many instances with more esoteric information which he was enjoined not to publish. After all, Egyptian cult and ritual as a whole was fundamentally esoteric, the privilege of a hereditary priesthood which was only too anxious to avoid profanation by the uneducated and illiterate masses. In dark, absconded chambers stood the cult statues which not merely represented but embodied in a magical way the venerated deity,

---

[1] Plutarch, *De Iside et Osiride* (= *Moralia*, 351 ff.: Loeb ed., vol. v, pp. 7 ff.). Cf. also Th. Hopfner, *Plutarch über Isis und Osiris*, Praha, 1940-1 (Monographien des Archiv Orientální ix).

the work of the sculptor being animated by a special ritual. Their daily liturgical attendance, meticulously prescribed, was the exclusive privilege of the priests and only on special occasions could the general public see them. The more profound theological doctrines and speculations were, of course, still less the concern of the man in the street; on the contrary, again and again we meet in the texts (admittedly particularly in those with magic contents) the commandment of strictest secrecy: 'Show it to no man, not even to your father or to your son!'[1]

Whatever the Hellenic mystery cults may or may not owe to Egypt (it has been pointed out that in Greece the initiated were personally involved, not just spectators as in the early Osiris mysteries—but after all every single deceased person could 'become' Osiris in later time), the Isis cult and its esoteric mysteries very soon conquered the ancient Graeco-Roman world, spreading to the remotest regions of the Roman Empire (Pl. 21). Stronger still than the Osiris–Dionysus–Bacchus mysteries with their promise of resurrection (Dionysiac emblems are perhaps the most frequent elements in Graeco-Roman funerary art) was the appeal of salvation[2] and security through the Mother-Goddess, an appeal instinctively felt by everybody born from woman. Just as all over the world we find the Mother-Goddess as the oldest (and for a long time the only) idol in prehistoric imagery, thus Isis, 'the one of ten thousand names' (*myrionoma*), claims for herself in Graeco-Roman times all the divine functions of all the goddesses venerated by the uninitiated under different names. Moreover, while in the classical Greek and Roman religions even gods and goddesses are ultimately powerless against the ruling of Fate, the Hellenized Isis proclaims that she 'conquers the Heimarmene, makes her obedient to herself'—a great comfort in a world riddled with the fears created by the widespread

[1] S. Morenz, *Ägyptische Religion*, pp. 237 f.

[2] C. J. Bleeker, 'Isis as Saviour Goddess', in *The Saviour God, Comparative Studies . . . pres. to E. O. James*, Manchester, 1963, pp. 1–16.

astrological determinism. It can hardly be doubted that the innumerable figures of the enthroned Isis nursing her son Horus (Pl. 19b) prepared the way for the Byzantine and later images of the Virgin Mary[1]—just as occasionally we find on early Christian monuments Horus, the young sun-god and conqueror of evil, identified with Christ (Pl. 12a).[2] Besides Isis her husband Osiris—in Graeco-Roman times gradually replaced by Serapis (Pl. 20), a rather artificial creation of Ptolemaic politics and Hellenic aesthetics—comes only second in real popularity. Serapis is fundamentally identifiable with Osiris although adopting features of Zeus, Hades, and Helios; and he serves as the expression of clearly monotheistic tendencies: '[there is] *one* god—Serapis', we read in Greek on numerous monuments.[3]

The authorities of the Roman Republic did their best to oppose and forbid this foreign cult of Isis, the mysterious secretness of which seemed to provide a cover for (occasionally manifest) moral and even political dangers[4]—just as at an earlier date the Senate had to outlaw the 'Bacchanalia', the mysteries of Dionysus, when such scandals blew up. But the Roman emperors had soon to give in to popular demand and the spirit of the age, conforming to what was accepted throughout the ancient world[5]. In the third century A.D. a Christian writer could state that 'what were once Egyptian are now Roman deities'. The festival of the *navigium Isidis* was still celebrated under Christian emperors of the fourth century in Rome (the ship-carriage of this lively procession most

[1] H. W. Müller, 'Isis mit dem Horuskinde', *Münchner Jahrbuch der bildenden Kunst*, xiv (1963), 7–38; 'Die stillende Gottesmutter in Ägypten', *Materia Medica Nordmark*, 2. Sonderheft, 1963.

[2] Cf. A. A. Barb, *Journ. Warburg and Courtauld Institutes*, xxvii (1964), 15 f.

[3] E. Peterson, Εἷς Θεός—*Epigraphische, formgeschichtl. und religionsgeschichtl. Untersuchungen*, Göttingen, 1926.

[4] Cf. A. A. Barb, in *The Conflict between Paganism and Christianity in the Fourth Century* (ed. A. Momigliano), Oxford, 1963, pp. 100 ff.

[5] A. Alföldi, 'Die alexandrinischen Götter und die Vota Publica am Jahresbeginn', *Jahrbuch f. Antike u. Christentum*, viii–ix (1965–6), 53–87.

likely gave the name to our 'carnival'),[1] and in the sixth century, when all pagan religion was outlawed in the Roman Empire, the Emperor Justinian had for many years to tolerate the Isis cult in its Egyptian centre of Philae.

There is one aspect of Isis which might have contributed to the initial resistance of Rome against her naturalization: the role she claimed as 'the Mighty in Magic'.[2] All through its history the authorities of Rome tried to keep religion separated and free from the evil arts of magic. The same was not the case in Egypt. Indeed, if a great Egyptologist called magic a cancerous growth in the body of Egyptian religion, one might add that there was a congenital proneness to this kind of cancer in the Egyptian way of thinking, where word and image were realities, not just symbols.[3] We realize how far this identification went when we see that since early times hieroglyphs representing living, and especially dangerous, beings appear mutilated or cut in two, or kept at bay by daggers to prevent them doing harm (Fig. 3).

Obviously the Egyptian must have been uncomfortably aware that his assurances of guiltlessness as formulated in the funerary texts, to be spoken by him before the judges in the nether world, were often very much at variance with his actual behaviour during his life on earth. Thus fear of the 'second death', of annihilation by the 'devourer', made him reinforce his lies by the power of magic, a power which, so he tried to convince himself, was a precious gift from the gods to defend himself against any evil, in this life as in the life hereafter. In his incantations he went so far as to pretend that he himself was one of the mighty gods, and to threaten and blackmail other divinities. His alleged knowledge of their real and secret names gave him power over them. It is

[1] A. Alföldi, *A Festival of Isis in Rome under the Christian Emperors of the IVth Century*, Budapest–Leipzig, 1937 (Dissertationes Pannonicae ii, 7).

[2] F. Sbordone, 'Iside Maga', *Aegyptus*, xxvi (1946), 130–48.

[3] S. Schott, 'Symbol und Zauber als Grundform ägyptischen Denkens', in *Studium Generale* (Heidelberg, etc.), vi (1953), 278–88.

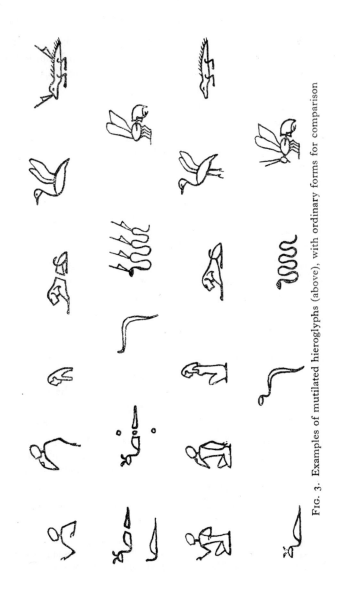

FIG. 3. Examples of mutilated hieroglyphs (above), with ordinary forms for comparison

this conviction that the name, even more than the image, is fully identical with the named, and that knowledge of it meant domination, which made Isis, so we are told, blackmail the aged creator-god Rē into telling her his secret true name—known so far only to himself; the knowledge of the name gave her the magic power of healing. We find this, like similar stories, told at length in endless incantation texts, composed in the conviction that the recitation of some mythological story of divine healing magic could effect the same result in any similar human emergency.

To recite such a lengthy litany (and, the longer it was, the more effective it was supposed to be) would, of course, have been a long and tedious job. But there was an easier way, that of writing it down and applying the scroll or amulet to the patient; this conviction, that the possession of such a magic text—never mind whether you could understand or even read it—meant protection, has been current at all times and in all places. There was an even more economical and ingenious way of magic healing. We find in Egypt large numbers of the so-called stelae of Horus, reliefs representing the young sun-god Horus holding serpents, scorpions, lions, and other poisonous and dangerous animals captive in his outstretched hands and treading down two crocodiles under his feet (Pl. 9). Besides this central figure the larger of these monuments show numerous other representations and magic texts (Fig. 4), leaving no empty space, and often in a position which would make the reading and reciting very difficult. But the latter was obviously not intended. These stelae were mounted on a basin as a pedestal (Pl. 10). Water was poured over them, which thus absorbed all the magic words and signs, and this magically saturated water, having collected in the basin, could then be used to protect and heal human beings: just as once upon a time the gods had worked magic—which the mythical stories on the stelae recalled.[1]

---

[1] P. Lacau, 'Les Statues guérisseuses dans l'ancienne Égypte', *Monuments et mémoires. Fondation Eugène Piot*, xxv (1921–2), 189 ff.; K. C. Seele, 'Horus on the Crocodiles', *Journ. Near Eastern Studies*, vi(1947), 43 ff.

Fig. 4. Magical representations on the back of the Metternich stela (upper portion)

One still finds the same idea in Arabic popular superstition, where bowls inscribed with magico-religious texts are similarly used, and also with Oriental Christians and Jews.[1]

We must not fall into the common 'evolutionist' error of assuming that Egyptian (or, indeed, all) magic is the residue of a primitive stage, preceding—and evolving into—religion. It might even be open to doubt whether polytheism represents the earliest stage of prehistoric Egyptian religion and not rather some kind of monotheism, which split up when 'powers latent in the creator were objectivated as distinct deities who now exercised power in their appropriate spheres', as a modern scholar has put it.[2] We see such a tendency in the cult of angels and saints, degenerating even in theoretically monotheistic religions, wherever and whenever orthodox theology slackens. When economic upheaval and moral decadence in later times undermined the Egyptian's reliance on descendants and priests for the services needed to ensure the well-being of the dead, people turned increasingly to the use of magic safeguards. What still made religious sense in the Pyramid Texts when applied to the divine nature of the king was gradually depraved and cheapened by application to everybody who could afford to buy his copy of the 'Book of the Dead' into base magic pure and simple. It has been similarly observed that we find the use of magic incantations less in early but increasingly in later and latest Egyptian medicine.[3] (Perhaps in a way a 'progress' to what we call today psychosomatic medicine? These charms could have proved in practice just as effective as the placebos prescribed by our physicians.)[4]

The alarming growth of the cancer of magic might also have something to do with the lowering of the social status of the

[1] T. Canaan, 'Arabic Magic Bowls', *Journ. Palestine Oriental Soc.* 1936, 79 ff.

[2] H. Frankfort, *Ancient Egyptian Religion*, p. 52.

[3] P. Ghalioungui, *Magic and Medical Science in Ancient Egypt*, London, 1963.

[4] Cf. H. E. Sigerist, *A History of Medicine*, i, New York, 1951, pp. 267 f.

Egyptian priest in Graeco-Roman times, when slowly and gradually (although, of course, never quite) he approached the role of
the gipsy (= 'Egyptian') in contemporary society. Thus we find
stark black magic in abundance in the great number of magic
papyri which the soil of Egypt has preserved for us. Although
the majority of those extant (apparently belonging to a late
period—third to fifth century A.D.) are written in Greek and the
Egyptian element is freely mixed with Greek liturgical hymns,
Neoplatonic 'theurgy', and an extraordinarily high percentage of
Jewish lore, we have also bilingual (Egyptian and Greek) and
later Coptic papyri of practically the same kind and fundamentally Egyptian character. The demotic texts can hardly have been
written by anybody but an Egyptian priest or scribe, the Coptic
ones were probably a lucrative sideline of unscrupulous monks,
while many of the Greek ones might have originated in the Greek-
speaking Jewish communities, mainly in Alexandria. The prescriptions in these papyri provide for all kind of human aims:
healing diseases, acquiring wealth, power, and fame, successful
pleading in court, finding out a thief, unveiling the future, pro-
curing love and sexual enjoyment of a desired person, or vice
versa estranging loving couples for one's own advantage, harming
and even killing an enemy. Innumerable, according to the belief
in the power of the 'real' name, are the Egyptian, Greek, Semitic
(even Babylonian), and abstrusely barbaric names of divinities,
demons, and angels, long formulae which seem senseless gibberish,
but which in a few cases specialist research has been able to interpret. The seven vowels of the Greek alphabet occur in rows of
endless permutations, perhaps—being connected with the seven
planets as well as with the heptachord—as some kind of powerful
magic tune.

These magical papyri correspond closely with a distinct class
of late-antique engraved stones (Pl. 11), which show the same
names and formulae, signs, and even occasionally representations
as put down in the papyri; they are commonly known as 'Gnostic'

or 'Abraxas' gems. Modern scholars prefer to call them magical or amuletic gems, disapproving of the earlier theory that these stones were monuments of the Gnostic heresy. However, all these denominations have some legitimacy. There is no doubt that most of these gems were used as amulets: 'protect the wearer' we even read on many of them, sometimes with the addition of his or her name. The word ABRAXAS (or, as we find it practically always on the stones, ABRASAX)[1] is—besides the Jewish IAO (= Jehovah—YHWH) and SABAOTH—one of the most frequent magic names invoked on them. We know also that the name Abraxas, the numerical value of whose Greek letters equalled 365 (the days of the year), was given to the highest of the 365 Aeons by the Syrian Basileides, who taught his Gnostic system in Alexandria at the time of the Emperor Hadrian. Also there are occasionally other exclusively Gnostic names engraved on these stones. That does not mean, of course, that these gemstones were a kind of propaganda material of the Gnostics—as earlier scholars thought; it only shows that Gnostic as well as Egyptian, Greek, and Jewish elements were freely (and not particularly intelligently) used by the magic practitioners. After all, considering the basic Egyptian mentality, it was no mere coincidence that Egypt became the country where Gnosticism flourished and proliferated more than anywhere else.[2] The inscriptions are in Greek letters—only very rarely do we see some hieroglyphic signs, far more often one finds as yet unexplained magic signs. They are also in Greek language, except the mysterious formulae, where occasionally a few Egyptian as well as Semitic words seem evident.

The representations are to a large extent—this is the very first impression we already gain from the abundance of human figures with animal heads—inspired by old-Egyptian imagery. Thus we find, for instance, the dog-headed Anubis and the ass-headed Seth

---

[1] A. A. Barb, 'Abraxas-Studien', in *Hommages à W. Deonna* (Collection Latomus xxviii), Bruxelles, 1957, pp. 67 ff.

[2] J. Doresse, *The Secret Books of the Egyptian Gnostics*, London, 1960.

(Pl. 11 *a–b*), the cow-headed Hathor and the ram-headed Amūn (Pl. 11*b*), Thoth with the head of an ibis, and many other divinities in their old-established familiar appearance. We find the Osiris-mummy standing or outstretched, attended by the sisters Isis and Nephthys or by Anubis, the young Horus-child (as the Greeks called him, Harpocrates) sitting, finger to his mouth, on a lotus-flower (Pl. 11*c*), Khnum as a serpent with lion's head, baboons worshipping, and other sacred animals. In many cases the images or a magic formula are surrounded by the serpent 'Uroborus' (Pl. 11 *b–c*) (a Greek word occurring in the magic papyri and later writers and meaning 'devouring its tail'); symbol of the endless cycle of time, i.e. eternity, it also represents the cosmic ocean, the chaos, encircling the created world, i.e. the universe. Few esoteric symbols have been and are being more used and misused, from late antique magic and theosophy, through alchemy (Fig. 6) and medieval occultism, right up to modern psycho-analysis, where it appears as an archetype of the all-embracing mother-complex.[1] Where figures of Graeco-Roman mythology occur, they are more often than not only a translation: Eros means Harpocrates, Aphrodite is Hathor or Isis, Zeus is Sarapis, and Hermes stands for Thoth or Anubis. Only the frequent cock- or lion-headed warrior with serpent-legs (Fig. 5), without sufficient reason formerly taken to represent the 'god' Abraxas, stands apart; possibly he represents the 'Adamas' of the Manichaean heresy.[2] Egyptian, however, is the curious figure of a winged pantheistic deity (Pls. 11*d*, 12*b*) combining features of Horus and the age-old popular gnome Bes (Pl. 6) with elements of various other divinities and sacred animals. Perhaps he stands for the Aion of late-antique theosophy; but we find a version of this figure on a Byzantine Judaeo-Christian-Gnostic amulet apparently meant to represent Christ (Pl. 12*a*),[3]

[1] E. Neumann, *The Origins and History of Consciousness*, New York, 1954 (Bollingen Series xlii).

[2] A. A. Barb, op. cit. (above, p. 161, n. 1), pp. 76 ff.

[3] Cf. A. A. Barb, loc. cit. (above, p. 154, n. 2).

while on the other hand it obviously influenced medieval representations of the Devil.

Although we have to look to Egypt, and probably to Alexandria, as the centre for the fabrication of most of these amulets, there

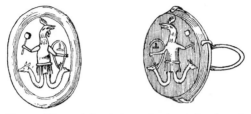

FIG. 5. The cock-headed anguipede on the ring of a thirteenth-century bishop. The intaglio may perhaps be antique, but the shape of the shield and the mace-like weapon replacing the usual whip (or sword) suggest a medieval copy.

are some which might have originated rather in Syria and Palestine. Anyhow, mainly from Egypt they found their way, like the Isis cult, into the remotest provinces of the Roman Empire.[1] Their intended use varies from general protection to that against poisonous animals, from curing gynaecological ailments and guaranteeing safe childbirth (Pl. 11 *a–b*)[2] to alleviating indigestion and sciatica and to securing the love of some person.

Amulets had been popular in Egypt long before the amuletic gemstones of Graeco-Roman times. In fact, as a glance at the Egyptian collections in any museum shows, their variety and number as well as their artistic excellence exceeds beyond comparison anything which other countries of antiquity have produced of this kind of monument. They were used not only to protect the

---

[1] Cf., for example, R. P. Wright, 'A Graeco-Egyptian Amulet from a Romano-British Site at Welwyn, Herts.', *Antiquaries Journal*, xliv (1964), 143 ff.

[2] A. A. Barb, 'Diva Matrix', *Journ. Warburg and Courtauld Institutes*, xvi (1953), 193–238.

living but—as the 'Book of the Dead' and the finds amply testify—
also quite extensively as essential objects in the care of the dead.
As well as tiny statuettes of divinities and sacred animals we find
symbolic hieroglyphs like the *ankh*, the ansate cross, sign of life
♀; later, in Coptic art, this sign was Christianized as a form of
the cross and its ubiquitous use in modern theosophy and
occultism is all too well known. There is the 'eye of Horus' ☜,
the 'knot of Isis' 🮲, the papyrus stem meaning 'thriving' ⸋.
There are meaningful parts of the body like the heart ♡, there
are symbolic objects of daily life like steps and ladders ⌐, mason's
and carpenter's squares ⌐, or the head-rest ⌣. The amulet *par
excellence*, however, was the scarab 🪲. We find these sacred
beetles since very early times as symbols of autogenous birth and
of the life-giving sun. Fashioned in glazed faience or cut from
gemstones, they not only are found in really amazing numbers in
Egypt but were exported in large quantities abroad. We find them
in pre-Hellenic sites all over the Mediterranean world, where
they were later copied and adapted to their taste by Phoenicians,
Etruscans, and Greeks. The originally smooth base of the Egyptian scarabs was soon adorned with lucky symbols and hieroglyphic inscriptions. Large scarabs inscribed with suitable formulae
were used to reinforce the heart of the dead against the ordeal of
the last judgement. It has been suggested that these engraved and
inscribed scarabs were the starting-point from which the 'Gnostic'
gems of the Graeco-Roman period developed. Among other clues
which would point in this direction is the fact that in both cases
the same kind of gemstones were used, with distinct preference
of certain materials for certain classes of amulets. Thus the shiny
black iron-ore, haematite ('bloodstone'—so called because its
powder turns out to be blood-red), which was never at all used
in classical Greek and Roman glyptic, but was a favourite material
for Mesopotamian and old-Egyptian seals and amulets, provided
the material for almost one-third of all the 'Gnostic' gems and
for the vast majority of all the 'gynaecological' ones. Only the

jasper (in green, yellow, brown, or red varieties), from which more than one-third of these gems are cut, is more frequently used. The idea of the distinctive magic powers of certain stones seems first to have been developed in Mesopotamia, but was apparently taken over in Egypt at a later date; a demotic papyrus in Berlin, for instance, contains a list of this kind[1] and the late antique stone-book of Damigeron, most popular throughout the Middle Ages, is described in the introductory letter, which pretends to be written by an Arab king to the Emperor Nero, as 'the best book to be found in *Egypt*'.

We learn from the magical papyri found in Egypt how the amuletic gem had to be not only suitably engraved but also cere-monially consecrated to become—like the statues of the Egyptian gods—'animated' by the divine being settling down in them. Part of the correct liturgical ceremonial was to choose the right day and hour according to their astrological qualification. Like the *Corpus Hermeticum*, Egyptian astrology[2] developed mainly from Hellenistic syncretism, owing more to the astrology of Mesopotamia than that of Egypt. An Egyptian creation, however, are the thirty-six decans[3] into which the celestial circle was divided, each ruling over ten days of the year. Represented as distinct divinities of fantastic, partly animal-headed appearance, originally conceived as elements of mathematical-astronomical chronology, they later played their role in the astrology of Graeco-Roman times and all the following centuries. Under Greek rule Egypt produced a mystic-astrological compendium, claiming (although written in Greek) to be the work of the pharaoh Nechepso and the priest Petosiris.[4] In the second century A.D.

---

[1] W. Spiegelberg, *Demotische Papyrus aus den königl. Museen zu Berlin*, Berlin, 1902, p. 29 (Pap. 8769) and pl. 98.

[2] F. Cumont, *L'Égypte des astrologues*, Bruxelles, 1937.

[3] W. Gundel, *Dekane und Dekansternbilder*, Glückstadt, etc., 1936 (Studien der Bibliothek Warburg xix). See also above, p. 46.

[4] Cf. E. Riess, 'Nechepsonis et Petosiridis fragmenta magica', *Philologus*, Suppl. vi, Göttingen, 1892, 328 ff. (reprinted, as 2nd ed., Darmstadt, 1969).

the great Egyptian-born astronomer Claudius Ptolemaeus wrote his *Tetrabiblos*, in which he tried to put astrology on a scientific basis. Consequently the astrology of the ancient world was handed down through Roman times and the Middle Ages as mainly 'Egyptian' wisdom. But what, for instance, successful French lady astrologers of our century imparted to their clients under their suggestive pseudonyms of Mme de Thèbes or Mme de Memphis is no more Egyptian than is the *Book of Fate* our English Mr. Kirchenhoffer produced a century earlier.

Closely related to astrology in its belief in the planetary influences, another occult science, alchemy, never had the universal appeal which made astrology so popular; but the origins of both run in many respects along very similar lines. For alchemy too Mesopotamia can claim anonymous priority of practical observation. However, in the same Hellenistic period in which Pseudo-Nechepso and Petosiris laid the foundations for Western astrology, Bolos(-Democritus) from Mendes in the Nile delta wrote his fundamental *Physica et Mystica* and in Roman Imperial times other Greek writers, referring to spurious Jewish, Persian, and preferably Egyptian authorities—from Hermes Trismegistus to 'Cleopatra' (*sic*) (Fig. 6)—built up their inextricable hermetic-technical-theosophical teachings on which centuries of Arabic and European science and pseudo-science elaborated. Enlightened later centuries developed our modern practical chemistry from these beginnings. They left behind what might be seen as the typical Egyptian element, that view of man and nature *sub specie aeternitatis*, as it were, concerning their ultimate destiny and trying (see above, p. 148) to behold the significant changeless behind the multiplicity of passing appearances—that fundamentally religious disposition which earned the Egyptians in the classical world the name of 'the most religious of all peoples'.

Jungian psycho-analysis of our times has found (admittedly often clumsily and unconvincingly) in alchemistic writings a

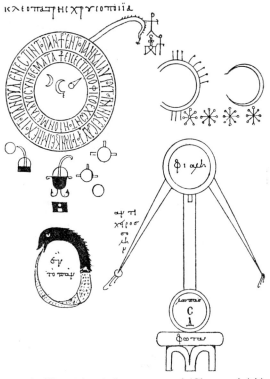

FIG. 6. The alchemical apparatus of 'Cleopatra' (*sic*), from a medieval manuscript of a Greek treatise of late antiquity.

veritable storehouse of important wisdom.[1] But after all, as we have seen, scientific Egyptology is hardly one and a half centuries old. We are in a way today in a similar position as regards the absorption of Egyptian thought as Europe was at the end of the Middle Ages regarding the assimilation of the legacy of Greece, when scholars of the Renaissance started to read Greek again. Perhaps the legacy of Egypt could somehow influence the thinking of the next generations in a similar way to that in which classical studies influenced the centuries of humanism up into our age.

A. A. BARB

[1] C. G. Jung, *Psychology and Alchemy*, New York, 1953 (Collected Works, vol. 12 = Bollingen Series xx, 12).

BIBLIOGRAPHY

J. BALTRUŠAITIS, *La quête d'Isis: introduction à l'égyptomanie*, Paris, 1967.

C. BONNER, *Studies in magical amulets, chiefly Graeco-Egyptian*, Ann Arbor, 1950 (University of Michigan Studies, Humanistic Series xlix).

E. A. WALLIS BUDGE, *Egyptian magic*, London, 1901 (Books on Egypt and Chaldaea ii).

F. CUMONT, *Les Religions orientales dans le paganisme romain*, 4ᵉ ed., Paris, 1929.

A.-J. FESTUGIÈRE, *La Révélation d'Hermès Trismégiste*, 4 vols., Paris, 1944–54 (vol. i, 2ᵉ éd. 1950).

H. FRANKFORT, *Ancient Egyptian religion: an interpretation*, New York, 1948.

T. HOPFNER, *Fontes historiae religionis aegyptiacae*, Bonn, 1922–5 (Fontes historiae religionum ex auctoribus Graecis et Romanis collectae ii).

—— *Griechisch-ägyptischer Offenbarungszauber*, 2 vols., Leipzig, 1921–4 (Studien zur Palaeographie und Papyruskunde xxi and xxiii).

E. IVERSEN, *The myth of Egypt and its hieroglyphs in European tradition*, Copenhagen, 1961.

F. LEXA, *La Magie dans l'Égypte antique de l'ancien empire jusqu'à l'époque copte*, Paris, 1925.

R. MERKELBACH, *Isisfeste in griechisch-römischer Zeit: Daten und Riten*, Meisenheim am Glan, 1963 (Beiträge zur klassischen Philologie v).

G. VAN MOORSEL, *The mysteries of Hermes Trismegistus; a phenomenologic study in the process of spiritualisation on the 'Corpus Hermeticum' and Latin 'Asclepius'*. Utrecht, 1955 (Studia Theologica Rheno-Traiectinai).

S. Morenz, *Ägyptische Religion*, Stuttgart, 1960.

——*Die Begegnung Europas mit Ägypten*, Leipzig, 1968 (Sitzungsberichte der Sächsischen Akademie, Leipzig, phil.-hist. Klasse, cxiii, 5).

—— *Die Zauberflöte: Eine Studie zum Lebenszusammenhang Ägypten-Antike-Abendland*, Münster, 1952 (Münstersche Forschungen v).

K. Preisendanz, *Papyri Graecae Magicae*, 3 vols., Leipzig, 1928–41.

G. Roeder, *Die ägyptische Religion in Texten und Bildern*, Bd. iv: *Der Ausklang der ägyptischen Religion mit Reformation, Zauberei und Jenseitsglauben*, Zürich, 1961.

V. Tran Tam Tinh, *Essai sur le culte d'Isis à Pompéi*, Paris, 1964 (Sér. 'Images et Cultes').

M. J. Vermaseren (ed.), *Études préliminaires aux religions orientales dans l'empire romain*, Leiden, 1961 and following.

7

THE HIEROGLYPHIC TRADITION

THE spread of Christianity in Egypt and its eventual victory towards the end of the fourth century represented the final stage of a long and continuous process during which the age-old traditions of Egyptian culture slowly deteriorated and succumbed to the fateful influence of Greek philosophy and thought.

Already before the advent of Christianity most of the gods of the Egyptians had, in the words of the Hermetist, departed from mankind, driven away by the new prophets Plato and Aristotle, who in the last centuries before our era had taught new approaches to new truths, and introduced new ways and methods of reasoning and new conceptions of cosmology and metaphysics incompatible with the particular 'pre-Aristotelian' logic of the Egyptians, based on an indomitable faith and belief in the magical nature of things and the aetiological reality of the myths. However, the ancient gods did not depart without resistance, and in the first centuries after its initial encounter with the Greeks—the period between the eighth and the fifth centuries B.C., representing the embryonic and receptive period of Greek civilization—the older culture had been able to exert a profound and fruitful influence upon the younger. Even at the time of its expiry Egyptian religion was suddenly to become expansive, and through the most universal and vigorous of its cults, the cult of Isis (Pl. 19a), was destined to exert a strong influence on the religious development of the West, where as a harbinger of the Virgin the goddess was even to leave her mark on Christianity.

In Egypt itself the national forces lost their centre of gravity by the Roman abolition of the monarchical tradition, the divine kingship, in which they had always, even during the Greek domination, found their highest manifestation, and the Christian victory severed all connections with the past, creating an unbridgeable abyss between the old traditions and the new. The ancient prophecy had come true, Egypt was dead, 'her children were known as Egyptians by their tongue alone, but by their actions they seemed to be men of another race, her religion had become an empty tale, and only the stones told of her ancient piety'. The ancient scripts were replaced by a Greek alphabet with the consequence that the old records were soon forgotten, and henceforward the only sources for the history and the traditions of the country were the various records of foreign writers. But, even so, the memory of ancient Egypt refused to die, and from the dead records grew a living *mythos*, which for centuries to come was to stir the curiosity and stimulate the imagination of artists and scholars.

Throughout classical antiquity Egypt remained a subject of inexhaustible historical interest in learned circles, and there arose an extensive literature dealing with Egypt and Egyptological subjects. After the Roman occupation this interest waned[1] and a substantial part of the Greek literature on Egypt would seem to have fallen into oblivion already before the end of antiquity. For our present purpose we are concerned only with what survived, the sources on which the classical conception of Egypt was based, and from which the scholars of the Middle Ages and the Renaissance drew their information. In so far as geography, history, and ethnography were concerned, the main sources were the works of Herodotus, Diodorus, and Strabo, in which much information was based on the lost works of other authorities such as Hecataeus and Manetho. For the *materia medica* and natural history Theophrastus, Dioscorides, and Pliny were quoted, and knowledge

---

[1] It is curious to compare the veneration and awe with which most Greek writers mention Egypt with the haughty scorn of a Lucan or a Tacitus.

on cult matters was generally derived from Plutarch, especially his treatise on Isis and Osiris, as well as from Apuleius, who in his *Metamorphoses* includes a widely read description of the initiation into the mysteries of Isis.

Particular importance became attached to two short passages in Plato stating, in accordance with a genuine Egyptian tradition, that 'a certain Theuth', that is, Thoth, the Egyptian god of learning and writing, had been the first to observe that 'the infinity of sound' could be divided up into distinctive elements such as vowels and consonants,[1] and was therefore considered not merely the discoverer of the concept of letters, but also the inventor of writing as such.[2] And from a further passage in Cicero, in which it is stated that 'Mercurius [the Latin name of Hermes or Thoth] . . . was said to have provided the Egyptians with laws and letters',[3] Thoth came to be considered in Roman times not merely the true originator of the art of writing, but also the primordial legislator—in Christian circles the Egyptian Moses.

Plato's interest in Egyptian letters had been purely historical. It arose from his interest in the origin of the Greek alphabet, which in common with most classical writers he considered a development of Phoenician writing, which again had been directly inspired by the hieroglyphs. But following the growing influence of speculative tendencies, especially in Neoplatonic circles, the hieroglyphic problem was soon transferred from a graphic to a philosophic sphere.

It is typical that no classical writer on Egyptological subjects ever took the trouble to learn Egyptian or to acquire more than a superficial hearsay knowledge of Egyptian writing.[4] The various reports about the hieroglyphs are therefore always erroneous and based on fundamental misunderstandings. Almost all of them

---

[1] *Philebus*, viii.   [2] *Phaedrus*, lix.
[3] *De Deorum Natura*, iii. 22. 56.
[4] Pythagoras was perhaps the sole exception.

agree that the Egyptians for the ordinary purposes of daily life used an 'ordinary' script called 'demotic', 'enchorial', or 'epistolographic', but for cult purposes and the registration of their esoteric teachings and sacred lore they were supposed to have used hieroglyphs, a divinely inspired system of writing, the secret knowledge of which was accessible only to the initiates. No one showed any interest in the ordinary writing, but the picturesque and enigmatic hieroglyphs proved of irresistible fascination and attraction, and gave rise to a special literary genre, the hieroglyphic compilations, of which several are known to have existed already in Hellenistic times, but of which only two have survived, that of Chaeremon, dating from the first century A.D., but preserved only in excerpts by the Byzantine grammarian Tzetzes, and the *Hieroglyphica* of Horapollo, in its original form probably compiled some time about the fourth century A.D.

The conception of the hieroglyphs propounded in these texts is everywhere the same, and always based on similar misconceptions arising from the Greek inability to understand the mythical logic of the Egyptians, their tendency to allegorical exposition of mythical material, and their efforts to 'translate' all information on Egyptian phenomena into the abstract terms of their own philosophy. So far as the hieroglyphs were concerned the Greek conception of their nature was already formulated by Diodorus, who states that 'their writing [i.e. the Egyptians'] does not express the intended concept by means of syllables joined one to another, but by means of the significance of the objects which have been copied and by its figurative meaning which has been impressed upon the memory by practice'.[1] The working of the system was illustrated by the expounding of the hieroglyphic picture of a hawk. 'Now the hawk signifies to them [i.e. the Egyptians] everything which happens swiftly, since this animal is practically the swiftest of winged creatures. And the concept portrayed is then

---

[1] Diodorus, *Bibliotheca*, iii. 4. The translation is that of C. H. Oldfather, Loeb Classical Library.

transferred, by the appropriate metaphorical transfer, to all swift things and to everything to which swiftness is appropriate . . .'[1]

Exactly the same allegorical conception of the signs is found in the works of Chaeremon and Horapollo, in spite of the fact that both were undoubtedly based on genuine Egyptian sources. This is obvious from the fact that even their most extravagant allegorical fancies can be traced to one of the established functions of the signs in their Egyptian use as graphic elements. One example will suffice to illustrate the theory as well as the practice. Horapollo tells us how the hieroglyphic picture of a vulture in Egyptian inscriptions was used to express the concept 'mother', which is perfectly correct. But in his explanation, the simple phonetic reason for the connection between the picture and the word is completely disregarded in favour of a rambling allegorical exposition, according to which the picture of a vulture is used metaphorically to express the abstract notion of motherhood because of the parthenogenetic nature of these birds of which only females were supposed to exist.

As a genre these collections of hieroglyphs are closely related to the so-called *Physiologus*, a curious collection of pseudo-zoological information combined with more or less fabulous stories about various animals. Each story is followed by a moral conclusion in which the fable is expounded as an allegorical illustration of the vicissitudes of a Christian existence. It dates from the second century A.D., and like the *Hieroglyphica* it was probably of Alexandrine origin; it spread with great rapidity to Asia Minor, Byzantium, and all over Europe, where it was translated into every conceivable language from Latin to Icelandic. A considerable proportion of its fables are directly borrowed from Horapollo, and both compilations became widely popular and exerted a profound influence on the development of early Christian symbolism in literature as well as in art.

[1] Diodorus, loc. cit.

This in itself astounding interest in the hieroglyphs and their alleged allegorical nature which is characteristic of late antiquity can be properly understood only as a result of their 'Platonization' and introduction as topical elements into the philosophical debate of Neoplatonism, the last universal philosophical and religious movement of pagan antiquity, which flourished from the third to the beginning of the sixth century A.D., and represented the final consummation of a ἱερὸς γάμος between Platonism and oriental mysticism. It is no coincidence that the final Neoplatonic defini-tion of the hieroglyphic problem was made by Plotinus himself, the undisputed head of the entire movement, who stated authorita-tively that the Egyptians 'either by exact science or spontaneously' had arrived at a method by means of which they could write with distinct pictures of material objects instead of ordinary letters expressing sounds and forming words and phrases. These pictures were not ordinary images of the things they represented, but endowed with certain symbolic qualities (*sophia*), by means of which they revealed to the initiated contemplator a profound insight into the very essence and substance of things, and an intuitive understanding of their transcendental origin, an insight which was not the result of reasoning or mental reflection, but was acquired spontaneously by means of divine inspiration and illumination. As artistic representations of the phenomenal ob-jects they revealed, in fact, their ideas.[1]

It is obvious that in this formulation the hieroglyphs had ceased to be merely objects of curiosity or historical interest. They had become illustrations of the Neoplatonic conception of the symbolic nature of things, revealing in a unique and un-paralleled way the true relations between matter and idea, body and soul, reality and art. As such they were considered one of the most essential and important Egyptian heirlooms, but by no means the only one. For the Neoplatonic literature itself, especially

[1] *Enneads*, v. 8, 6.

books such as the treatise on the Egyptian mysteries ascribed to Iamblichus, but also the very works of Plato and Plotinus, was considered to be inspired and influenced by Egyptian sources, and in the so-called *Corpus Hermeticum*, a collection of syncretistic treatises dating from about the third century A.D., Egyptian 'philosophy' was, in the opinion of Neoplatonic scholars, found in its purest and most uncontaminated form. Purportedly written by Thoth, the Egyptian god of wisdom and letters, who under his Greek title of Hermes Trismegistus gave his name to the compilation, it represents a blend of oriental mysticism, Gnosticism, and Greek philosophy, which the ancients considered genuinely Egyptian, and akin to the esoteric knowledge taught in the Egyptian mysteries of Isis and Serapis.

The various treatises were widely read and acquired great popularity, being generally studied in connection with the Neoplatonists themselves. They became of the highest importance for the development of the myth about ancient Egypt, because their esoteric teachings and cosmological conceptions were considered directly borrowed from Egyptian sources, and to represent genuine Egyptian notions and ideas. To their readers in antiquity, and to the Neoplatonic scholars of the Renaissance as well, they represented in fact the reputed, and otherwise lost, secret teachings of the ancient Egyptians, and thus explained and expounded they contributed essentially to the development of the widespread and still living myth of Egypt as the original home of all true esoteric knowledge, the cradle of revealed metaphysics and divinely inspired mystical wisdom.[1] This was combined with a vague and romantic idea of a mysterious Egypt of immemorial age and antiquity, inhabited by a people who, in the words of Herodotus, 'made themselves customs and laws of a kind contrary to other

[1] An utterly unmetaphysical, essentially romantic and idyllic conception of Egypt is found in the *Aethiopica* of Heliodorus, and this is also the Egypt we find in the Roman mosaics and paintings of the early Empire (Pl. 22).

men', but in reward of their fervent piety had become blessed with special magical insight and secret knowledge of God and the Universe.

This conception was corroborated by the Biblical references to Egypt, and so inherited by the Christians. But while the pagan tradition had stressed the venerable antiquity of the country, praised the piety and wisdom of its inhabitants, and exalted the knowledge and skill apparent in their pyramids and temples— even if deploring their lack of liberty and shocked by what they considered the cruel despotism of their tyrannical rulers—the Christian writers emphasized the basic wickedness, the idolatry, and the magical practices, as well as the sinful opulence and renowned lasciviousness of 'this thrice-wretched human race',[1] though introducing a romanticism of their own by elaborating on the colourful Biblical legends of the country.

From the beginning of the sixth century A.D. Neoplatonism began to wane as an independent spiritual force, but continued to exert a powerful influence through its impress on Christianity. Unlike many other pagan traditions, the myth of Egypt did not die, but survived the transplantation from paganism to Christianity in adapting itself to the new spiritual climate by subtle changes and modifications.

The resemblances between the teachings of the Hermetic corpus and those of Christianity were first pointed out by medieval scholars,[2] and through the *Physiologus* and the Bestiaries hieroglyphic material was continually spread in fables, legends, and the decorative arts, where many of the most popular motifs were of hieroglyphic origin—such as the eye symbolizing divine justice, the snake biting its tail used metaphorically for eternity, the pelican plucking its breast for Christian charity, and the heron carrying a stone in its claw for vigilance. They were used side by

[1] Eusebius, *Praeparatio evangelica*, iii. 5.
[2] They are even noted in encyclopedias such as the lexicon of 'Suidas'. Cf. W. Scott, *Hermetica*, i, Oxford, 1924, p. 34.

side with the new Christian symbols, and had in fact themselves become completely Christianized, expressing religious and moral teachings and ideas which were purely Christian in principle and purpose. Although Horapollo himself was continually copied right down until the fourteenth century, the Egyptian origin of the individual signs was generally ignored or forgotten, sharing in this respect the fate of other Egyptian relics, even the obelisks of Rome (Pl. 14), among which the Vaticanus was throughout the Middle Ages considered the sepulchre of Julius Caesar, and the Capitolinus a memorial of Octavian. Generally speaking, Egyptian phenomena were always considered in their Biblical aspect,[1] and it is typical that in the mosaics of San Marco in Venice even the pyramids appear as the 'granaries of Joseph'.

By one of the curious incongruities of literary tradition the Biblical accounts of Joseph, undoubtedly more folkloric than spiritual, and of which elements were certainly borrowed from old Egyptian sources, suddenly acquired an unprecedented popularity, almost an independent artistic existence of their own, and became an inexhaustible source of popular legends, about Joseph and Asenath, Joseph and the wife of Potiphar, Joseph and his brethren, all of which spread in countless versions and variants through the popular traditions of East and West, keeping a romantic memory of Egypt alive. The stories remained in favour right down to the invention of printing, when they were among the earliest printed, the most frequently translated, and the most widely read of popular books. Even in modern times they have remained a distinct motif in literature as well as in art.

Nor was the important question of the origin of letters and laws forgotten, but it received, like all other problems, a new orthodox formulation. The ancient explanation of Plato, repeated by Cicero and several other authors known to medieval scholars, that the

[1] A notable exception is Tzetzes, mentioned above (p. 173), who used the hieroglyphs of Chaeremon to illustrate a symbolic exposition of the *Iliad*.

Egyptian Hermes had invented the former and instituted the latter, was felt to clash with the Hebrew doctrine of the divine authority of Moses, and already Philo had strongly defended the priority of the Hebrew tradition against the Egyptian. The didactic literature of the Middle Ages was less explicit, and apparently reluctant to side openly with Philo against Plato. A cautious compromise was therefore proposed, for instance by Isidorus, who, in one of the most widespread and popular encyclopedias of the period, states that Moses was the first among the Hebrews to explain the divine laws 'by sacred letters', just as Phoroneus was the first among the Greeks, and Hermes among the Egyptians. In this way the awkward question about the relative age of the Hebrew and Egyptian traditions was diplomatically avoided.

Generally speaking, these scattered references to an Egypt which was primarily that of the Bible were merely faint offshoots of a tradition which was not entirely dead, but lay dormant in a period ardently occupied with metaphysical and theological problems of its own. It is significant, though, that wherever we meet the traces of the hieroglyphic tradition itself, as opposed to the folkloric one, it is always in the wake of Neoplatonic ideas, which throughout the Middle Ages continued to make their influence felt as a frequently concealed, but always active, source of inspiration. Nothing demonstrates with greater clarity this indissoluble connection between the Neoplatonic and the Egyptian traditions than the almost eruptive upsurge of interest in the latter, in the wake of the Neoplatonic revival of the fifteenth century.

The transformation of one cultural epoch into another is always a complicated and gradual process in which it is dangerous to give prominence to individual agents and symptoms, but few events were destined to exert a greater influence on the spiritual development of an epoch than the visit paid to Florence in 1438 by the Byzantine scholar Gemisto Plethon. Invited as an expert to attend the Council which was to try in vain to reconcile the Churches of the East and West, he used his stay in Florence to give a series of lectures on Platonism in which he violently attacked the scholastics and their Aristotelianism, and rarely has a message been delivered at a more appropriate moment or received with greater attention. In their political form, as the background to an ambitious scheme for a radical reform of the Church which in orthodox circles was called a 'paganization', his efforts to combine Platonism in its Neoplatonic form with Hebrew and other oriental mysticism were condemned by the Church, but they became the first inspiration of the Florentine scholars' study of Greek and of those Neoplatonic studies which were to dominate the entire spiritual and philosophical outlook of the following generations.

The discussion of a direct historical and spiritual connection between Christianity, the philosophy of Plato and his Neoplatonic successors, and the 'Egyptian' wisdom of the Hermetic literature, which had already occupied medieval scholars, was reawakened by Marcilio Ficino, who in 1471 published a Latin translation of some of the Hermetic treatises, about 1483 a translation of Plato, in 1486 a translation of Plotinus, followed in 1491 by an extensive commentary, and in 1497 an edition of Iamblichus. The origin and mutual relations of these works were explained by Ficino thus: that Pythagoras had studied in Egypt at the time of Hermes, whom on the authority of Lactantius he considered an Egyptian sage comparable to the sibyls and the prophets, and a contemporary of Moses, and that Plato had also studied there and derived his knowledge of Egyptian wisdom directly from Pythagoras and the original Hermetic corpus. Thus considered, the Graeco-Egyptian tradition could be used in support of Ficino's efforts to reconcile Christianity and paganism, religion and philosophy, which in his opinion aimed at the same ultimate goal, the revelation of God, who alone was truth. Christianity as revealed in the Gospels was the highest and final manifestation of religion, but the philosophies of Plato and Hermes were merely weaker emanations of the same essence. The pagan tradition had been inaugurated by Hermes, just as Moses had founded the Hebrew tradition, and both of them were entitled to the same amount of reverence, since they represented two different, but parallel, roads towards the same universal revelation.

It is characteristic that the scholars of the Renaissance continually called the Hermetic treatise *Poimandres* 'the Egyptian Genesis', and Hermes 'the Egyptian Moses', and that this was more than learned rhetoric is clear from the famous representation decorating the pavement of Siena cathedral (Pl. 13), where Hermes—explicitly called 'a contemporary of Moses' in the accompanying inscription—is seen resting his left arm on a slab carrying a Latin inscription with a paraphrase of a passage from the Hermetic treatise *Asclepius* frequently used to demonstrate that the doctrine of the Holy Trinity had been foreshadowed by Hermes.[1] With his right hand he is presenting a tablet carrying the inscription 'Take up O Egyptians, letters and laws' to two men representing the native and the Greek populations of Egypt. It is obvious that this representation in a Christian church of the Egyptian Hermes as lawgiver, in an attitude and function normally reserved for his Biblical counterpart Moses, bears strong witness to the importance attached to the Hermetic tradition towards the end of the fifteenth century,[2] even in theological circles. It was in fact so strong that it proved dangerous, for, among scholars who did not have Ficino's unshakable and absolute Christian conviction, it supported, and almost authorized, the belief in the existence of an Egyptian wisdom, combining occult science with mystical insight and magical practices, an Egyptian cabbala, which could profitably be studied independently, not for Christian but for secret and esoteric purposes of its own.

---

[1] *Asclepius Lat.*, i. 8. According to Scott, *Hermetica*, i, p. 32, n. 1, the passage is translated from Lactantius; cf. also pp. 298–9.

[2] The pavement, generally ascribed to Giovanni di Maestro Stefano, dates from 1488.

In this respect it is extremely interesting to see the historical sequence established by Ficino attacked by the Hermetic scholars of the following generation, not because it was felt to infringe on the Biblical tradition and the authority of Moses, but because it did not do justice to the Egyptian one and to Hermes. Such is the case in the Greek preface to Turnebus's edition of the Greek text of *Asclepius* and *Poimandres* of 1554,[1] where Vergicius launches a polemic against the contemporaneity of Hermes and Moses, asserting that the former must necessarily 'have lived before Pharaoh and, consequently, before Moses also.[2] In his preface to the edition of 1574[3] Flussas accepts the full consequences of this presumed priority of Hermes. He adduces an extensive list of quotations in order to illustrate the extent to which the teachings of Hermes—which Flussos explicitly states that he considers translations from an Egyptian original—had anticipated those of the Scripture, and the preface concludes ecstatically 'What more is made known to us by those who were instructed by Our Saviour himself? And yet this man [i.e. Hermes] was anterior in time not only to the disciples of Our Lord, but also to all the prophets . . . and, as the Ancients say, to Moses himself.'[4] To Flussos it was obvious that Hermes had been divinely inspired, and had attained a knowledge of divine things surpassing that which was revealed to the Hebrew prophets, and equalling that of the apostles and the evangelists,[5] and this was the historical and philosophic conception of the so-called wisdom of the Egyptians in Neoplatonic circles until the end of the seventeenth century.[6]

[1] *Mercurii trismegisti Poemander seu de potestate ac sapientia divina*, Paris, 1554.   [2] Scott, *Hermetica*, i, p. 33.

[3] *Mercurii trismegisti Pimandras utraque lingua restitutus*, Bordeaux, 1574.   [4] Scott, *Hermetica*, i, p. 35.   [5] Ibid.

[6] It was by no means uncontested, especially by Reuchlin, who strongly advocated the priority of the Hebrew tradition, and by Casaubon, who was the first to date the Hermetic texts to about the third century A.D.

Concurrently with this historical and philosophical interest in the Egyptian Hermes there developed a fainter, but by no means insignificant, interest in Osiris, inspired mainly by the accounts of Diodorus, Plutarch, and Apuleius. Plutarch's story of the suffering god, unjustly killed, his resurrection as 'King of the dead' and 'Saviour', and his relationship with his loving wife Isis and his son Horus, contained a profusion of elements which were considered mythical anticipations of the Christian passion, but what especially caught the fancy of the Renaissance was Diodorus' account of the 'laughter-loving', Dionysian Osiris, 'fond of music and the dance', who in the company of Apollo, Hermes, and Pan roamed the world, surrounded by satyrs, musicians, and young maidens propagating his cult, and spreading Bacchic enthusiasm through the teaching of viticulture and the dance.

Angelo Poliziano gave lectures on Osiris during his stay in Venice towards the end of the fifteenth century, and Annius of Viterbo (1432–1502) used Diodorus' version of the myth as a background to his curious efforts to establish a heroic genealogy for his papal patron Alexander VI Borgia, identifying the bull of the papal coat of arms with the Osirian Apis, and making the Pope a descendant of the god himself. The divine genealogy thus established was celebrated by Pinturicchio in the delightful ceiling decorations of the Borgia rooms of the Vatican, depicting scenes from the life of Osiris as recorded by Diodorus.

However, the influence on the learned debate of the purported philosophical inheritance from Egypt was completely overshadowed by the interest in what among the period's artists and men of letters was considered its most important cultural contribution to posterity, its hieroglyphs.

We have seen that wherever a Neoplatonically inspired interest in Egypt was aroused the hieroglyphic problem was always in the air, and the direct incitement to the revival of the classical hieroglyphic tradition came in 1414, when the fragments of the history of Ammianus Marcellinus were found in a German monastery by Poggio Bracciolini. In a digression about obelisks Ammianus quotes an extensive Greek translation of the hiero-glyphic inscription of one of the Roman obelisks, which to Florentine scholars proved that the ancient reports about the symbolical nature of Egyptian writing were true and this concep-tion of the script was confirmed four years later when Christoforo Buondelmonti found on the Greek island of Andros a manuscript copy of Horapollo's *Hieroglyphica*. This manuscript too was brought to Florence, where the text, circulated in numerous copies, was studied with avidity and compared with the other classical accounts of the script, and these activities resulted in the formulation of the 'hieroglyphic theory' of the Renaissance, based on Plotinus' already-mentioned definition of the hieroglyphs, which once more were explained as a unique form of symbolic writing revealed to the Egyptians by divine inspiration. They were supposed to be basically different from all other graphic systems operating with words and letters, and each sign was con-sidered a symbolic entity of its own, revealing its true meaning only to the initiated. The meaning thus revealed involved a spontaneous insight into the very essence of things, an esoteric understanding of their ideas, and the process by which this enlightenment was effected was supposed to reflect the dynamic process of divine intelligence. Thus defined, the hieroglyphs became once more divine illustrations of the symbolic nature of things, and were introduced into the allegorizing art of the period as means by which the essence and idea of material objects could be indicated and revealed, and only against this background is it possible to understand the subsequent importance of the hiero-glyphic question, and its unparalleled influence on art and letters.

Leone Battista Alberti (1404–72) already used a hieroglyphic emblem for the decoration of his medal, the winged eye sym-bolizing the swiftness or promptitude of divine justice, and was the first to recommend authoritatively the use of 'sacred Egyptian letters' for architectural and ornamental purposes. Giving

Etruscan writing as an example, he pointed out how ordinary letters had a tendency to become obsolete and forgotten, and proposed the use of allegorical hieroglyphs for all monumental inscriptions, since these could always be read and interpreted by initiated scholars. Alberti's proposal was first put into practice by Francesco Colonna (1433–1527) in his curious publication the *Hypnerotomachia Polifili* written in the latter half of the fifteenth century and published by Aldus in 1499. It abounds in elaborate illustrations of sententious hieroglyphic inscriptions from imaginary ruins and monuments, which in spite of their purely fictitious character are all painstakingly translated and commented upon in the text as if they were genuine and original. The individual signs used for the writing of these inscriptions are explicitly called '*coelati hieroglyphi, ouero characteri aegyptici*', but are nevertheless entirely free inventions made from Colonna's descriptions by the unknown illustrator of the book. Only in one single inscription are there signs obviously copied from genuine Egyptian hieroglyphs, which Colonna must have either seen on the hieroglyphic monuments of Rome, among which the Capitoline and the so-called Mahutaean obelisks were at the time the most conspicuous, or possibly known from copies of hieroglyphic inscriptions brought back from the Orient by Ciriaco de'Pizzicallo. All the other signs were invented by Colonna himself, and it is typical of the spirit of the period, and its lack of historical *Stilgefühl*, that no efforts were made to stress or even indicate their presumed Egyptian origin. As decorative elements they were in no way distinguished from other ornamental designs of the early Renaissance. From this general rule there was only one exception. In the Roman church of San Lorenzo fuori le Mura was kept an antique Roman temple frieze, representing cult objects and sacred emblems such as were known from many other monuments of the same kind, but for unknown reasons these particular signs were considered genuine Egyptian hieroglyphs, and were continually represented as such not only by Colonna, but by a series of distinguished artists from Mantegna and Heemskerck to du Cerceau and Piranesi.

The allegorical and symbolic meaning of all these reconstructed hieroglyphs was derived from their appearance, more or less according to the same principles used in our rebus. The picture of a rudder was used for the verb 'to govern', and two fish-hooks meant 'to keep'. Occasionally a more subtle exposition was necessary, as when a tankard with a narrow spout was used to signify 'little by little', or the patera to mean 'liberality'. Very often the metaphors were even more far-fetched, as for instance when the picture of an eye drawn on the sole of a sandal meant 'subject to God', or a ball of yarn 'conducting', evidently with reference to the story of Ariadne and Theseus. When the original hiero-glyphs of Chaeremon and Horapollo were used, they retained the allegorical meaning ascribed to them by these authors, but in their outward appearance, as reconstructed by the period's artists and craftsmen, these signs also were made in the traditional style of the period. With the various translations and illustrated editions of the *Hypnerotomachia* and Horapollo they spread all over Europe, and exerted a profound influence on the decorative arts, and also, through their influence on Alciati, who explicitly stressed his dependence on the hieroglyphic tradition, on the emblematic literature of all European countries.

It became fashionable to put into practice Alberti's demand for the use of hieroglyphs in official monumental inscriptions, and we know that hieroglyphic decorations, often made by distin-guished artists, on obelisks, arches, and transparencies, were characteristic features of innumerable 'triumphs', processions, and pageants throughout the Renaissance. Almost all of them have disappeared without trace, but Dürer's monumental triumphal arch, dedicated to the Emperor Maximilian about 1517, was a typical specimen of the genre. It represents a classical triumphal arch decorated with episodes from the Emperor's life, and a variety of allegorical and symbolical representations alluding to his aspirations, virtues, and ideals. The focal point of the entire monument is the so-called *tabernaculum*, a panel inserted immediately above the main gate of the arch, called 'the gate of honour and authority'. In accordance with the practice of the period this panel was supposed to express in quintessence the symbolic significance of the entire monument, and at the same time provide an allegorical key to its understanding. It portrays the Emperor enthroned, surrounded by a variety of animal figures and ornamental objects, almost all of which had been reconstructed by Dürer from Horapollo's descriptions. Translated in accordance with the latter's expositions they represent a pompous and long-winded panegyric upon the Emperor, describing him among other things as a 'hero of undying fame, a descendant of age-old nobility, a prince of exalted virtues, strong, courageous, and circumspect, and adorned with all the gifts of nature and the arts'. The 'tabernacle' was explicitly called 'a mystery in sacred Egyptian letters' by the Emperor's historian Stabius, and is a typical example of the way in which these 'hieroglyphical' enigmas, inserted as decorative details into allegorical art by the combined efforts of artists and theoreticians, were seen as secret indications of the esoteric meaning of the work as a whole. They were considered of equal importance for artist and spectator, for by indicating the artistic intentions of the former they inspired the latter to serious contemplation, initiating and preparing him for the ultimate revelation of the artist's idea, the final miracle of understanding, and in this respect 'the sacred language of the hieroglyphs' became the language of art itself.

The final formulation of this hieroglyphic theory is found in the most compendious of all hieroglyphic compilations, the *Hieroglyphica* of Pierio Valeriano, which from its appearance in 1556 until the disappearance of the entire tradition towards the end of the seventeenth century remained the Bible of the allegorizing hierogrammates of arts and letters. Outlining in a preface the origin and purpose of the book, Valeriano recalls '*questi giorni santi'* when in Rome he discussed the burning problems of his youth with Giovanni Grimaldi, the later Patriarch of Aquileia, especially 'this mysterious knowledge, used in the paintings and the architecture of the Ancients, who—undoubtedly on the authority of Egyptian priests—had invented a silent language, conceivable by means of pictures of things alone without any sound of the voice or combination of letters'. It was the fervent ambition of Valeriano to reconstruct 'this sacred language of ideas', and the fifty-eight books of the *Hieroglyphica* were the result of his efforts to transcribe the totality of his period's philosophical and theological knowledge into a *magnum corpus* of hieroglyphic pictures and fables.

Although greatly admired by contemporaries, and reprinted in numerous translations and revised editions, the book of 'the divine Pierio' very quickly lost its influence among the learned, but became an inexhaustible source of inspiration for emblematic art and literature—which would probably not have appealed to the author, who saw a higher destiny for his hieroglyphs, for, as he himself states, 'to speak hieroglyphically is to disclose the true nature of things divine as well as humane'. The truth was that the book represented at the same time the culmination and the end of a tradition. The suppression and gradual disappearance of the Neoplatonic tradition was one of the most conspicuous and fateful results of the new approach to scientific and spiritual problems heralded by the Counter-Reformation, and new generations of critical and sober-minded Jesuit scholars had little patience with hieroglyphic extravaganzas which they considered superflous, profane, and slightly dangerous in their esoteric exuberance. But deprived of their Neoplatonic background and *raison d'être*, the Egyptological studies lost their very essence and spirit, and their philosophical and artistic significance as well. The interest in Egypt remained, but the hitherto purely artistic and philosophical tradition was transformed into a historical and archaeological discipline. The focus of interest shifted from

Egyptian ideas to Egyptian objects and it was more than a coincidence that this change coincided with the new interest in the obelisks (Pl. 14).

In an ambitious effort to vie with the ancients, and a pious desire to extol the glory of the Church of Rome, Sixtus V in 1588 had the Vatican obelisk removed from its ancient place on the *spina* of the Vatican Circus to its present position in front of the Basilica of St. Peter, in order to let the last witness to the martyrdom of the apostle partake in the triumphant completion of his new sanctuary. The removal was considered an epoch-making achievement, admired and celebrated all over Europe, and was followed by the removal of other obelisks and new finds of Egyptian antiquities, such as the famous *Mensa Isiaca*, or *Tabula Bembina* (Pl. 15), which gave rise to an extensive literature and a new archaeological approach to Egyptological problems.

Mercati's scholarly treatise *De gli obelischi di Roma* of 1589 already bears evidence to this change in attitude. The author is still absorbed by the ancient problems about the origin of writing, the relative importance of Noah, Moses, and Hermes in its development, and the nature of the hieroglyphs, but he has an unconventional and critical approach to most of them. He is the first to draw a clear distinction between the reconstructed hieroglyphs and the real ones used in original inscriptions, and it is significant that his conception of the latter is based on the account of Egyptian writing given by Clement of Alexandria, and not primarily on the Neoplatonists. It is also characteristic that he should compare Egyptian hieroglyphs with the newly discovered Mexican ones, and he makes some remarkably shrewd observations on the pictorial, but in his opinion completely unmetaphorical, use of the signs in ideographic writing.

Even more critical and independent was Lorenzo Pignoria in his scholarly publication of the Isiac table, which appeared in Venice in 1605 under the title *Vetustissimae tabulae aeneae . . . explicatio* (Pl. 16). Since its discovery in 1525 the table had occasioned endless discussions and learned controversies, based on the weirdest interpretations of its symbolic significance, but Pignorius refused to consider it allegorically and treated it as an ordinary archaeological object. By adducing comparative material such as gems and seals, he tried to establish an objective archaeological basis for an evaluation of its ornamental and decorative designs, as well as for its dating, which he estimated to be the time of Augustus, and in so doing he became an undisputed pioneer.

At about the same time there appeared another publication, in its own way equally epoch-making: Hoerwart von Hohenburg's *Thesaurus Hieroglyphicorum*, which gave fairly accurate copies of hieroglyphic inscriptions from obelisks, tablets, and statuary, and for the first time spread the knowledge of original hieroglyphs in wider circles. However, as is frequently the case, the course of evolution was not straight, but fluctuating, and before its final eclipse the old tradition was once more to experience a short but vigorous revival in the extensive Egyptological production of Athanasius Kircher (1601–80), which represents a curious conglomeration of old ideas and new, a combination of Renaissance esoterics and Baroque science.

One of history's last true polyhistors, Kircher was professor of mathematics in the University of Rome, but at the same time an adept, in many cases even a pioneer, in a number of widely divergent fields such as music, geology, astronomy, and Sinology. A proficient philologist, he was well versed in that *philologia sacra* on which most of the academic activities of the Baroque were based, and his publication of the first Coptic grammar and vocabulary, from manuscripts brought to Europe from the Orient by Pietro della Valle, made him the founder of modern Egyptology. His Coptic studies had aroused his interest in pagan Egypt also, and, when Innocent X Pamfili decided to let Bernini erect the obelisk in the Piazza Navona (Pl. 14*b*), Kircher was called in as an expert, which resulted in his first Egyptological publication, *Obeliscus Pamphilius* (1650), followed by the monumental *Oedipus*

Aegyptiacus in three folio volumes (1652–4), *Ad Alexandrum VII Obelisci Aegyptiaci . . . interpretatio hieroglyphica* (1666), and *Sphinx mystagoga* (1676).

Few scholars have suffered more than Kircher from the complacency and lack of historical sense among his successors in a science to the foundation of which he offered no mean contribution, and for centuries he has been whipping-boy of Egyptology, his Egyptological life-work censured and ridiculed, and himself denounced as a fraud and a humbug. Nothing is more unhistorical or more unjust. Having made an extensive study of the Neoplatonic classics, the Hermetic literature, Iamblichus, and the other traditional sources, which now included the cabbala, Kircher had formed strong opinions on what he considered to be Egyptian philosophy, and was convinced that his conception of it was correct and unassailable, in that it was based on the best traditions and authorities. He was therefore sure that he knew, so to speak in advance, the content of all original inscriptions, in which according to the same authorities Egyptian philosophy and wisdom had found their final esoteric expression. By establishing the symbolic connection between the individual hieroglyphs and the elementary concepts and ideas on which his conception of Egyptian thought was based, it was in Kircher's opinion possible not merely to decipher the hieroglyphs, but also to obtain irrefutable confirmation of the classical accounts of Egyptian philosophy.

From the very outset Kircher had therefore a clear idea of how to proceed, and by a symbolic analysis of the individual hieroglyphs, he combined them with the basic philosophical, cabbalistic, and demonic concepts of his 'Egyptian' cosmology, revealing what he considered their inner connection and true esoteric meaning, their *lectio idealis*, by means of subtle expositions and elucidations. In this way he succeeded in making the hieroglyphic inscriptions conform perfectly with his own preconceived ideas of Egyptian wisdom, by a method which is certainly indefensible, but not without a certain logic and consistency when judged on its own premisses. To discard it as fraud and swindle is merely to show a lack of judgement and historical sense, and by drawing attention to the original inscriptions and signs Kircher's efforts will always mark a turning-point in the history of Egyptology.

In fact it was not merely his methodological shortcomings which were responsible for Kircher's rapid decline in reputation, but also the fact, already mentioned, that the Neoplatonic tradition of which he was such a typical representative was on the wane in polite academic circles. It is indeed characteristic of the general attitude that less than fifty years after Kircher's death Warburton could dismiss both Kircher and Neoplatonism with the same indulgent smile. 'It is pleasant to see him [Kircher] labouring thro' half a dozen Folios with Writings of the late Greek Platonists and forged Books of Hermes, which contain Philosophy, not Egyptian, to explain and illustrate old Monuments not Philosophical. Here we leave him to course his Shadows of a Dream thro' all the fantastic Regions of Pythagoreic Platonism.'[1]

Warburton's attitude was typical, for not only had the Neoplatonic myth of Egypt become unfashionable among the enlightened scholars and dilettanti of the eighteenth century, but the former enthusiasm for the wisdom of Egypt had turned into a critical and often disdainful attitude towards its art, already apparent in the period's first publication of Egyptological material, Montfaucon's voluminous catalogue *L'Antiquité éxpliquée et représentée en figures'*, which appeared in 1719. This contains reproductions of almost all Egyptian antiquities known at the time, including also those which had already been published by Boissard and Bonanni, but the reproductions are mostly bad and give a poor and distorted impression of Egyptian art, strongly corroborated by Montfaucon's commentary, in which he explicitly states that he has only reluctantly included the 'mostly hideous and at most bizarre' Egyptian objects, and that he has done so

---

[1] W. Warburton, *The Divine Legation of Moses*, London, 1741, p. 110.

not for aesthetic but merely for chronological reasons. Nevertheless, the book did undoubtedly arouse a considerable interest in Egyptian archaeology, and it was followed by a similar compilation published by de Caylus,[1] who included additional material, and took a slightly less apologetic attitude towards the Egyptians. But the general conceptions of the history and evolution of art were decidedly unfavourable to an objective evaluation of their artistic achievements.

The final verdict, generally accepted until the middle of the nineteenth century, was pronounced by Winckelmann, who had seen only the very limited number of Egyptian antiquities gathered in Italian collections, of which the greater part were Hellenistic pastiches or else of inferior quality (Pl. 4*b*). He considered them all bizarre and barbarous curiosities rather than art, and deemed them unfit for a modern aesthetic analysis. Generally speaking, they were in his opinion manifestations of an inferior and preliminary stage of artistic development, which might be of a certain historical interest, but could never be compared to the final and unsurpassable perfection that was Greece.

With certain modifications this was the general view of Egyptian art among artists and scholars until modern times, with two notable exceptions, Piranesi and Zoëga.

The former based an 'apologetical essay' in defence of Egyptian art[2] on a comparison of the monumental sculptures of lions decorating the Roman fountain Acqua Felice, of which two were 'naturalistic' Greek and two 'stylized' Egyptian (Pl. 5*a*). It was the thesis of this short but remarkable paper that those qualities of Egyptian art which were generally held against it—its purported lack of grace and charm, and its 'unnatural' stylization—were not in fact artistic shortcomings, but essential manifestations

---

[1] *Recueil d'antiquités égyptiennes, étrusques, grecques et romaines* Paris, 1752–67.

[2] G. B. Piranesi, *Diverse maniere d'adornare i cammini*, Rome, 1769, preface.

of its specific nature. The positive aspects of this were strongly emphasized by Piranesi, who stressed the unemotional immobility of Egyptian sculpture, which he rightly considered a direct result of its ornamental 'architectural' character and function. In Piranesi's opinion its lack of grace, in the conventional meaning of the word, was far outweighed by its gravity, wisdom, and modification of parts, and his congenial and inspired analysis makes his article one of the most fascinating and penetrating evaluations of Egyptian art ever made by any artist. In his practical efforts to introduce Egyptian motifs and ornament into the decorative arts he was not equally successful, and his Egyptian furniture, chimney-pieces, wall-paintings, and candelabra were mostly rather unfortunate and in dubious taste; they became, however, the harbingers of the curious Egyptian fancy which was to spread over Europe in the wake of the French expedition to Egypt.

Zoëga's entire life-work represents, almost volume by volume, a subtle and unpolemical corrective to the extravaganzas which Winckelmann's often unbridled enthusiasm introduced in his various numismatic, archaeological, and art-historical publications. In his book *De origine et usu obeliscorum* he replaced Winckelmann's aesthetic condemnation of Egyptian art by a historical analysis, which made a clear distinction between the Hellenistic pastiches and the Egyptian originals, and demonstrated for the first time that Egyptian art also was subject to distinct changes of form and style, characteristic of definite epochs and periods. Through their influence on Champollion these observations became of the greatest importance for the subsequent conception of the entire history of Egypt.

Egyptian influence on the philosophical and scientific debate of the century was otherwise characterized by the same remarkable lack of inspiration as in the arts, degenerating into etymological absurdities, and dilettante efforts to solve the riddle of the hieroglyphs by comparisons with Chinese and Armenian. But the ancient *mythos* still refused to die completely, and in the dark sub-terranean strata of eighteenth-century society never penetrated by the rays of enlightenment, it lived on as a potent element in strong undercurrents of occultism and demoniac superstition, suddenly to be brought to light in the criminal activities of a Cagliostro.

The various Theosophical, Rosicrucian, and Masonic societies of the period, which combined a humanitarian 'enlightened', idealism with an ambiguous belief in an initiation by stages into a vaguely defined, but allegedly gradually revealed, esoteric knowledge, based on popularized Neoplatonic ideas, were also pro-foundly influenced by the last emanations of the ancient myth as expounded, for example, in a curious piece of literature, 'the Egyptian Télémaque', Terrasson's moralizing novel *Séthos, histoire ou vie tirée des monumens anecdotes de l'ancienne Égypte.* This book, which between 1731 and 1825 saw no less than thirteen editions, was based on extensive studies in the Neoplatonic classics, and describes how its noble hero passes through the vicissitudes of human existence, but is admitted to 'the realm of light and truth' after his gradual initiation into the sacred mysteries of Isis. It was widely read, and gave rise to an impressive series of Egyptian pastiches in literature, ballet, and opera, among which the most celebrated was Schikaneder's text to Mozart's *Magic Flute.* In its theosophical and Masonic offshoots faint reminis-cences of the ancient tradition have survived to the present day, when the belief in mysterious Egypt has even shown enough vitality to lapse into the new aberrations of modern Pyramid philosophy—but otherwise the myth of Egypt died with Neo-platonism.

The new revival came from archaeology, for with the finding of the Rosetta Stone towards the end of the eighteenth century the hitherto sterile and stagnant Egyptological studies received a new impulse, which inspired the genius of Champollion, and inaugurated the development of modern Egyptology.

ERIK IVERSEN

BIBLIOGRAPHY

G. Boas, *The hieroglyphics of Horapollo*, New York, 1950 (Bollingen Series xxiii).

M. V.-David, *Le Débat sur les écritures et l'hiéroglyphe aux XVIIe et XVIIIe siècles et l'application de la notion de déchiffrement aux écritures mortes*, Paris, 1965.

R. Enking, *Der Apis-Altar Johann Melchior Dinglingers*, Gluckstadt–Hamburg–New York, 1939 (Leipziger ägyptologische Studien xi).

K. Giehlow, 'Die Hieroglyphenkunde des Humanismus in der Allegorie der Renaissance', *Jahrbuch der kunsthistorischen Sammlungen des allerh. Kaiserhauses*, xxxii. 1, Wien–Leipzig, 1915.

L. Hautecoeur, *Rome et la renaissance de l'antiquité à la fin du XVIIIe siècle*, Paris, 1912 (Bibliothèque des Écoles françaises d'Athènes et de Rome cv).

E. Iversen, *The myth of Egypt and its hieroglyphs in European tradition*, Copenhagen, 1961.

S. Morenz, *Die Begegnung Europas mit Ägypten*, Leipzig, 1968 (Sitzungsberichte der Sächsischen Akademie, Leipzig, phil.-hist. Klasse, cxiii, 5).

—— *Die Zauberflöte: Eine Studie zum Lebenszusammenhang Ägypten-Antike-Abendland*, Münster, 1952 (Münstersche Forschungen v).

E. Panofsky, '"Canopus Deus". The iconography of a non-existent god', *Gazette des beaux-arts*, lvii (1961), 193–216.

W. Scott, *Hermetica*, 4 vols., Oxford, 1924–36.

L. Volkmann, *Bilderschriften der Renaissance: Hieroglyphik und Emblematik in ihren Beziehungen und Fortwirkung*, Leipzig, 1923.

8

LANGUAGE AND WRITING

CONSIDERING the great and protracted part which Egypt played in the development of human civilization it is strange that the Egyptian language made so relatively small an impact on the tongues of the ancient world. In modern European languages there is hardly a score of words whose origin can be traced back to ancient Egypt—and yet the Greeks gladly, and almost with pride, acknowledged their indebtedness to Egypt for many elements of their culture. There is ample archaeological evidence, too, for the influence which Egypt radiated into neighbouring countries—slight perhaps in the vast desert to the west, but considerable in Nubia and the Sudan to the south and in Palestine and Syria to the east, all of which were for centuries under direct Egyptian rule.

The lack of Egyptian linguistic influence to the west and south is not surprising, for the native languages spoken there left no written record themselves and were later superseded by the languages of invading or immigrant newcomers. But in the east the Egyptians were, from time immemorial, in contact with Semites who have left written records almost as old as the Egyptian ones. The Amarna tablets which have preserved the diplomatic correspondence of Palestinian and Syrian rulers with the Kings of Egypt of the later Eighteenth Dynasty contain a number of Egyptian words, but these are restricted almost entirely to the names of objects requested from Egypt and to Egyptian administrative or military terms.

When, in the eleventh century B.C., an Egyptian official, Wenamūn, went to Byblos in Syria to acquire some much-sought-after pine timber, and, having been robbed of his money on the way, was unable to pay, the King of Byblos refused to supply the timber without adequate compensation, but admitted loyally: 'True, Amūn fitted out all the lands. He fitted them out after having earlier fitted out the land of Egypt whence you have come. And craftsmanship came forth from it reaching to the place where I am. And learning came forth from it reaching to the place where I am.' In Wenamūn's time the ruler of the Egyptian town of Tanis kept a considerable fleet to trade with Syria. Egyptians were settled there, like the Egyptian singing woman employed by the King of Byblos whom Wenamūn met, and even at Cyprus Wenamūn found in a crowd a man who understood Egyptian. But the political might of Egypt had gone, and a century later, when the oldest part of the Bible was written, the past Egyptian rule was no longer remembered. Words of Egyptian origin in these parts of the Hebrew sacred writings are few, but even then, and down to the time of the prophets, the words for measures of capacity *hīn* and *ēpha* (from Egyptian **hīnaw* and **aipat*) were still in use, although, it seems, these measures were different in size from their Egyptian originals.

Before, however, we pursue further the words which have come down to us either through the medium of the Bible or through the Greek world, it is advisable to give some account of the ancient Egyptian language itself. The origin of Egyptian is obscure, but many Semitic features in the language suggest that at some time the language of the inhabitants of the Nile valley, who were probably of African origin, was strongly influenced by Semitic immigrants from Asia. Egyptian, as we know it, is a mixture of these African and Asiatic elements. The beginning of its written records coincides with the beginning of Egyptian history, some time before 3000 B.C., and it survived until the final defeat of paganism by Christianity shortly before A.D. 500. The writing, that is hieroglyphs (and their formal simplification called hieratic), and also the further simplified form called demotic which dates from the seventh century B.C., expresses only the consonants of the words; it is only Coptic, the stage of the language spoken by Egyptian Christians (Copts) from the third century A.D. and written in Greek letters with a few additional signs for sounds unknown to Greek, that writes the vowels of words as well. Consequently, it is possible to reconstruct the approximate sound of only such ancient Egyptian words as were preserved down to Coptic or are by chance known from Greek or cuneiform (Assyrian and Babylonian) transcriptions. Such reconstructed forms are here throughout preceded by an asterisk (*) to stress their hypothetical character, the greater in that Egyptian possessed several consonants unknown to European languages and therefore difficult or impossible to indicate by means of our alphabet. Coptic, the last form of Egyptian, died out some time during the Middle Ages, but one of its dialects is still used as a liturgical language in the Egyptian Christian (Coptic) Church.

Let us now return to the Egyptian words which passed the frontiers of their country of origin and which, through the Bible, have been handed down and are with us still. The first to be noted is the feminine proper name Susan, taken from the apocryphal story preserved only in a Greek translation and added to the book of the prophet Daniel. There *Sousanna* is the beautiful wife of King Joacim of Juda and her name is a Graecized form of the Hebrew *Shūshannā*. This latter again is a feminine form of the Hebrew *shūshan* derived from the Egyptian *shōshen*, 'lotus', a water-plant highly esteemed by the Egyptians for its beauty and pleasant smell. The word penetrated into the Near East in the thirteenth century B.C. or later, and is known not only from Hebrew but also in other Semitic languages, designating everywhere 'lily', or rather any lily-like flower. From the Near East it passed with this same meaning into Greek (*souson*) and, a convincing testimony to its widespread popularity, the winter residence of Persian kings, the famous town of Susa, in reality bore its name, *Shūshan*.

The continuous tradition of the generic name of Egyptian kings, Pharaoh, is also due entirely to the Bible. The exact Hebrew form of the word is *Parᶜō*, our Pharaoh being the Greek transcription *Pharaō* of the Septuagint. It is strange that Greek authors never used the word prior to the date of this translation. Pharaoh goes back to the Egyptian expression **par-ᶜo*, lit. 'great house', which was originally applied, in accordance with this literal meaning, to the king's palace and his court. It is only from the Eighteenth Dynasty that it was used exclusively to refer to the king's person, though never in conjunction with the king's name; this latter use is attested for the first time about 950 B.C. and is thenceforward common. It is interesting to note that the Biblical use of the word conforms with this development; the earlier parts of the Bible (Genesis and Exodus) use the word Pharaoh without any name, and only in the later prophet Jeremiah do we meet Pharaoh Hophra and Pharaoh Necho. It was undoubtedly because the Pharaoh of the Jewish oppression acquired a bad reputation that he had a Mediterranean card game of chance named after him—*pharaon*, 'faro' in English. In this the part of banker is very lucrative: 'There was no other way left for me but to steal; I act as banker of *pharaon*', says one of Beaumarchais's figures.

It is difficult to see on what grounds the name of two Biblical characters called Phinehas, the grandson of Aaron and the son of Eli, was revived as the Christian name Phineas in seventeenth-century England, a name found occasionally even in modern times in America. The name, however, is indisputably of Egyptian origin, for Phinehas, as it is spelt in the Revised Version, is nothing else but the Egyptian proper name *Pꜣ-Nḥsy* (**Pineḥas*), 'The Nubian', not uncommon during the New Kingdom.

An Egyptian origin of the name of Moses is still a matter of dispute. It has been accepted by many serious scholars, though they differ as to which Egyptian word or words are involved, and a number of daring suggestions have been made since the beginning of the Christian era, when Egyptian was still a living langu-age. The personal name *Msw* (**Mose*) often met with in Egyptian texts of the New Kingdom seems to have the best claim, though no more than this; *Mose*, meaning 'is born', is itself an abbrevia-tion of some such common name as Amenmose, Ptaḥmose, Ramose—'(the god) Amūn, Ptah, Rē is born'. The *s*-sound which it contains is regularly expressed in Hebrew by the letter *samekh* ס, but the *s* in the name of Moses is written by means of the letter *shīn* ש. To the layman this may seem a trifling difficulty, but to a linguist and philologist it is a warning, if not, indeed, an insuperable obstacle.

Czechs sometimes apply the disapproving term *putifarka* ('Potiphar's wife') to married women behaving like the disrepu-table wife of the officer Potiphar in the story of Joseph. The name of Potiphar is a good Egyptian proper name which has survived in this form since the time of the Massoretes, the Jewish Biblical scholars who in the fifth century A.D. fixed the pronunciation of the Hebrew text of the Bible, which hitherto lacked any indication of vowels. The Massoretes were unaware that the name ought to have been *Peteprēꜥ* ('He whom (the god) Rē has given'), to which *Petephrē* of the Septuagint is a very close approach.

Having thus exhausted the small number of Egyptian words which have reached us through the Bible we can now turn to such words as have been handed over to us by the Greeks. Here 'ebony' and 'gum' seem to be among the earliest which started their journey to us from the shores of Egypt. The tree (*Dalbergia melanoxylon*) which supplied the highly valued hard black 'ebony' wood did not grow in Egypt itself but in the countries to the south, and it is possible that the Egyptian name of the wood, *hbny*, from which the Greek *ebenos* and Hebrew *hābnīm* are derived, is not a native Egyptian word but a loan-word from some language of the Sudan or Central Africa. Whatever the truth may be, it is, however, certain that the word 'ebony' comes from the Greek and thus indirectly from Egypt. The same is also true of the word 'gum', which acquired this form having passed through the French *gomme* and the Latin *gummi* from the Greek *kommi*. This was at first only the viscous secretion of various species of the acacia tree which is found fairly plentifully in Egypt, where the gum was called *kmyt* (pronounced perhaps **komyet*), of which the Greek word is but a very slight modification, its use, like that of 'gum' now, being later extended to include the resinous secretions of numerous other trees and shrubs growing outside Egypt. These gum-resins were used in various ways, chiefly as preservatives in mummification, as incense, and as adhesives. The words *ebenos* and *kommi* were current in Greek as early as the fifth century B.C. and their reception probably goes back at least to the time of the foundation of the first Greek trading settlements some two centuries earlier.

Contemporary with these two words was the Greek *sakkos* or *sakos*, the ancestor (through Latin *saccus*) of our 'sack', designating a bag of rough cloth, *sakkos* itself being apparently nothing else but the Egyptian **sak*, 'receptacle', a derivative of the verb **sōk*, 'to gather', 'to collect'. There is, however, a possibility that the Greeks acquired their word indirectly from their Phoenician competitors in trade, for the Egyptian word had already penetrated into Palestine and Syria and *sak* is also present in Hebrew.

It has been suggested, too, that our 'lily' (in Old English *lilie*) is, through Greek *leirion* and Latin *lilium*, a loan-word from Egyptian **hrēre*. Linguistically the suggestion is quite plausible, though the Egyptian word designates a flower in general; the meaning of 'lily', especially its white variety, was defined by the Greeks. If the derivation is correct we can observe in its history the work of two mutually opposed linguistic tendencies, namely, dissimilation by which two identical sounds in the same word become different, and assimilation, by which an originally different sound obtains the same value as another. The final part of the Greek word, *-ion*, is, of course, a diminutive ending, but instead of *reirion* the word by dissimilation turned out as *leirion*, while this in Latin through assimilation became *lilium*. The Egyptian **ḥrēre* was in its country of origin used also as a feminine proper name, though our Lilian is not, needless to say, derived directly from it, but is a more recent formation from *lilie*, probably the Anglo-Saxon genitive *lilian*, '(she) of the lily'.

The Greeks might have been expected to adopt or adapt native Egyptian words for things peculiar to, or characteristic of, Egypt. Instead, however, they preferred their own words, which in turn passed into our languages. For the Nile, the only river of the country, they adapted the Semitic word *naḥal*, 'river'; the pyramids are thought to have been so named because they resembled *puramides*, small cakes of wheat and honey of similar shape; obelisks they called *obeliskoi*, 'little spits'; and crocodiles were but *krokodeiloi*, 'lizards'. On the other hand, although they knew about the Egyptian practice of mummification from a detailed description by Herodotus, for mummy they had no special word, our own term having been acquired only in the Middle Ages through later Greek and Latin from the Arabic *mūmīya*, 'asphalt', 'bitumen'.

There remain only two animals, the ibis and the uraeus, whose Egyptian names have been transmitted to us. The former, the stork-like bird sacred to the god Thoth, is the Egyptian **hībey*. The latter, the Egyptian *i͗rt*, had its name considerably changed into *ouraios* as if it came from the Greek *oura*, 'tail'. To these two may here conveniently be added our phoenix, Greek *phoinix*, a term by which several things were designated, though only in two connotations has the word in fact survived. 'Phoenix', a fabulous eastern bird (and hence a paragon of excellence) comes surely from the Egyptian **boinew*, a species of heron sacred to the Egyptians. As to the other connotation, 'Phoenician', formed from the Latin name of the country *Phoenicia*, an attempt has been made to relate it ultimately to the Egyptian term *Fnḫw*, by which, from about 2500 B.C., the Egyptians referred to a race in the lower lands of Palestine and Syria; but the reasons which have been adduced for this etymology are far from convincing. The remaining three meanings of *phoinix*, though not accepted in modern languages may none the less be mentioned here: *phoinix* meaning 'purple' or 'crimson' is simply 'Phoenician' (sc. colour), owing to the technique developed by the Phoenicians of dyeing textiles with a special kind of mollusc; *phoinix*, 'date palm', comes from the Egyptian name of that palm **benret*, while the musical guitar-like instrument *phoinix* is the Egyptian harp **boinet*.

One of the most important words of Egyptian origin is the name of the country itself, our 'Egypt' being descended from the Greek *Aiguptos*, which in turn comes from the Egyptian expression **Ḥi-ku-ptaḥ*, meaning literally 'Mansion of the soul of (the god) Ptah'. Since Ptah was the local god of Memphis, this expression was one of the alternative names of that town, but the Egyptians never used it as a name for the whole country. That application is entirely due to the Greeks, for whom, at the time of their first acquaintance with the country, Memphis was evidently its most representative city. The reader will probably know that 'gipsy', a shortening of an earlier *gipsyan*, is in reality simply 'Egyptian', for when gipsies appeared in England in the sixteenth century they were believed to come from Egypt. It may, however, be less well known that 'Copt', the name applied to Egyptian Christians, is a shortening of the Greek adjective *Aiguptios*, 'Egyptian'.

Among the native names of Egypt the most common was **Kēme(t)*, 'black one'—that is the area so called on account of the colour of its alluvial soil deposited by the Nile. **Kēme(t)* is, indeed, believed by some to be at the root of the word alchemy, but the derivation remains doubtful. It is true that 'alchemy' can be traced through the Old French *alquimia* and the medieval-Latin *alchimia* back to the Arabic *alkimia*, where *al-* is the Arabic definite article, but there is little to suggest that the element *kimia* comes either from the Egyptian **Kēme(t)* itself, through Coptic, or from a Greek equivalent of it.

As far as the Egyptian town of Memphis is concerned, it has disappeared almost completely from the surface of the earth. Memphis is the Greek form of its name, of which the Egyptian prototype was *Mennefer*, meaning properly 'is established and well' (or 'beautiful'). This in itself is but an abbreviation of the full name of the pyramid and residence of King Pepy I of the Sixth Dynasty, which was situated near the town and whose full name was *Mennefer-Piōpey* ('Piōpey [Pepy] is firm and well'). In its shortened form it was later applied to the town, whose original name was, however, quite different. The name is now perpetuated by Memphis in the state of Tennessee in the U.S.A. Located in territory acquired by the U.S.A. in 1797, it was renamed Memphis in 1819 on account of the similarity of its situation on the Mississippi to that of ancient Memphis on the Nile.

That the Greek word *oasis*, which is still a current geographical term, was of Egyptian descent was already known in antiquity to the Greek geographer Strabo. It is, however, not quite half a century since it was established that the underlying original was *waḥet*, which literally means 'cauldron' and must somehow refer to the low level of the oasis in relation to the surrounding desert, though travellers assure us that oases do not give the impression of a cauldron at all.

We may now turn to the field in which Egyptian has left relatively more traces than elsewhere, namely, that of mineralogy. On reflection it is not surprising that this should be so, for Egypt possesses a wide variety of excellent stones, a happy circumstance which greatly fostered the development of Egyptian architecture and sculpture.

Two stones, syenite and basalt, have in comparatively recent times been given names of Egyptian origin, though in neither case justifiably, as we shall see. When the founder of modern geology, A. G. Werner (1750–1817), was looking for a name for a dark rock he had encountered in the vicinity of the town of Plauen in

Saxony, he remembered the stone described by Pliny and called by him *syēnitēs lithos*, 'Syenite stone', because it was quarried near the town called by the Greeks *Syēnē*, at the southern frontier of Egypt. But in coining the name 'syenite' for his discovery he was doubly in error, for the stone referred to by Pliny is different not only in composition but in colour, being in fact none other than the common Egyptian red granite. It is therefore by a misnomer that the geologist's 'syenite' now calls to mind the ancient town *Syēnē*, in Egyptian *Swēn or *Swan, which, prefixed by the Arabic article, became the modern Aswan, famous for its Nile dams.

The word basalt was introduced into modern terminology somewhat earlier by Georg Bauer, better known under his Latin name Agricola, father of mineralogy (1490–1555). He gave the name to a black compact rock, consisting of an aggregate of various minerals, believing that this was the stone which according to Pliny had the colour and hardness of iron and was found in the desert mountains east of the Nile. Pliny says that they called it *basalten* and from this accusative Agricola, who was an excellent classical scholar, coined his 'basalt'. *Basalten* is, indeed, the reading of the majority of manuscripts of Pliny, but the best manuscript reads *basaniten* and it is thus clear that the stone ought correctly to have been called 'basanite'. Pliny so calls it because it had the same qualities as 'basanite', *basanites lithos*, from Lydia in Asia Minor, the stone used for 'probing' (in Greek *basanizein*) gold, since only genuine gold can mark a visible line on it. The stone from Lydia is, however, a kind of schist and so is that from the Egyptian desert, the more precise mineralogical name being greywacke—not at all the stone which we, following Agricola's example, call basalt. The Egyptians called the greywacke in question *bḥn*, and, since in later times the sound *ḥ* (pronounced originally as *kh*) changed into *š* (pronounced as *sh*) it seems likely that the late pronunciation of the name of this stone was *bashan and that the Greeks, whose language possessed no *sh* but expressed this sound regularly by *s*, took it over as their *basan(ites lithos)* 'basanite (stone)'.

While syenite and basalt are Graecized Egyptian words introduced into modern languages only fairly recently, alabaster differs in so far as its survival is due to an uninterrupted tradition, for it has come down to us through the Old French, and previously the Latin, *alabaster*, from the Greek *alabastros* or *alabastron*. The earlier Greek form, however, is not this, but *alabastos*, and denotes not the stone itself but a vessel made from it. The stone itself was called *alabastrites*, 'of alabaster', by the Greeks; the Egyptian word for it, **shēs*, penetrated into Hebrew and occurs in the Old Testament as *shēsh* or *shīsh*, though with a slightly altered meaning. The place from where most of the alabaster came was called by the Greeks and Romans *Alabastra*, that is 'alabasters' (plural) or *Alabastrōn polis*, 'town of alabasters', and lay in Upper Egypt, though its exact position is uncertain. These 'alabasters' are precisely the vases made from the stone, and greatly favoured by both Egyptians and Greeks as receptacles for oils, perfumes, and ointments, since according to Pliny they preserved these perishable materials very well in the hot climate. The name of the stone, *alabastrites*, therefore means properly 'the stone serving for making *alabastos* vases'. In Egypt these vases had a peculiar and characteristic form; they were called **bas* and the picture of such a vase was also used to write the name of the Egyptian cat-headed goddess *Baste(t)* in hieroglyphs. It therefore seems probable that the word *alabastos* ultimately comes from an Egyptian expression **anebaste*, 'vase of (the goddess) Baste(t)'.

The name 'stibnite' given to the common ore mineral of antimony and the occasional use of the term 'stibium' for the metal itself are further examples of the misapplication of words derived ultimately from Egyptian. Though both are immediately due to the Latin *stibium*, from the Greek *stimmi*, terms which were indeed applied principally to antimony compounds, the Egyptian words **mestēme*, **stēme*, which lie behind the classical forms, are known to have had a rather different meaning, referring generally to black eye-paint, and in particular to galena (lead sulphide), the mineral most commonly used in this connection.

'Nitre', which is another name for saltpetre (potassium nitrate), and 'natron', a carbonate of soda, are both derived, through French and Latin, from the Greek *nitron*, the former preserving more faithfully its Greek form, the latter modified by the Arabic *natrûn*. Greek *nitron* had only the meaning of carbonate of soda and is derived from the Egyptian **netrey*. **netrey* in Egypt and *nitron* (Latin *nitrum*) in the classical world were widely used for washing in place of soap, as also the Hebrew *neter*, equally a loan-word from the Egyptian. Egypt had extensive deposits of this chemical, and its export largely, if not exclusively, covered the ancient needs, hence the universal spread of the Egyptian term **netrey*. This latter means literally 'divine'—it comes from the same root as **nūter*, 'god'—because of its important use in religious ablutions.

The gas 'ammonia', its adjective 'ammoniac', 'of ammonia', and the fossil mollusc 'ammonite' have handed down to posterity the name of the chief Egyptian god Amūn. In classical times there was a temple and oracle of this god (called Zeus Ammōn and Jupiter Ammon respectively by the Greeks and Romans) in the oasis now called Sîwa far west of the Nile valley, and *sal ammoniacus*, 'ammoniac salt', which was found near the temple, was thought to have been extracted from the dung left by visitors' camels. This was, of course, wrong since the said salt is an inorganic, not organic, substance. Ammonite, the mollusc, obtained its name through its resemblance in shape to the ram's horns with which the figures of Jupiter Ammon, and earlier of Amūn, were represented.

In order to make this survey of the survival of the ancient Egyptian language in the modern world complete, it is necessary to deal, however briefly, with the influence it has exercised through its last stage, Coptic, on the language of present-day Egypt, namely, Arabic as it is spoken in that country. When the Arabs conquered Egypt in A.D. 641, Coptic began to yield to the language of the conquerors, slowly at the beginning, but, as time went on, with increasing speed. This was due partly to a constant immigration of Arabic tribes into a country which tempted them by its fertility, and partly to the acceptance of Islam, the religion of the conquerors, by the native Christian population, since adherence to Islam brought with it material advantages, especially an exemption from taxes. One might, nevertheless, expect some imprint to have been made on Arabic by the great mass of the Coptic population, especially in view of its long cultural tradition and its high degree of civilization. In fact, however, the influence of Coptic in the spoken Arabic of Egypt is small, and as to phonology, i.e. pronunciation, and structure, i.e. grammar, quite insignificant. As far as vocabulary is concerned some hundred words can with confidence be accepted as originating in Coptic, though not all of these go back to ancient Egyptian and some were Semitic or other loan-words even in Coptic. Of the rest a few are technical terms connected with the Coptic church, while the majority refer to agriculture, and not all of them are used or understood all over the country, but are limited to the out-of-the-way villages in Upper Egypt. To the peasant's environment belong, e.g. *barsîm*, 'clover' (Coptic *bersīm*); *shamar*, 'fennel plant' (Coptic *samahēr*); *tûrya*, 'hoe' (Coptic *tōre* from Egyptian **djōret*, lit. 'hand'); *wêba*, 'a grain measure' (ultimately from Egyptian **aipat* mentioned earlier in this chapter); *tâsh*, 'border of a field' (Coptic *tash*); *shûna*, 'granary' (Coptic *sheune*); *nabâri*, 'winter crop of maize' (from *napre*, 'grain'); and *damîra*, 'time of inundation' (from *t-emēre*). Three names of animals enjoy a great antiquity: *timsâh*, 'crocodile' (from *t-emsah*), *ba'rûr*, 'frog' (from *pe-krūr*), and *handûs*, 'lizard' (from *hantūs*). Any visitor interested in antiquities soon becomes acquainted with *birba*, 'temple ruin', which is simply the Coptic *p-erpe*, 'the temple', the underlying Egyptian *r-pr* appearing as early as the time of the great pyramid-builders. In its *wâha*, 'oasis', Arabic has preserved the original Egyptian **waḥet* more faithfully than the Greek *oasis* and our own word.

One Egyptian word, **djobʿet*, '(sun-dried mud) brick', has in its Arabic form made a long journey to America and back again. Having become *tōbe* in Coptic it passed into Arabic as *ṭūba*, and the Arabs then carried it on their conquest of north Africa to Spain, where, prefixed with the Arabic definite article *al*, it penetrated into Spanish as *adobe*. The Spanish conquest of Mexico brought it into the New World and from the United States it came back to Europe as the architectural term *adobe, (a)dobie*.

Though Muslims have Arabic names for the twelve months of the year, their calendar is lunar and consequently shorter (only 354 days) than the natural solar year, and as a result the Muslim months are constantly shifting their position within the year, namely, by eleven days every year. Muslims and Copts alike, therefore, use the Coptic month names of the Coptic Julian year whenever a reference is to be made to some natural phenomenon linked with an annual season. Thus, speaking of the windy February spell, they say *Fil-'amshîr fi hawa keṭîr*, 'in *'amshîr* there is much wind', a case in which it would be impossible to substitute the Muslim month for *'amshîr*, since this would have to be changed every three years. The names of the Coptic months go back to names given to them in the New Kingdom at Thebes. These referred to the most important festivals celebrated in each month, the names of some being attested since the Old Kingdom, like that of the first month, now *Tût*, the ancestor of which is **Djḥowt*, '(the month of the god) Thoth', a festival **Dḥwtyt* having been celebrated in this month as early as the pyramid age. The month of *Baremhât* perpetuates the name of King Amenhotpe I who reigned *c.* 1530–1510 B.C. In the Nineteenth and Twentieth Dynasties he became a favoured oracular deity at Thebes, and after a festival of his in the seventh month this month was called **Pa-amenhotpe* ('That (sc. festival) of Amenhotpe'), from which *Baremhât* descends.

It is well known that throughout the whole world place-names are most tenacious and that very ancient names of rivers, mountains, and towns have often survived several changes in the language of the inhabitants within whose territory they are situated. Since there is only one river and no individual mountain in Egypt, it is the names of towns which confirm this phenomenon. Over the whole country, from Aswan, already mentioned, in the south, to the Mediterranean, names of towns, villages, or deserted hills occur in great numbers which reach back into the more or less distant past, sometimes as far as written records extend. A mere handful will suffice as illustrations. The town of Edfu when regular sound-changes have been taken into account still bears the name *Edjbō under which it was known in the twentieth century B.C., while at some distance north of it Esna seems to have had the name of *Snē only since the Ptolemaic period. A little further north again, however, Aṣfûn was founded as *Ha-Senfōrew, 'Mansion of Senforew', around 2600 B.C. by the first king of the Fourth Dynasty whom we call rather incorrectly Snofru. The town of Qifṭ is met with as *Gebtōyew in the inscriptions of the Sixth Dynasty, and Asyûṭ appears as *Siowtey as early as the Pyramid Texts, thought to have been composed centuries before they were written down in the pyramids of the kings of the Fifth and Sixth Dynasties. Unlike the names of these and many other, sometimes small and fairly insignificant places, the names of the three capital cities of Egypt fell into complete oblivion. In Upper Egypt *Woꜣset*, which the Greeks, as early as the time of Homer, called *Thēbai*, was resuscitated as Thebes only in modern times; the name of Memphis was given, as already mentioned, to an American town a century and a half ago; and that of *Djaꜥnet* in the Delta, the Zoan of the Bible, has survived only as the first part of the name of its ruins Ṣan el-Ḥagar ('Ṣân of the stones').

All three kinds of writing in which the ancient Egyptian language was written, hieroglyphic, hieratic, and demotic, were extinct by the end of the fifth century A.D. How their mystery occupied the minds of the Middle Ages and the Renaissance prior to their decipherment in 1822 has been discussed elsewhere (see Chapter 7). Only the decipherment revealed that seven letters of the Coptic alphabet, those for sounds unknown to Greek, had been borrowed from demotic writing and thus had continued to be used all the time, and that of these again, one (that for *sh*) had found its way into the alphabet of the eastern Slavs, Russians, Bulgarians, and Serbs. Much more important than this, however, is the part which Egyptian hieroglyphs played in the invention of our own alphabetic writing. That the alphabet we use is derived from the Greek is probably known to every reader. It may not, however, be a matter of common knowledge that the Greeks were not the inventors of their alphabet, but themselves took it over ready-made from the Phoenicians some time about the beginning of the ninth century B.C. The Phoenician writing was but a variety of that used at the time among the Semitic population all over Syria and Palestine and can therefore be called Canaanite. This is the earliest known alphabetic writing—that is, one in which each sign denotes one simple sound, as opposed to ideographic writing, where a sign expresses a whole idea or the word corresponding to it, or to syllabic writing, where signs denote whole syllables, each again an agglomeration of a consonant or consonants with a vowel or vowels attached to them. Since the number of signs in an ideographic writing (like Chinese) is very great and in a syllabic writing still considerable, it is clear that the alphabet which expresses only a very limited number of the separate sounds present in any given language is a great boon. Indeed, owing to its very simplicity, it has made a wide spread of literacy possible so that our civilization owes an incalculable debt to its unknown inventor.

That the Greeks were correct in deriving their alphabet from Phoenicia is confirmed by a comparison of the Greek and Canaanite alphabets in their earliest known forms. The forms of the letters, if not identical, are at least closely similar, their order is fixed and the same in both alphabets, and so is the total number of letters, namely twenty-two, together with their names. Moreover, before they eventually adopted the left-to-right direction of writing, the Greeks wrote, like the Phoenicians, from right to left. In one important point, however, the two alphabets differ substantially; the Canaanite writing expresses only the consonants of words, while the Greek writing includes vowels as well. The peculiarity of writing consonants only was due to the structure of the Canaanite language, or of any Semitic language for that matter, where the meaning of words was inherent in the consonants and their order, while vowels had the minor function of merely modifying the basic sense. The nature of the Greek language, however, required vowels as well to avoid the utmost ambiguity which would otherwise ensue, and the Greeks therefore greatly improved the accepted Canaanite alphabet by attributing the value of vowels to six letters representing consonants which were absent from the Greek language and for which they would have had no use. In this way, for instance, they gave the value of *a* to the very first letter of the alphabet, *alpha*, which originally denoted a guttural consonant ' (*'ālef*) peculiar to all Semitic tongues.

The dependence of the Greek alphabet on the Canaanite being established beyond any doubt, the question arises whether the invention of the Canaanite alphabet was a spontaneous one, or whether its inventor took it over from elsewhere or modelled it on some other writing already existing. A number of rival theories have been propounded in the last hundred years or so, seeking the origin of the Canaanite alphabet in various known writings from the ancient Near East. Among them was the attempt of de Rougé in 1857 to derive the alphabet from Egyptian hieratic writing, the simplified derivative of Egyptian hieroglyphs as written in ink with a rush pen. De Rougé's attempt was quite unconvincing, and if during the last fifty years the balance has tilted heavily in favour of the Egyptian hieroglyphs as the model, though not the origin, of the alphabet, this is due to the research of two Egyptologists, Kurt Sethe and (Sir) Alan Gardiner. Independently, and at about the same time during the First World War, they arrived at results mutually complementary and corroborative. Sethe pointed out the fact, which had previously been considered insufficiently or not at all, that among the ancient writings of the Near East, Egyptian was the only one that expressed consonants only, the character of Egyptian being similar to that of the Semitic languages; in creating an alphabet of consonants, therefore, the inventor of the Canaanite alphabet was clearly influenced by the Egyptian example. Secondly, the Egyptian writing alone, though a mixture of ideographic and phonetic signs, possessed signs denoting single consonants, in other words, signs which could be called alphabetic; the great feat of the unknown inventor was that he imitated the Egyptians only as far as the alphabetic signs were concerned and completely disregarded the great bulk of other signs which expressed either groups of two or three consonants or whole conceptions (ideograms). Last but not least, Sethe was able to advance a highly probable suggestion as to the original form of the signs of the Canaanite alphabet.

The names of the Greek letters, *alpha, bēta, gamma, delta*, etc., have no other meaning, but their counterparts in the Canaanite alphabet are all common Semitic words: *'ālef*, 'ox', *bēth*, 'house', *gimel*, 'camel', *dāleth*, 'door', etc. Even in the earliest Semitic inscriptions then known on stone (about the middle of the ninth century B.C.) the Canaanite signs already showed rather cursive forms suggesting a long previous use for recording on a different writing material, such as papyrus or leather, but even then some signs still seemed to betray their original form, a picture of the object which the letter name denoted. The principle followed was acrophony—that is, the picture denoted the consonant with which the Semitic name of the object began. Sethe therefore argued that when the alphabet was first formed all its signs were pictures of objects similar to Egyptian hieroglyphs and in this, too, he saw an Egyptian influence. For various reasons of a historical character Sethe was inclined to date the formation of the alphabet to the beginning of the sixteenth century B.C. and to attribute it to a Semite living either in Egypt or in a country near to Egypt, Sinai, or Palestine.

Such considerations led Gardiner to postulate for the common ancestor of the various known Semitic writings a picture writing which, following him, we can now call proto-Semitic. He was led to the problem when in 1917 he was preparing for publication the inscriptional material brought in 1905 by Sir Flinders Petrie from his excavation in an ancient Egyptian site, now called Serâbît el-Khâdim, in the peninsula of Sinai. The site in question was an Egyptian temple consecrated to the goddess Hathor, 'lady of the turquoise', for it was this favourite semi-precious stone that the Egyptians came here to seek, and accordingly the bulk of the inscriptions was in Egyptian hieroglyphs. Eleven inscriptions, however, all short, damaged, and indistinct, though written by means of pictures somewhat resembling Egyptian hieroglyphs, were clearly not Egyptian. The total of different signs occurring in them was low, not more than thirty-two, and possibly fewer, since some of them might have been variants of others, and this indicated that the writing was neither ideographic nor syllabic, but alphabetic. In view of the state of preservation and the smallness of the material, the chances of decipherment seemed slight, but Gardiner observed that among the various signs of these inscriptions were some which were consistent with the theory that the letters of the original alphabet were pictures of the objects designated by the letter names. There was not only the ox-head $\forall$ required for '*ālef* ('ox'), but also the water-line $\wedge\wedge\wedge$ for *mēm* ('water'), the snake $\searchable$ for *naḥāsh* ('snake'), the human head Ω for *rēsh* ('head'), the eye $\triangle$ for the Semitic sound called '*ayin* ('eye'), and $+$ for *tāw* ('cross-mark'). This could hardly be a coincidence, and thus encouraged Gardiner concentrated on

a group of four signs already noticed by Petrie which occurred
five, or possibly six, times among the eleven inscriptions:

The first sign resembled very much the Egyptian hieroglyphs ⊏⊐ and ⊓ both depicting the plan of a house, and
might therefore be *b*, called *bēth* ('house'). The second sign
would then be ʻ, *ʻayin* ('eye') and the last *t*, and Gardiner
thus obtained *bʻXt*, For the unknown sign *X*, which in one example of the group was inverted as ⟩, the best possibility seemed
the old Canaanite *l* ⁊, *lāmed* ('ox-goad'(?)), the Greek *lambda*. The
whole group was then *bʻlt*, 'mistress, lady', pronounced *Baʻlat*, as
the Canaanites called the supreme goddess, a feminine counterpart
of the god Baʻal so well known from the Bible. Here she was
evidently identified with the Egyptian goddess Hathor, at whose
temple all the inscriptions were found, a coincidence which would
seem to confirm the correctness of Gardiner's reading. For the
rest of the inscriptions Gardiner was unable to suggest any satisfactory interpretation, nor were his many followers much luckier,
though some of them proposed utterly unwarranted and fantastic
explanations. No help either has been afforded by several other
inscriptions in the same writing, again imperfectly preserved,
found since at Sinai, and there is at present little hope for further
progress unless a larger and better preserved text turns up. The
extensive digging which took place between the two World Wars
in Palestine and Syria, however, produced a number of small
objects inscribed with signs some of which were identical with
those occurring in the Sinai script, especially the picture of a
human head supposed to be the letter *r*, the majority of the signs
again approaching the signs already known from the earliest
Semitic inscriptions. It seems therefore that the Sinaitic writing
gradually spread north through Palestine and Syria, and on the
way, through frequent use in ink and on a different writing
material, probably papyrus or leather, gradually acquired the
cursive forms with which modern scholars were already well
acquainted before the Sinai writing was discovered.

The inventor of the Sinai alphabet must have been a Semite, since the term *ba'lat* is Semitic and no other race is ever recorded in this region. As to the date of the invention, only two possibilities can be envisaged, corresponding to the two periods during which Egyptian activity in the turquoise mines of Serâbît el-Khâdim is proved by hieroglyphic inscriptions of the site, that is during the Twelfth Dynasty and again during the Eighteenth to Twentieth Dynasties. Only during the earlier period, more particularly in the reign of Amenemhet III (*c.* 1842–1797 B.C.), is the presence of Semites actually guaranteed by references to them in the Egyptian inscriptions in the local temple of Hathor. They were engaged as miners, perhaps also as guards, and the presence or visit of a brother of the ruler of Retjenu, that is southern Palestine, is repeatedly mentioned. It would seem therefore that a date about 1800 B.C. is most likely for the invention, and this earlier date is also confirmed by that of the alphabetic cuneiform writing known from Ras Shamra, the ancient Ugarit, in northern Syria, an alphabet which has no connection with the cuneiform writing of the Sumerians and Babylonians except in the use of the stylus for writing on clay tablets. It seems unthinkable that an alphabet was here invented independently a second time and it is more likely that the principle of the alphabet established at Sinai was only reapplied to suit the different writing material current in the region of Ras Shamra. Since the Ras Shamra tablets are agreed to belong to about the fourteenth century B.C. their date supports an earlier date for the Sinaitic hieroglyphic alphabet, for which then the beginning of the eighteenth century B.C. becomes quite plausible.

We are therefore entitled to claim that Egyptian hieroglyphic writing has played, as a model, a considerable part in the formation of the Semitic, and through this of our own, alphabetic writing. Yet the service which the alphabet has rendered to civilization would have been considerably reduced in importance if the Egyptians had not handed over to the Near Eastern countries, and through them to Greece and Rome also, an excellent writing material, lighter than stone or clay tablets and cheaper and more plentiful than leather, namely papyrus. Papyrus was made from the aquatic plant, also called papyrus, *Cyperus Papyrus* being its botanical name, which was extremely plentiful in Egypt in ancient times, especially in the marshes of the Nile delta, though at the present day it is found only in the Sudan and equatorial Africa. By cutting thin slices from the stem of the plant, laying them crosswise in two layers, and beating these together, the Egyptians, from the beginning of the third millennium B.C., produced pliable sheets of whitish writing material on which they wrote with a fine brush from the rush *Juncus maritimus*, using black ink made of soot and gum and red ink similarly prepared from ground red ochre. Any number of sheets pasted together formed a strip which could easily be rolled to form the papyrus roll which was the ancient book. It was indubitably the invention of the alphabet which prompted the export of papyrus to Syria, especially through the port of Byblos, and it is after this town that the Greeks first called papyrus *byblos*, later differentiating from it *biblion*, 'book'. The origin of the name papyrus itself is not certain, though the suggestion that it is the Egyptian *pa-pūro, 'that (i.e. the plant) of the king', is attractive in view of the fact that under the dynasty of the Ptolemies, and probably before, the fabrication of papyrus and its sale and export were royal monopolies.

Owing to the extremely dry climate of the country, manuscripts or documents on papyrus have often been preserved in Egypt down to our time, while elsewhere, because of its nature, papyrus perished unless carbonized by fire. The contemporary use of leather and more particularly of parchment in time affected the popularity of papyrus, but for many centuries it was the main vehicle of Greek and Roman written thought and remained so down to the eighth century of our era, when it was gradually ousted from use by a new writing material coming from the East, the paper made from old linen rags. But even so the newcomer has a name derived from that of its predecessor.

It can be seen that the transmission and preservation of the Greek and Roman literary works which were the basis of our modern civilization are largely if not wholly due to an Egyptian invention and it is clearly here that our world has contracted its greatest debt to ancient Egypt.

J. ČERNÝ

BIBLIOGRAPHY

On various Egyptian words preserved in modern languages:

W. B. BISHAI, *The Coptic influence on Egyptian Arabic*, Baltimore, 1959.

A. H. GARDINER, 'The Egyptian origin of some English personal names', *Journ. American Oriental Soc.* lvi (1936), 189–197.

K. SETHE, 'Der Name des Phönix', *ZÄS* xlv (1908), 84–5.

—— 'Die ägyptischen Bezeichnungen für die Oasen und ihre Bewohner', *ZÄS* lvi (1920), 44–54.

—— 'Die Bau- und Denkmalsteine der alten Ägypter und ihre Namen', *Sitzungsberichte der preuss. Akademie der Wissenschaften, Phil.-hist. Klasse*, 1933, 864–912.

H. WIESMANN, 'Adobe', *ZÄS* lii (1914), 130.

On the origin of the alphabet:

G. R. DRIVER, *Semitic writing* (Schweich Lectures), London, 1948.

A. H. GARDINER, 'The Egyptian origin of the Semitic alphabet', *JEA* iii (1916), 1–16.

K. SETHE, 'Der Ursprung des Alphabets', *Nachrichten von der Gesellschaft der Wissenschaften zu Göttingen*, 1916, Heft 2, 81 ff.

—— 'Die neuentdeckte Sinaischrift', *Nachrichten . . . Göttingen*, 1917, 437 ff.

On papyrus:

J. ČERNÝ, *Paper and books in ancient Egypt*, London, 1952.

A. LUCAS, *Ancient Egyptian materials and industries*, 4th ed. (J. R. Harris), London, 1962, pp. 137–40.

W. SCHUBART, *Das Buch bei den Griechen und Römern*, 3rd ed., Leipzig, 1961.

9

LITERATURE

IT is clear from a rereading of the first edition of the present work that the idea of 'legacy' may be interpreted in a number of different ways. In approaching Egyptian literature, the subject of this chapter, it is possible first to consider the whole, to view it as something complete in itself, in which case it represents a stage on a long road stretching on down to our own times and which, without it, would not have been quite the same, or, if you prefer, a tributary which has served among many others to create the course we still follow. This contribution, however indirect and slender it may be, does constitute a form of heritage. But in addition to this historical role of Egypt in the development of world literature there is also the fact that the labour of scholars has made accessible to modern man the works of imagination and thought created by the ancient Egyptians. A source of capital, exploited in its own day, has thus been brought back into circulation like an inheritance long deferred. That many pharaonic writings are of little interest or positively alien to contemporary taste—as also for that matter are many of those surviving from classical antiquity and the Middle Ages—does not alter the fact that Egyptian literature, brought to life once more, will as a whole constitute for the future 'a part of the stock-in-trade of literary criticism' (Glanville).

Our debt to Egypt increases, and the concept of legacy becomes at the same time more personal and intimate, when in reading translations of pharaonic literature we find that there are works still capable of giving us pleasure, arousing our interest, or stirring our emotions. Their effect cannot be compared with that produced by Egyptian plastic art, but the fact remains that the 'Story of Sinuhe', some tales and poems, and certain maxims of wise men succeed in moving the modern reader by their intrinsic qualities. Considerations quite unrelated to the true worth of these works, in particular their antiquity, their provenance, and their exotic nature, endue them with a peculiar lustre common to everything coming from the banks of the Nile. The fascination exercised by ancient Egypt is responsible for modern novels which take it as their setting or borrow ideas from it, adapting them to different genres of writing—romantic, sentimental, *risqué*, occult, or detective. This too is an indirect form of the legacy of Egypt, and one which in many cases we could well do without.

The influence exercised by pharaonic literature while it was still a living force and the borrowings made from it in antiquity are of greater interest. Here again it is a question of Egypt's contribution to the development of world literature, but in a direct and more tangible form. Definite examples of such borrowings and influences are few, and are chiefly to be found in the wisdom texts—to which we shall return later. All too often there remains room for doubt. In the first place themes, ideas, and images which are common to Egyptian texts and, for example, the Bible may not necessarily have a single origin; some may have come into being spontaneously and independently under different skies. Psalm 104 to the glory of the Creator shows similarities with Akhenaten's hymn to the sun, yet even an indirect connection may be disputed. Moreover, Egypt is not the only possible claimant to the role of initiator and inspirer. Other civilizations, to begin with that of Mesopotamia, are in a position to contest this honour. It is not easy to establish who was the first to create or innovate in this or that field, and even if priority in time be established it does not of itself constitute proof of paternity.

In the face of so many uncertainties, and rather than launch into dubious rivalry in the manner of the *panbabylonistes* and their successors, it is better not to endeavour at any price to make

Egyptian literature the fount from which drank all other peoples
of antiquity. One should not therefore dwell upon Egypt's possible contribution to other nations, but concentrate rather upon
those elements which find a parallel in genres exploited later, in
themes treated elsewhere, and in literary forms employed down
to the present. The Egyptians will be seen to have been pioneers
or forerunners in many fields, and their credit is no less if others
were not able to benefit from their discoveries. An achievement,
even if not followed up, has also its place in the legacy.

Whatever idea one may form of the pharaonic heritage, it is
in the end the background and particular interests of any one
reader which will determine what in Egyptian literature represents for him a real legacy. The choice of each individual is of
necessity subjective; the reverberations and their intensity depend
on his taste and experience. In the following pages the reader
will himself discover what conjures up for him a familiar image
or a specific memory.

Conventionally one should take account in this outline only of
texts which are known, but in so doing one would inevitably give a
distorted picture of Egyptian literature, for the lacunae are many.
The gaps in our knowledge are due primarily to the fragile nature
of papyrus, the material principally used for writing literary
texts. Papyrus is not strong and cannot long withstand damp.
The best conditions for its preservation are found in the peace
of the tombs cached in the arid desert, and as a result innumerable funerary texts have survived to the present day. But, if the
dead considered it useful to equip themselves with these *grimoires*
for the after-life, they were not in the habit of taking their secular
literature on their last journey, unless for a particular reason.
Literary papyri have indeed been found in cemeteries, but this
was not where they were normally deposited. Their proper
environment, the towns, did not offer the same advantage of
security and dryness. With rare exceptions it is the few centres
situated beyond the land flooded by the Nile that have provided

papyri. If Western Thebes with its villages and cemeteries is the place where the harvest has been the richest in all Egypt, the actual city of Thebes itself, because of its proximity to the river, has not produced a single specimen. The same is true of the Memphis area, where the ancient capital has not yielded one manuscript, while excavation on the Saqqara plateau has brought to light a good many. One can only conclude that the great majority of literary papyri have perished.

Each new discovery of manuscripts supplies an appreciable quota of new texts. A jar unearthed in 1891 near El-Hiba concealed three rolls including the 'Misfortunes of Wenamūn' and an obscure narrative in epistolary form. The box discovered by Quibell in 1895-6 in a tomb beneath the magazines of the Ramesseum contained, among many other manuscripts, two new ethical writings. The most recent of the great discoveries, made about 1928 at Deir el-Medina, brought to light two stories, the 'Conflict of Horus and Seth' and the 'Blinding of Truth', as well as some fine love poems. If our knowledge of literature were approaching completeness, the number of unknown works in these batches of new manuscripts would not have been so great. Nor does it diminish as time goes on and discoveries accumulate. In the last few years we have become aware of the existence of a new tale of the Middle Kingdom and of a wisdom text of the Late Period. We are still far from reaching the end.

The extent of the losses suffered, and thus of our ignorance, may further be gauged from the unsatisfactory state of such texts as are known. Of about seventy different works noted up to the present, only some fifteen are preserved more or less complete, and of these several exist only in a single manuscript, while the better copies of some others are partially defective—facts which do not make the study of them any easier. Turning to the less fortunate group we find about twenty-five works surviving in too fragmentary a condition for their plots to be reconstructed or their exact nature or significance established, to which may be added those 'classical' authors who are no more to us than names, and works of which almost nothing remains but the title. How many more are there of whose very existence we have not the least suspicion?

This lamentable state of affairs compels us, if not to speculate on the gaps, at least to take them broadly into consideration, and in order to be in the best position to do this we must try to see how they are distributed. The first question to be asked is which works were most frequently copied and so had the best chance of coming down to us. In this respect the literature of the schools occupies a particularly favoured position. For centuries students learned to write by copying the same textbooks on to tablets and ostraca (potsherds and flakes of limestone). Examples of the same texts written on papyrus and belonging to teachers and men of letters sometimes came to be added to these classroom exercises. To give some idea of the total which this might represent, let us take the example of a manual called *Kemyt*, written about the year 2000 B.C. and copied, to our knowledge, more than any other, which despite the ravages of time has survived in some 400 partial copies. Certain major works of literature, too, appeared in the curriculum, such as the 'Story of Sinuhe', the 'Instruction of Amenemhet I', or the 'Prophecy of Neferty', and of these we also have a considerable number of duplicates. Next to this favoured group may be classed the works which, although little used in the schools, or not at all, enjoyed nevertheless a particular esteem among the learned and enlightened dilettanti. Here copies are less numerous, but such as survive are generally of better quality than the school versions. This is particularly the case with papyri containing the 'Complaints of the Peasant', the 'Instruction of Ptahhotpe', and the 'Instruction for Merikarē'. The smaller and less lasting the popularity of a work, the more uncertain inevitably are the chances of preservation.

Sheer accident may, however, upset one's estimate of probabilities. A papyrus has thus preserved for us a large part of an obscure work, the 'Dialogue between a Man Weary of Life and His Own Soul', while of the 'Instructions of Hardjedef', one of the most admired works of Egyptian literature, we possess no more than scraps. There is, nevertheless, one literary genre in which one may presume particularly extensive gaps, namely, in the field of popular stories which were commonly transmitted by oral tradition and which only appear accidentally in written literature—no doubt in a civilized and embellished form. It is significant that nearly all the stories we possess are extant in single manuscripts; about twenty are thus known, the majority reduced to shreds. In this connection myths and legends as well as the stories handed down by classical authors no doubt provide a useful supplement. One must, however, resign oneself to the idea that a large part of Egyptian folklore is lost beyond recall.

In the light of what has been said it will be appreciated that it is not easy to retrace the history of Egyptian literature. One has to be content with a rough outline. We do not possess a single literary manuscript dating from the Old Kingdom, though we know from later copies and from tradition that literature was already flourishing in the Memphite period. It was then that the wisdom genre came into being, represented chiefly by the *sbōyet*, 'Instruction', which a wise man is supposed to address to his son in order to pass on his experience and instruct him in the art of living. The oldest known author was the famous Imhotep, adviser to King Djoser (Third Dynasty, *c.* 2650 B.C.), who was to be deified in the Late Period, yet nothing remains of his didactic work. It is quite probable that some of his maxims survive, reproduced and commented upon by later writers, or quoted in biographies, but they cannot be identified, for the Egyptians had an unfortunate habit of not indicating their sources even when they knew them perfectly well, nor did they make use of any equivalent of our inverted commas to indicate quotations. So the maxims of Imhotep are lost, maxims which were still current at least half a millennium after his death. The situation is a little better in the case of another celebrated moralist, the prince Hardjedef, considered to be a son of Khufu (Cheops). A few fragments of his 'Instruction' have come down to us in school copies of some 1,500 years after his time. We read that a man of means should set up a home and build a house for his son; that he should take care to make his tomb excellent and to set up a landed estate. In the badly preserved continuation of the text, we gather too that it is well to enlist a mortuary priest who is worthy of being endowed with the best fields, for 'he is more useful to you than an heir'; after all, 'death is the haven of all men'. In the little that remains of this wisdom text there is, as may be seen, much concern with death and preparations for the next life—a sign of the times; we are in the period when the great pyramid of Giza was built. A less illustrious individual than Imhotep and Hardjedef has been luckier than they; the last two pages of his 'Instruction' survive intact in a good copy. We gather the name of his son Kagemni, but the name of the author, who was vizier, is lost; it is thought that his name was Kaires. As for the date, Egyptologists do not agree with the text itself, which ascribes the work to the end of the Third Dynasty; they would prefer to bring it down towards the end of the Fifth. In the extant portion of this wisdom book we find in particular advice on how to behave at table. The invitation to frugality illustrates 'the call to suppression of self, to modesty, and to moderation permeating the book' (Gardiner). Here clearly formulated is the ideal of Egyptian moralists, a blend of reserve and discretion; the wise man is already called 'the silent one'.

The only writing of the Old Kingdom that has survived intact is the 'Instruction of Ptahhotpe', also a vizier, who lived at the end of the Fifth Dynasty (c. 2350 B.C.). Here for the first time we are able to appreciate a wisdom text in its entirety. It is a learned work, verbose and affected, the product of an already long tradition which the author is concerned to hand down by quoting maxims of his predecessors which he comments upon and develops. He teaches good manners and also the art of eloquent speaking so dear to the Egyptians, and which often consisted in knowing when to keep quiet—which brings us back to 'the silent one'. The art of listening is the essential counterpart of speech; he who knows how to listen gains knowledge, is obedient, and carries out instructions well. Like Kaires, Ptahhotpe addresses himself to his son, whom he is preparing to succeed him, the 'Instruction' being, in other words, designed primarily to mould the higher cadres of the state. So it is that a great part of these maxims is taken up with rules of etiquette, obedience, and faithfulness to superiors, the way to treat inferiors, how to give orders, and how to give judgement; they are also concerned with private life, the wife, the son, and friends. The aim is to succeed in one's career and in life, enjoying universal esteem and respect. In this context religion has little part to play; in speaking of God the writer principally has the king in mind. But opportunism is not inconsistent with moral sense. Some maxims are not without nobility, as when, at the beginning, Ptahhotpe declares that 'the limits of skill cannot be reached', or when, later, he exalts the primacy of truth and justice (*ma'at*), a theme which recalls a passage in the first of the two apocryphal Books of Esdras.

The writers whom we know from the Old Kingdom all belonged to the immediate entourage of the Pharaohs and were exponents of the didactic genre. The position changes with the collapse of the Memphite state. The First Intermediate Period (*c.* 2181–2052 B.C.) brings misery, insecurity, and restlessness; social equilibrium is replaced by conflicts and upheavals which find their reflection in literature. Kings begin to speak, and so do peasants. The literary genres multiply. We see the appearance of political and social diatribe, of philosophic discussion in dialogue form, of a type of discourse which is both a complaint and a critique, of the royal testament, of prophecy—and so on. The prevalent tone is sombre. Of this rich harvest, as of the output

of the Old Kingdom, we possess only the few writings preserved
and recopied by succeeding generations, in so far as such copies
have survived.

Though formal proof is lacking, it is to this troubled period
that the 'Admonitions of an Egyptian Sage'—or at least the subject
treated in this work—is commonly assigned. The sage, who was
called Ipuwēr (?) and was perhaps a chief singer, moans interminably about the anarchy which reigns in the land, about the lost
monarchy, about the misery of the propertied classes and the
arrogance of the yokels who have appropriated their riches. It
is the eternal jeremiad of the conservative. In his hands the reversal
of material fortunes already savours of the literary form and provides an opportunity for rhetorical exercises. The theme was to
find favour for quite a long time to come. It seems that in his
indignation the sage even goes so far as to blame the Creator himself and to reproach him for having arranged things badly so that
he bears a measure of responsibility for the miseries of Egypt.
To about the same period belongs, it is thought, the 'Dialogue
between a Man Weary of Life and His Own Soul', a text of which
the interpretation remains uncertain. The man, disheartened by
the wickedness which surrounds him and tired of living, wants
to put an end to his existence; he is afraid his soul will desert him,
since it is opposed to his design. The soul will have the last word
in the discussion, but the man, and with him the author, has all
the time he wants to give vent to his grievances in stanzas of real
beauty. Death again is the subject of the 'Song of the Harper'
from the tomb of King Inyotef. The writer expresses his doubts
as to the chances of survival and urges enjoyment of life and the
pleasures which it offers so long as one is on earth. Such ideas are
exceptional in Egyptian literature. The text was destined to enjoy
a certain vogue in the New Kingdom and to provoke a reaction;
death and the hereafter were to be exalted in funeral-banquet
songs no less remarkable than it.

It is justice which is the theme of the 'Complaints of the

Peasant', the action of which is set at the end of the First Intermediate Period (*c.* 2070 B.C.). The story of the oasis dweller,
beaten and deprived of his property, who demands restitution,
provides a vehicle for nine petitions in which the oppressed man
stigmatizes dishonesty and exalts equity. One needs a taste for
flowery eloquence, with its imagery, repetitions, periods, and
apostrophies, to appreciate the pleading of the peasant, 'a fine
speaker indeed', and the Egyptians, for whom the mode of expression was often of equal or greater importance than the substance
of the thought, certainly relished these speeches. This form of
oratorical art, of which another very incomplete specimen survives,
must have been widely practised in Egypt, to judge from the
refinements and artifices of the one text of this type which has
been preserved intact. The 'Complaints of the Peasant' is also
remarkable for the skilful combination of the narrative portions
and the monologues—to which we shall have occasion to return.
Of similar date and also belonging to the decline of the kingdom
of Herakleopolis, which seems to have been a literary centre, the
'Instruction for Merikarē' is among the most outstanding works
which Egypt produced. To some extent an apologia, the text is
the testament of a Pharaoh, designed to instruct his successor to
the throne in the art of governing without injuring one's good
name or one's eternal salvation. It contains historical insights,
describes the political situation, and tells how to treat one's subjects, great and small, civil and military, and how to combat
enemies at home and abroad, as well as touching upon problems
of morals and religion—relations between man and God, piety,
ethical principles, the nature of the royal office, even a cosmogony,
unique of its kind, which makes man the goal of creation, and
finally the fundamental concept, nowhere so clearly expressed, of
the posthumous judgement which even the king himself cannot
escape. The idea of inevitable expiation haunts the writer, who
has faults with which to reproach himself. His advice, tinged with
resignation and pessimism, returns continually to the necessity of

inspiring affection, of practising justice, and of leading a pious and exemplary life. One is conscious that the Herakleopolitan kingdom is nearing its end.

With the Middle Kingdom, the state grows strong again, and Egypt gradually recovers its prosperity and power, but this restoration is not brought about without difficulties. After a long period of confusion the central authority lacks experience and reliable servants, and it is no mere coincidence that the beginning of the Middle Kingdom sees the appearance within a short time of two texts designed to school the officials of the renascent state and to instil in them a sense of the responsibilities and dignity of their office. One may imagine that these educational manuals were drawn up in response to an urgent need. They were to remain in use for some thousand years and it is only later copies of them that we possess. The first of these writings was called *Kemyt*, which seems to mean 'The Whole'. It is not impossible that a vague memory survived to the end of antiquity, and that the word 'chemistry', which first appears at that time, owes its origin to it. Contrary to late tradition, *Kemyt* contained nothing mysterious except perhaps for us who do not understand it very well. We find in it an impressive collection of epistolary formulae and pieces of advice on practising self-control and working hard at one's studies in order to become a well-to-do official of the central government. More imposing in scope, the second book, known as the 'Satire of the Crafts', is the work of the scribe Khety, of whom it was later to be said that he was 'the first' of Egyptian authors. It is a sign of the changing times that Khety bears no high-sounding titles and his 'Instruction' is addressed not to a future vizier, but to a student, his son, who is to enter the central school for scribes. The text begins with a quotation from *Kemyt* which is commented upon and developed. The underlying idea is that the career of a bureaucrat has no equal, and to illustrate this the author reviews different professions, pointing out their drawbacks and the miserable condition of those who follow them. In this way he describes the wretched existence of the potter, the stone-mason, the weaver, the barber, the fisherman—seventeen crafts in all, each one worse than the last according to him. After this comes some advice and reflections on the advantages of study. It is the motif of satire above all which was to be retained by posterity, to be taken up again and greatly exploited by the scribes of the New Kingdom and handed down as far as the Book of Ecclesiasticus (38: 24–30).

Also going back to the beginning of the Middle Kingdom is the 'Prophecy of Neferty', an apocryphon put into circulation to support the cause of a usurper, Amenemhet I, the founder of the Twelfth Dynasty. The narrative which introduces the prophecy and serves as its pretext places the prediction in the happy times of Snofru, the father of Khufu (Cheops). This device allows the seer to predict things which, at the time of the composition of the text, belong in fact to the past and the present. Drawing inspiration from the literature of pessimism he thus describes the trials and tribulations which await Egypt following the Old Kingdom and announces the coming of the Golden Age with the advent of Amenemhet, who takes on the appearance of a messiah. The interest of the text, which is skilfully constructed, is twofold. As an instance of the secondary use of the prophetic genre, it shows first that the latter flourished in Egypt before the Middle Kingdom. It will readily be acknowledged that messianic literature came into being in the First Intermediate Period when men had need of hope. There are even allusions to prophecies of this period, and very much later we shall find prophetic texts written in demotic or preserved in Greek versions. The apocryphon attributed to Neferty is the only pharaonic example of the genre to be preserved intact, a fake no doubt, but certainly for that very reason adhering to the rules of the divinatory style. It may be doubted whether any other people can boast of having used a similar artifice at so early a date. This leads on to the second point: the composition with a political bent, which we saw appearing in the previous period, has here become a propaganda tract. The Twelfth Dynasty is, at the very outset, mobilizing the resources of literature to establish itself in the country; it will make use of them again in other circumstances.

Amenemhet I died the victim of a conspiracy. His son, Senwosret I, succeeded in seizing power, but found himself in a difficult position. He therefore commissioned Khety, the author of the 'Satire of the Crafts', to draw up in the name of the deceased Pharaoh a political testament in such terms as to strengthen the throne. So at least may be reconstructed, with some degree of probability, the origin of the 'Instruction of Amenemhet I'. In accordance with the conventions of wisdom literature, the old king is regarded as giving instruction to his son and heir. He advises him to be firm and to trust no one, and gives as an example the ingratitude of the conspirators, all of whom were under obligation to him. He describes the attempt on his life and speaks of all that he accomplished during his reign. At once an apologia and an indictment, this work, full of bitterness, gives without doubt the most human picture of a Pharaoh to be found in Egyptian literature.

If the 'Prophecy' and the 'Instruction' we have mentioned belong to the literature of propaganda, the same cannot be said of the 'Story of Sinuhe', although this work is wholly favourable to Senwosret I. A product of circles close to the royal court, it expresses their feelings. The reverential attitude which is characteristic of it is also appropriate to its form, that of an autobiography, which relates it to the inscriptions in tombs. Although short by our standards—but Egyptian literary texts are never long and rarely amount to more than about twenty of our pages—this composition deserves to be called a novel. Adventure, psychology, and sentiment all play their part in the story of a servant of the queen who flees from Egypt on the tragic death of Amenemhet I, leads a dangerous existence in Syria, and returns home, covered in honours, to end his days at the royal residence. A hymn to the glory of Pharaoh, letters exchanged with Senwosret I, and a description of home-sickness set off a lively narrative, which reaches its climax with a duel between Sinuhe and a Syrian champion, and which ends with the triumphal finale of the reception at court, sketched skilfully and with spirit. It is not surprising that Rudyard Kipling appreciated this story.

The loyalist tendency is more sustained in two 'Instructions' which can be reconstructed in part with the aid of fragmentary extracts and copies. The first, whose author was a high dignitary, which gives some idea of its intended audience, explains the secret of happiness and success, consisting in veneration of the sovereign whose power is boundless and in fighting for his cause; this section contains a panegyric of the Pharaoh. There follows a recommendation to solicitude for the happiness of the people, without whom the propertied classes would be nothing. The second, entitled 'Instruction of a Man to his Son', was addressed, so far as one can see, to a large, popular audience to whom it held up the prospect of a better life if they too would revere the king. Add to these wisdom books a great hymn to Senwosret III, not to mention several texts of lesser importance, and one has some idea of the extent of the loyalist movement, which was undoubtedly not altogether spontaneous.

Apart from writings of this kind, there remain from the Middle Kingdom a few stories and some compositions of a moral and philosophical nature. It is difficult to speak of the latter because of their miserable state of preservation; even their date often remains uncertain and the same is true of their contents. In one of the best-preserved, it is evident that a certain scribe Sisobek has met with misfortunes which prompt him to discourse. The text appears to be put together in the manner of the 'Complaints of the Peasant', but the theme of the 'discourses' is different. Sisobek meditates aloud about life and death and about the uncertainty of human destiny; like other Egyptian sages, he dwells on the advantages of restraint in speech. Not a single line of this text, which was a long one, survives intact. There is less to be said about a collection of largely pessimistic maxims dealing with the nature of man and human relations, and less still about the 'discourse' of a fisherman of the Southern City (Thebes) or that of the priest of Sekhmet, Renseneb, of which only the opening words remain. There are other fragments too, also didactic, of which it is not known whether they come from lost works or from incomplete texts which are extant. One thing at least is certain, that in the field of wisdom literature the output was considerable, so that towards the middle of the Twelfth Dynasty Egypt had in this respect reached a certain degree of saturation both in subject-matter and manner of expression. The priest of Heliopolis, Khakheperrē'sonb, who knew the literature better than we do, complains in his 'Collection of Utterances'—of which only some twenty lines survive—of the difficulty of finding something new to say, and then, addressing himself to his heart, launches resolutely into a description of the troubles of his time, showing without a doubt that he knows his authors well.

Turning to the stories, we find, first, one in which a god has a great deal to say and a man dies in his garden from a snake bite; another is concerned with a vizier and the loading of a boat, then a gang arrives and someone is thrown into the water; a third refers to a certain Hay and a murder. A mythological narrative tells of the advances which Seth made to Horus, while, in a different text, a goddess seems to be interested in a shepherd who feels nothing but terror for her and thinks only of his flock. These pitiful fragments, in which there are glimpses of interesting plots and rapid action, excite the curiosity without ever satisfying it. Even more exasperating are the fragments of a story, sufficiently large and numerous to justify hopes of grasping the thread but which only reveal that the actors are all gods, involved in an adventure which vaguely recalls the myth of the eye of Rē. Equally unsatisfactory are the extensive fragments which describe the pleasures of fishing and fowling, or those, full of inane talk, which deal with a sporting king, Amenemhet II, who goes to seek relaxation in the Faiyûm. They are, in any case, scarcely stories.

Fortunately we possess the whole of the 'Story of the Shipwrecked Sailor'. A sailor recounts an extraordinary adventure which happened to him during a voyage in the Red Sea. His ship is destroyed in a storm, and the waves cast him up on an enchanted island ruled by a giant serpent. He receives the castaway kindly and sends him back to Egypt with lavish gifts, upon which the island disappears in the waves. The reader will already have noticed that the tale is reminiscent of several well-known stories; it is related to those of Sindbad the Sailor and Prince Zeyn Alasnam in the *Thousand and One Nights* or to the episode of the arrival of Odysseus among the Phaeacians in the *Odyssey*. It is, indeed, an archaic example of the fabulous tale of adventures at sea. The manuscript dates from about the nineteenth century B.C. and reproduces a more ancient text, which in turn goes back to an oral tradition. The narrative has the characteristics common to popular tales: simplicity of style and a taste for repetition. A remarkable detail is that the narrator addresses himself to a prince with whom he is returning on the Nile from Nubia to Egypt. The prince is apprehensive about the welcome the king has in store for him, and it is to give his master courage that the shipwrecked sailor relates his past experience which, after a tragic beginning, ends with the congratulations of Pharaoh. The story does not have the effect anticipated; the text ends with a cynical and disillusioned rejoinder from the listener. This brief narrative which forms the setting of the tale does not reveal the reason for the prince's fears. The manuscript begins *ex abrupto*, and it is probable that the text is not complete. It is an episode in a long story which must have begun with an account of the prince's expedition and his misfortunes, and ended with the audience before the king, preceded perhaps by some incidents which retrieved the situation. One may even suppose that, within this broad framework, several adventures were recounted to the prince and that the 'Story of the Shipwrecked Sailor' was one of a series of stories all of which had a common pretext.

Indeed, ancient Egypt was already familar with the literary device of setting separate stories into a narrative which served to connect them and provided a reason for their telling—a form made famous by, among other works, the *Thousand and One Nights*. The Westcar papyrus even shows that the Egyptians had perfected the idea. The beginning and end of the manuscript are lost, but for once they can be reconstructed in broad outline. The story begins at the court of Khufu (Cheops) of the Fourth Dynasty, who, doubtless to amuse himself, asks his sons to tell him tales about the feats of magicians. The princes oblige in turn, the result being a series of short, simple stories. It is not known how much is lost. In the part which survives there is the end of an adventure occurring in the time of King Djoser (Third Dynasty). The next marvel is the vengeance of a cuckolded sorcerer in the reign of Nebka (Third Dynasty) who makes a crocodile of wax, brings it to life, and makes it carry off his successful rival. In the third tale a magician folds back the water of a lake like a cloth in order to recover a piece of jewellery lost by one of the girls rowing Snofru, the father of Khufu, in a barge. The stories follow one another in chronological order; this last one finishes with the past, and the next is set in the present. A magician brought before Khufu replaces the heads of decapitated geese and restores them to life. This little tale, complete in itself, is comparable to the others, but it is linked with the prologue and serves as a transition to what follows. His feats performed, the magician prophesies incidentally to Khufu the end of his dynasty and the imminent birth of three children of Rē, destined for the throne. This birth of the Kings of the Fifth Dynasty, in which some goddesses intervene as midwives, is described at length, and the manuscript breaks off soon after. The lost conclusion of the papyrus will have told of the vicissitudes which led to the change in the ruling family. The tales are thus bound closely together, in such a way that eventually the narrative which forms the pretext becomes in its turn a tale of wonders. One cannot but admire the cleverness of the arrangement, while wondering whether the montage was not accomplished at the stage when scribes made a written collection of these stories of ancient times.

The Westcar papyrus dates from the Hyksos period (1652–1554 B.C.) and, to judge from the language, the text which it reproduces is not much older, though the stories which it contains take place during the Old Kingdom, some thousand years earlier. Despite this long lapse of time, the text is not without historical value. It preserves, transposed into legend, the memory of the devotion of the Fifth Dynasty to the cult of Rē, and all the kings and princes named really existed. Some even have substance: Hardjedef shows learning and urbanity, as becomes the author of a wisdom text; the good King Snofru is pleasantly familiar, as popular tradition demands; Khufu is arrogant and hard— Herodotus too preserves this unsympathetic impression of the builder of the great pyramid.

The history of another text makes it possible to appreciate in a tangible way how a tradition concerning a king of the Old Kingdom could be handed down right to the time when the Greeks, coming into the Nile valley, became acquainted with Egyptian tales. We have two, perhaps three, fragmentary manuscripts of the 'Story of Neferkarē and the General Sisene'. The more recent dates from the eighth to sixth centuries B.C., the older from the fourteenth century; the composition must go back another two to four centuries, and the action of the plot is set in the time of King Neferkarē, probably Pepy II of the Sixth Dynasty (*c.* 2200 B.C.). The route is thus clearly marked, and it is evident that the story came down to classical times in written form. Only two episodes of the tale are known. In one, some musicians and singers by performing prevent a plaintiff from making himself heard before the court. In the other, Neferkarē makes clandestine visits to the general at night, shadowed by an amateur detective who tries to get to the bottom of these queer goings-on. Without knowing the remainder of the text, we cannot tell whether in the end these comic stories did not take a tragic or edifying turn. Irreverent as they are, they belong to the same ribald genre as certain stories retailed by Herodotus, such as the experience of King Pheron or the treasure of Rhampsinitus, a famous tale attested in about twenty versions throughout Europe and Asia. The similarity in inspiration to the 'Story of Neferkarē' makes it probable that all these anecdotes first saw light on the banks of the Nile, and ancient Egypt thus appears as a great creative force in the realm of folklore.

With the last story we are already approaching the New Kingdom. The Second Intermediate Period, unlike the First, was not distinguished for its literature, so far as one can tell, and it is in the time of the Empire that output revives in the literary field, without, however, attaining the brilliance and originality which it enjoyed in the past. To the New Kingdom, nevertheless, must be credited the creation of a genre not previously attested—the love poem. Of these, two collections on papyrus are known, as well as two other groups and a number of fragments. These texts, which are not earlier than the Nineteenth Dynasty, have a number of points in common; already a developed form of poetry, it obeys its own conventions, makes use of word plays, and has its own themes and imagery. It knows the sickness of love, it invokes the dawn, the moment of separation, and has its stock hero, the prince Mehy, who seems to have had the reputation of a Don Juan. The lovers are never named; they are called 'brother' and 'sister', as in the 'Song of Songs', which is similar in inspiration to these poems. Nature occupies an important place; the trees talk and the flowers and birds are an accompaniment to the lovers' passion; the affairs are set in rustic surroundings or take place by the water's edge. The lovers describe their feelings in high-flown words, express their desire and impatience in artful comparisons and speak gracefully of their joys and hopes and deceptions. One must read these poems to appreciate their quality.

'Despite all their defects, they are of inestimable value for the world history of lyric expression' (Gardiner). This mannered, and even precious, artistry, almost totally devoid of sensuality, is well attuned to the refined tastes of the New Kingdom. The banquets which were then in vogue provided an opportunity ideally suited to the performance of love songs, perhaps in mime and to a musical accompaniment. If such was their genesis and original purpose, they quickly attained the status of written literature. They were read for pleasure in themselves just as the stories were read. The two principal collections are found in papyri which also contain works of fiction, to which we shall refer anon.

Among the numerous stories which from their language or subject-matter may be attributed to the New Kingdom, none is distinguished by a compositional skill comparable to the linking of the tales in the Westcar papyrus; none includes even an introductory narrative. Nevertheless, one of the two Late Egyptian stories which have survived intact is peculiar in combining in a single story two narratives of quite different origin. The first part of the 'Story of Two Brothers' in fact makes use of the situation made famous by the episode of Joseph and Potiphar's wife or the conflict between Phaedra and Hippolytus. The second part adapts a basic tenet of Egyptian theology, that of the self-creating demiurge. The story here follows the successive deaths, rebirths, and transformations of the hero until his final triumph, and one may note several themes attested in the folklore of Europe and Asia. The first part is a human drama set in the milieu of the fellahin, whose life and habits are realistically described, the marvellous playing only an insignificant part. The second half, on the other hand, is steeped in the strange and the supernatural. The hero, Bata, is in the first part at variance with his elder brother Anupu, and has analogies with the god Seth, but in the sequel his tribulations recall the figure of Osiris. The formal connection of these very different narratives is established through the person of the principal character and his brother, who appear throughout the story, yet this would not be sufficient to make the two parts hang together were the theme of the plot not the same in both—the persecution of a righteous man by an evil woman. She appears first in the form of a peasant woman who tries to seduce her young brother-in-law and who, on his refusing, falsely accuses him to her husband, and then we find the wife of Bata, who becomes the favourite of Pharaoh and persecutes her husband with her hatred. In both cases the machinations miscarry just in time, and the treacherous woman receives the punishment she deserves. The story is clearly addressed to a male audience and the view of the weaker sex is scarcely flattering; nor is it more so in certain other narratives. It is, however, of some interest that at no point does the story-teller comment on the conduct of his characters, or express an opinion about even the most unsympathetic of them. In Egypt the tone of stories is always objective—it is the rule—and only the behaviour of the protagonists and their remarks make it possible to distinguish the good from the bad.

In the 'Conflict of Horus and Seth', this rule is applied with particular strictness. The text, also practically intact, deals in an off-hand manner with an important mythological theme of which a fragment has already been encountered in the Middle Kingdom, the rivalry existing between the two divine claimants to the throne of Egypt. There is an interminable trial before the ennead convened under the presidency of Rē, a trial continually interrupted by all kinds of incidents involving magic, violence, trickery, and indecency. Certain of the anecdotes reappear later among other peoples; thus the lewd gesture of Hathor, who displays her nakedness before her father Rē to cheer him up, is found in Greece and Japan. The story-teller does not seek to edify his audience with the sacred story; he merely wishes to amuse them and make them laugh at the expense of the gods. It is mythology 'somewhat in the spirit of Offenbach' (Gardiner). The denizens of the Egyptian Olympus are here completely lacking in that majestic serenity to which one is accustomed; on the contrary, the picture given is often one of common mediocrity. The irreverent manner of representing the Pharaoh has already been noted in connection with another story. It is thus that the stories serve as an outlet of relief against conformity and devout humility. One must not be too surprised or embarrassed by the attitude of mind which such texts reveal; this mild form of impiety is found among the Egyptians precisely because they were 'the most pious of men'. The 'Conflict of Horus and Seth' is not devoid of moral sense. Right triumphs over might, and Horus ultimately wins the case and receives the inheritance of his father Osiris.

The triumph of right over injustice is also the subject of another story, 'Truth and Falsehood', the beginning of which is lost. Its pattern is that of the Osirian myth, the villain ill-treats his brother and the latter's son revenges him. This theme, freely treated, is transposed into the human sphere and in some ways gives a faithful picture of Egyptian life. But the two brothers have allegorical names; they personify the concepts of justice and iniquity, a device much exploited in many literatures. Moreover, the court which in the beginning condemns Truth and which in the end reinstates him thanks to his son's subterfuge, is made up of the divine ennead—which takes us back to the conflict of Osiris, Seth, and Horus. This story, more than any other, finds parallels in the folklore of different countries, not only as regards the basic plot, but also in specific incidents. Its mythological ties, evidence of greater importance than its date, give it an undoubted priority among all such tales.

In contrast to this story, that of the 'Doomed Prince' has no obvious mythical antecedents, though it includes many marvellous features. The tale, one of the most successful of those extant, has as its theme man and his destiny. At the birth of a prince of the royal house, certain goddesses declare that 'he shall perish by the crocodile, by the serpent, or by the dog'. When he grows up, the young man goes off to Syria, where he conceals his identity and, victorious in a contest, wins the hand of a princess, as in

R

many popular romances. His wife saves him from the serpent, but the other two threats remain and are closing in upon him when the manuscript breaks off. There has been much discussion as to the possible outcome of the story, but in fact there is no great cause for anxiety about the hero. A legend preserved by Diodorus provides a parallel for the last surviving episode and suggests that all ended for the best. The innate optimism of the Pharaohs' subjects allowed for a compromise with destiny which, under the Egyptian sun, ceased to appear inescapable.

In the 'Doomed Prince', the king, the hero's father, is a fictional and anonymous character, as so often in folk literature. The same does not apply to the following three stories, which have a historical basis. The 'Quarrel of Apopi and Seqenenrē' takes us back to the period of the Hyksos domination in Egypt. In the preamble, which alone survives, the King of Avaris sends an embarrassing message to the Theban Pharaoh, who is at a loss how to reply. It is probable that the conflict, which is over some hippopotami, was of a religious nature. However that may be, one may rest assured that the Theban ruler eventually had the better of it, even though the mummy of Seqenenrē, preserved in Cairo Museum, is riddled with wounds and shows that in fact he died in battle—doubtless against the Hyksos. The 'Taking of Joppa' (the modern Jaffa) relates to the campaigns of the great conqueror Thutmose III. The general Djehuty, the hero of the story, is a historical character, but the end of the story, all that remains, belongs to legend. There is a description of a *ruse de guerre* not unlike the Trojan Horse or the jars of the forty thieves in the story of Ali Baba in the *Thousand and One Nights*. It may be noted in passing that there is also another tale concerned with the Syrian wars of Thutmose III, the King appearing in person in the meagre fragments it has been possible to put together.

Since we chose to begin our review of the stories of the New Kingdom with the best-preserved, we now come to the most fragmentary texts, among which the 'Legend of Astarte' takes pride of place. It took all the knowledge and insight of Sir Alan Gardiner to discover the thread of this mythological narrative from the mutilated remains of a large roll of some twenty pages. The legend traces the conflict between the gods and the insatiable sea who exacts tribute, demands that Astarte be given to him as wife, and threatens to engulf everything, only, it seems, to be subdued eventually by Seth. A Late Egyptian version of an older myth concerning the struggle against the watery element, the story has parallels in other literatures, particularly in the Ras Shamra tablets. Passing from this text to the 'Story of the Ghostly Revenant' we descend from high mythology to the legend of popular superstition. Its protagonists are a high priest of Amūn and a dead man who lived in the time of the Eleventh Dynasty; the latter's tomb is in ruins and the priest attends to its restoration. The tale is clearly Theban and must have originated among the inhabitants of the necropolis. We also have a few fragments of another ghost story; conjured up by a Pharaoh, the spirit appears floating in the air. . . Such are the meagre remains of a class of tale which was certainly very common among a people as pre-occupied as the Egyptians with the dead and their existence.

There are also extant fragments of a few other stories. The best-preserved, consisting of two unpublished pages, introduces the god Herishef, and a goddess, who play tricks on each other. A goddess appears again in some scraps of narratives primarily concerned with a Pharaoh. A king and a young beauty are also involved in a text of which so little remains that it is impossible to tell whether it is the same story as that just mentioned. In yet another excerpt, a female being appears to a man while he is asleep; the result is bloodshed and tears. Of other fragments, lastly, it is possible to read just enough to be sure that they came from stories.

We have kept two texts until the end because they are of a distinct type and of later date, belonging to the end of the Ramessid period (*c.* 1075 B.C.). The 'Misfortunes of Wenamūn' represents, properly speaking, a report of a mission; even the actual arrangement of the sole-surviving manuscript is characteristic of a document of this nature. But the numerous dialogues, certain of the incidents, and the descriptions and reflections which intersperse the narrative, not to speak of its vivacity, are hardly suited to the official style. There can be little doubt that this is a case of the literary elaboration of a genuine report, just as it may be assumed that the 'Story of Sinuhe' is derived from an autobiographical tomb inscription. 'Wenamūn' is the story of a Theban envoy who goes to Byblos to buy wood intended for the sacred bark of Amūn. Egypt enjoys little prestige abroad at the time, and the mission proves difficult, even dangerous. Theft, pursuit by sea, attempted murder, and endless discussion and bargaining mark the stages of the journey, which takes the Egyptian from port to port as far as Alasia (? Cyprus), when the manuscript breaks off. This 'most fascinating of all Egyptian tales' (Gardiner) is a sort of minor *Odyssey*, without the marvellous element, and the hero, astute, stubborn, and energetic, calls to mind Odysseus. In the jar which contained this papyrus was also another roll which, though intact, is not of the same interest. The text is corrupt often to the point of being unintelligible. Against a background of anarchy, revolt, and foreign invasion, the author describes his misfortunes and his wanderings throughout Egypt. There is thus a certain parallelism between 'Wenamūn' and this narrative, which is presented in the form of a letter.

The Egyptians had, indeed, raised the epistolary genre to the level of a literary form. Already under the Old Kingdom one sees the importance they attached to the art of composing their correspondence. It is in the New Kingdom that the idea develops of diverting the letter from its original purpose and employing it for other ends. This development takes place in scholastic circles to serve the needs of teaching. From the Middle Kingdom, following the pattern of the book of *Kemyt* (above, p. 230), teachers compose collections of model letters to put before their pupils. The process of evolution leads to 'Epistolary Instructions', in which, besides letters borrowed from the archives or entirely invented, there are included little compositions of all kinds, whether introduced as epistles or not—hymns and prayers, royal protocols and official titularies, and reprimands and encouragements addressed to students in the hope of awakening their dormant enthusiasm. It is here that the 'Satire of the Crafts' (above, p. 230) is revived and blossoms; certain pieces describing the misfortunes of the peasant or the unhappy lot of the soldiers are instinct with life and full of animation. The 'Satirical Letter of the Scribe Hori' (Pap. Anastasi i) reveals a different concept; a variety of subjects are here treated in one and the same letter, so that it assumes exaggerated proportions—twenty-eight pages. The text takes the form of a reply to a malicious epistle; the writer counter-attacks, makes fun at the expense of his correspondent, and poses tricky and difficult questions, particularly on Syrian geography, which, interspersed with descriptions and even bits of narrative, form in effect a miscellany of information and problems intended for students. The pill is sugared, and it is not surprising that no Late Egyptian composition was so frequently copied as this.

The collections to which we have just referred might on occasion include moral precepts. There is even a hybrid text, in which wisdom takes up more space than the pieces about the advantages of a bureaucratic career or the drawbacks of the military profession. This 'Instruction', of which the beginning and part of the end are lost, was perhaps composed by a certain scribe Amennakhte. The principal interest of the work lies in a long eulogy in honour of the great moralists of former times. This passage, so far unique in Egyptian literature, is evidence of a taste for literary history, and reveals sound knowledge. The theme is that the fame of a writer ensures his immortality better than the pyramids. The author is here offering a new solution to the problem of survival which others, of whom he is aware, had tried to solve since the

Old Kingdom. Thus it is that thinkers echo one another down through the centuries.

Apart from this composition, and disregarding some small fragments, there are extant only two wisdom texts, and these of the traditional type, which may be attributed to the New Kingdom, the one to the beginning, the other to the extreme end of this period. The 'Instruction of the Scribe Any', which dates probably from the Eighteenth Dynasty, is well preserved, save for the first pages, in versions of indifferent quality, in which the language has been modernized. So far as it is possible to follow the author's thought, it is not distinguished by any peculiar elevation. Any's ideal is limited to cultivating his garden, both literally and metaphorically; family, home, and daily work are the centre of his interests. A scribe in a Theban chapel, he belongs to a limited circle. The prudent and reserved wise man, so dear to Egyptian moralists, becomes in his hands a timorous being. One of the most successful passages in the book is that in which he commends filial piety and recalls all that a mother does for her child. In the matter of religion, questions of ritual come first; it is, however, necessary to 'pray with a loving heart, all of whose words are hidden'. Any is as superstitious as he is pious, and devotes a whole paragraph, unique of its kind, to the harm which can be done to the fields and in the house by a spirit one has not succeeded in placating. At the end of the book, a discussion takes place between the sage and his son and disciple, who finds the 'Instruction' difficult to follow for a beginner, while the father insists on the value of the training. The dialogue form, which we have already encountered in the 'Man Weary of Life' (above, p. 228), appears to have been quite widely employed in the literature of the New Kingdom, though the 'Instruction' of Any is the only text to preserve a good example.

With the 'Instruction of Amenemope' we come to one of the most interesting and controversial texts in Egyptian literature, for this work, preserved complete in a good copy and in some partial versions, shows striking parallels with part of the Biblical

Book of Proverbs (chiefly 22:17–23:11). The analogies are such
that a connection is beyond doubt, and the question is to know
in which direction the borrowing took place. All the probabilities
are in favour of the priority of Amenemope. The passages common
to both have precedents, sometimes of great antiquity, in the
wisdom tradition of Egypt, and there are even specific pointers
back to Amenemope, as in the mention of 'thirty chapters' (Prov.
22:20) which corresponds to the number of sections in the former.
It may therefore be regarded, without much risk of error, as a
purely Egyptian book. The themes treated are for the most part
age-old; there are some among them we have met before—
reserve, prudence, discretion, frugality, obedience to superiors,
respect for age, and the need to inspire affection in people. As
a high official in the administration of agriculture and land
registration, Amenemope stresses the sanctity of weights and
measures, respect for landed property, and strictness in drawing
up deeds, which is nothing very new either. If the book has some
features which are peculiar to it, the same has been seen to be
true of many others. As regards the form of the work, Amenemope
resorts more to similies and imageries than his predecessors; as
regards the substance he is distinguished by his charitable disposition, by his uncompromising sense of honesty, by the clear-cut
distinction he makes between 'the silent one' and 'the impas-
sioned one', that is between the upright sage and the perverse
fool, and above all by his profound religiosity. His whole thought
is permeated with it. The conviction that the ways of God are
unfathomable, that 'man proposes, God disposes', leads to a
certain passivity. Optimism and self-confidence belong to the
past, the pursuit of success is replaced by quiet happiness 'in the
hand of God'. The text dates from the eleventh or tenth century
B.C., when Egypt in decline had lost her exuberant vitality never
again to recover it.

Before passing to the Late Period, two compositions at least
remain to be mentioned. We have from the New Kingdom a

few items from a collection of short maxims which as a rule take up a line each and all begin in the same way, with a negative injunction. Simpler and less sophisticated than the maxims of the wisdom books, these pieces of advice may represent the popular wisdom which was to occupy a position of no small importance in demotic literature. In a very different genre, the 'Case of the Stomach *v.* the Head' is a dispute over precedence. The beginning of the text, which is all that remains, gives only the opening of the speeches, and one cannot tell whether the arguments of the parties alone were sufficient to decide whether stomach or head was superior, or whether in the end some evidence was produced— unless of course, the conclusion was that the parts of the body, being interdependent, were useless one without the other. Such at least is the moral suggested by parallels, for this is a theme well known in fables since classical antiquity. It is doubtful whether the 'Case' is properly speaking one of these, for at present they are definitely attested only from a much later period, in demotic literature.

With the dark ages of the Libyan hegemony (tenth to eighth centuries B.C.) we enter upon a barren period which until the last few years could be considered totally destitute of original literary works. Quite recently, we have become aware of the existence of a fragmentary wisdom text, to be dated to about the middle of the first millennium. It is much concerned with relations with superiors and the role and duties of a leader. A whole page is devoted to agriculture and the peasant, whose social function is extolled, a change from the derision of the scribes of the New Kingdom. This work, which cannot have been isolated, at present represents the last extant literary text of importance in hieratic. The manuscript belongs to the time when demotic is already in current use and preparing to make itself felt in literature.

The creative genius of Egypt does not dry up with the loss of independence. If under the successive domination of Persians, Greeks, and Romans, the country submits to history instead of making it, demotic literature shows that imagination and thought remain alive and that change continues even if traditions endure. The old genres still remain in favour, with of course wisdom literature to the fore. We possess an imposing gnomic work known as the Insinger papyrus after one of the manuscripts. The text is divided into chapters like the 'Instruction of Amenemope' and is similarly imbued with a deep religious feeling. The conviction that God controls the destiny of all things is expressed in particular in a concise formula which recurs as a refrain at the end of each section. The god Thoth maintains the balance of the world and man in his turn must hold to the middle path. Moderation and the art of self-control constitute the secret of happiness and the essence of wisdom as understood by the author of the book. A little before his premature death the late S. R. K. Glanville published the 'Instruction of 'Onkhsheshonqy', an important didactic work the existence of which was not even suspected. Introduced by a narrative in the manner of certain older writings, it consists of a collection of short maxims rather untidily arranged and which in their terseness have often the pungency of popular sayings. The thought which is thus expressed is concrete and of no exalted moral level. It is essentially 'practical wisdom' designed 'for the guidance of the peasant farmer' (Glanville).

A caustic description of an inept musician, drunken and half starved, has as its distant ancestors the satires of the crafts. The beast fables, of which several demotic specimens exist, have not as yet been encountered in earlier texts, but numerous drawings of the Ramessid period are evidence of the existence of animal stories. Moreover, the lives of animals and their habits had long served as an allegory from which a moral was drawn. The elements were thus assembled for the formation of the didactic genre of the fable. In demotic literature, several animal stories both entertaining and moralizing are in particular found incorporated in a long text which is a variation of the 'Myth of the Eye of the Sun', the distant goddess. The divine protagonists are represented by their sacred animals, in this case the cat and the monkey, the latter telling fables to the former and succeeding in bringing her to Egypt. This method of adaptation has no known precedent in the texts, but the idea of making an entertaining story out of a legend is an old one, as we have seen. As for the device whereby stories are introduced by a narrative which serves as a pretext and brings in historical characters, this too is no novelty. Thus in a demotic fragment we find King Amasis, drunk and debauched, as Herodotus too describes him, incapable of working the day after a drinking-bout and having stories of love affairs told to him.

The exploits of magicians, illustrated by the Westcar papyrus (above, p. 236), remain popular. In demotic literature they take a strange, macabre, and grandiose turn, a chauvinistic tinge. The 'Cycle of Setna Khaemwēse' uses this son of Ramesses II, famous for his learning and who here becomes a magician, as a peg for tales of dead men who set themselves against the living, of an accursed *grimoire* which spreads death, and of ancient wizards who come back to life and engage in a contest on which the fate of Egypt depends. A descent to hell is centred on a story which might almost be the prototype of the parable of Dives and Lazarus. A remarkable passage describes Setna's passion for a diabolical beauty. The author skilfully contrives a build-up from a banal encounter to a monstrous crime, which breaks off abruptly when the tension reaches its climax—the whole adventure turns out to be a nightmare. One is not accustomed, in demotic literature, to stories of this quality. More often than not the narration is diffuse and drags on slowly, and the composition lacks cohesion. This is particularly true of the never-ending 'Cycle of Petubastis', which is derived ultimately from recollections of the troubled times of the Twenty-third Dynasty and takes the form of a kind of epic. Civil conflicts and wars, even adventures in the land of Amazons, are recounted with pathos and at great length in a succession of episodes in which speeches alternate with single combats. Homeric influence is probable in this longwinded chronicle, the inspiration of which is foreign to classical Egyptian literature.

Following this brief survey of Egyptian literature as it appears in the light of present knowledge, one may perhaps venture a few general remarks. In the first place, the reader, if he is new to the subject, will hardly have failed to be surprised by the general tenor of the chapter. At a remote period when one might have expected to find mostly myths and legends recounted in majestic poems, works of a priestly origin, one has in fact encountered a body of literature devoid as a whole of epic inspiration and independent of the cult. If Egyptian art developed in relation to religion and always remained subservient to it, Egyptian literature was, as we have seen, essentially secular in its *raison d'être*. It had an independent existence and was cultivated for its own sake, for the mere pleasure it gave, and for the benefit of society and mankind.

Ancient Egypt also, of course, possessed a vast religious literature —a subject on which we have not touched—and among the wide variety of texts which it includes there are hymns to the gods and Pharaohs which show undoubted poetic qualities. The Egyptians themselves acknowledged their intrinsic value and looked upon them as works of art. Some are found incorporated in secular writings and many appear in school copies. It is quite possible that Khety the author of an 'Instruction' (above, p. 230) also wrote a hymn to the Nile, a classic composition which was learned in the schools. To get a complete picture of Egyptian tastes and ideas in the realm of literature it is necessary to bear these facts in mind. The lyric, which the reader might have expected to be somewhat neglected by the people of the Pharaohs, was on the contrary widely cultivated and found its chief source of inspiration in religious faith. In this respect the impression which emerges from the preceding pages needs to be complemented and modified.

But religion did not overrun literature and swamp it. So far as one can tell, mythology did not inspire the poets, nor do we know of any epic text extolling the deeds and exploits of the gods which enjoyed any popularity among the literati. Leaving aside one or two doubtful cases, myths only penetrated into literature stripped of their glory and reduced to the level of tales in which the interest of the story takes precedence over the theological content. Moreover, even in religious texts themselves, systematic accounts of mythology are extremely rare.

As regards the epic genre, it is not really attested except in official inscriptions which relate the feats and achievements of kings, the most famous example being the poem describing the battle of Qadesh fought by Ramesses II against the Hittite confederation. Texts of this nature rarely appealed to the educated, as evidenced by the very small number of copies which we possess on papyri or tablets. Epic assumes an appreciable place in literature only with the 'Cycle of Petubastis', at a time when Egypt was no longer ruled by native Pharaohs.

The literary genres which were employed at all periods and which gave Egyptian literature its distinctive character are the story and the wisdom text, the two fields in which Egypt made its greatest contribution to world literature. In spite of the obvious inadequacy of our knowledge, it is evident from the fragments we possess how rich the folk literature of the country was. Every people has its treasury of popular tales. The thing which distinguishes the Egyptians is their having freely and at an early stage allowed such tales to find their way into written literature. Nor did this early promotion fail to advance the art of narration. The manuscript of the 'Shipwrecked Sailor' is among the oldest known literary papyri, if indeed it is not the oldest, yet the tale is given a setting; it is no longer a case of simple story-telling. The scribes contributed largely to the development of narrative and were responsible for its advancement well beyond the level of folklore; 'Sinuhe' and 'Wenamūn' bear witness to this. A rare imagination, a taste in this field shared equally among different levels of society, and the general regard in which the genre was held, made Egypt a great centre of the narrative art in its different forms, from the unsophisticated tale to the novel of real life.

The Egyptians loved to moralize as much as they liked story-telling. The wisdom genre appeared in Egypt when writing was not yet entirely suited to the expression of thought, and remained in vogue for 3,000 years. One wonders whether there is any other people which has produced so many wisdom texts. The form of the 'Instruction' favoured this multiplication, its flexibility permitting treatment of the most varied subjects provided only that they were given an edifying twist. Indeed, the satire of the crafts, the political testament, loyalist propaganda, biography, etc., all find their place in these texts. Moreover, the genre was not confined to the *sbōyet* (above, p. 225). As is clear from the eulogy of the great authors (above, p. 245), the Egyptians included in the same category as the 'Instructions' the meditations of a Khakheperrē'sonb and even the 'prophecy' of a Neferty. One might say that the term 'wisdom' was broadly interpreted. In this vast ensemble, analysis of the texts reveals notable differences. It also makes it possible to distinguish main lines of development and a complex web of interrelationships which give unity to this body of literature. Seen from outside it must appear monolithic and impressive. It is by no means irrelevant to the reputation which Egypt enjoyed in neighbouring countries. The Bible speaks of 'all the wisdom of the Egyptians' (1 Kgs. 4: 30=5: 10; Acts 7: 22) and, if we are to believe Wenamūn, the Prince of Byblos said of Egypt: 'It is from her that wisdom came forth to reach the landin which I dwell.'

If stories and wisdom literature are the secular genres most favoured by the Egyptians, it may be said that in the art of com-position it is the introductory narrative, the setting, which is the particularly characteristic element in their literature. The device was used to furnish a pretext for the telling of a story or several stories, and to knit them together, as we saw in the case of the 'Shipwrecked Sailor', the Westcar papyrus, and the demotic tale about Amasis. An embryonic form of introduction is found in the 'Story of Sinuhe', which is prefaced by the words 'so-and-so says', going back to the autobiographical inscriptions which begin in this way. The artifice of the setting owes its origin to the universal desire for titles, introductions, and prefaces, but its development was the result of the Egyptians' penchant for story-telling. It was duly carried over into wisdom literature, permitting the linking of the story and the wisdom text and so giving rise to a mixed genre which thus represents the synthesis, in both form and substance, of specific trends of Egyptian literature.

Our sources illustrate the formation of this hybrid genre, showing how the narrative developed out of the title of the wisdom text. We see a subordinate clause being added to the title to indicate the circumstances in which the 'Instruction' was given ('Satire of the Crafts'). This element is then somewhat extended ('Instruction of Ptahhotpe') and becomes a proper introductory anecdote ('Prophecy of Neferty') which ends as a framework enclosing the gnomic text. The 'Complaints of the Peasant' provides a fully developed example; here the narrative consists of a true plot which is resolved only in the last lines of the story. The hero, wretched and ill-used, presents petition after petition and in the end succeeds in obtaining justice. This formal arrangement is of advantage to both constituent elements of the text, for they set each other off. The moral dissertations postpone the denouement and create a feeling of suspense in the narrative, while the latter gives the speeches a personal interest and a certain emotion which they do not of themselves possess.

The method employed in the 'Peasant' to enhance speeches of a rather academic kind was also employed in purely wisdom literature. At present we know of two examples, which have already been mentioned. In the Middle Kingdom, the discourses of the scribe Sisobek have a long introduction and are interspersed with narrative; it appears from the meagre remains of the text that the sage, doubtless imprisoned, is in danger of death and owes his safety only to the intervention of a dancer. In demotic, the 'Instruction of 'Onkhsheshonqy' begins with a long narrative. The author, involved in a plot against the Pharaoh, is cast into prison; separated from his son, whom he wishes to educate, he writes down pieces of advice for him on potsherds, for lack of papyrus.

The feature common to these books and to the 'Peasant' is their showing the sage persecuted and overcome by misfortune. The theme of the righteous sufferer was familar and traditional among a people who worshipped Osiris, and was particularly appropriate for adding weight to a work of moral instruction. The Egyptians appreciated this and knew how to exploit this potential; they were drawn to it quite naturally, as we have seen. If one cannot be sure that the authors of the 'Romance of Ahiqar' or the Book of Job profited from Egyptian tradition in this respect, it is at least certain that it was developed on the banks of the Nile without outside influence. It is one of the most interesting Egyptian accomplishments in the field of letters and together with others noted in the preceding pages goes to make up the literary legacy of Egypt.

GEORGES POSENER

BIBLIOGRAPHY

Sir Alan Gardiner, several times cited in the foregoing chapter, has more than any other scholar advanced our knowledge of Egyptian literature. Yet all that he has written on the subject is intended for the specialist and cannot therefore be included in this bibliography. The works here listed owe much to his publications.

H. BRUNNER, *Grundzüge einer Geschichte der altägyptischen Literatur*, Darmstadt, 1966.

E. BRUNNER-TRAUT, *Altägyptische Märchen*, Düsseldorf–Köln, 1963.

S. DONADONI, *Storia della letteratura egiziana antica*, Milano, 1957.

A. ERMAN, *The literature of the ancient Egyptians*, tr. A. M. Blackman, London, 1927 (reprinted New York, 1966, as *The ancient Egyptians: a sourcebook of their writings* (with introduction by W. K. Simpson)).

G. Lefebvre, *Romans et contes égyptiens de l'époque pharaonique*, Paris, 1949.

B. Lewis (ed.), *Land of enchanters*, London, 1948 (Egyptian texts translated by B. G. Gunn).

T. E. Peet, *A comparative study of the literatures of Egypt, Palestine, and Mesopotamia*, London, 1931.

J. B. Pritchard (ed.), *Ancient Near-Eastern texts relating to the Old Testament*, 2nd ed., Princeton, 1955 (Egyptian texts translated by J. A. Wilson).

S. Schott, *Altägyptische Liebeslieder*, Zurich, 1950 (tr. P. Kriéger, *Les Chants d'amour de l'Égypte ancienne*, Paris, 1956).

B. Spuler (ed.), *Handbuch der Orientalistik*, Bd. I, *Ägyptologie*, Abschnitt II, *Literatur*, Leiden, 1952 (various authors).

10

EGYPT AND ISRAEL[1]

BECAUSE of the unique position of Syria-Palestine as a bridge between Egypt and Western Asia, across which the military roads and trade routes passed, it was continually subject to the cross-currents which flowed from these centres of culture. As early as about 3000 B.C., for instance, there are evidences of Egyptian influence in Byblos. Indeed, from the time of the Old Kingdom right down to the Empire period, an Egyptian temple was to be found in this Phoenician city.

During the Middle Kingdom (c. 2052–1786 B.C.) Egypt exercised an economic if not political domination over Syria-Palestine. To this period belong the movements of the Hebrew patriarchs to and from Egypt recorded in the Old Testament (Gen. 12: 10 ff.). A wall painting in a tomb at Beni Hasan, from the reign of Amenemhet II (c. 1900 B.C.), depicts a group of thirty-seven Semitic tribesmen (Pl. 17). Their leader bears the Hebrew name Abishai (cf. 1 Sam. 26: 6, etc.), and they are described as *ḥḳꜣw-ḫꜣswt*, 'rulers of foreign lands', an appellation which was the source of the later name Hyksos. That such visitors to Egypt often remained is clear from a Thirteenth Dynasty papyrus to be

---

[1] The transcription of Hebrew in the present chapter does not coincide with that employed for Egyptian (see table). The following letters have different values or are used solely for Hebrew.

a as in s*a*loon	*ḏ* = th as in *th*is
ꜣ a short 'Murmurvokal'	*ṭ* = an 'emphatic' t
ɛ as in m*e*t	*ḵ* = ch as in lo*ch*
ɔ as in n*o*t, *a*we	*p̄* = f
ḇ = v	*ś* = a sound between s and sh
ḡ = a palatalized gh	*ṯ* = th as in *th*ink

dated about 1740 B.C., now in the Brooklyn Museum, which contains a list of ninety-five workmen, many of them Semites. Their gradual assimilation to Egyptian ways is shown by the fact that they gave their children Egyptian names.

From the end of the Twelfth or the beginning of the Thirteenth Dynasty, comes a group of documents known as 'Execration Texts'. These are pottery bowls and clay figurines bearing curses directed against the enemies of the state, whether actual or potential. They contain many names of places in Syria-Palestine, such as Achshaph, Askelon, Jerusalem, and Shechem, as well as those of persons, and serve as a valuable source for determining the unsettled political conditions of the time. Not long afterwards Egypt was to be invaded and occupied by the Asiatic hordes known as the Hyksos. The period of their domination witnessed the movement of Semitic tribes into Egypt, and the Biblical account of Joseph is probably to be placed at the end of the Hyksos era.

The contacts between Egypt and Syria-Palestine became still closer when, during the New Kingdom, the latter territory became part of the newly created Egyptian Empire. The topographical lists of Thutmose III carved on the temple at Karnak, and later copied by Ramesses II and III, bear witness to his conquests. Through the machinations of the wily Hittite ruler Suppiluliumas, who took advantage of the invasion of the area by the Habiru, Egypt's Asiatic possessions were lost for a time during the reigns of Amenhotpe III and his dreamer son Akhenaten (c. 1403–1348 B.C.). This is graphically portrayed in the state archives discovered at (Tell) El-Amarna in Middle Egypt. The nearly 400 clay tablets written in Akkadian, the lingua franca of the day, include letters from the rulers of the city-states of Syria-Palestine which were under Egyptian suzerainty, and copies of the replies. From them we learn that one of the royal scribes of Abimilki, the ruler of Tyre, was himself an Egyptian.

The soil of Palestine has also yielded evidence of Egyptian

domination in the form of hieroglyphic inscriptions found at various sites. For example, at Beth-shan three stelae from the reigns of Sety I and Ramesses II have been excavated. One of them refers to the '*ʿprw* of Mount Yarumtu', a term cognate with Ugaritic *ʿprm* and Akkadian *Ḫab/pirū*. We have already encountered these Habiru as the invaders who accomplished the collapse of Egyptian authority in Syria-Palestine. This designation, which probably meant 'transient', 'nomad', was later adopted in the form *ʿibrîm* as a name of the Hebrew people. As *ʿprw* it appears on monuments in Egypt to designate foreigners employed in the labour corvée. The earliest mention of these people in hieroglyphic inscriptions comes from the reign of Thutmose III.

Not all Semites in Egypt were of the labouring classes, however. One of the sons of Ramesses II, for instance, was married to the daughter of a Syrian ship captain named Ben-Anath. Some attained to positions of trust and responsibility in the court. During the Nineteenth Dynasty a Semite by the name of Ben-Ozen served Merenptah as chief herald, and in the following dynasty a royal butler called Mahar-Baal served as a judge at the harem conspiracy trials.

It was probably during the Nineteenth Dynasty that the Exodus took place, when the Hebrew tribes that had been living in the Delta returned to Palestine. Merenptah (*c.* 1212–1202 B.C.), early in his reign, had a series of hymns of victory inscribed on a stela which was placed in his mortuary temple at Thebes, a duplicate being carved on the temple at Karnak. In the closing lines we find the only mention of the name Israel in Egyptian texts:

> The princes lie prostrate, saying, 'Hail!'
>   Not one lifts his head among the Nine Bows.
> Destruction for Libya! Hatti is pacified;
>   Canaan is plundered with every evil;
> Askelon is taken; Gezer is captured;
>   Yanoam is made non-existent;
> Israel lies desolate; its posterity is no more;
>   Hurru has become a widow for Egypt.

Indicative of the close ties between Egypt and Palestine is the salutation in the first line quoted above, which is a Canaanite loan-word cognate with Hebrew *šālōm*.

Contacts between Egypt and the Hebrew people become increasingly important during the period of decline which followed the New Kingdom. In the time of David, a member of the Edomite royal house named Hadad fled to Egypt and was given political asylum by an unnamed Pharaoh (1 Kgs. 11: 14–22), who may have been Siamūn (*c.* 990–974 B.C.) or Psusennes (Psibkhenne) II (*c.* 974–940 B.C.) of the Twenty-first Dynasty. When Solomon succeeded to the throne, Hadad returned to Palestine to plague him. In similar fashion Solomon's enemy Jeroboam later took refuge under Sheshonq (O.T. Shishak) I (*c.* 940–919 B.C.) of the Twenty-second Dynasty (1 Kgs. 11: 40).

The account of Solomon's own marriage to an Egyptian princess again fails to name the Pharaoh who was her father (1 Kgs. 3: 1); perhaps this too was Psusennes II, or less probably Sheshonq I. At any rate, Solomon received the city of Gezer (or should Gerar be read?) as a wedding gift (1 Kgs. 9: 16). This alliance is a clear indication of the growing importance of the Israelite state on the one hand, and the waning power of Egypt as contrasted with her position in the Eighteenth Dynasty on the other. We need only recall the proud words of Amenhotpe III quoted by Kadashmanenlil I, King of Babylon, in a letter to the Pharaoh: 'From of old no daughter of a king of Egypt has ever been given to anyone' (*EA* 4/6 f.). In the fifth year of his successor Rehoboam, about 930 B.C., a campaign was conducted against Palestine by Sheshonq I (1 Kgs. 14: 25 f.), who listed on a wall of the temple at Karnak 156 cities of Syria-Palestine which he claimed to have captured.

In the eighth century, during the time of the prophet Hosea, a pro-Egyptian party had arisen in the Northern Kingdom, and many adherents eventually made their way to Egypt where they settled (Hos. 7: 11; 9: 6). By the end of the same century, Isaiah clearly indicates the presence of a similar group partial to Egypt in Judah during Hezekiah's reign (Isa. 30: 1–5; 31: 1–3). A century later Egyptian troops were again on Palestinian soil in a vain endeavour to save the tottering Assyrian Empire from collapse before the forces of Babylonia and Media. As fate would have it, the Judean king Josiah met his death at the hands of Necho during this campaign, in 608 B.C. (2 Kgs. 23: 29). The Pharaoh then proceeded to depose Josiah's rightful heir Jehoahaz and replace him with his brother, who was given the throne name Jehoiakim and reduced to the role of a vassal, paying tribute to Egypt. A few years later, after the fall of Jerusalem to Nebuchadrezzar in 587 B.C. and the subsequent murder of Gedaliah, whom the Babylonians had installed as governor, there was a large-scale emigration to Egypt (Jer. 41: 16 ff.). At the time the prophet Jeremiah referred to earlier Hebrew colonies in the Delta and Upper Egypt (Jer. 24: 8; 44: 1).

Late in the seventh century a colony of Jewish mercenary soldiers was established on the Island of Elephantine at Aswan, which was to continue in existence through the sixth and fifth centuries. From this site as well as others, such as Saqqara, Edfu, and Hermopolis Magna, have come a great mass of letters and business and legal documents written in Imperial Aramaic on papyrus, ostraca, and leather. They contain much evidence of Egyptian influence, especially in the matter of names and religious practices. A particularly instructive example of the latter occurs in a papyrus which reads, 'I bless you by Yahweh and by Khnum'![1] Yet, as the correspondence at Elephantine shows, the Jews of that place were in close communication with the religious and civil authorities in Jerusalem.

In 301 B.C. Palestine came under the control of Ptolemy I, and was to remain so for a century. Many prisoners were brought

---

[1] ברכתך ליהה ולחנב: A. Dupont-Sommer, 'Le Syncrétisme religieux des Juifs d'Éléphantine d'après un ostracon araméen inédit', *Revue de l'histoire des religions*, cxxx (1945), 17–28.

back from his Palestinian campaigns, and during the third century he also imported Jewish soldiers to Egypt as mercenaries, granting them lands to be held under military tenure. Jewish settlers tended more and more to drift into Alexandria until, by the first century B.C., they formed the largest body of Jews outside Judaea. After the deposition and subsequent murder of the High Priest Onias IV, about 160 B.C., a further group of Jews emigrated to the southern Delta, where they built a temple at Leontopolis, which was eventually destroyed during the first century A.D.

In view of these numerous contacts between the two cultures, occurring in both Egypt and Palestine, it was inevitable that Israel should fall heir to many features of Egyptian civilization. It will be our task in the following pages to draw attention to some of these.

Of paramount significance for all subsequent ages was the creation of the first true alphabet. This was not an accomplishment of the Egyptians, but of a Semite working in the Egyptian turquoise mines in the Sinai Peninsula (above, p. 215). Nevertheless, this linear script was clearly derived from Egyptian hieroglyphic, employing the acrophonic principle. That is to say, the hieroglyph depicting a house plan was read as the Semitic word *bayit/bēt*, 'house', and given the phonetic value *b*; the wavy line representing water, and possessing in Egyptian the phonetic value *n*, was read in Semitic as *mayim/mēm*, 'water', and employed to indicate the sound *m*. This revolutionary step was taken about 1500 B.C., and it is possible to trace the development of the signs from these proto-Sinaitic inscriptions to the later Hebrew forms, and ultimately through Greek to our present alphabet.

As we have already observed, Semites living in Egypt tended to give their children Egyptian names, and sometimes even to adopt them for themselves. Some of these names went with them to Palestine, and a few have survived even to the present day, such as Moses, derived from *msw*, 'child', Phinehas, from *pꜣ nḥsy*, 'the negro', and Susanna, from *ssn* (earlier *sššn*), 'lotus'. Other Egyptian names which were current in Biblical times are Hophni, from *ḥfnr*, 'tadpole', Merari, from *mrry* or *mrrw*, 'beloved', Pashhur, representing *pš* (‹*pss*›)-*Ḥr*, 'portion of Horus', and Putiel, which is Egyptian in form, beginning with the familiar element *pꜣ dì*, but substituting the Hebrew word *'ēl*, 'God', for the name of an Egyptian deity, and thus meaning 'he whom God has given'.

The Egyptian language, as might well be expected, also left an indelible mark on Hebrew vocabulary, and a number of loan-words are preserved in the Old Testament.[1] Some of these are titles, such as *par'ō* from *pr-rꜣ*, hence Greek φαραώ and English 'Pharaoh', and *ḥarṭummīm*, 'magicians', probably from *ḥry-tp*. Names of water-plants, which were such a common feature of the Egyptian landscape, also found their way into Hebrew. Such are *'ꜣḥū*, 'reeds', derived either from *ꜣḥ*, 'papyrus-thicket', or from *ìyḥ/ìḥy*, 'reeds'; *gōmē*, 'papyrus', from *ḳmꜣ*, 'reeds'; *sūp̄*, 'reeds', from *twfy*, 'papyrus-marshes' (Copt. ϫοοϥ); *šūšan* or *šōšannꜣ*, 'blossom', 'lily', from *ssn* (‹*sššn*›), 'lotus' (Copt. ϣωϣεн). Terms for materials also occur: *šēš* or *šayiš*, 'white marble', from *šs*, 'alabaster'; *šēš*, 'byssus', from *ssr-nsw*, 'royal linen' (Copt. ϣεнc, ϣ̄нc); *'ēṭūn*, '(Egyptian) linen', from *ìdmì*, 'red linen', whence Greek ὀθόνη; *šiṭṭꜣ*, 'acacia', from *šnḏt* (Copt. ϣοнтε); *hoḇnīm* from *hbny*, whence Greek ἔβενος and English 'ebony';[2] *neṭer* from *nṭrì*, producing Greek νίτρον, Latin *nitrum*, and English 'natron'.

Two Egyptian measures were adopted by the Hebrews: *'ēp̄ꜣ*, 'ephah', from *ìpt* (Copt. ειοπε), and *hīn*, 'hin', from *hnw*, 'jar', used as a liquid measure. Other words borrowed were *yꜥ'ōr*, 'river, Nile', from *ì(t)rw*, 'river' (Copt. ιοορ); *qeseṭ*, 'scribal kit', from *gstì*; *qōp̄*, 'ape', 'monkey', from *gìf/gwf*, whence Greek κῆπος, κῆβος; *maṭṭē*, 'staff', from *mdw*, 'staff'; *'eḇyōn*, 'poor', from *bìn*,

---

[1] T. O. Lamdin, 'Egyptian Loan Words in the Old Testament', *Journ. American Oriental Soc.* lxxiii (1953), 145–55.

[2] It may be, however, that *hbny* was itself a loan-word from the Sudan.

'bad', 'miserable', pronounced **ĕbyūnĕ*¹ (Copt. eϩιнп); *ṭabba'aṯ*, 'seal', 'signet-ring', from *ḏb't*, 'signet-ring' (Copt. ⲧϩϩe).

The debt, of course, was not all one way, and during the Eighteenth and Nineteenth Dynasties especially the Egyptian language was enriched by a very large number of loan-words from Canaanite sources. Among them are such words as *ym*, 'sea' (Heb. *yɔm*), which survived into Coptic as eιⲟⲙ; *mrkbt*, 'chariot' (Heb. *mɛrkɔḇɔ*), Copt. ϩepeϭⲱⲟⲩⲧe; *mktr*, 'fortress' (Heb. *miḡdɔl*), Copt. ⲙeϭⲧⲟⲗ; *ṯpr*, 'scribe' (Heb. *sōp̄ēr*); *ktm*, 'gold' (Heb. *kɛṯɛm*); *šbd*, 'rod' (Heb. *šeḇɛṯ*), Copt. ⳙϩⲱⲧ; *mkmrt*, 'net' (Heb. *mikmɛrɛṯ*); *krr*, 'holocaust' (Heb. *kɔlīl*), Copt. ϭⲗⲓⲗ; *ʿgrt*, 'wagon' (Heb. *ʿᵃḡɔlɔ*), Copt. ⲁϭⲟⲗⲧe; *brt*, 'covenant' (Heb. *bᵊrīṯ*); *ʿšg*, 'to misuse' (Heb. *ʿɔšaq*); *iṯɔ*, 'which?' (Heb. *'ē-zɛ̄*).

The influence of Egyptian may also be seen in some idiomatic expressions. In Eccles. 12: 5 occurs the term *bēṯ 'ōlɔm*, 'eternal home', used of the tomb, familiar also from Phoenician and Palmyrene inscriptions². This recalls the Egyptian *pr n nḥḥ* (*Beni Hasan* i. 26/180), or *pr n ḏt* (*Urk.* iv. 1200/5). A similar expression appears in Tobit 3: 6, τὸν αἰώνιον τόπον, with which may be compared Egyptian *st nt nḥḥ* (*Urk.* iv. 1200/4).

In Eccles. 4: 8 we also find the word *šēnī*, 'second', employed in the sense of 'companion'. This is unparalleled in Hebrew, but common with Egyptian *sn-nw*, 'second' (e.g. *Urk.* iv. 151/4). Again, *mahēr šɔlɔl*, the first half of the compound name Maher-shalal-hash-baz, given by Isaiah to his son as a reminder of his prediction that the Syro-Ephraimite coalition would be overthrown (8: 1, 3), brings to mind the Eighteenth Dynasty Egyptian term *is-ḥɔk*, 'plunder', 'easy prey' (*Urk.* iv. 6/4, 613/16). This latter likewise consists of an imperative (*is*, 'go') followed by a substantive (*ḥɔk*, 'plunder').³

---

¹ The vocalization indicates that the borrowing could not have been later than the twelfth century B.C.   ² Ph. בת עלם, Palm. בת עלמא.

³ S. Morenz, 'Eilebeute', *Theologische Literaturzeitung*, lxxiv (1949), 697–9.

Another instance of a borrowed idiom may be found in 1 Kgs. 18: 42, where Elijah, in a time of severe drought, ascended to the summit of Mount Carmel, where he 'put his face between his knees'. This takes on a particular significance when we remember the common Egyptian phrase *ḏꜣḏꜣ ḥr mꜣst*, 'head on lap', a sign of mourning (e.g. *Sinuhe*, R 10; *P. Westc.* 12/20 f.), and the derivative compound *ḏꜣḏꜣ-mꜣst* (*Med. Habu*, 86/22; *P. Bremner-Rhind*, 4/17; *P. Sall.* iv. *rt.* 16/5). The same idiom was also transmitted to Syria, where it turns up in the Ugaritic texts: 'The gods lowered their heads upon their knees' (Text 137, 23–9).[1]

A frequent expression in Egyptian is *sꜣw-ꜥ*, 'broken of arm', in the meaning 'weak', 'disabled', 'incapacitated', as contrasted with its opposite *nḫt-ꜥ*, 'strong'. It may be traced back to the First Intermediate Period and the Middle Kingdom (*Merikarē*, 136; *Neferty*, 54), but it becomes more frequent in Late Egyptian (*P. Anast.* i. 8/8, 9/3; *Urk.* iv. 1078/1; *Amenemope*, 4/5). This idiom clarifies the Biblical use of *zᵉrōaꜥ*, 'arm', with the verb *šibber*, 'break' (Pss. 10: 15; 37: 17; Job 38: 15; Jer. 48: 25; Ezek. 30: 21 f., 24) or with *dikkꜣ*, 'crush' (Job 22: 9).

An example of the reverse tendency is the borrowing into Egyptian of the term *hdm rdwy*, 'footstool' (*Truth and Falsehood*, 6/3 f.), from Hebrew *hᵃḏōm raḡlayim* (Pss. 99: 5; 132: 7; 1 Chr. 28: 2; Isa. 66: 1).[2] A second instance comes, not from the New Kingdom as in the preceding case, but from the late fourth century B.C. In one of the inscriptions from the tomb of Petosiris, to which we shall refer later, we encounter the unique expression *snḏ(t) nt nṯr*, 'fear of god' (*Pet.* 62/2), which is certainly a rendering of the Hebrew *yirʾat ʾᵉlōhīm* (Gen. 20: 11; 2 Sam. 23: 3).

Several metaphors have also found their way from Egyptian

---

[1] A. Jirku, '"Das Haupt auf die Knie legen". Eine ägyptisch-ugaritisch-israelitische Parallele', *Zeitschrift der deutschen morgenländischen Gesellschaft*, ciii (1953), 372.

[2] F. Hintze, '*Hdm rdwj* "Fussschemel"', *ZÄS* lxxix (1954), 77.

into Biblical Hebrew. For instance, Yahweh's promise to Jeremiah to make him a 'fortified wall of bronze' to the people (Jer. 15: 20; cf. 1: 18) reminds us of the Egyptian use of *inb n ḥmt*, 'wall of copper', to describe Senwosret III (*P. Kahun* ii. 14), or *sbty ꜥꜣ n ḥmt*, 'great wall of copper', with reference to Sety I (Champ., *Not. descr.* ii. 76).[1] In demotic texts the metaphor appears as *sbt ḥmt*, 'copper wall', descriptive of Pesnufe in the Petubastis Cycle (*P. Spieg.* 12/13), and in the saying 'He is a copper wall to his master in the darkness' (*P. Ins.* 11/15). In similar vein, Ramesses II is portrayed as *sbty n bꜣꜣ n pt*, 'a wall of iron' (Kuentz, *Bat. de Qadech*, p. 299, § 262; cf. Lepsius, *Denkm.* iii. 187e, 7), and Thutmose III as *sbty m bꜣꜣ [n pt]*, 'a wall of iron' (*Urk.* iv. 1233/6). The briefer expression *sbty n bꜣꜣ* for 'wall of iron' is also employed as an epithet of Sety I (Mar., *Abydos* i. 52/17) and Ptolemy II (*Urk.* ii. 36/1). Rekhmirē, the vizier of Thutmose III, is even called *ḏri nbw*, 'a wall of gold' (*Urk.* iv. 1087/10).

Of special interest is the fact that during the fourteenth century B.C., in a letter written to the Egyptian ruler in the Akkadian language, Abimilki of Tyre calls the Pharaoh *dūri siparri*, 'a wall of bronze' (*EA* 147/53). We have already observed that Abimilki's scribe was an Egyptian. Since the demotic instances quoted show that the figure was still current in Egypt during the first century A.D., it is perhaps permissible to see Egyptian influence in the words of Horace, *'hic murus aeneus esto'*, 'let this be a copper wall' (*Epist.* i. 1/60). The expression is unique in Latin literature. The description of the 'Field of Reeds', the Egyptian prototype of the Greek Elysian Fields, as being surrounded by *inb m bꜣꜣ*, 'a wall of iron' (*CT* ii. 369a), is strikingly paralleled in the much later Homeric account of the island of Aeolia, which was encircled by τεῖχος χάλκεον (*Odyssey*, x. 3 f.). It is also reminiscent of Ezekiel's 'wall of iron' (Ezek. 4: 3).

Another frequent metaphor in Egyptian texts is the 'way of

---

[1] A. Alt, 'Hic murus aheneus esto', *Zeitschrift der deutschen morgenländischen Gesellschaft*, lxxxvi (1933), 33–48.

life'.[1] It occurs in the form *wзt n ʿnḫ* (*P. Ch. Beatty* iv. *vs.* 6/4; *Instr. of Amennakhte*, 1; *Urk.* iii. 19/14; *Stela of Ta-Hebt*, 13), or *wзt nt ʿnḫw*, 'way of the living' (*Khety*, 11/4), as well as *mtn n ʿnḫ* (*Harmhab Edict*, 5, left) and *mìt n ʿnḫ* (*Amenemope*, 1/7, 16/8). The Hebrew equivalents, which are all to be found in books which elsewhere reveal Egyptian influence, are *dɛrɛḵ (ha)ḥayyῑm* (Jer. 21: 8; Prov. 6: 23) or *'oraḥ ḥayyῑm* (Ps. 16: 11; Prov. 2: 19; 5: 6; 15: 24; cf. Prov. 10: 17).

In this connection it is interesting to note the words which Jeremiah ascribes to Yahweh (21: 8): 'I am setting before you the way of life and the way of death.' Nearly a century and a half earlier Piankhi (*c.* 751–730 B.C.) of the Twenty-fifth Dynasty had recorded on his stela (*Urk.* iii. 26/1–4) the words which he addressed to the besieged inhabitants of Medum: 'See, two ways are before you; you must choose as you wish: open up, and you shall live; close, and you shall die.' We are reminded also of the words in Deut. 30: 15, 19.

An Egyptian source has also been claimed for the maxim contained in Prov. 25: 22 (cited by St. Paul in Rom. 12: 20) which advises one to feed an enemy, 'for you will heap fiery coals on his head'.[2] This is a custom mentioned nowhere else in Hebrew literature, but the Old Testament does speak of sprinkling ashes on the head as a sign of mourning (Pss. 11: 6; 140: 10 [Heb. 11]). In the demotic tale concerning Setna, written in 233–232 B.C., we read that he must pay for his misdemeanour in appropriating the magical book from the tomb of Naneferkaptah: 'I will make him bring this book here, with a forked staff in his hand and a fiery brazier on his head' (*I Kh.* 4/35–7, 5/37–9). Here it is clearly a rite of penance, and suggests for the Biblical passages a higher motivation for kindness than the usual exegesis allows. The

---

[1] B. Couroyer, 'Le Chemin de vie en Égypte et en Israël', *Revue biblique*, lvi (1949), 412–32.

[2] S. Morenz, 'Feurige Kohlen auf dem Haupt', *Theologische Literaturzeitung*, lxxviii (1953), 187–92.

interpretation offered here is supported in a remarkable way by a maxim in the 'Wisdom of Amenemope' (5/3–6) which counsels the reader to treat the wicked man thus:

> Lift him up, give him your hand,
>> Leave him (in) the arms of the god;
> Fill his stomach with the bread which you have,
>> That he may be sated and weep.

In the Old Testament Yahweh is often referred to as a potter (e.g. Isa. 29: 16; 45: 9; 64: 8 [Heb. 7]; Jer. 18: 2 ff.; Job 10: 9; 33: 6). In three passages from later Jewish literature, however, the deity is portrayed as fashioning men at his pleasure for different purposes. In Sir. 33: 13 we read:

> As clay in the potter's hand—
>> Since all his ways are according to his pleasure—
> So are men in the hand of him who made them,
>> To repay them as he decides.

The second passage is found in Wisd. 15: 7:

> For a potter, kneading the soft earth,
>> Painstakingly moulds each vessel for our use;
> Yet he shapes from the same clay
>> Both the vessels that serve clean purposes
>> And those for opposite purposes, all alike;
> But which shall be the function of each of these
>> The worker in clay decides.

St. Paul adopts this figure in Rom. 9: 21: 'Has the potter no authority over the clay, to make out of the same lump one vessel for noble and another for ignoble use?' For this striking metaphor also an Egyptian prototype may be adduced.[1] In a work to which we have already had occasion to refer, and to which we shall return again, the author says (*Amenemope*, 24/13–8):

> As for man—(mere) clay and straw!—
>> The god is his builder.

[1] S. Morenz, 'Eine weitere Spur der Weisheit Amenopes in der Bibel', *ZÄS* lxxxiv (1959), 79–80.

> He tears down and builds up daily,
>> He makes a thousand poor men at will,
>> And makes a thousand men into inspectors,
>> While he is in his hour of life [i.e. actively engaged].

Another metaphor found in this important work runs (*Amenemope*, 20/3–6):

> Be resolute in your mind; keep your intellect steadfast;
>> Do not steer with your tongue.
> A person's tongue is the steering-oar of a boat—
>> The Universal Lord is its pilot.

A late instance of the same thought occurs in a demotic text: 'Do not let your mind be a steering-oar. A man's tongue is evil which leads him like the steering-oar of a boat' (*Krugtexten*, A, 14 f.). This has survived into Biblical literature in Jas. 3: 4 f.: 'Look at ships, too: though they are so great and are driven by strong winds, they are steered by a very small rudder wherever the will of the pilot chooses. So also the tongue is a little member and yet makes great boasts.'[1]

Perhaps the most influential contribution of Egypt lay in the area of literary types and motifs. Peet, in his Schweich Lectures of 1929, made the statement that Egypt was 'the home of the short story, and one of her claims to literary recognition is that she produced the first short stories to be told for their own sake'.[2] If by the term short story we mean a well-told tale characterized by its brevity, with only the bare essentials, shorn of superfluous details, outlined in a few deft strokes, and often revealing a feeling for the dramatic, then the Egyptians were indeed its creators. This literary form they transmitted to the Hebrews, who developed it to a remarkably high degree.

Folk-tales often provided the material for such compositions.

---

[1] S. Herrmann. 'Steuerruder, Waage, Herz und Zunge in ägyptischen Bildreden', *ZÄS* lxxix (1954), 106–15.

[2] T. E. Peet, *A Comparative Study of the Literatures of Egypt, Palestine and Mesopotamia*, London, 1931, p. 27.

An outstanding example of the Egyptian genius for story-telling is known as the 'Tale of the Two Brothers', contained in a Nineteenth Dynasty manuscript written about 1225 B.C. (*ANET* 23–5). The theme of the first part of the work has survived into Greek and Latin literature, being found in the *Iliad* (vi. 156–65), Euripides' *Hippolytus*, Aristophanes' *Clouds* (1063–8), and Horace's *Odes* (iii. 7). Most striking, however, is the close resemblance it bears to the account of the attempted seduction of Joseph by Potiphar's wife recounted in Hebrew sources (Gen. 39: 6–20).

The Joseph narratives are characterized by their Egyptian colouring,[1] a feature especially noticeable in the case of the proper names which they contain. According to Gen. 41: 45, Joseph adopted the name Zaphenath-paneah (Eg. *ḏd-p₃-nṯr-iw·f-ꜥnḫ*), his wife was called Asenath (Eg. *ns-Nit* or *iw·s-n-Nit*), and his father-in-law was Potiphera (Eg. *p₃-di-p₃-Rꜥ*). The last-mentioned Egyptian name is also the source of the form Potiphar, borne by Joseph's master (Gen. 37: 6; 39: 1). We note too the Egyptian practice of embalming in the case of Jacob (Gen. 50: 2 f.) and Joseph himself, who lived to the ripe age of 110 (Gen. 50: 26), a figure well attested as the ideal length of life in Egyptian sources.

Another folk-tale motif which found its way into Biblical literature has survived in the 'Second Tale of Khaemwēse', which is contained in a demotic papyrus of the first century A.D. Despite the late date of this manuscript, the tale is of purely Egyptian character, and preserves elements of great antiquity. The story tells of a priest who was led through the halls of the underworld by his son Si-Osiris. Seven later Hebrew or Aramaic versions of the theme are known. One such may have formed the basis for Jesus' parable of Dives and Lazarus (Luke 16: 19–31).[2] It is

[1] J. Vergote, *Joseph en Égypte* (Orientalia et Biblica Lovaniensia, 3), Louvain, 1959.

[2] H. Gressmann, 'Vom reichen Mann und armen Lazarus', *Abhandlungen der preussischen Akademie der Wissenschaften zu Berlin, Phil.-hist. Klasse*, 1918, no. 7.

possible that the account of Moses' dramatic division of the waters of the Sea of Reeds (Exod. 14: 21 f.) owes its inspiration to the similar feat of the ancient Egyptian magician Djadjaemonekh, as related in the Westcar papyrus (6/7–13).

There may be evidence in this area also that the cultural flow was not only in one direction. The 'Astarte papyrus' of the thirteenth century B.C., now pitifully fragmentary, contains a mythological tale of Yam, the sea, and Ashtoreth/Astarte (*ANET* 17 f.). Although too badly damaged for a complete understanding of its contents, enough has survived to suggest to some scholars that we are dealing with a Canaanite myth now familiar from the Ugaritic texts. Posener, however, has argued that the theme can be traced much earlier in purely Egyptian sources.

Some scholars have also claimed that the so-called 'Famine stela' was influenced by the Hebrew account of Joseph. This inscription, of the Ptolemaic period, dates perhaps from the end of the second century B.C., although the scene is set in the reign of Djoser of the Third Dynasty, more than two and a half millennia earlier (*ANET* 31–2). The theme of a seven-year period of famine, followed by years of prosperity, could have been inspired by the Biblical story, since it originated at Elephantine, where, as we have seen, a Jewish colony had been in existence for some centuries.

Before passing on to the next literary genre bequeathed by the Egyptians to the Hebrews, we must digress briefly to consider the important developments in the administration of the nascent Hebrew state under David and Solomon. During the reign of the former, Israel became the leading power in Syria-Palestine, and consequently required the creation of a military, economic, and governmental organization. It was only natural that David should look to Egypt for his models, either directly or through Phoenician intermediaries.

Foremost among the titles held by the royal officials were two which have Egyptian antecedents: the first, *sōp̄ēr*, 'scribe', combined the functions of private secretary to the ruler and secretary of state, and corresponds to the Egyptian *ss̆* (*nsw*), '(royal) scribe'; the second, *mazkīr*, 'recorder', or chief of protocol, is equivalent to the Egyptian *wḥmw*, usually rendered 'herald'.[1] These officials first appear under David (2 Sam. 8: 16 f. = 1 Chr. 18: 15 f.; 2 Sam. 20: 24 f.), continue during the reign of Solomon (1 Kgs. 4: 3), and last until the time of Hezekiah and Josiah.

The title *rēᶜē/rēᵃᶜ* (*hammɛlɛk̲*), '(royal) companion', current in the time of David (2 Sam. 15: 32 [LXX], 37; 16: 16; 1 Chr. 27: 33) and Solomon (1 Kgs. 4: 5) calls to mind, as has long been recognized, the common Egyptian titles *smr* (*wᶜty*), '(unique) companion', or *rḫ nsw*, 'royal confidant'. To these officials David added a council of thirty (2 Sam. 23: 18–39), which likewise harks back to an Egyptian institution, the *mᶜbᵌyt*, a group of thirty which has been called the 'traditional Grand Jury of Egypt' (cf. *P. Anast.* v. 9/5; *Med. Habu*, 96/1; *Amenemope*, 20/18; *Harmhab Edict*, 6, right).

Solomon's reign witnessed a great economic expansion, accompanied by new social and political developments. His determination to establish himself as an oriental potentate with a large harem, a well-organized court, and extensive international relations, combined with his lavish building schemes, required both wealth and manpower. In order to levy taxes, as well as to conscript men into military service and labour corvées, the land was divided into twelve districts under prefects. The device of employing the labour force in three-monthly shifts (1 Kgs. 5: 13 f. [Heb. 5: 27 f.]) was inspired by Egyptian practice, if we can trust Herodotus (ii. 124). For administrative purposes a greatly enlarged bureaucracy was essential. Solomon's close ties through marriage would inevitably lead him also to turn to Egypt for

---

[1] R. de Vaux, 'Titres et fonctionnaires égyptiens à la cour de David et de Salomon', *Revue biblique*, xlviii (1939), 394–405; J. Begrich, 'Sōfēr und Mazkīr', *Zeitschrift für die alttestamentliche Wissenschaft*, lviii (1940/1), 1–29.

assistance. The description in 1 Kgs. 7, for example, shows that both Solomon's palace and that constructed for his Egyptian wife were of Egyptian design.

It may be that scribal schools on the pattern of those in Egypt were set up in Jerusalem, and youths were trained for the civil service. In addition to the functionaries already mentioned, Solomon instituted a new office, the bearer of which was described as one *'al habbayit̲*, 'over the household' (1 Kgs. 4: 6). His duties appear to have been those of a royal steward or comptroller, but later, in the case of Shebna, who held the office during the reign of Hezekiah (Isa. 22: 15), or of Jotham, who acted as regent (2 Kgs. 15: 5), the incumbent exercised almost the same powers as those of the Egyptian vizier. It is noteworthy that Joseph is also described by the Pharaoh as being *'al bēt̲ī* (Gen. 41: 40).

During the reigns of David and Solomon this Egyptian influence manifested itself in yet another literary form, to which A. Hermann has given the name *Königsnovelle*, or royal romance. In Egypt this is a reflection in literature of the concept of the divine, invincible king depicted in heroic style on the wall reliefs of many a temple. The pattern became a stereotyped one: first, the motivation is given for some royal activity, often of a ritual or military nature, and is frequently received through the medium of a dream; next, the king's plans are outlined to a gathering of courtiers and officials, who are usually sceptical or hesitant; and, finally, the exploit is successfully accomplished. In this way the myth of the divine might and majesty of the Pharaoh is portrayed.

The earliest known example belongs to the Twelfth Dynasty. It concerns the building of a temple to the god Atum at Heliopolis by Senwosret I (*BAR* i, §§ 501–6). Other examples which may be cited are the celebrated 'Sphinx stela' of Thutmose IV (*ANET* 449), the recital of Kamose's expulsion of the Hyksos preserved on the Carnarvon Tablet (*ANET* 232 f.), and the account of Thutmose III at the battle of Megiddo (*BAR* ii, §§ 419–37).

It should occasion little wonder, then, when this literary convention turns up in Hebrew narratives of the reigns of David and Solomon.[1] The account of David's proposal to build a temple (*bayit*) for Yahweh in 2 Sam. 7, resulting in the divine promise to build a *bayit*, here in the sense of 'dynasty', for David, shows how the Hebrew religious genius skilfully adapted the form. The expression *'ŝŝ šēm gāḏōl* (vs. 9; in the parallel passage 1 Chr. 17: 8 the adjective is omitted) is particularly instructive, for it is an exact reproduction of the Egyptian phrase *iri rn (wr)*, 'make a (great) name', the formula for proclaiming the royal titulary (*Urk.* iv. 261/13–262/1, 199/8).

In passing, we may note that this phrase, followed by the motif of the Egyptian fivefold titulary, is employed by the eloquent peasant in his first speech before the chief steward Rensi (*Peas.*, B1, 64–8), as Ranke first pointed out. A similar rhetorical use of the motif in Hebrew literature has been demonstrated by Alt for Isa. 9: 2–7 [Heb. 1–6].[2]

A second instance of the royal romance in Hebrew sources concerns Solomon's dream (1 Kgs. 3: 4–15), and the subsequent demonstration of the divine gift of wisdom which he received. Perhaps the same form also underlies the account in 1 Kgs. 8: 1–5, 66.

It has been suggested that the custom of anointing kings on their accession in Syria-Palestine owes something to Egyptian practice.[3] The Biblical narratives recount the anointing of Saul, David, and Solomon, as well as Joash and Jehoahaz of Judah and Jehu of Israel.

---

[1] S. Herrmann, 'Die Königsnovelle in Ägypten und in Israel', *Wissenschaftliche Zeitschrift der Karl-Marx-Universität Leipzig, Gesellsch. und Sprachwiss. Reihe*, 3 (1953/4), 51–62.

[2] A. Alt, 'Jesaja 8,23–9,6. Befreiungsnacht und Krönungstag', *Festschrift Alfred Bertholet*, Tübingen, 1950, pp. 29–49; reprinted in *Kleine Schriften zur Geschichte des Volkes Israel*, ii, Munich, 1953, pp. 206–25.

[3] R. de Vaux, 'Le Roi d'Israël, vassal de Yahvé', *Mélanges Eugène Tisserant*, i, Rome, 1964, pp. 119–33.

The Pharaohs were not themselves anointed, but their officials and vassals were, as a sign of subjection to their overlord. Although explicit evidence for the anointing of officials in Egypt is scanty, it is none the less clear. A stela now in Florence, probably of the First Intermediate Period, describes the functionary Simentuwosre as 'one who anoints the officials in the house of the ruler' (No. 6365, 2). The only other written reference is in a lengthy demotic document of the reign of Psammetichus (Psamtik) I (664–609 B.C.) of the Twenty-sixth Dynasty, in which the 'Prophet' of Amūn Peteēse is 'taken before Pharaoh and anointed with lotus-oil' (*P. Ryl.* ix. 8/15). The ceremony is also recorded in scenes on tomb walls.

The anointing of Canaanite vassals is alluded to in a cuneiform letter from Addu-nirari to a Pharaoh, probably Akhenaten: 'When your grandfather Manakhpi(r)ya (Thutmose IV), King of Egypt, made my grandfather Ta[ku] king over Nukhasshe, and put oil on his head, he said the following: "As for him whom the King of [Egy]pt has made king, [and on whose head] he has put [oil], no one [may depose him]"' (*EA* 51/4–9). Archaeological evidence is also forthcoming, since the tomb of a King of Byblos contained a handsome obsidian jar with gold inlay bearing the throne name of Amenemhet III. The traces clearly show that the oil this royal gift once contained had been slowly poured from it.

If the custom of anointing rulers in Syria-Palestine, which symbolized their position with respect to their Egyptian suzerain, was adopted by the Hebrews, they applied to it a new and most significant interpretation. For them it meant the recognition that their king was a vassal of Yahweh.

Egypt had long been renowned for her wisdom, as both Old and New Testaments affirm (1 Kgs. 4: 30 [Heb. 5: 10]; Acts 7: 22). She had a long tradition of didactic treatises designed for the edification of the sons of officials who were trained to enter government service. The earliest work of this nature to be mentioned in Egyptian sources is attributed to Imhotep, the

celebrated vizier of Djoser, first king of the Third Dynasty. This
has not survived, but books of instruction by an unnamed vizier
who wrote for his son Kagemni, also of the Third Dynasty, by
Hardjedef of the Fourth Dynasty, and above all by Ptahhotpe of
the Fifth Dynasty, are still extant. During the First Intermediate
Period, Khety III of the Tenth Dynasty compiled such a work
for his son and successor Merikarē. The New Kingdom produced
two treatises, those of Any and Amenemope, and the demotic
'Instruction of ʿOnkhsheshonqy' and the Insinger papyrus show
that this type of literature was still in vogue as late as the first
century A.D.

Such works, entitled *sbꜣyt*, 'teaching', in Egyptian, provided
the material of instruction in the scribal schools, and were used
to teach reading and writing, to inculcate rules of etiquette and
ethical conduct, and to develop habits of correct speech. We have
noted above that the tenth century, which witnessed the rapid
development of the Israelite state under David and Solomon, was
especially receptive to Egyptian influences, and perhaps saw the
introduction of similar scribal schools.

By the end of the eighth century, after the fall of Samaria to
Assyria, Hezekiah of Judah was once more the sole ruler of the
Hebrew state. His reign was marked by a nationalist revival which
looked back admiringly to the days of Solomon. It is not surprising
that Egyptian influence once again became strong. We have
alluded earlier to the presence of a pro-Egyptian party at this time
which roused the ire of Isaiah (Isa. 19: 11 f.). The *hᵃkᵃmīm*, 'wise
men', do not emerge as a professional group until this time, when
they are denounced by Isaiah (Isa. 29: 14). Scribal activity was
certainly a mark of the period, according to Prov. 25: 1. Perhaps
it would not be an exaggeration to describe Hezekiah as a patron
of literature. It is worthy of note that Egypt also was experiencing
an archaistic revival at the same time, beginning at least as early
as Piankhi, and continuing throughout the Twenty-sixth Dynasty.

Hebrew literature is permeated with concepts and figures

derived from the didactic treatises of Egypt, as we shall demonstrate in a moment. Yet works of a similar nature, composed by a father for his son, were also produced in Mesopotamia. It is surely significant that, apart from the 'Wisdom of Ahiqar', they appear to have had little appreciable influence on the Old Testament, whereas Akkadian sources contributed much in the areas of law, theodicy, psalmody, and mythology.

The most striking example of borrowing from Egyptian texts is found in Prov. 22: 17 to 23: 14. This small collection within the Book of Proverbs bears a remarkable similarity to the 'Wisdom of Amenemope', to which reference has already been made. The existence of an ostracon containing a schoolboy's copy of a portion of the text is clear evidence of the fact that the original work is much earlier than the actual British Museum papyrus, which has been dated by some scholars as late as the sixth century B.C. The work may, indeed, be as early as the thirteenth century.[1] It is characterized by a high ethical tone and an emphasis on personal piety which is a mark of the late Nineteenth Dynasty.

We turn first to a bold simile in *Amenemope* (9/14–19, 10/4 f.):

> Do not exert yourself to seek gain,
>> That your needs may be secure for you;
> If riches are brought to you by robbery,
>> They will not spend the night with you;
> At daybreak they are not in your house;
>> Their places can be seen, but they are not there! . . .
> They have made themselves wings like geese,
>> And have flown towards the sky.

This is adapted in Prov. 23: 4 f. as follows:[2]

---

[1] The attempt of Drioton to make both 'Amenemope' and Prov. 22: 17–23: 14 dependent on a common Semitic source (*Mélanges bibliques . . . André Robert*, Paris, 1957, pp. 254–80; *Sacra Pagina*, Paris, 1959, i. 229–41) has been answered by the present writer (*JEA* xlvii (1961), 100–6) and B. Couroyer (*Revue biblique*, lxx (1963), 208–24).

[2] In vs. 4 read מִבִּינָתְךָ for מִבִּינָתֶךָ, and in vs. 5 probably עָשֵׁר should be substituted for עָשֹׂה.

> Do not toil to become rich;
>> Cease from your plundering!
> Do your eyes light upon it?
>> It is gone!
> For riches make themselves wings,
>> Like an eagle which flies to the sky.

The Hebrew adapter has substituted the eagle, or more accurately the griffon-vulture, a familiar bird in Palestine, for the Egyptian goose, which is unknown to the Old Testament.

Another instance of the substitution of a Palestinian figure for an Egyptian occurs in Prov. 22: 24 f.:

> Do not be friendly with a hot-tempered man,
>> Nor go with a passionate man,
> Lest you learn his ways,
>> And get a snare for yourself!

The snare is a well-known metaphor in Biblical literature (e.g. Isa. 8: 14; Prov. 18: 7; 29: 6; Ps. 106: 36), and here replaces the lasso, peculiar to Egypt, which appears in the parallel in *Amenemope* (11/13 f., 17 f.):

> Do not fraternize with the passionate man,
>> Nor go too near him for conversation . . .
> Do not make him cast his speech to lasso you,
>> Nor be too free with your answer.

Here we encounter the Egyptian concept of the *šmm*, 'passionate man', as contrasted with the *gr*, 'silent man'. This antithesis is found as early as the Old Kingdom, and refers to the unbridled, unrestrained man as opposed to the man of self-control. To render the Egyptian term *pꜣ šmm*, the Hebrew writer has coined the expression *'iš ḥēmōṯ* (appearing once more in Prov. 15: 18 as *'iš ḥēmɔ̄*). The natural Hebrew equivalent is *qᵉṣar 'appayim* (cf. Prov. 14: 17).

Another passage from *Amenemope* reproduced in this section of Proverbs runs thus (3/9–16):

Give ear, hear what is said,
  Set your mind to interpret them;
It is profitable to fix them in your mind,
  But detrimental to him who ignores them.

Let them rest in the casket of your body,
  That they may be a door-post in your mind;
Indeed, when there is a gale of speech,
  They shall be a mooring-post for your tongue.

The Hebrew equivalent is found in Prov. 22: 17 f.:

Give ear, and hear my words,
  Set your mind to know them;
For it is fine that you keep them within you,
  That they be fixed as a tent-peg on your lips.

In vs. 17, as the Septuagint shows, *dibrē ḥᵃkᵊmīm*, 'the words of the wise', is a misplaced title, having taken the place of the original *dᵊbārᵊy*, 'my words'.[1]

This is not the only place where the Egyptian document has suggested a superior reading for the Hebrew text. In Prov. 22: 20 a strange form[2] appears, which has perplexed generations of scholars. The puzzle was finally solved when the concluding lines of *Amenemope* were examined (27/7–10):

Observe these thirty chapters:
  They divert; they instruct;
They constitute the foremost of all books;
  They inform the ignorant.

The work is indeed divided into thirty numbered chapters. Erman was the first to realize that the enigmatic Hebrew word should be read simply as *šᵊlōšīm*, 'thirty', and the Biblical verse rendered:

Have I not written thirty (sayings) for you,
  Consisting of sensible counsels?

---

[1] On the basis of the Egyptian passage, the unlikely word יַחְדָּו, 'together', in vs. 18, has been emended to (כְּ)יָתֵד.

[2] שָׁלְשׁוֹם.

Scholars have pointed out that, if the introduction, consisting of 22: 17–21, be excluded, the remainder of the collection consists of thirty distich lines. This was undoubtedly an attempt to conform to the pattern of the earlier work.

The influence of the 'Wisdom of Amenemope' is not confined to this section of the Book of Proverbs. In the former we read (19/14–17):

> The god is (always) given to success,
>> While mankind is given to failure;
> The words which men say are one thing,
>> The things which the god does are another.

As early as the Old Kingdom the sage Ptahhotpe had said (*Ptah.* 115 f.):

> The plans [lit. preparations] of men have never come about;
> It is what the god ordains that comes about.

His maxim became proverbial, for centuries later it was quoted on a stela of the Twenty-fifth Dynasty (*Urk.* iii. 72/33). The same sentiment was also expressed a little before Amenemope in the 'Instruction of Any' (8/10):

> Their [i.e. men's] plans are one thing;
> (Those of) the Lord of life are different.

Finally, the demotic 'Instruction of 'Onkhsheshonqy', of the Ptolemaic period, shows how persistent this belief was (26/14):

> The designs [lit. calculations] of the god are one thing;
> The thoughts of men are another.

In these passages we find the earliest expression in literature of the dictum of Thomas à Kempis, *Homo proposuit, sed Deus disponit*, or 'man proposes, but God disposes'. The sentiment is to be found in Prov. 16: 9 (cf. also 19: 21; 20: 24):

> Man's mind plans his way,
> But Yahweh directs his steps.

Another passage in *Amenemope* which is echoed in Biblical literature is the following (19/11–13):

> Do not pass the night fearful of the morrow;
>   When day dawns, what is the morrow like?
> Man is ignorant of what the morrow is like.

Again Ptahhotpe has anticipated the thought. One version runs, 'No one knows what may happen when he (tries to) perceive the morrow' (*Ptah.* 343); another, 'There is no one who knows his [*or* its] plans when he thinks about the morrow' (*Ptah.* 345). This too became a proverb which was later quoted in the Ramessid age (*P. Ram.* i. B i. 6 f.). In the well-known tale from the First Intermediate Period, the eloquent peasant says: 'Do not prepare for the morrow before it comes, for no one knows what trouble may be in it' (*Peas.*, B i. 183).

A similar sentiment is expressed in a series of maxims preserved on a New Kingdom ostracon: 'Do not prepare yourself on this day for tomorrow before it comes. Is yesterday not like tomorrow in the hands of god?' (*O. Petrie* 11, *rt.* 1). Compare with this Prov. 27: 1:

> Do not boast about tomorrow,
> Because you do not know what the day will bring forth.

Still later versions of this saying in the New Testament will quickly spring to mind (Matt. 6: 34; Jas. 4: 14).

A very fine simile concerning the silent and the passionate man forms the fourth chapter of *Amenemope* (6/1–12):

> As for the passionate man in a temple,
>   He is like a tree growing in a courtyard:
> In but a moment (comes) its loss of foliage,
>   And its end is reached in the timber-yard [?];
> It is floated far from its place,
>   And the flame is its burial shroud.
>
> The truly silent man keeps to one side;
>   He is like a tree growing in a plot [?]·

> It is verdant, and doubles its yield,
>   And (remains) before its owner;
> Its fruit is sweet, its shade pleasant,
>   And its end is reached in the grove.

This would appear to have been the source of Jer. 17: 5–8, a passage composed at a period when Egyptian influence was strongly in evidence. The theme turns up again in the Psalter (Pss. 1; 92: 12–15 [Heb. 13–16]).

An Egyptian milieu is also apparent in Prov. 25: 23: 'The north wind brings forth rain; a secretive tongue, a vexed countenance.' As is well known, the winds which produce rain in Palestine come from the west (cf. 1 Kgs. 18: 41 ff.; Luke 12: 54). It is in Egypt that such rains blow from the north.

The Book of Job has affinities with Mesopotamian literature, for it was there that the problem of theodicy first found expression. However, there are traces of Egyptian influence even here. Apart from references to papyrus and marsh reeds (8: 11) and reed skiffs (9: 26) in the dialogue, the clearest evidence comes from the later portions of the work. In Job's monologue (29–31) we encounter the phoenix (29: 18) and ostriches (30: 29). The description of Job's philanthropy in 29: 12–17 recalls the tomb inscriptions and stelae from the Old Kingdom. In the Sixth Dynasty, Harkhuf of Elephantine writes: 'I gave bread to the hungry, clothing to the naked; I brought to land him who had no ferryboat' (*Urk.* i. 122/6–8; cf. 133/2 f.). The eloquent peasant, during the Tenth Dynasty, addressed the chief steward Rensi thus: 'You are a father to the orphan, a husband to the widow, a brother to the divorcee, an apron to the motherless' (*Peas.*, B1, 62–4). The same statements continue into the Ptolemaic period, as the stela of Ta-Hebt shows (line 15). Job 31 calls to mind the 'Affirmation of Innocence' contained in Chapter 125 of the 'Book of the Dead' (*ANET* 34–6).

The Yahweh Speeches (38–42) also refer to Egyptian fauna, the ostrich, crocodile, and hippopotamus. The survey of natural phenomena in Chs. 38–9 has been compared by von Rad to the 'Onomastica', lists of birds, animals, plants, minerals, meteorological and geographical terms, compiled for the use of Egyptian scribes.[1] Babylonian scribes also composed similar lexicographical lists, but the great ḪAR-ra-ḫubullu has quite a different arrangement. The impressive series of questions by which the Deity interrogates Job is reminiscent of the teacher's sarcastic cross-examination of a pupil contained in Pap. Anastasi i (*ANET* 475–9) of the Nineteenth Dynasty.

The *carpe diem* motif appearing in Ecclesiastes (2: 24 f.; 3: 12 f., 22; 5: 18 f.; 9: 7–9) finds parallels in Egyptian literature. The earliest are to be found in the Harpers' Songs, one of which (*Khai-Inheret*, 10–2, 15 f.) counsels:

> Make holiday, in very truth!
> Put both incense and fine oil by you,
>> Wreaths of lotus and *rrmt*-flowers on your breast.
> The woman whom you love,
>> She it is who sits beside you. . . .
> Set your mind on drunkenness every day,
>> Till that day comes when there is mooring.

This text is carved on a tomb of the time of Ramesses III, but other versions go back to the Eighteenth Dynasty. The theme survived in Egypt for many centuries, so that in the tomb of Petosiris, from the end of the fourth century B.C., we read: 'Drink and be drunken; do not cease from festivity. Follow your desires while you are on earth. . . . When a man goes, his possessions go' (127/3 f.). The funerary stela of Taimhotep, dated 42 B.C., runs: 'May your heart not weary of eating or drinking, of drunkenness or the joys of love! Make holiday and follow your desire always. Do not set care in your mind' (*B.M. Stela* 146).

Early in the Twelfth Dynasty the renowned scribe Khety, son of Dwauf, composed a teaching addressed to his son Pepy (*ANET*

[1] G. von Rad, 'Hiob xxxviii und die altägyptische Weisheit', in *Suppl. to Vet. Test.* iii, Leyden, 1955, pp. 293–301.

432–4). In this he developed a new genre, the satire on the trades, in which various occupations are described and contrasted unfavourably with the noble office of the scribe. As might be expected, the theme became a very popular one in the scribal schools, and during the New Kingdom many imitators rang the changes on it (e.g. *P. Lansing*, *P. Anastasi* v, *P. Sallier* i). It was natural that a Hebrew teacher of Wisdom, acquainted with this literary tradition, should adapt it for his own use. Thus it was that Jesus ben Sira, about 190 B.C., incorporated it into his book (38: 24 – 39: 11).

The Egyptians showed a particular aptitude for lyric poetry. This found its finest expression in several collections of love songs from the later New Kingdom (*P. Harris* 500, *P. Ch. Beatty* i, and a papyrus in Turin; cf. *ANET* 467–9). An excellent example is the following (*P. Ch. Beatty* i. *vs.* C4/6–C5/2):

> Seven days till yesterday I have not seen (my) sister,
>> And illness has assailed me;
> I have become heavy of body,
>> Forgetful of my own person.
> If the leading physicians come to me,
>> My mind is displeased with their medicines;
> The lector-priests are without resource,
>> And my illness cannot be determined.
> To tell me, 'Here she is!' is what will revive me,
>> Her name is what will elate me.
> The coming and going of her messengers
>> Is what will revive my spirit.
> My sister is of more use to me than any medicines;
>> She is more to me than the medical corpus.
> My health is her coming in from outside;
>> The sight of her leads to fitness.
> She opens her eye, and my body is rejuvenated,
>> She speaks, and then I am invigorated.
> When I embrace her, she drives evil far from me—
>> But she has been gone from me for seven days!

This gift for lyricism, which was not characteristic of Akkadian literature, was transmitted to the Hebrews. Although the latter did not preserve much literature that might be regarded as secular, some of their love poetry has survived in the Biblical collection known as the Song of Songs. The marked resemblance of these poems to their Egyptian counterparts is unmistakable. With the above song, for instance, we might compare S. of S. 2: 5 and 5: 8. The Egyptian custom of employing the terms 'brother' and 'sister' for one's beloved is reflected also in the Hebrew work (4: 9–12; 5: 1 f.).

It is probable that Israel owed as much to Mesopotamia as to Egypt in the area of hymnology, but her debt to the latter civilization was by no means inconsiderable. Indeed, literary dependence on the great Hymn to Aten (*ANET* 369–71) has been claimed for Ps. 104. It cannot be denied that the similarity is impressive between this psalm and the hymn which was composed in the reign of the heretic king Akhenaten (*c.* 1365–1348 B.C.). Three examples must suffice. In the first, the terrors of darkness when Aten, the sun-god, has withdrawn himself are described (*Bibl. aeg.* viii. 93/17–94/3):

> When thou dost set in the western horizon,
>   The earth is in darkness, like to death.
> Men sleep in a bed-chamber, their heads covered,
>   One eye unable to behold the other.
> Were all their goods beneath their heads stolen,
>   They would be unaware of it.
> Every lion has come forth from his lair;
>   All the reptiles bite.
> Darkness prevails, and the earth is in silence,
>   Since he who made them rests in his horizon.

This is paralleled by Ps. 104: 20 f.:

> Thou appointest darkness, that it may be night,
>   In which all the beasts of the forest prowl:
> The young lions roaring for their prey,
>   To seek their food from God.

A little further on in the hymn we read (*Bibl. aeg.* viii. 94/8–10):

> Ships sail up and down stream alike,
> > Since every route is open at thine appearing.
> The fish in the river leap before thee,
> > For thy rays are in the midst of the sea.

With this we must compare Ps. 104: 25 f.:

> Here is the great and vast sea,
> > Wherein are teeming masses without number,
> > Living things both great and small.
> There the ships go,
> > Leviathan which thou didst create to play in it.

Finally, the Egyptian poet declares (*Bibl. aeg.* viii. 94/16 f.):

> How manifold is that which thou hast made, hidden from view!
> > Thou sole god, there is no other like thee!
> Thou didst create the earth according to thy will, being alone.

Ps. 104: 24 similarly affirms:

> How manifold are thy works, O Yahweh!
> All of them thou hast made by wisdom,
> > The earth is full of thy creations.

It must be admitted, however, that it is difficult to see how the psalmist could have been familiar with the Hymn to Aten. The latter composition, written more than 500 years earlier, was the product of a religious movement which later ages anathematized and sought to obliterate from their memory. For the text we are dependent on a single copy carved on the wall of the tomb of Ay at (Tell) El-Amarna. Is the resemblance, then, purely fortuitous?

The answer is to be found in the fact that, despite the rapid eclipse of Atenism, its influence lived on in art and literature. Just as the Aten hymn itself owed much to the earlier hymns to Amon-Rē, so later Egyptian sun-hymns incorporated ideas and phrases from that of Akhenaten. Dramatic proof of this is found in the tomb of Petosiris, constructed in the late fourth century B.C. Text No. 60, as Lefebvre has pointed out, echoes passages of the Aten hymns contained in this very Amarna tomb of Ay.

A further example of the same influence may be cited in **Ps. 34: 12** [Heb. 13]:

> Who is the man who desires life,
> Craving (many) days in order to enjoy good?

This can hardly be other than a reproduction of the line which occurs in a text inscribed in the same tomb at (Tell) El-Amarna: *ỉ wꜥ nb mr ꜥnḫ ꜣbỉ ꜥḥꜥw nfr*, 'O every one who loves life, desiring a long life of good' (*Bibl. aeg.* viii. 99/16).[1]

Before leaving the subject of psalmody, we should draw attention to the fact that here too Biblical literature has exercised an influence on that of Egypt. The tomb of Petosiris, High Priest of Amon-Rē at Hermopolis, to which we have already alluded on several occasions, is inscribed with a great body of texts. Earlier we noted that one contains the Hebraic expression 'fear of god'. Lefebvre, who edited the texts, has shown that No. 61 also betrays Jewish influence, especially from Ps. 128.

We have now passed in review the evidences for Egyptian influence on the Hebrews in the political, economic, linguistic, and literary spheres. We should expect to find at least as great a debt on the part of Israel in the area of religion. This would appear to be all the more likely in view of the adoption of Canaanite deities such as Astarte, Anath, Qadesh, Resheph, Horon, and even the title Baal, into the Egyptian pantheon. The remarkable fact is that the Egyptian contribution here is but negligible.

It has long been held by some scholars that Hebrew monotheism owed its origin to the Atenist heresy of Akhenaten. We have observed above that this religious movement soon disappeared after the death of Akhenaten, when the Egyptians assiduously attempted to expunge all traces of it. But far more disastrous to this theory is the fact that Atenism was probably not monotheistic at all. The introductory lines of the Hymn to Aten itself equate

---

[1] B. Couroyer, 'Idéal sapientiel en Égypte et en Israël (à propos du Psaume xxxiv, verset 13)', *Revue biblique*, lvii (1950), 174–9.

Aten with the deities Rē, Rē-Harakhti, and Shu. The line from the same hymn quoted above, 'Thou sole god, there is no other like thee' (*Bibl. aeg.* viii. 94/17), has been cited as testimony for such a monotheism. Yet the earlier Hymn to Amūn (*ANET* 365–7), which all scholars would accept as the product of a polytheistic faith, addresses the god Amon-Rē with crass tautology as 'The only sole one, who has no peer' (8/5), or again (6/2 f.):

> Thou art the sole one, who madest [every]thing,
> The only sole one, who madest what exists.

It is quite evident that this has become a mere literary cliché, and is not to be taken literally. Similar sentiments are expressed in the polytheistic sun-hymns from the post-Amarna period (such as *P. Ch. Beatty* iv. *rt.* and *P. Leiden* 350). They arise from the syncretistic and universalistic tendencies which mark the Empire period, and at the most could be described only as incipient monotheism. We can hardly do more than employ the term monolatry even for Atenism.

A Hebrew doctrine which may owe something to Egyptian sources is that of the creation of man in the image of God (Gen. 1: 26 f.; 5: 1; 9: 6; cf. 1 Cor. 11: 7; Jas. 3: 9). Attempts to show a dependence on Babylonian mythology are most unconvincing. However, in a work of the Tenth Dynasty in which the sun-god Rē is described as a beneficent creator, we read: 'They [i.e. mankind] are his likenesses [*snnw*] who have come forth from his body' (*Merikarē*, 132). The concept appears again in the New Kingdom. At the end of the 'Instruction of Any', in a lively exchange of letters between Any and his son, the latter writes: 'Men are in the image [*sn-nw*, lit. second] of the god ⟨because of⟩ their custom of hearing a man in regard to his reply. It is not the wise alone who is in his image [*sn-nw*], while the multitude are dumb beasts' (*Any*, 10/8 f.). Later still, during the Twenty-fifth Dynasty, Taharqa's sister Shepenwepet is described in a text at Karnak as the 'image' (*tit*) of the god Rē (*Rec. Tr.* xxii [1900], 128).

In the text just mentioned Rē is called *mniw nfr n rḫyt*, 'good shepherd of the people'. This is a common figure in Egyptian texts, going back to the First Intermediate Period. The sage Ipuwēr says of Rē: 'He is the shepherd of everyone, in whose mind there is no evil. His herds are diminished, (yet) he has certainly spent the day caring for them' (*Ipuwēr*, 12/1). Mankind is referred to as 'this noble flock' (*P. Westc.* 8/17), and Merikarē says: 'Men, the flock of the god [i.e. Rē], are (well) provided for' (*Merikarē*, 130 f.). In the New Kingdom sun-hymns Rē is spoken of as a good shepherd who is tireless, capable, and loving (*P. Ch. Beatty* iv. rt 3/4, 4/3, 10, 7/9, 8/6; cf. *B.M. Stela* 826, lines 7 and 11). The Biblical parallels are obvious (Isa. 40: 11; Mic. 2: 12; Jer. 31: 10; Ezek. 34: 11 ff.; Pss. 23: 1; 78: 52; 80: 1 [Heb. 2]; 95: 7, etc.). However, it should be noted that Mesopotamian texts also occasionally employ the word *rēʾū*, 'shepherd', in speaking of the gods, although it is much more commonly used with reference to human rulers.

During the First Intermediate Period in Egypt, the idea emerged of a final judgement of the deceased. Somewhat later Osiris became the final judge of all men. In the later copies of the 'Book of the Dead', vignettes frequently portray the scene of psychostasia, in which the heart of the deceased is weighed in the scales against *maʿat*, 'truth', 'justice', 'righteousness', while Anubis and Thoth preside over the proceedings (Pl. 18). The Hebrew belief in a doctrine of immortality is late, however, and consequently the idea of a final judgement does not appear before the second century B.C. (Dan. 7: 10; 12: 1–3; Enoch 47: 3; 90: 20 ff.; Heb. 9: 27; 1 John 4: 17; Jude 6; Rev. 20: 4, 12–15). However, a few earlier passages in the Old Testament may reflect Egyptian ideas concerning psychostasia (Job 31: 6; Prov. 16: 2; 21: 2; 24: 12). Certainly the motif of scales in which the good and evil deeds of men are weighed in the final judgement appears in later Jewish writings (Enoch 41: 1; 61: 8; 2 Esd. 3: 34; Apoc. of Elias 13: 13 f.).

It does not fall within the scope of this chapter to trace the further contributions of Egypt to the development of early Christianity. Nevertheless, enough has been said to show that Hebrew culture did not emerge in a vacuum, but was subjected to influences from many quarters, not the least of which came from the valley of the Nile.

RONALD J. WILLIAMS

BIBLIOGRAPHY

A. ALT, *Israel und Aegypten*, Leipzig, 1909.

A. CAUSSE, 'Sagesse égyptienne et sagesse juive', *Revue d'histoire et de philosophie religieuses*, ix (1929), 149–69.

P. HUMBERT, *Recherches sur les sources égyptiennes de la littérature sapientiale d'Israel*, Neuchâtel, 1929.

P. MONTET, *L'Égypte et la Bible*, Neuchâtel, 1959.

W. O. E. OESTERLEY, *The wisdom of Egypt and the Old Testament*, London, 1927.

T. E. PEET, *Egypt and the Old Testament*, Liverpool–London, 1922.

E. H. SUGDEN, *Israel's debt to Egypt*, London, 1928.

R. WEILL, 'Les Transmissions littéraires d'Égypte à Israël', *Cahier complémentaire à la Revue d'Égyptologie*, 1950, pp. 43–61.

11

THE CONCEPT OF LAW IN ANCIENT EGYPT[1]

In daring to speak of 'law' in ancient Egypt one tends to lay oneself open to a number of criticisms. In the opinion of some authorities it is nonsense to talk of law before it was elaborated by the Romans, and this view, which holds for the whole of the ancient Orient, applies particularly to Egypt owing to the lack of documentary evidence. We have, after all, collections of Sumerian, Akkadian, Hittite, and Neo-Babylonian laws—but nothing of the kind from Egypt. Even documents relating to legal practice are rare, and the few traces that are preserved are in religious contexts, thus encouraging the theory, so dear to sociologists, of the progressive *désacralisation* of institutions, a process completed only in the classical era. Moreover, in their legal deeds the Egyptians use everyday language with the addition of only a few technical terms, and even these had several applications and were frequently imprecise, giving rise to suspicion of a lack of clarity in their concepts. The problem is thus, in short, to determine whether they had really progressed beyond a vague legal empiricism.

[1] In the present chapter I have tried to give an over-all picture of the legal and judicial institutions of ancient Egypt and their evolution, having regard to the historical background and endeavouring wherever possible to include and analyse extracts from actual documents. A more detailed study of the law of the Old Kingdom is to be found in J. Pirenne, *Histoire des institutions et du droit privé de l'ancienne Égypte*, and a systematic account of the material, with a precise chronological summary of the sources, in the various works of Erwin Seidl dealing with pharaonic Egypt (see the Bibliography). In the following notes, $RIDA = Revue internationale des droits de l'antiquité$.

In reply it must be said that if Egypt ever went through the stages which ethnologists call 'tribal' and 'gentilic', she had certainly passed out of them by the time she entered upon the historical era at the beginning of the third millennium B.C. The social and administrative system then encountered in the Nile valley is based on the family and even on the individual, and, as far as institutions are concerned, there is developing at the same time a strong civil organization.

This organization existed at an early period. To realize this, one has only to refer to the Palermo Stone, which proves that from the dawn of the historical period the Egyptian administration recorded, for instance, the annual level of the Nile flood, and that, as well as the census of population, a biennial census 'of gold and fields' was made, at least from the Second Dynasty onwards. What does this imply, if not that the transfer of both personal and landed property from one owner to another was considerable, and that private property must therefore have existed?

From the evidence of documents of legal practice, so often damaged and handed down in an incomplete form in funerary inscriptions, it thus appears that private property did indeed exist, that it was transferable, and further that there was real equality between man and wife in the eyes of the law. Children were supposed to inherit an equal share of their parents' estate, unless the latter had made other dispositions, for the practice of making a will was known. A wife was not her husband's legal heir, but she could be made his legatee, and provision could be made for legacies to third parties.

The state guaranteed the execution of deeds of conveyance by registering them, as is shown for example by the document called 'the contract for the sale of a small house' (in the pyramid city of Khufu (Cheops) of the early Fourth Dynasty). This I should prefer to regard as evidence of a legal dispute following upon the sale, and such an interpretation would give additional support to the view that, from the Old Kingdom, sale in Egypt could be by consent.[1] If the plaintiff had in his possession the order for recovery of the property which established his right to it, it is evident that the sale was completed once agreement had been reached. Moreover, it should be noted that, despite the inadequacy of our documentation, there are clear indications of the bilateral nature of such transactions. The *Stèle Juridique* from Karnak (of the Seventeenth Dynasty, *c.* 1600–1570 B.C.) reveals that at that period the parties concerned were given a year to fulfil their obligations, with the possibility of requesting a renewal of the time allowed.[2]

The Fourth Dynasty contract had been prepared before the local council, which had registered it, and in the presence of several witnesses, all ordinary people, principally artisans, who therefore enjoyed full civil rights. Workers were, indeed, respected and remunerated, and a document shows that even a queen of the glorious Fourth Dynasty had paid those who constructed her tomb.

Again in the same dynasty, an important individual named Heti made a will (or, more literally, gave out an 'order' from his 'living mouth'), expressing himself in the following terms (*Urk.* i. 162 f.):

As for all my children, truly, that which I have constituted for them, as assets of which they shall enjoy the usufruct, I have not granted any of them the right to dispose of his (share), as a gift or in consideration of payment (?) . . . an exception being made for the son he may have and to whom he shall transfer (it). They are to act under my eldest son's authority as they would act with regard to their own property; for I have appointed an heir against the day—the latest possible—when I shall go to the West.

These funerary priests who shall act under his authority, he shall call upon them for my funerary offering each day and on (such-and-such) festivals . . ., but I have not granted him the right to require of them any service whatever, other than the funerary offering (which shall be made) for me each day . . .

[1] J. Pirenne, *Histoire des institutions*, ii, pp. 293 f.; *Archives d'histoire du droit oriental*, i (1937), 9–11.

[2] A. Théodoridès, *RIDA* ix (1962), 102–15.

We gather that the author of the will is turning property, the source of which he does not reveal, into an endowment to provide for his mortuary cult. Some of his contemporaries made contractual agreements with priests, but Heti wishes to avoid letting any part of the endowment's revenues be lost to his heirs. This is why he makes his children into a family syndicate, placed, as a consequence of his dispositions, under the authority of his eldest son, who is to administer the estate. The deed of foundation makes it clear that each member of the said syndicate will himself receive only the revenue from this estate, which has been made indivisible in perpetuity.

The founder transfers the property in question to an association of individuals, but it is evident none the less that the association is conceived as such and that it has its own legal personality.[1] The same is true also of temples, whose estates are regarded as belonging to the gods to whom they are dedicated and which may be represented at law. And so it is too with the state, which we see, for example, paying out revenues allocated for religious purposes that are a perpetual charge on government assets. As the beneficiaries from these incomes can dispose of them in various ways, we are faced at this early date with a remarkable system of credit.

However, from the Fourth Dynasty precisely there was a change in the concept of royal power. The king had become the head of a very strong centralized government, the machinery and regulation of which (the ladder of promotion, the hierarchy of officials), by the very fact of their existence, inhibited any tendency he might have to act arbitrarily. The same king was in supreme control of legislation, but laws were conceived as expressions of ideal justice. A law promulgated in the proper way remained in force so long as it was neither modified nor abrogated, and we see the king rescinding decisions made by his administration in opposition to established laws.

[1] J. Pirenne, *Histoire des institutions*, ii, pp. 327 f.; G. Thausing, *Wiener Zeitschrift für die Kunde des Morgenlandes*, li (1948), 14–20.

But the king, descendant of the gods and divinely inspired—especially in his legislative work—succeeded in obtaining acceptance, in his role of Horus, no longer merely as the son of Rē, but as the incarnation of Rē himself. The consequent creation of a religious cult of royalty disorganized the administrative system, in that the king, henceforth all-powerful and absolute, placed himself above it. The cult weakened the administration and at the same time the king himself, since the royal priesthood he appointed was endowed with revenues and benefices (in the form of ever more extensive estates) which could not but impoverish the crown. And, when the very administrative functions themselves were handed over to the royal 'privileged', we witness the break-up of territorial rule. The provincial governors arrogated the rights of royalty and became princes, and the king was then no more than *primus inter pares*.

Several mastabas have preserved representations and descriptions of life in the great seigneurial domains, in which, in the Sixth Dynasty, a closed economy was established and individuals were no longer equal in law. It is wrong to attempt to form a picture of social, economic, and legal life in Egypt during the Old Kingdom on the basis of evidence from these representations; they are valid only for one class (the nobility) and for a particular period.

It is in the general context of the Sixth Dynasty, with its altered social conditions, that we must place Pap. Berlin 9010, which reveals a new state of affairs on the occasion of a succession.[1] The translation is as follows:

(A) Title (missing);

[On such and such a date . . . opening of legal proceedings on behalf of Sebekhotpe against Tjau by . . .]

(B) Arguments of the parties involved:

This Sebekhotpe [has produced a documen]t [which the royal noble], the overseer of caravans, User [is alleged to have had] made,

---

[1] K. Sethe, *ZÄS* lxi (1926), 67–79.

[by which] his wife, his children and all his property [were placed (?)] in his power (?) in order to satisfy by (this) means [all] the children of this User, treating the old and the young according to their age.

But this Tjau has replied that his father never made it (this document) in any place whatever.

(C) Interlocutory judgement:

If this Sebekhotpe produces unimpeachable and trustworthy witnesses who will take oath (in these terms): 'Let your might be against him (i.e. Tjau), O god, in so far as this document was truly made in accordance with the declaration of this User', these things shall be in the power of this Sebekhotpe, when he shall have produced these witnesses in whose presence this utterance (of User) was voiced, while this Sebekhotpe shall be the usufructuary.

But if he does not produce the witnesses (*irw*) in whose presence this utterance was voiced, none of the said User's property shall be kept in his possession; it shall be kept in the possession of his son (i.e. the eldest son of User), the royal noble, the overseer of caravans, Tjau.

The fundamental question here raised is whether on the basis of this text one can argue that at this point of time a woman no longer enjoyed more than a reduced legal status, which, in particular, placed her under the tutelage of her husband, and after his death under that of his eldest son, or, indeed, of a third party designated by her husband in a will.

Pirenne has been criticized for holding this view, but it must be noted that his theory does not rest on this single document. The interpretation he gives results from the combination of various deductions drawn from all the sources relating to the institutions of this period, and thus throws light on the evolution which has taken place in public and family law since the Fourth Dynasty.

The appearance of 'benefices', the enrichment of privileged families, the proliferation of endowments, the concentration of property into a few hands, had the effect of making the constitution of landed property more rigid and of strengthening ties within the propertied families. Proof of this is to be found in the appearance of the idea of the 'eldest son', to whom the administration of the funds of the joint property was entrusted. On the death of the eldest in a family, the title and duties of 'eldest son' devolved upon the next in age, though in fact a daughter was not called upon to hold a position equivalent to that of 'eldest son', for she was not 'eldest' in relation to her brothers.

The legal equality which existed among children during the Third and Fourth Dynasties had altered, which does not in any way imply that at the close of the Old Kingdom daughters, or women in general, no longer had any rights. Moreover, these observations hold only for members of the land-owning nobility which had come into being at that time. Just as the nomes had changed into principalities, so the domains became seigneurial properties, with the juridico-social position of those who were in possession of them established on a hereditary basis.

Tjau, whom we have already encountered through Pap. Berlin 9010, belonged to the nobility; as a 'royal noble' he was qualified to receive the benefice with which his father, or a more distant ancestor, had been favoured by the king. He had inherited his father's title, his function ('overseer of caravans'), and likewise his property, which he had to preserve undivided, with the duty of administering it for the whole family. It is worth noting that it was no longer necessary, as in earlier times, to insert a special clause in a will so that he should acquire the rights and duties of an elder son. The succession to his father's estate was legally vested in him, which amounts to saying that if his father had died intestate Tjau, by virtue of his status as eldest son, would have administered the property, and in this connection have exercised control over his own mother, as well as over his brothers and sisters. From the way the document is constructed it may be inferred that he had already begun to act in this way as administrator and guardian, since he is the defendant in the case, which a third party, named Sebekhotpe, has brought against him. The latter opposes the administration of Tjau on the basis of a will which User is said to have made without his son's knowledge, and to his disadvantage.

It has been said that this Sebekhotpe would not have been a guardian but a 'usufructuary' who would have had to divide the estate among User's children. It should, however, be noted that this is not stipulated in the document and that, moreover, the right to a life interest in a property does not imply a state of transition towards the division of such property. This may be verified from the extract from the contracts of Hapidjefai, quoted below, in which he expressly provides that the usufructuary shall be forbidden to 'share' the property entrusted to him.

It has also been maintained that, if, in spite of everything, one has to admit that Sebekhotpe was indeed called upon to exercise tutelage over User's wife, it is not absolutely necessary to take this as an indication that women suffered legal disability: User's wife might in the event have been 'much too young'. This hypothesis cannot, however, be defended, since the woman was, after all, the mother of Tjau, who, in that he had inherited his father's position, was certainly of age—and, if the author of the will had put forward a specific reason for placing his wife under tutelage, would he not have had to justify this measure? This is not at all the case, especially in that if it were not Sebekhotpe who was to exercise the tutelage it would be User's own son, and this in complete accordance with the law.

In actual fact, at the time of the lawsuit the tutelage is not at issue. Neither Tjau nor the magistrate disputes the legality of the will's provisions. What has to be established is a question of fact: did User really compose the 'deed'?

It may be noted that there is reference only to a 'writing', and not to an *imyt-pr*, the expression which designates a certified deed of conveyance. Moreover, according to the evidence of Egyptian texts, the author of a deed of this kind 'makes' his *imyt-pr*, whereas in this case it seems that User 'had his "writing" made', so that perhaps the document in question was of a special kind which would not have been registered. This, to my mind, would explain why the magistrate required the production not of an abstract of this 'writing', but of the testimony of persons who were alleged to have been present when it was drawn up.

The term *irw* which has been translated 'witness' is unusual, if not unique. Etymologically it could refer to 'those who made' the writing, the 'co-authors' of the document who had a hand in drawing it up, for, as we have seen, User 'had his "writing" made'; he must have dictated (?) it at a time when—because of his state of health (?)—he could not do otherwise. At all events, the method employed is recognized as valid. It rests with Sebekhotpe to prove the authenticity of the 'writing' he has produced. The tribunal gives the terms of the oath the witnesses will have to swear: they will have to testify that the 'writing' was really made 'in conformity with the declaration of User'.

My personal view is that we may here be at the stage of the preliminary investigation of the dispute. Sebekhotpe has probably lodged a complaint with the office of the clerk to the tribunal, which has undertaken to notify Tjau. The examining magistrate has pronounced the judgement, which orders a further inquiry (in the form of summoning witnesses, the summoning to be the plaintiff's responsibility). Proceedings will then have been adjourned until further notice. The papyrus gives us the official report of this sitting, in which the clerk to the tribunal began by summarizing the arguments of the plaintiff and then of the defendant, and ended with a note of the magistrate's decision.

We have now only to return for a moment to the word 'usufructuary' contained in the first part of the judgement. Provided of course that his plea is not dismissed, Sebekhotpe will become the 'usufructuary', but the fact must not be overlooked that, legally as well as grammatically, the proposition containing this term is secondary to the essential element: 'these things shall be in [his] power' (these being the wife, children, and property of User). In practical terms, 'usufructuary' specifies the method of administration, if not of remuneration, envisaged. Sebekhotpe 'shall consume' the fruits of the assets 'to which he may not cause any loss'; he is to handle it like a good father of the family. It may be deduced from the information given in the text that this would continue so until his death, after which the rights of administration and tutelage, which would have been conferred on him by the disputed will, would return to Tjau, or to his legal heir. The last line of the papyrus seems to emphasize once again the right of 'possession' which Sebekhotpe would exercise over the property. It is precisely the same formula as is used for Tjau, who, as User's eldest son, and in default of the will invoked by his opponent, will be the administrator of the benefice, which has become a joint family asset he cannot dispose of, since he does not own it entirely.

In giving this account—which may already seem long enough, though certain details might still be further amplified—I have tried to point out the difficulties encountered in interpreting texts of this kind, which consist of reports of hearings too laconic for our appreciation. And it is worse still with the great majority of ostraca (notably of the Ramessid period, Nineteenth–Twentieth Dynasties), which give mere extracts of deeds or official reports, keeping strictly to essentials, and which were intended to serve as memoranda for litigants.

At the same period, following the break-up of the Old Kingdom, some texts shed a few gleams of light upon the activities of the 'middle class'. Pirenne has defined their status and pointed out that their appearance cannot have been the result of spontaneous generation.[1] By definition, documents relating to the 'domains' take no account of them, which does not in any way indicate that they did not exist at that time. It was when domanial

---

[1] J. Pirenne, *Archives d'histoire du droit oriental*, iii (1948), 125–43.

and seigneurial rule was tending to establish itself all over the country, stifling the economy, that the middle class of the towns rebelled: 'Every town says: "Come, let us put down the powerful ones among us. . . . The vessel of Upper Egypt is adrift; the towns are destroyed and Upper Egypt is a desert." ' There is no question of similar destruction as far as towns of Middle and Lower Egypt are concerned, and Memphis, the displaced capital of the Old Kingdom, was even to remain the centre of commercial activity within the compass of urban institutions.

Little by little, however, the reunification of Egypt came about, this time, during the Eleventh Dynasty, at the hands of the princes of Thebes.

In the letters of Hekanakhte,[1] which date from this period (*c.* 2000 B.C.), one senses a kind of feverish urge to accumulate wealth. The funerary priest Hekanakhte is a landed proprietor; he has property in various parts of the country and travels about much more for business reasons than in connection with his office. On his principal estate, to the south of Thebes, live several people, who seem to be members of his family: his mother and her servant, another person, who may be an aunt, also with her servant, . . . and his children (boys and girls). The eldest, Merisu, is in charge of the people and property there in his father's absence, but this duty does not appear to give him any legal or economic privileges. All are paid in proportion to the work they do, independent of age or sex. These payments are personal acquisitions, and as a consequence they entail financial responsibilities. If, for example, some head of cattle are lost, their 'price' will be debited to such of the children as were in charge of them. Hekanakhte likes to use commercial terms!

[1] T. G. H. James, *The Hekanakhte Papers and Other Early Middle Kingdom Documents*, New York, 1962. Cf. assessments by K. Baer, *Journ. American Research Center in Egypt*, i (1962), 34 f.; *Journ. American Oriental Soc.* lxxxiii (1963), 1–19; A. Théodoridès, *Chronique d'Égypte*, xli (1966), 295–302.

But let him speak for himself, occasionally with a certain acrimony, in a letter addressed to his mother and his son Merisu. He reproaches the 'household' for not accepting readily the reductions in payment which he has fixed for them:

See, you yourselves are people who eat until you are satisfied, . . . the whole land is dying (of starvation), but you are not hungry. See, I came here upstream and determined your rations for the best. Will the inundation be very great? See, our rations will be fixed for us according to the state of the inundation.

Be patient, all of you . . . Avoid being angry about this (fixing of rations). See, the whole household is (treated) like [my] children, but all the property is mine, and, as they say, it is better to be half alive than to die outright . . . and see, . . . they have started to eat men here; see, such rations are not given to them (i.e. people) anywhere (else). Conduct yourselves (therefore) with stout hearts until I reach you, for I shall spend the season of *shomu* here . . . You shall give this payment to my people according to how they are doing (their) work. Attend to it strictly . . . Be very diligent, since you are eating my rations . . . Now as for anyone among the women and men who shall reject these rations, let him come to me here to live with me as I live; but there will certainly be no one who will come to me here.

It is clear from his correspondence that Hekanakhte wants to get the maximum return from his agricultural enterprise by taking advantage of a situation which may not be quite as alarming as he would like to make out. He seems to be speculating on the demand for cereals, which he sells at a good price, and with the metal obtained 'in exchange' he takes out leases on other estates which he exploits in the same way. One gets the impression that Hekanakhte wants to get people to work harder and at a lower wage in order to make higher profits. He is not simply a landowner, but a businessman actuated by the profit motive, who speculates on the price of foodstuffs. Unfortunately, the information provided by the letters is too summary for one to be able to determine the legal status of the members of the 'household' (or of the 'domain') with any precision.

At all events, the right of primogeniture, which, as we have seen, had become the rule after being introduced in the form of a testamentary provision from the Fourth Dynasty, fell into disuse. And consequently, in order to maintain the indivisibility of an estate set up as an endowment, Hapidjefai, nomarch and high priest of Siut in the Twelfth Dynasty, addresses his funerary priest as follows: 'May you watch over all my assets which I have placed in your charge, and of which this is the document. The one you shall favour among your children, and who shall act as funerary priest for me (after you), shall enjoy the usufruct of it, and he alone, under prohibition of sharing it out among his children, in accordance with this will which I have expressed to you.'

The same Hapidjefai drew up various contracts with the priesthood of the temple of Siut, all for the benefit of his personal cult. It has been said of one of these contracts that it was made between Hapidjefai in his capacity as a private individual, and the high priest, which he also was. But in fact it is with the high-priesthood of Siut that he, as nomarch and high priest, concludes an agreement relating to certain offerings which are to be made to his statue in the temple—on his side he makes over properties which he affirms are part of his patrimony and do not come from the 'house' of the nomarch—and thus he binds the high-priesthood for the future. The text adds that he agreed to this in the presence of the temple council, over which, as high priest, he presided at the time and which was thus answerable for the honouring of the agreement by future high priests.

Then again, a passage in Pap. Brooklyn 35. 1446 (beginning of the Thirteenth Dynasty, *c.* 1785 B.C.) shows the married woman enjoying a completely independent legal personality, in that she brings a lawsuit as plaintiff against her father in order to protect strictly private interests: 'My father has committed an irregularity (?). He had in his possession objects belonging to me and [which] my husband [had given me], but he (my father) made them over to his (second) wife Senebtisi. May I obtain restitution (thereof).'[1] She is thus free to go to law without in any way being under marital authority.

The *imyt-pr* was, during the Old Kingdom, a deed of transfer by gift, but later became the generic term covering all kinds of conveyance: thus in Pap. Kahun ii. 1 (end of the Twelfth Dynasty), the plaintiff wishes to recover an outstanding debt inherited from his father and relating to a credit sale which had been concluded by *imyt-pr*. An *imyt-pr*, which provides for a unilateral transfer of property through arrangements consequent upon death, corresponds to what we know as a will. It is to be noted that the *imyt-pr* are made in the form of a declaration to the local council of the *srw* (**sar*: representatives of public authorities), who register it and send a minute to be kept in the vizieral archives. Transfers are sometimes accompanied by conditions (e.g. indivisibility or entailment). The taking of an oath is not required for the drawing up of an *imyt-pr* valid as a will, because it can be revoked, but it is necessary in the case of deeds which involve liabilities for the future.

An instance of this is to be found in Pap. Kahun vii. 1,[2] of which a translation and discussion here follow:

Year 39 (of Amenemhet III, Twelfth Dynasty, *c.* 1834 B.C.), the 4th month of (the season) *akhet*, the 19th day.

Deed of transfer (*imyt-pr*) which the 'phylarch' Mery-son-of-Inyotef, called Kebi, drew up in favour of his son Inyotef-son-of-Mery, called Iuseneb.

I transfer my office of 'phylarch' to my son Inyotef-son-of-Mery, called Iuseneb, on condition of his being for me 'a staff of old age', in that I have grown infirm. Let him be appointed to it immediately.

As for the deed of transfer which I drew up in favour of his mother previously, it is revoked; and as for my house situated in

---

[1] W. C. Hayes, *A Papyrus of the Late Middle Kingdom in the Brooklyn Museum*, Brooklyn, 1955, pp. 114 f., pl. xiv; A. Théodoridès, *RIDA* vii (1960), 87–8, 92–3.

[2] F. Ll. Griffith, *Hieratic Papyri from Kahun and Gurob*, pp. 29–31, pl. xi [= K. Sethe, *Aegyptische Lesestücke*, Leipzig, 1928, p. 90, ll. 1–11]; A. Théodoridès, *RIDA* v (1958), 38–43.

the region of Hatmadet (?), it is for the children who may be borne (*msy*) to me by Satnebneninesu, the daughter of the guard of the councillor of the district, Sobekemhat, together with all that it contains.

List of the names of the witnesses present at the drawing up of this deed of transfer: (three names).

This *imyt-pr* annuls a previous deed with the same title which was a will, but it does not itself constitute a will, since it is expressly laid down by the wish of the settlor that it shall take effect immediately. It may be noted that the revocation applies only to the second part of the text and that, consequently, the first clause has nothing to do with it. But why then was it brought into the present *imyt-pr* of which the son is made beneficiary when it does not concern him, or so at least it would appear? What, in other words, was the *raison d'être* of the first *imyt-pr*?

Apart from his religious function, still a family affair at this period and so hereditary, the father reckoned among his assets a house and its furnishings. On his dying intestate, the whole would have passed to his son, but he must have made a legacy to his wife and it is this disposition which will have necessitated the drawing up of the first *imyt-pr*. It may be supposed that the will in question would have become void on the death of the legatee; in fact, it is by the present deed that the husband annuls his previous liberality. One wonders whether the revocation may not conceal a repudiation. At all events, the father speaks of the 'mother' of his son and not of his own wife; but neither does he give the title of wife to the second woman, though from the context it would seem unlikely that he had only an irregular relationship with her. It would be tempting to assume therefore that the deed was drawn up at the time of a remarriage. The form *msy(w)* would then be better taken as a prospective participle ('the children who *may be* borne to me . . .'), which would be consistent with the fact that the children of the second liaison are neither named nor even enumerated. By the terms of the first *imyt-pr* the legacy had evidently been entailed and the son named as beneficiary of his mother, and it is in this respect that he was affected by the revocation of the will.

It was not therefore because of the first wife that the previous *imyt-pr* was annulled (it would in fact have remained effective even after her death and the hypothesis of a possible repudiation would be pointless), but because the father, at the time of the apportionment which he now makes, is also concerned about the children he may have by the other woman. As he stipulates that his (eldest) son should serve him as 'staff of old age' (which amounts to saying that he has to make him a good allowance), the apportionment we have here would correspond, as Maspero noted, to what under the *Ancien Régime* was called a *démission de biens*.

Quite apart from the fact that the present deed modified, fundamentally, the terms of the first *imyt-pr*—a codicil would otherwise have been sufficient, as is clear from another Kahun papyrus[1]—the father was bound to draw it up because he was in fact transferring his assets before his death and because, moreover, as far as his eldest son was concerned, he was doing so conditionally.

The kings of the Twelfth Dynasty reconstituted the administrative system, with its unifying force. But the Hyksos invasion in the time known as the Second Intermediate Period (1678–1554 B.C.) must have afforded the great lords of Upper Egypt a new lease of independence, to the extent that the principate of El-Kab could still be regarded by its holder as a transferable patrimony. However, if during the seigneurial period which followed the Old Kingdom a prince was master of his province, this is no longer the case under the Seventeenth Dynasty. The prince has as his counterpart a military chief directly dependent upon the king (Petrie,

[1] Pap. Kahun i.1, 14; cf. A. Théodoridès, *Annuaire de l'Institut de phil. et d'hist. orientales et slaves*, xiv (1954–7), 94; *RIDA* v (1958), 42–3; viii (1961), 52–3.

Koptos, pl. viii), and Pap. Berlin 10.470 shows us the vizier's administration introducing its legal machinery everywhere so as to centralize procedure.[1]

. . . Such (therefore) are the prescriptions. See, the parchment from the vizier's office is brought to you, so that you may know all the measures (?) of justice in this (matter) . . .

See that, having been interrogated, they (the interested parties) approve it, and also that they take oath on the matter. See that the prescriptions (of the rescript) are presented to the slave Senbet (the subject of the litigation). See that (a report) is sent so as to make it known to the prince of Elephantine . . .

This is sent to make it known to them (that is to say, as instructions to the administrative officials of Elephantine).

The prince is kept informed of legal proceedings in his province, but he no longer controls them.

As regards slaves, who were not very numerous in Egypt—the reference here is not to prisoners of war—and who were bought and transferred from owner to owner like chattels, it is evident that they enjoyed a legal status which made them more like serfs. They could acquire property and bear witness at law, even against their masters. . . ;[2] they seem also to have been able to marry easily with free individuals or to be adopted by them, so becoming free themselves, the process of manumission being unknown.[3]

Ahmose, the founder of the Eighteenth Dynasty after the liberation of Egypt, rapidly completed the territorial and administrative unification.

Thanks to the 'Instructions' given by the king to his vizier we are familiar with the principles which inspired the royal works. Their composition must go back to the Thirteenth Dynasty, but the outstanding copy which we possess, that in the tomb of

[1] P. C. Smither, *JEA* xxxiv (1948), 31–4, pls. vii–viii; A. Théodoridès, *RIDA* vi (1959), 131 f.
[2] A. Bakir, *Slavery in Pharaonic Egypt*, Cairo, 1952, pp. 84 f.
[3] A. Théodoridès, *RIDA* xii (1965), 79–142.

Rekhmirē, dates from the Eighteenth Dynasty. There we find first a veritable ethic of viziership, in which it is laid down that justice is to be rendered in public and in such a way that every individual shall always secure his rights. To this end, appeal is made to a sense of equity and also, by implication, to jurisprudence, since it is pointed out that the records of all judgements are kept in the vizier's archives, where they could certainly have been consulted:[1]

> . . . See, if a petitioner presents himself, from south or north, (in a word) from anywhere in the country, equipped (with his papers?), seeking an audience at the vizier's office, take care that you judge every case in conformity with the provisions of the law and (also) judge every case with the correctness which is proper to it, [giving every person] his rights.
>
> See, with regard to the magistrate who gives judgement in public the water and the wind report on all that he does. And if he does something unjust . . .
>
> See, it is the refuge of the magistrate to judge cases in conformity with the instructions and by putting into execution what has been decided. A petitioner who has received judgement [should not say: 'I have] not [been given my rights'].
>
> See, it is a maxim found in the 'collection of Memphis' . . . Beware of that with which they reproached the vizier Khety, namely that he dealt unfavourably with his kindred to the advantage of strangers, fearing that it might be said of him: 'He [judges] with partiality' . . . that is more than justice. Do not (therefore) judge [inconsistently]; the abomination of the god (i.e. the king) is partiality.
>
> Such is the doctrine (*sbȝyt*: 'instruction'). You must act accordingly: you shall look upon him who is known to you in the same way as him who is unknown to you; him who is close to you in the same way as him who is far from you . . .
>
> Do not send a petitioner away before giving attention to his words. If there is a petitioner who has recourse to you, do not [reject] what he says, arguing that it must have been said (already); you shall dismiss him (only) after letting him hear the reason why

---

[1] R. O. Faulkner, *JEA* xli (1955), 18–29; A. Théodoridès, *RIDA* xiv (1967), 148–51.

you dismiss him, for it is maintained that a petitioner would rather that you pay attention to what he says than see judgement given on that for which [he has] come.

Do not be angry with a man without justification; be angry (only) because of that for which there is reason to be angry. Inspire fear of yourself, so that you are feared, for he is (truly) magistrate, the magistrate who is feared. But the reputation of a magistrate lies in his practising justice; and if a man makes himself feared excessively, there is something of injustice in him in the opinion of people who cannot say of him: 'He is a man' (in the fullest sense of the word) . . . As for the office in which you hold audience, it includes a large room which contains [the records] of [all] the judgements, for he who must practise justice before all men is the vizier . . . Do not act as you please in cases where the law to be applied is known . . .

The whole of the first section of the text of the 'obligations of the vizier' deals with the jurisdictional rights of this highest official in administrative matters:[1]

Now with regard to the general procedure of the vizier holding audience in his office: whosoever [is not] perfect in any service (?) ought to be heard by (the vizier) with regard to the matter; he who does not then himself put from him the fault (which has been committed) after he (the vizier) has heard the circumstances shall be entered in the register of malefactors which is kept in the great prison, and it shall be the same for him who does not put from him the fault (committed) against the (vizier's) messenger.

In case of backsliding on their part, the first thing to be done is to send their criminal record to the vizier.

The same text then deals with civil cases relating to land trans-actions in the country, for all land registration comes within the vizier's jurisdiction. That is why the *imyt-pr* have to be sent to him.

In relation to judicial procedure one may cite a papyrus dated

---

[1] N. de G. Davies, *The Tomb of Rekh-mi- rēʿ at Thebes*, i, New York, 1953, p. 91; W. C. Hayes, *A Papyrus of the Late Middle Kingdom in the Brooklyn Museum*, Brooklyn, 1955, pp. 40–1; H. W. Helck, *Zur Verwaltung des mittleren und neuen Reichs*, Leiden–Köln, 1958, pp. 33–4; A. Théodoridès, *RIDA* vi (1959), 120–1; vii (1960), 135.

in the reign of Thutmose III (Eighteenth Dynasty, *c.* 1490–1436 B.C.) where, although the first part is damaged, there is preserved the conclusion of a case under review in which the petitioner's appeal is dismissed. The statement given as to the grounds of the decision embraces the factors taken into consideration, followed by the legal basis of the sentence and the enacting terms, in which we find the time-honoured formula: 'A is right, B is wrong.' It is apparent from this report that the law invoked envisaged respect for the *res judicata*. It made provision for a 'hundred strokes' for any reckless litigant.[1]

It is to be noted that there was no higher jurisdiction to which appeal could be made against a judgement pronounced by an inferior court. It was the same tribunal or court which reviewed the cases in the light of fresh evidence, although perhaps the assessors were not the same (?).

During the reign of Ramesses II (Nineteenth Dynasty, *c.* 1290–1224 B.C.), a scribe of the treasury of Ptah at Memphis, called Mes, had likewise lodged an appeal, which in his case was allowed.[2] The military benefice given to his ancestor Neshi by the king Ahmose should have been kept as a joint property, but its transmission provoked disagreement, for out of personal interest all members of the family had soon claimed their individual share, which, notwithstanding the terms of the constitutive clause, they were allowed to have by the vizieral court under Horemheb (end of the Eighteenth Dynasty). However, at the time of these difficulties and of the division finally achieved, irregularities crept into the procedure, to the extent that the mother of Mes found herself dispossessed of the share which should have come to her—the land-registration documents and the archives had been falsified even in the registry of the central administration!

[1] W. Spiegelberg, *ZÄS* lxiii (1928), 105–15; E. Seidl, *Einführung in die ägyptische Rechtsgeschichte*, pp. 25, 38; A. Théodoridès, *RIDA* xiv (1967), 126–7.

[2] A. H. Gardiner, *The Inscription of Mes: A Contribution to the Study of Egyptian Judicial Procedure*, Leipzig, 1905 (*Unt.* iv, Heft 3).

Mes, in asserting his claims, had to begin by lodging a petition with the vizier, in which he set out the grounds for them. When this petition had been declared admissible and notified to the defendant, who in turn made known his own case, and after each had replied, the vizier opened the hearing. He directed the proceedings, beginning in all probability by making known the arguments of the two parties, questioning them, referring to the evidence, and reserving the right to require fuller information. The vizier presided over the court (there was not normally only one judge in Egypt), but was not acting simply as an arbiter; he was the defender of the pharaonic order.

There were no professional lawyers pleading instead and in place of their clients, but legal representation was known, and there must, moreover, have been specialized scribes who placed themselves at the disposal of the interested parties.

At the close of his plea, which is remarkable, Mes marshals his arguments very methodically, demanding that his rights to the property in dispute be recognized, even though his mother's name does not figure in the appropriate registers. He undertakes to prove that these have been falsified, by citing evidence in confirmation and by producing an earlier *procès verbal*. From this it may be inferred that in Egypt legal decisions were made on the basis of documentary proof, supported by witnesses' evidence.

As regards criminal justice, local councils—and likewise the workers' council of the Theban necropolis—were as competent as in civil matters, but only up to a certain point. Thus it is that a particular case examined by the workers' council is expressly stated to fall within the competence of the vizier so far as the judgement is concerned.[1]

It is important to note that when the council of the Theban necropolis sat as a tribunal its members were called *srw* (**sar*), like

[1] Ostr. Nash 1 (= Ostr. B.M. 65930), vs. 14–15 (J. Černý and A. H. Gardiner, *Hieratic Ostraca*, i, pl. xlvi, 2).

the highest government officials. The humblest workman[1] was at this moment and by the authority of the vizier charged with a small part of the executive power. The vizier, for his part, was the supreme representative of the king, the *sr par excellence*, and remained so, except, of course, in the event of dismissal.

But powerful law officer though he was, it occasionally happened that the vizier himself was not qualified to pronounce judgement. In the most serious cases, such as crimes of pillage in the royal necropolis, it appears to have been on royal indictment that the vizier instituted public proceedings. He began by appointing a commission of inquiry, which inspected the scene of the crime and reported its conclusions. The suspects, after being arrested and imprisoned, appeared before the court, which apart from the vizier was composed of high officials, who must have been endowed with judicial authority *ex officio*.

To complete the preliminary investigation, the vizier ordered a re-examination, with a visit to the scene of the crime, in which he took part. The preliminary investigation being then at an end, the conclusions were set down in writing, with the charges upheld against the guilty; while as regards the others the vizier was competent to dismiss the case. The file was sent by the court to the king, and those who had been convicted were held in prison 'until Pharaoh should decide their punishment'. Thus, after an examination of *questions of fact* under the direction of the vizier, the king,[2] doubtless with his privy council, of which the vizier might be a member, judged the case in *law* and imposed the penalty.

At the stage of the preliminary investigation, the accused had the right to defend themselves as best they could (though without

[1] J. Černý, *ASAE* xxvii (1927), 183 f.; *From the Death of Ramesses III to the End of the Twenty-first Dynasty* (*CAH*[2], ii, Ch. XXXV), pp. 21-2.

[2] According to Pap. Abbott (T. E. Peet, *The Great Tomb Robberies of the Twentieth Egyptian Dynasty*, Oxford, 1930, pp. 37 f.) and Pap. Leopold II—Amherst (J. Capart, A. H. Gardiner, and B. van de Walle, *JEA* xxii (1936), 169 f.).

the help of lawyers, as stated), by producing witnesses to exculpate them, and even on occasion by requesting additional inquiries.

It may be added that some cases were tried by extraordinary means. Thus, after the plot hatched against his person, Ramesses III (Twentieth Dynasty, *c.* 1190–1158 B.C.) appointed a special commission, instructing its members to judge the guilty severely but justly, and without referring the matter to him. In this way, the special tribunal which the king set up was delegated with a discretionary power of life and death. This is made clear by the text itself (the 'Judicial papyrus of Turin'), which indicates that it was the magistrates that had brought the case against the guilty who then inflicted their punishment. Usually in criminal cases authority for the examination of a case was distinct from authority to pass judgement.

Several papyri found in the region of the Faiyûm constitute what might be called the 'Messuia dossier', from the name of the individual cited therein.[1] This Messuia, a cowherd, is frequently approached by the local people, who—save for the time when the herdsman Nebmehyt offers him three arourae of land—propose to sell him 'days (of work)' of slaves. Thus the same Nebmehyt says to Messuia on another occasion: 'Hand over to me the price of the four days (of work) to be done by the (female) slave Henut.' All the agreements for 'hire of services' are executed in the form of a sale of labour, and we are provided with a clause of guarantee given under oath—since it consists of an undertaking for the future. The guarantee provides for compensation in case the work cannot be done as agreed. The papyri do not always give the contracts themselves, but copies of deeds of discharge which

[1] The extant documentation provides us with seven deeds covering the period from year 27 of Amenhotpe III to year 4 of Amenhotpe IV (first half of the fourteenth century B.C.). These are preserved in Pap. Berlin 9784 and 9785 and Pap. Gurob ii. 1 and ii. 2 (A. H. Gardiner, *ZÄS* xliii (1906), 27 f.; J. Pirenne and B. van de Walle, *Archives d'histoire du droit oriental*, i (1937), 17 f.; A. Théodoridès, *RIDA* xv (1968), 39–104).

certify among other things that the undertakings entered into have been adhered to.

It is interesting to note that the cowherd Messuia delivers as 'payment' for the 'days (of work)' which he buys not only oxen, cows, calves, and other kinds of small cattle, but also grain, metal (silver, bronze), and fabrics or clothes, from which it would appear that he probably managed an agricultural enterprise, with an annexe devoted to weaving. But why did he not engage on a more permanent basis the menial labour upon which he relied?

It may be observed that the work of the slave Kharyt, like that of the slave Henut already mentioned, is offered to Messuia by different people. From this Gardiner deduced that slaves could easily change hands, unless one were to assume that there was a question of co-ownership. In fact, in one of the papyri of the Messuia we read: 'Have me some cattle delivered, and I will pay you what may be due by means of Maatnofret, the slave *who belongs to me*'—a formula which is repeated on the four occasions when the slave Maatnofret is mentioned. There can be no doubt that she does in fact constitute a private property.[1] Since such indication of ownership never occurs in the case of the slaves Henut and Kharyt, and since the days of work to be furnished by them are always few in number (2, 4, 6: the reading is not certain in a case of '17' days), one may be justified in asking whether these slaves did not rather belong to a town[2] or to some other community, being then placed at the disposal of the inhabitants at the rate of so many days per month or year. It would then be their right to days of the slaves' work that the inhabitants of the Faiyûm

[1] At least she is alleged to be such, for some irregularity, not explicitly stated, gave rise to the lawsuit related in Pap. Berlin 9785 (A. Théodoridès, *RIDA* xv (1968), 74 f., 99–100).

[2] In this connection it may be recalled that in Pap. Berlin 10.470 (seventeenth century B.C.), the over-all interpretation of which is very difficult, a slave-girl who has more than one owner is in process of becoming the property of 'the town' of Elephantine (P. C. Smither, *JEA* xxxiv (1948), 31–4).

were selling to Messuia,[1] and it was up to him to make something out of it.

Now, it is the words *ḥm*, 'slave', and *hrw*, 'day (of work)', that are here used to designate the corresponding rights,[2] and it is likewise evident from the testamentary dispositions known from Pap. Turin 2021 that *rdi*, to 'give' or 'surrender' a thing, is similarly employed to express the giving up of a right[3] over a particular thing, and that *iri sḫr*, lit. 'make a plan', is used of dispositions made by an individual and of the sanction or legality which the vizieral authority gives them. Everyday vocabulary could therefore embrace legal notions, with the result that one must beware of concluding from the apparent absence of technical terms that there were no juridical concepts.

Thus, the word *snḥ*, which has been noted only in the concrete sense of 'tie' or 'bind', is undoubtedly used with the legal meaning of 'obligation' in an ostracon of year 3 of Ramesses IV (Twentieth Dynasty): '(The pot of fresh fat which I am buying), I will repay you for it in barley, through the agency of this my brother whom one has the right to pursue in order to acquit (lit. "loose") *my obligation.*' In the event, the brother in question did not respect the agreement for which he was surety, and it was the buyer himself who was pursued. The reference he had made to his brother had not therefore freed him from the debt, but the brother may none the less be considered as a guarantor, and we thus touch

---

[1] It may be noted, similarly, that workmen of the Theban necropolis, at whose service the administration placed female slaves for certain household duties, sometimes sold their colleagues 'days (of work)' to which they were entitled from the slaves, in order to make some profit (information kindly supplied by Prof. J. Černý).

[2] In Ostr. Gardiner 90 a father cedes to his son 'all the *days*' of the slaves whom he himself has obtained from his mother and 'who are in the town'. For the son it must mean the right to collect whatever the work of the slaves brings in, though they themselves remain the property of the father (J. Černý and A. H. Gardiner, *Hieratic Ostraca*, i, pl. li, 2).

[3] Cf. A. Théodoridès, *RIDA* xi (1964), 69, n. 75; *JEA* liv (1968), 149–54.

upon one aspect of personal security in ancient Egypt[1]—not forgetting that we seem also to find indications of real securities.

In the relations of the Egyptians with foreigners, rules of law also came into being, perhaps from an early period, although the date cannot be fixed. The interested states created the basis of international law, beginning with the mutual recognition of their gods, which amounted to admitting divine sanction as a guarantee of pacts and contracts. It is in this spirit that the *entente* between the Hittites and the Egyptians was concluded in the time of Ramesses II (*c.* 1270 B.C.). The instrument of the treaty had been prepared, discussed, and exchanged through diplomatic channels; the Hittite version survives, drawn up in Akkadian, and some copies of the hieroglyphic version.[2]

The fundamental clause of non-aggression which the treaty contains is strengthened by a defensive alliance, and the text provides, on the part of each of the states, for the extradition of political refugees, whether they are ordinary people or persons of high standing. It is, moreover, clearly stipulated that those extradited shall enjoy a complete amnesty: '. . . and likewise if a man flees from the land of the Hittites . . . and comes to the great King of Egypt, (he) shall scize him and have him taken back to the great chief of the Hittites. But the great chief of the Hittites shall not reproach him with his fault; his house, his wives, his children shall not be destroyed, . . . no accusation shall be made against him.'

The treaty constitutes an act of public law, the more so since it is concluded between the reigning sovereigns for 'the land of Egypt and the land of the Hatti', so that the 'children's children' on both sides shall for ever be 'in peace and fraternity'.

It is upon the same kind of ideas that the foundations of private international law were based. Thus, a treaty made in the fifteenth

---

[1] Ostr. Chicago (Or. Inst.) 12.073, 3 (J. Černý and A. H. Gardiner, *Hieratic Ostraca*, i, pl. lxxvii; A. Théodoridès, *RIDA* xv (1968), 44–55).

[2] J. Pirenne, *Histoire de la civilisation de l'Égypte ancienne*, ii, Neuchâtel–Paris 1962, pp. 354–67; cf. pp. 228–43.

century B.C. between the King of Alasia (? Cyprus) and the King of Egypt defined the rights of succession of Alasian nationals who died in Egypt. By the application of an existing agreement to a particular case the King of Alasia indicates to Pharaoh the nationality of the deceased, and the identity and domicile of his heirs, so that these may be properly possessed of the property left by the deceased on Egyptian soil.[1]

When, in the eleventh century B.C., Wenamūn, the envoy of the Theban high priest, disembarked at Dor on the Phoenician coast, he complained of having been robbed in the port to the ruler of the region. 'You are the prince of this country', he explains to him, 'and it is you who are its controller; search therefore for my money.' Benevolent, but also careful to respect the established law, the prince of Dor replies to him: 'I have no knowledge of this affair of which you tell me. If the thief who went down into your boat and robbed you of your money had been a national of my country I should have reimbursed you from my treasury, until your thief himself had been discovered. . . .' The prince answers Wenamūn's complaint with a demurrer, but he justifies it on the basis of a rule of law obtaining in the country, and relating to dealings with foreigners.

From the period of the great imperialistic expansion under the Eighteenth Dynasty, and in times of internal strife, the kings began to advance the fortunes of military men, by granting them fiefs, and greatly to favour the priesthood, particularly that of the temple of Amūn at Thebes, in order to obtain their support in dynastic disputes.

Before long, judicial procedure underwent a change to the extent that plaintiffs could appeal to the oracle for judgement in civil cases and those involving minor offences.[2] It is clear

[1] J. Pirenne, op. cit., pp. 243–6.
[2] Oracular procedure is attested from the Nineteenth Dynasty. The following is an example of the Twenty-second Dynasty (*c.* 775 B.C.): 'They began to dispute again today concerning the payment for the

nevertheless that this practice did not impair the jurisdiction of ordinary tribunals dependent on the central authority, and that criminal cases remained the exclusive province of the vizier's court until the end of the New Kingdom.[1]

With the increase of these material advantages and privileges (immunities), the state again became weaker, and at the beginning of the Twenty-first Dynasty (1075 B.C.) a sort of theocracy was established at Thebes and throughout Upper Egypt to the advantage of the high priest of Amūn, while seigneurial rule reappeared over the rest of the country (Twenty-first to Twenty-sixth Dynasties, 1075–664 B.C.).

A stela of the Twenty-second Dynasty records that a complaint relating to certain springs (in Dakhla oasis) was received and investigated by the governor of the region, who gave a ruling on the basis of land-registration documents, but that the judgement proper was pronounced by the oracle of the local god. This decided in favour of the plaintiff and against the state, at the same time, however, imposing a statute of mortmain on the properties recovered: 'Establish them for him, these springs, so that they may be established for his son's son and his heir's heir (that is to say: that they may be handed down solely by male primogeniture) and for his wife and children, without any other (of his brothers) sharing it with them.'[2] We thus witness the formation, by the wish of the priesthood and not of the owner, of a family property,

parcels of land of the townswoman Ipip, which Paneferher, the son of Harsiesi, her employee (?), sold to Ikeni. They went before (the god) Hemen of Hefat, and Hemen said concerning the two written documents (which were placed before him): "Ikeni is right. He has handed over to Paneferher the money which reverted to the [woman Ipip], . . . It is (therefore) paid."' (Pap. Brooklyn 16.205: R. A. Parker, *A Saite Oracle Papyrus from Thebes*, Providence, 1962, p. 50).

[1] A. Théodoridès, *Actes de la deuxième journée des orientalistes belges*, June 1964, pp. 179–94.

[2] A. H. Gardiner, *JEA* xix (1933), 19–30, pls. v–vii; J. Pirenne, *Histoire de la civilisation de l'Égypte ancienne*, iii, 1963, pp. 34–5; A. Théodoridès, *RIDA* xii (1965), 120, 126–8.

entailed with the provision that it shall remain undivided, and the establishment of the right of primogeniture which involves as a consequence a reduction in the legal competence of women, at least in respect of the property so entailed.

However, the urban centres of Lower Egypt could not tolerate this state of affairs, which was further accentuated during the times when the country suffered invasion. After Psammetichus I had expelled the Assyrians and founded the Twenty-sixth Dynasty (664 B.C.) the Greeks came into contact with the culture of the Nile valley, and according to tradition it was in Egypt, in the towns of the delta, that they acquired the ideas of liberty and democratic equality. The fact is that the vigorous work of Bocchoris (*c.* 715–710 B.C.) and Amasis (570–526 B.C.) had had its effect, in the suppression of, among other things, imprisonment for debt and the privileges of the priests, and in the reorganization of the central administration. Egypt was then caught up in the great economic expansion of the Mediterranean world and brought into contact with Lydia and the Greek cities. Despite the occupation of the country by the Persians, the fundamentally Egyptian institutions based on the individual were revived, and tradition even attributed to Darius a new codification of the existing laws. And, when under the Ptolemies, in the second century B.C., judgement was given in Upper Egypt between conflicting interests in a succession, the procedure followed, although adapted to the new conditions, retained several elements of the old tradition. Attention has in particular been drawn to the right of the Egyptian married woman to go to law freely, without the backing of a κύριος.[1] It was, however, left to the Greeks to introduce into Egypt such an idea as that of mortgage, to judge at least from the extant sources relating to real securities.

In making a close study of the institutions of ancient Egypt, one is struck by some peculiarly characteristic features.

[1] H. Thompson, *A Family Archive from Siut*, Oxford, 1934, Text, p. xvi.

The skilful government which the country enjoyed throughout the vicissitudes of its history guaranteed to individuals certain rights which together may legitimately be described as the Egyptian 'law' of the period, a law embodied in statutes and protected by courts. The law is independent in the sense that it is not smothered by a host of primitive or religious notions. On the contrary, it is religious life which, in spite of the pomp and circumstance it preserved and even intensified, expresses itself in legal terms—the setting up of foundations, contracts providing for religious observations, donation, etc. Indeed, the entire day-to-day business of existence in the Nile valley is regulated by law.

But this law being a living thing, like the institutions it upheld, did not remain identically the same over the centuries. Human aspirations conditioned by new circumstances caused it to change, and it evolved between the pole of equality and liberty and that of inequality, the latter being determined above all by the system of land tenure. Egypt passed through three such evolutionary 'cycles', as Pirenne has called them, but even in the periods when individualism waned, when family groupings were restored with several members sometimes associated in the same cult, the country never witnessed the reappearance of a 'gentilic' regime.

In short, what is striking is the modernity of this law. It gives Egyptian civilization, though remote in time, a structure close to that with which we are familiar. The sources do not in any sense confront us with a mentality *sui generis*, with concepts and reactions alien to our own.

The Nile valley has given us no code, nor any copious theoretical treatises, but the application of law is coherent, despite peculiar features of procedure—the important point being that there was a procedure, with laws to organize it.[1] We do not know how the Egyptians defined their various legal categories, but they seem to proceed as though they had defined them as we do: a

[1] Cf. A. Théodoridès, *RIDA* xiv (1967), 107–52, instancing laws whose existence is known or can be inferred from extant deeds of practice.

property transfer on death, or inheritance, is clearly distinguished from a property transfer between living persons, either in consideration of payment or as a gift, in particular by the fact that the property does not change hands at the same juncture. A husband or wife is not an heir, but can be made a legatee, thanks to the freedom to make a will, under the terms of which the person making the settlement modifies the legal destination of the property. This freedom to make a will gave rise to new social and legal circumstances, which led to the creation of new law, until such time as it evolved further.

The history of ancient Egypt does not present an example of the 'secularization' of law. On the contrary—and this is what is miraculous—it attained from the outset, during the Old Kingdom, a high level of institutional and juridical development, which was subsequently distorted by the intrusion of religious practices. Not only did Egypt not surpass this level in the later phases of her development, she may even perhaps have failed to reach it again, despite the efforts of her rulers and thinkers.

Finally, it may be added that the processes of public law and all decisions of a political nature were hedged about by an impressive formalism and surrounded with a whole ritual of solemn words and gestures, but that the processes of private life were without these and rested essentially upon the consent of the parties. There could, indeed, be nothing more simple yet effective than an Egyptian will conceived as a declaration of a last intent.

ARISTIDE THÉODORIDÈS

BIBLIOGRAPHY

For a complete bibliography see J. Pirenne and A. Théodoridès, *Droit égyptien (Introduction bibliographique à l'histoire du droit et à l'éthnologie juridique, A/1)*, Bruxelles, 1966.

G. CARDASCIA, 'Chronique des droits de l'antiquité: Égypte pharaonique', *Revue historique de droit français et étranger*, 1963, 496–504; 1964, 504–6; 1965, 507–12; 1966, 503–7; 1967, 521–8.

C. CHEHATA, 'La notion de contrat dans l'ancien droit égyptien', *Studi Arangio-Ruiz*, iii, Naples, 1952, pp. 493–500; 'Le testament dans l'Égypte pharaonique', *Rev. hist. de droit fr. et étr.*, 1954, 1–22.

H. GOEDICKE, *Königliche Dokumente aus dem alten Reich*, Wiesbaden, 1967.

I. HARARI, *Contribution à l'étude de la procédure judiciaire dans l'ancien empire égyptien*, Le Caire, 1950.

M. MALININE, 'Un jugement rendu à Thèbes sous la xxvᵉ dynastie', *Revue d'égyptologie*, vi (1951), 157–78. *Choix de textes juridiques en hiératique 'anormal' et en démotique*, i, Paris, 1953.

M. MALININE and J. PIRENNE, 'Documents juridiques égyptiens', *Archives d'histoire du droit oriental*, v (1950–1), 11–91.

A. MORET and L. BOULARD, 'Donations et fondations en droit égyptien', *Recueil de Travaux*, xxix (1907), 57–95.

P. W. PESTMAN, *Marriage and matrimonial property in ancient Egypt*, Leiden, 1961.

J. PIRENNE, *Histoire des institutions et du droit privé de l'ancienne Égypte*, 3 vols., Bruxelles, 1932–5; 'L'administration civile et l'organisation judiciaire en Égypte sous la Vᵉ dynastie', *Annuaire de l'institut oriental de l'université de Bruxelles*, iii (1935), 363–86; 'Introduction à l'histoire du droit égyptien: les trois cycles de l'histoire juridique et sociale de l'ancienne Égypte', *Archives d'hist. du droit oriental*, ii (1938), 11–62; 'La preuve dans la civilisation de l'Égypte antique', in *Recueils de la Société Jean Bodin*, xvi: *La Preuve*, Bruxelles, 1965, pp. 9–42.

—— and M. STRACMANS, 'Le testament à l'époque de l'ancien empire égyptien', *RIDA* i (1954), 49–72.

—— and B. VAN DE WALLE, 'Documents juridiques égyptiens: vente et louage de services', *Archives d'hist. du droit oriental*, i (1937), 3–86.

E. SEIDL, *Einführung in die ägyptische Rechtsgeschichte bis zum Ende des neuen Reiches*, 2nd ed., Glückstadt, 1951; *Aegyptische Rechtsgeschichte der Saiten- und Perserzeit*, 2nd ed., Glückstadt, 1968; *Ptolemäische Rechtsgeschichte*, 2nd ed., Glückstadt, 1962; 'Altägyptisches Recht', in B. Spuler (ed.), *Handbuch der Orientalistik*, Abt. I, Erg. iii, *Orientalisches Recht*, Leiden, 1964, pp. 1–48; 'Juristische Papyruskunde', regular reviews in *Studia et Documenta Historiae et Juris*, Rome.

W. SPIEGELBERG, *Studien und Materialien zum Rechtswesen des Pharaonenreiches der Dynastien XVIII–XXI*, Hanover, 1892.

12

GRAECO-ROMAN EGYPT

IF at the very outset of this essay one wanted to sum up the legacy of Hellenistic Egypt, one might say that, because she was made use of by the Greeks, Egypt has handed down to us, in a medium intelligible throughout the Roman Empire, namely, the Greek language, institutions which go back either to pharaonic Egypt or to the Greek city state. I have phrased it that Egypt was 'made use of' by the Greeks rather than that she was 'Hellenized', for although there were several areas of contact it can, I think, be shown that the Egypt which, through its Greek kings and immigrants, realized some of the aims of the classical city state and that other Egypt which remained centred upon its temples and villages existed side by side without mixing at all closely. There are thus two distinct legacies which have been handed down, that of Alexandria and that of the country at large, compared to which the legacy resulting from a fusion of the two is slight indeed. Within the limited framework of the present study I shall select some of the lines of survival which seem the most significant.

To begin with, the Ptolemaic kings, by the way in which they conducted themselves both as Pharaohs and as Greeks, assured the survival of several social and cultural institutions. As Pharaohs, by ostentatiously assuming religious offices, by lavishing estates and tax revenues on the Egyptian temples for the upkeep of new cults[1] and thus perpetuating a tradition which the Roman

[1] For donations to the temples see, for example, the decree of Rosetta (*OGIS*, no. 90) and other sources collected in my *Économie royale*, pp. 47–52. A bibliography of Ptolemaic and Roman work in the temples of Egypt has been compiled by N. Sauneron, *Temples ptolémaïques et romains d'Égypte: études et publications parues entre 1939 et 1954*, Le Caire, 1956.

emperors were to continue, the Ptolemies ensured that religion, the very backbone of Egyptian civilization, would long survive. This preservation of religion, and with it of a class of native Egyptian scholars and scribes,[1] secured in turn the survival of the language and consequently of an Egyptian pattern of thought. And the importance which the Egyptian language retained in Graeco-Roman Egypt is shown by the emergence of a specifically Coptic Christianity.

Moreover, in spite of the royal control at first imposed on the temples,[2] the maintenance of their revenues, and later the immunities they were granted, continued to their advantage a form of economy based on the principle of capital accumulation. This helped to preserve archaic social patterns and the ties between men and the soil which were to reappear in the Byzantine period. The survival of an intellectual class in the temples also kept alive a way of thinking which held fast to non-rational patterns and was associated with the glamour of magic, something which the Greek world was to take over at the close of antiquity.

This maintenance of the Egyptian religious element, through the respect shown to it by the Ptolemies, has in turn carried down to the present time, in Christianity, a little of the country's religious sensibility. Indeed, monasticism, which was in particular a demonstration of anti-Greek feeling and of hostility to the seductions of urban life, achieved in the admirable rule of St. Pachomius the combination of anchoretic and communal existence. This rule served as a model for that of St. Benedict, which still remains in force in the Benedictine order and, to a certain extent, in several others.

The Greek desire not to admit Egyptians to the privileges of citizenship at Alexandria or in other cities also helped to keep the

[1] The large number of demotic contracts found in the Theban area is evidence of the survival of the Egyptian scribes.

[2] Cf. J. Bingen, *Sammelbuch griechischer Urkunden aus Ägypten*, Beiheft I, Göttingen, 1952, cols. 33, 37, 50, 51, 56.

Egyptian element in the population separate. If, even in the time of Caracalla, it attempted to infiltrate into Alexandria it could still be distinguished 'by its language and by its way of life, the rusticity of which is far removed from the urban style of living'.[1] The distinction firmly laid down by the Prefect of Egypt, Appius Sabinus, in a judgement given in A.D. 250, between the fiscal burdens of the peasants and those of the town-dwellers must have accentuated this anti-urban—i.e. anti-Greek—feeling of the Egyptian population. Its Christianity of the heart with its edifying virtues had little in common with that of the Greek theologians of Alexandria. Cut off from the world by its language, which had no universal currency, Coptic Egypt did not attempt to rally to catholicism and persisted in the monophysitism which even today separates it from the main body of the Christian Church.

Paradoxically, or so at least it appears at first sight, the adoption of Greek characters for writing Egyptian, a development of which the first signs may be detected in the second century B.C., helped to spread, among the people who still spoke the language, the habit of reading which, according to Diodorus (i. 81. 7), was denied to them by the difficult scripts of the pharaonic period. Thus Hellenization and the consequent dissemination of writing preserved for Egyptian the status of a written language which it would otherwise have lost with the disappearance of pharaonic religion, and this in its turn ensured the survival of Coptic culture. Language and religion, each supporting the other, set out upon a new career under Christian auspices, and, though they now speak Arabic, the Copts, being Christians, have retained down to the present day a separate consciousness which has prevented their being submerged in Islam and which made them, in the nineteenth century, the intermediaries between the West and Muslim Egypt.

We may now pass to the Greek inheritance which the Ptolemies, as Greek kings, developed and whose survival they ensured. From

[1] Pap. Giessen 40, col. 2, ll. 27–9 (*Select Papyri*, ii, no. 215).

his Macedonian and Greek heritage Alexander had gathered several concepts of kingship. Surrounded by his companions, he was the king chosen by the armies he led into battle, for the Greeks had entrusted him with the conduct of war as a commander-in-chief with absolute powers. His literary background, on the other hand, presented him with the Homeric models of royalty, and, in the tragedies of the fifth century, warned him against the excesses of tyranny, which Plato and Aristotle also described. In the *Republic*, Plato had conceived the idea of a royal nature capable by its intellectual grasp of perceiving the order of the universe and of drawing inspiration from it, while Isocrates, in his advice to Nicocles, provided a definition of royal morality which was no more than the rule of conduct of the honest citizen knowing how to combine prudence with justice. At the same time, and over-riding the particularism of the city states, a pan-Hellenic ideal, even a universal humanism, had gradually arisen out of reflections on the relativity of human conduct. Here one need only recall what Antiphon had said about the common nature of Greeks and barbarians—and Alexander had picked up this trend of thought as well. Indeed, all these elements are combined in the Stoic ideas of royalty which closely follow the synthesis accomplished in Alexander's own career.

The Hellenistic period thus witnessed a crop of 'treatises on kingship',[1] one of which is particularly connected with the Ptolemaic dynasty. This is the one inserted in the form of questions and answers in the mythical account of the translation of the Old Testament, the 'Letter of Aristeas to Philocrates'.[2] It is, of course, a document to be used with caution, for although it purports to have been written in Alexandria under Ptolemy II its actual date is not known and its author may be representative only of

[1] Cf. E. R. Goodenough, 'The Political Philosophy of Hellenistic Kingship', *Yale Classical Studies*, i (1928), 55–102.

[2] Cf. the edition of A. Pelletier, *Lettre d'Aristée à Philocrate*, Paris, 1962 (Sources chrétiennes 89), with full bibliography.

Hellenized Jewish circles. In it, however, we find attributed to the divine model invoked by the Jewish scholars all the elements of a royal code of conduct based upon self-control, justice, and love of humanity—the *philanthropia* commended by the Stoics. This tradition of royal ethics, deeply rooted in Pythagoreanism, in Platonism, in the advice of Isocrates to Nicocles, and in his eulogy of Evagoras, as well as in Stoicism and Cynicism, is clearly not peculiar to the Ptolemies. What is important is that it provides the inspiration for the statements of motive underlying several of their orders and instructions to higher officials (*UPZ*, no. 110).

The thing that characterizes the royal virtues is their excellence. Their very perfection proclaims the power of the king, and it was this that the Ptolemies wished to assert and which their eulogists praised in them. It was in fact by their munificence that they revealed their royal nature to the Greeks. The Ptolemies have given our civilization one of the prime examples of ostentatious display as an expression of sovereign power, and through the Roman emperors[1] something of the royal style which they created was to pass to the great monarchies of the West as well as to Byzantium. The lavishness of their hospitality, the luxury of their palaces, the size of their courts, the exotic brilliance of their festivals and of the processions in which they paraded their riches, the generosity of their gifts to Hellenic sanctuaries and to various cities, all this caught the imagination. And the figure of Cleopatra, the very epitome of it, magnified by the fear she inspired in Rome, has marvellously lived on until the present day. Through her, propaganda by luxury, which the Ptolemies carried to its extreme, has never ceased to be an active force and to exert its seductive influence.

---

[1] Philo, *Leg. ad Gaium*, 338, was conscious of the attraction that Alexandria had for the Emperor Gaius and of the ideal of deification he sought in Egypt. Cf. E. Köberlein, *Caligula und die ägyptischen Kulte*, Meisenheim am Glan, 1962 (Beiträge zur klassischen Philologie 3).

But this form of excellence is a far cry from the philosophic virtues recommended in the treatises on kingship. Conscious no doubt of not being sufficiently philosophical themselves, the Ptolemies gathered around them counsellors who were, and who, coming from Greece, provided them with the style of thought and the intellectual language developed in the Greek city states. Athens had dreamed, through Pericles, of making herself the teacher of the world (Thucydides, ii. 37); Isocrates had set himself up as an educator of kings (*Ad Nicoclem*, 6). Each one of the Hellenistic courts had its philosophers and men of learning. At the court of the Ptolemies, Aristotelians, first among them Demetrius of Phalerum, as well as Stoics and Cynics, encountered engineers such as Sostratus of Cnidus, the architect of the lighthouse of Alexandria, of doctors like Herophilus and Erasistratus. To the engineer, as to the doctor or philosopher, the king entrusted diplomatic missions and with them too he deliberated about political matters, for it was generally accepted that knowledge was of universal validity. Thus the Peripatetic natural philosopher Strato of Lampsacus was the mentor of Ptolemy II, and the librarian Aristarchus of Samothrace, grammarian and Homeric scholar, was tutor to the son of Ptolemy Philometor.

To the Aristotelian plan for a systematic inventory of knowledge the Ptolemies—and this is their greatest merit in the eyes of posterity—gave the backing of their immense financial resources. On their orders, and within the framework drawn up by Demetrius of Phalerum, an encyclopedia of learning and the arts was set up under the auspices of the two institutions housed in the precincts of the palace itself, the Museum, a research establishment in which worked men of learning living at the king's expense, and the Library—to which must be added the zoological gardens and the royal nursery gardens. The fame of the Museum and the Library has echoed down the centuries, and the Ptolemies, together it is true with the Kings of Pergamum, have thus bequeathed to subsequent kings and sovereigns a moral obligation to encourage research. The founding of royal academies from the seventeenth century onwards, the libraries formed by kings and princes from the time of the Renaissance, their collections of antiquities, and their zoological gardens, all go back to these Hellenistic models.

In their recruitment the Museum and Library were international in spirit. The men of learning called to Alexandria by the Ptolemies came from all over the Greek world; Euclid no doubt from Athens, Aristophanes from Byzantium, Callimachus and Eratosthenes from Cyrene, Aristarchus from Samothrace, Herophilus from Chalcedon, and Erasistratus from Ceos. Moreover, in adopting this pan-Hellenic concept of culture, the Ptolemies did no more than follow the practice of the Greek city state, whereby the Sophists who founded and taught the science of argument in Periclean Athens came from many different cities. The Kings of Persia also had surrounded themselves from the fifth century B.C. with Greek advisers, notably Demaratus, the King of Sparta, and the physician Democedes, whose influence is mentioned by Herodotus (vii. 101–5, 234–5; iii. 125–37), and Philip and Alexander of Macedon had done the same. This unrestricted movement of men of learning summoned to the courts of kings, this recruitment by universities and academies, on an international basis is still a living tradition. Inherited by the Ptolemies from the Greek city states and from earlier kingdoms, and subsequently taken up by Rome, it thus acquired an aura of prestige that ensured its survival.

In investigating the problems formulated by Greek science of the classical period, the Museum advanced research in several fields. In medicine, detailed anatomy and physiology called for experiments on living subjects, and as early as the fifth century B.C. Alcmaeon of Croton, working on living animals, had discovered the source of motor impulses. But for a precise knowledge of the specific anatomy of man and his physiology animals were not enough. 'One needs to know', says Celsus, 'what is the normal colour of an organ in order to judge what is undamaged and what has undergone change when the organ is laid bare through injury' (*De Medicina*, introd. 25). 'It is said that Herophilus and Erasistratus advanced knowledge of the internal organs the most when they practised dissection on living men—criminals whom the King allowed them to have from the prisons—and were able while their subjects were still breathing to observe parts of the body which nature had previously kept hidden' (ibid. 22). (The ethics of this regal liberality were, indeed, the subject of some discussion, which Celsus also reports.) Thus it was that at the beginning of the third century B.C. Herophilus of Chalcedon and Erasistratus of Ceos, summoned to teach at Alexandria, were able to bring about several major advances in the knowledge of the human body. The discoveries of Herophilus about the pulse were fundamentally new, while to Erasistratus we owe the precise distinction between motor and sensory nerves as well as research into the physiology of digestion. Their work, of which we have only fragments and summaries in ancient textbooks like that of Celsus or in the books of Galen, remained through these intermediaries a stimulus and inspiration to such as Vesalius in the Renaissance, while the translation of Galen's work into Arabic caused something of the heritage of research pursued at Alexandria under the early Ptolemies to live on in Islamic science.[1] Later, in about 200 B.C., it was at Alexandria that Sarapion founded the Empiricist school which had such great success in Italy, and even the figures in antique style which illustrate certain Byzantine medical manuscripts may date back to antiquity and to the Alexandrian book trade, themselves inspiring, as has been shown by Sarton (*History of Science*, ii. 402), the earliest illustrated editions of the Renaissance.

The construction of a map of the world on scientific principles is another of the important works to be credited to the Alex-

[1] On medical science at Alexandria, see C. Singer, 'Medicine', in R. Livingstone, *The Legacy of Greece*, Oxford, 1921, pp. 237–41.

andrian Museum. The explorers sent by Alexander in search of the regions where tropical rains prevailed and those whom the early Ptolemies had commissioned to reconnoitre the elephant-hunting country and the coastal areas of the Red Sea—Timo-sthenes, Philon, and Ariston—brought back precise determinations of the latitude of several towns, notably Meroe. These observations provided the foundation for Eratosthenes' map, itself the basis for that of Ptolemy which was our own until the seventeenth century. Moreover, the investigations of the ethnographers Agatharchides of Cnidus and Artemidorus of Ephesus, made on behalf of the Ptolemies in the Red Sea region, established human geography on a rational basis.[1]

Of advances made in astronomy one should mention the increasingly accurate determination of the duration of the year, in which a part was played by the great Aristarchus of Samos, the author of the heliocentric theory, who came to Alexandria at the beginning of the third century B.C. These researches culminated in the reform of the calendar promulgated by the decree of Canopus in 239/8 B.C. (*OGIS*, no. 56), a reform which instituted the year of $365\frac{1}{4}$ days, the quarter days being taken together as an intercalary day every four years. It is this year which provided the basis for the revision of the calendar in 45 B.C. by Julius Caesar, prompted by his experience in Egypt at the time of the Alexandrian war, and the Julian calendar, taking into account the Gregorian adjustment, is still the basis of the one that we use today.

It must not be forgotten that it was at Alexandria and Syene (Aswan) that Eratosthenes set up one of the most elegant systems for measuring the terrestrial meridian. It was Eratosthenes too who affirmed his belief in the possibility of reaching India via the West (Strabo, i. 64), while a century later Eudoxus of Cyzicus, again in order to reach India, attempted the circumnavigation of

[1] On Alexandrian geography, see J. O. Thomson, *A History of Ancient Geography*, Cambridge, 1948, pp. 123–68.

Africa (Strabo, ii. 98–102). These discoveries were not lost. The Renaissance, avidly scouring the writings of antiquity, brought them to life again, and there is thus a direct link between these Alexandrian researches and the discovery of America by Christopher Columbus.

Heron of Alexandria, whose date is difficult to fix, has also left a prolific heritage, for the greater part of his work has been preserved, if only in Latin or Arabic translations. In addition to his mathematical and geometrical works, the treatises on mechanics in which he describes automata of his own invention, some of them based upon the principle of the steam engine, enjoyed a revival in the Renaissance, while through his works translated into Arabic he had considerable influence on Islamic science, notably in the work of an-Nairizi (ninth to tenth century A.D.).[1] The inventions of Hellenistic engineers also became known in Rome through Vitruvius, and this in turn ensured that they were handed down.

We know too what influence Alexandrian mathematics exerted in the India of the Guptas; and from these Indian sources some of it passed, through Persia, into Arabic science.[2] The researches of Bolus of Mendes into dye-stuffs and substitute materials are the beginnings of alchemy, the first suggestion of chemistry, and it may be that through the medium of Arabic the very name of this science is derived from the name of Egypt, *Kēme(t)*.

The list of scientific advances made in Alexandria which survived as fruitful additions to knowledge could well be extended. Here I have done no more than bring together a few achievements whose legacy is both obvious and important.

In addition to fostering such scientific innovation the Ptolemies were anxious to store up knowledge already acquired, and it was

[1] On the transmission of the work of Heron of Alexandria, see M. R. Cohen and I. E. Drabkin, *A Source Book in Greek Science*, New York–Toronto–London, 1948, p. 197.

[2] Cf. De Lacy O'Leary, *How Greek Science Passed to the Arabs*, London, 1949, pp. 104–9.

upon the Library in particular that this task devolved.[1] The most specific contribution of this royal institution was in the realm of philology. The gathering together, in the best available text, of all intellectual and literary works, the effort to trace the authentic text among the mass of variants of which Homeric quotations made in the fifth and fourth centuries B.C. give some idea, and to banish from the venerable text of Homer (the basis of Greek education) the additions with which it had become encumbered— all this work, the origins of which go back at least to Pisistratus, precursor of the kings in many fields, had without doubt already been begun at Athens. But it was Alexandria that gave the enterprise the force and effectiveness which only the wealth its kings extracted from Egypt could provide.[2]

Together with Pergamum, Alexandria bequeathed to the world the technique of organizing a great research library and the basic outlines of the librarian's task. Once the works had been assembled —we hear of 490,000 rolls in the main library under Callimachus and 42,800 in the library of the Serapeum, though neither statement can possibly be verified—and the best text established by strict critical examination, it was necessary to compile catalogues, and such in fact were the famous '*pinakes*' of Callimachus. Thereafter biographies and commentaries were composed, the latter the basis of the scholia we still use, as well as summaries and select lists of all that was worthy to be taken as a model.

In Alexandria, and in provincial towns, there must have been many large publishing houses to meet the demand of a considerable reading public, if, indeed, we are to judge from the number of copies of certain works—not to speak of Homer—which have

---

[1] For the Library, see W. Schubart, *Das Buch bei den Griechen und Römern*, 2nd ed., Berlin, 1921.

[2] The high proportion of texts of Homer among 'school' papyri indicates the poet's importance in education. Cf. P. Collart, 'Les Papyrus de l'Iliade', in P. Mazon, *Introduction à l'Iliade*, Paris, 1942, pp. 37–73; H. I. Marrou, *Histoire de l'éducation dans l'antiquité*, 4th ed., Paris, 1958, pp. 231–8, and Index, p. 591 s.v. Homère.

been found among the Greek papyri.[1] It is to this diffusion of literature, a result of the educational programme, that we owe the survival of the best part of classical Greek literature, for it is certain that the manuscripts copied in Greece in the Middle Ages, and which reached the West during the Renaissance, owed their origin to Alexandrian texts. We are also indebted to this publishing industry for the recent resurrection of several works found among the papyri, for example, Hypereides, Herondas, Aristotle's 'Athenian Constitution', and Menander, whose *Dyscolus* restores to us the model for all European comedy of intrigue and character. Finally, the very format of our large diplomatic documents, 33 cm. in height, is that of the 'royal papyri' of Alexandria.

But the programme of preserving works of the past was not restricted to Greek literature alone. It also included collecting the traditions and the best of the thought of foreign nations, and first and foremost those of Egypt. Under Ptolemy I, Hecataeus of Abdera wrote a monograph on Egypt, of which Diodorus has preserved fragments showing the same great admiration for the wisdom of the country already professed by Plato. Under Ptolemy II, the Egyptian priest Manetho was commissioned to compile from existing lists of kings a history of Egypt, the chronological framework of which, handed down through Josephus and the Greek chronographers, has served as a basis for our reconstruction of the pharaonic period. It may indeed be said that Egypt owes her survival in the memory of men to the presence of Greeks upon her soil and to their curiosity. Without Herodotus, without the monographs used by Diodorus, Strabo, and Josephus, without Graeco-Egyptian bilingual texts such as the Rosetta Stone, without the survival of Coptic written in the Greek alphabet— and therefore readable—without Clement of Alexandria's short treatise on the hieroglyphs, this script would not have been deciphered, and the monuments of the Nile valley, covered as they

[1] Cf. R. A. Pack, *The Greek and Latin Literary Texts from Greco-Roman Egypt*, 2nd ed., Ann Arbor, 1965.

are with inscriptions, would have remained as silent as have been for so long those of the Maya and the Incas. The translation of the Old Testament into Greek, which will be discussed below, reflects the same basic desire to get to know the wisdom of the barbarians, and it is no coincidence that, at about the same time, Berosus, the priest of Bel, was writing a history of Babylon for Antiochus I.

Alexandria was a centre for poetry as well as for learned and scientific literature, and so set the fashion, that all Hellenistic poetry is frequently referred to as 'Alexandrian'. The *poetae novi* of Rome imitated its style, and we now know from a papyrus that the *Coma Berenices* of Catullus was a translation from Callimachus. This survival through the Latin lyric poets of the gracious mythology and allusive style of such as Theocritus and Callimachus led to a revival in the Renaissance of something of the pleasing imagination and elegance which adorned the court of the early Ptolemies.

No estimate of the legacy received by posterity from the Greek kings of Egypt would be complete without mention of the progressive sacralization both of their functions and of their persons, a process which in less than a hundred years made them into living gods.[1] It is a question not of their divine nature as Pharaohs, but of the divinity they acquired in the Greek fashion by the setting up of dynastic cults. Although the relationship between the Greek dynastic cult devoted to the Ptolemies and those at first rejected and later encouraged by the Roman emperors cannot be traced back with certainty, the example of the Ptolemies may at least have been one of those which provided the inspiration for Rome, as Philo believed (*Leg. ad Gaium*, 338). Complex as it was, the sacred character of the Ptolemies, especially from Philopator

---

[1] On the sacralization of the Ptolemies, see L. Cerfaux and J. Tondriau, *Le Culte des souverains dans la civilisation gréco-romaine*, Louvain, 1957; F. Taeger, *Charisma*, i, Stuttgart, 1957, pp. 171–440; and for the Imperial cult, Taeger, op. cit., ii, Stuttgart, 1960.

onwards, derived one of its elements from Dionysiac influence and the mystique of sacred frenzy. There is a Dionysiac aspect in the 'inimitable life' with which Mark Antony scandalized Rome, just as there is also in the life of Nero.

We may now turn to the legacy of Alexandria as a city, although it is perhaps difficult to isolate what is really peculiar to a city so intimately connected both with the king and with Egypt. And if one refers exclusively to Alexandria it is because the other cities of Egypt—ancient Ionian Naucratis, Ptolemais, the foundation of Ptolemy I in Middle Egypt, Antinoë, founded by Hadrian also in Middle Egypt, and the very Hellenized Oxyrhynchus, Hermopolis, and Arsinoë, whose economic and cultural importance has been revealed by the papyri—all these, even at their best, could do no more than imitate her. As for the ancient capitals of Memphis and Thebes, centred respectively upon the Serapeum and the temple of Amūn and serving each its necropolis, they seem to have added nothing new to the heritage already handed down to posterity under the Pharaohs.

The city of Alexandria, on the other hand, is in itself one of the legacies of Hellenistic Egypt to the world.[1] The Greeks selected and founded the majority of the great ports now in existence in the Mediterranean and the Levant—Marseilles, Naples, Syracuse, the Piraeus, Istanbul, and Alexandria—the foundation of a great coastal port in Egypt being a stroke of genius on the part of Alexander. The old ports were inland, Pelusium was hemmed in by desert and marshland, and the existence of a pre-Hellenic port to the west of the Canopic branch of the Nile cannot be accepted. Of all the Alexandrias founded by Alexander, the Egyptian was the most impressive, and the one too with the most brilliant future. Through Alexandria, Egypt, which under

[1] For the site of Alexandria and its description, see Strabo, xvii. 791–8, and the bibliography of A. Calderini, *Dizionario dei nomi geografice e topografice*, Cairo, 1935, s.v. Ἀλεξάνδρεια (for the Pharos, ibid., pp. 156–64). Cf. also A. Bernand, *Alexandrie la grande*, Paris, 1966.

Persian domination had retired within itself, was suddenly given a gateway on to the world, but of this gateway the Greeks alone guarded the door. Alexandria '*ad Aegyptum*', jealous of its rights as a city, knew how to shut itself off from the Egyptians, and, if its population seemed to Polybius (in Strabo, xvii. 797) to be debased by native elements 'ill suited to political life', this state of affairs was the outcome of a process of infiltration which Alexandria wished to eliminate and which, moreover, the kings and the Roman emperors helped to restrict.

The port of Alexandria was to a large extent created artificially by a dyke which linked the mainland with the island of Pharos and formed two adjoining basins. The entrance to the eastern channel was marked by the lighthouse, one of the seven wonders of the world, the work of Sostratus of Cnidus, which was so much higher and more powerful than all other beacons that its name has remained the term for lighthouse in most Mediterranean languages (e.g. French *phare*). This eastern harbour was dominated by the royal palaces and provided ships with one of the finest approaches in the world. From the Nile was brought the fresh water necessary for a population whose numbers we unfortunately cannot estimate, but which, given the size of the enclosed area and the length of the streets as mentioned by Diodorus (xvii. 52), may well have been of the order of 500,000–1,000,000 inhabitants. At the present day it is the western harbour that is used, the eastern one having been submerged, along with the palaces, through a gradual subsidence of the shore, but broadly speaking the outline of the port of Alexandria still survives.

In the time of Strabo, Alexandria was 'the greatest port in the world' (xvii. 797), one of the focal points of international trade. From a self-sufficient Egypt it exported the immense corn surpluses which, from the time of Ptolemy II, the representatives of Greek towns thronged to buy (Pap. Cairo, Zenon, 59021), and at a later date it was in the form of taxes that the corn was sent first to Rome, and then to Byzantium. Alexandria also exported papyrus, glass—Alexandrian glass has been found in China from the second century B.C.—and the finest fabrics of Egyptian linen.

From the period of Ptolemy II, Alexandria sought to organize trade routes to Africa and the East.[1] Competing with the Arab caravan merchants, she made the sea a factor in relations between East and West. In the second century B.C., as we have seen, Agatharchides recorded and described the coastal regions of the Red Sea and the customs of the inhabitants, and in so doing he no doubt made use of the travel accounts of the second Ptolemy's explorers. At this period too, a Greek papyrus shows us a group of Greek and foreign financiers, among them a Marseillais, approving a maritime loan for a voyage to the Spice Coast. The discovery by Hippalus, at the end of the Ptolemaic period, of the conditions governing the monsoons was to open up the possibility of a direct sea route to India. From then onwards, as Strabo points out (xvii. 798), whereas under the later Ptolemies

barely twenty ships dared to pass the cape beyond the straits at the foot of the Arabian Gulf, now (under Augustus) immense fleets sail to India and the capes of Ethiopia, whence they bring back to Egypt the most precious cargoes, which from there are re-exported. Customs duties are therefore levied twice, on both import and export, the duties being calculated in proportion to the value of the merchandise. Moreover, Alexandria has the monopoly, for it is the only port to receive and export the majority of these commodities.

Strabo notes also that this trade left Alexandria with a trading surplus, for the vessels returned from Puteoli loaded with sand.

A little later the 'Periplus of the Erythraean Sea', doubtless compiled at Alexandria by an anonymous merchant,[2] enumerates not only all the ports of call on the long route to India, but also the merchandise bought and sold there and the character of the

[1] Cf. E. H. Warmington, *The Commerce between the Roman Empire and India*, Cambridge, 1928, pp. 5–18, 35–83.

[2] Cf. the edition of H. Frisk, *Le Périple de la mer érythrée*, Göteborg, 1927, together with W. H. Schoff, *The Periplus of the Erythraean Sea*, New York, 1912.

inhabitants. From the coasts of Africa, Arabia, and India came spices, incense, aromatic and medicinal gums, textiles, pearls, medicinal plants, perfumes, and precious stones and metals. Alexandria gave the world a glimpse of the riches of India, and fostered a taste for exotic luxuries. But she was not content merely to reship as raw materials the precious commodities which her ships brought back; she worked them, set the gems in beautiful pieces of jewellery, steeped the spices in oil to extract the perfume, compounded the incense, made up the medicaments into remedies from her pharmacopoeia, exporting them in boxes of carved ivory, and mingled the gold among the threads of her woven garments. The delicate work of Alexandrian craftsmen was thus sold abroad and the products of her industry journeyed to kindle good taste at the ends of the earth—to Denmark, to the shores of the Sea of Azov, and as far as Begram, where a glass vessel has been found decorated with a representation of the Pharos light-house.[1]

Nor did Alexandria export only material things. The cult of Isis (Pl. 19), Hellenized by the Greeks in Egypt, and that of Serapis (Pl. 20), introduced by them, spread throughout the Graeco-Roman world in the wake of her ships, and with them went all the paraphernalia of the cult and the statuettes representing the deities. Thus it is that the *ambo* of Henry II in the cathedral of Aix-la-Chapelle preserves ivory ornaments one of which represents Isis, patroness of the Alexandria lighthouse (Pl. 21). A product of the art of Alexandria in late antiquity, this plaque may possibly have stimulated the imagination of some medieval sculptor, and the importance of Oriental objects, notably fabrics and ivories, in the development of medieval iconography has been amply demonstrated.

[1] For the Begram vessel, see, C. Picard, 'Nouveaux documents figurés concernant le phare d'Alexandrie', *Revue des études grecques*, lxiv (1951), p. xvi; 'Sur quelques représentations nouvelles du phare d'Alexandrie et sur l'origine alexandrine des paysages portuaires', *Bull. de correspondance hellénique*, lxxvi (1952), 61–95. On Alexander's contacts with India, see S. Lévi, 'Alexandre et Alexandrie dans les documents indiens', *Mélanges Maspero*, ii, Le Caire, 1934–7 (Mém. IFAO lxvii), pp. 154–64.

Temples of Isis and Serapis (Pl. 8) are frequent in the Graeco-Roman world,[1] for, together with the worship of Dionysus, and later Mithraism, the cults answered the need for salvation which Christianity was to satisfy. The Greeks in Egypt, and others in turn throughout the rest of the world, became interested in the Egyptian concept of the universe and in the revelations, attainable only through mystical initiation, which were handed down in Greek by adapters who doubtless moved in Alexandrian circles. The great corpus of Hermes Trismegistus, in which Egyptian esotericism is presented in Greek garb,[2] is one such legacy of Graeco-Roman Egypt, a vehicle for magic and the irrational, which gained an increasing hold on the imagination of late antiquity. Franz Cumont has shown how much the writings of Greek and Latin astrologers owe to Hellenistic Egypt,[3] and magical intaglios, many of them no doubt engraved in Alexandria, also travelled to the West, bringing with them the hopes of power which nourished the Jewish Cabbala and the 'black arts' of the Middle Ages.

Through Alexandria too the Egyptian landscape found its way into the repertoire of 'escapism' in the Graeco-Roman world. At Ain Tabgha on the shores of Lake Tiberias, as at Praeneste in Italy and in so many other places, mosaicists broadcast Nilotic themes upon the ground (Pl. 22)—the festivals of the inundation with nonchalant, flower-decked vessels floating between the

---

[1] For the diffusion of the cults of Isis and Serapis, see F. Cumont, *Les Religions orientales dans le paganisme romain*, 4th ed., Paris, 1929, and the volumes of the *Études préliminaires aux religions orientales dans l'empire romain*, ed. M. J. Vermaseren, Leiden, 1961 and following. Cf. also P. M. Fraser, 'Two Studies on the Cult of Sarapis in the Hellenistic World', *Opuscula Atheniensia*, iii (1960), 1–54; 'Current Problems Concerning the Early History of the Cult of Sarapis', *Opuscula Atheniensia*, vii (1967), 23–45.

[2] Cf. A. J. Festugière, *La Révélation d'Hermès Trismégiste*, i: *L'Astrologie et les sciences occultes*, Paris, 1944; A. D. Nock and A. J. Festugière, *Corpus Hermeticum*, 4 vols., Paris, 1945–54. The treatise of Iamblichus, *De Mysteriis*, may also be noted.

[3] Cf. F. Cumont, *L'Égypte des astrologues*, Bruxelles, 1937.

towers of a village surrounded by the waters, or crocodiles hiding among the lotus from which the Nile birds rise, or, again, pygmies, symbolic of darkest Africa, pygmies in whom Strabo did not believe (xvii. 821), riding on hippopotami or fighting cranes, a theme which we find again on a capital at Autun, and lastly (at Ain Tabgha) a nilometer to complete the local colour. And yet the Alexandrian art of Egypt did not as a whole differ from Hellenistic art in general; it is simply that the world took from it Egyptian themes, to which in fact it was not especially dedicated.

A keen taste for exotic Egyptian objects grew up in high Roman society, the emperors themselves setting the trend by going sight-seeing to the strange land of the Nile.[1] Hadrian, who paid a lengthy visit to Egypt, had the landscape of Canopus re-created in his palace at Tibur, and, at great expense, the emperors had obelisks brought to Rome, and later to Constantinople, a practice which European sovereigns were to revive from the Renaissance onwards (Pl. 14a). This presence of Egyptian monuments in Europe thus guaranteed the survival of at least a symbolic acquaintance with Egypt. At great expense too, Rome sent to fetch from *Mons Porphyrites* and *Mons Claudianus* in the eastern desert the purple-pink imperial porphyry for its colossal statues and the black and white granite for its most precious columns. At Meroe a kind of nymphaeum depicts an uncouth Apollo playing the cithara, and several bronze objects of Alexandrian origin have been found in the Sudan, not to mention the magnificent head of Augustus from Meroe now in the British Museum. Even the Egyptian garden with its sources of water for irrigation has lived on in Arab gardens,[2] and particularly in those of Spain with their Mexican offshoots.

In the realm of escapism, Egyptian exoticism allied itself with the practices and prestige of Hermetic magic, and several Greek

[1] Cf. N. Hohlwein, 'Déplacements et tourisme dans l'Égypte romaine', *Chronique d'Égypte*, xv (1940), 253–78.

[2] For the influence of Graeco-Oriental gardens upon the Arab garden, see P. Grimal, 'Le Jardin de Lamon à Lesbos', *Revue archéologique*, xlix (1957), 211–14.

romances have their characters journey to Egypt or even Ethiopia, where they are made to encounter some sorceress.

One should not, of course, attribute to Alexandria every product of so-called 'Alexandrian' art, although even the local imitations bear witness to a certain influence. And, if among ancient silver work or glassware it is rather difficult to distinguish between a Syrian and an Alexandrian product, this is because the latter shared a style disseminated throughout the Hellenistic world, the product of an art evolved from Greek origins. Whether made in Syria or in Alexandria, the glass vessel found at Begram bears a picture of the Pharos lighthouse, which at least indicates an Alexandrian connection. Among the objects of opaque glass decorated with white motifs there is one, the Portland Vase, which, reaching Europe in the eighteenth century and passing to the British Museum, had a notable influence and, as the inspiration of the 'cameo' style of Wedgwood Jasper ware and other pottery, was responsible for the dissemination of Hellenistic taste.

Finally, one should not confine the present list of Alexandrian influences, however summary, to Europe. Through its relations with the Sudan and Abyssinia—where apart from the famous inscription of Euergetes I at Adulis (*OGIS*, no. 54) there have been found several others in Greek—Alexandria prepared these countries for the reception of Christianity in the Greek language as it was brought to them in the sixth century A.D. by missionaries sent from Constantinople by the Empress Theodora. Even in the eleventh and twelfth centuries, epitaphs, found in the Sudan, at Wadi Ghazali, were still being composed in Greek, and thus a country as Byzantine as Christian Abyssinia, where the calendar is still that of the decree of Canopus, has preserved its peculiar character down to the present day. In the field of theology, Alexandria, the centre of Neoplatonism, played an essential part in the process of integrating Hellenism with Christian theology through the work of Clement of Alexandria and Origen—whatever discussion the latter may have aroused in other respects.

Among Alexandrian institutions which had a profound influence on the future, a special place must be given to the treatment accorded the considerable Jewish population.[1]

At the same time as the first Greek settlers, some Jews had established themselves in the new city, or so at least they claimed. They came there in considerable numbers and quickly became Hellenized as far as language and culture were concerned, but clung fiercely to the 'iron bulwark' of their religion, as Aristeas calls it, and with it to everything which depended upon it—a morality dominated by very ancient taboos, a private law conforming to the prescriptions of the Bible, and numerous ritual prohibitions. A strict Jew could not marry a non-Jewish partner, eat at the table of a non-Jew, or frequent the gymnasium or theatre, and naturally he was forbidden to take part in public observances connected with the cult of the kings and, later, of the emperors.

However, the idiosyncratic nature of the Jews does not appear to have been as serious a matter in the Ptolemaic period as it was to become in Roman times, and it is possible, moreover, that some Jews were fairly liberal, like those who earlier, under the Persian domination, had been established at Elephantine. In the first century A.D. a number of Jews were among the most influential men, for example, Philo and, from the same family, the Prefect of Egypt, Ti. Julius Alexander, but one may nevertheless refer to the Jews as a 'nation', since their status was clearly defined by a system of laws, by their religion, and by the fact that they did not intermingle with other groups.

Yet although firmly resolved to retain the things which thus set them apart and were preserved by the specific institutions of their autonomy—an ethnarch (abolished by Augustus), a gerousia, a Jewish system of jurisdiction—they still claimed, by virtue of

[1] The most recent treatment of the subject, with bibliography, is that of V. Tcherikower and A. Fuks, *Corpus papyrorum judaicarum*, 3 vols., Cambridge Mass., 1957–64 (historical introduction in vol. i, pp. 1–111). Cf. also H. I. Bell, *Cults and Creeds in Graeco-Roman Egypt*, Liverpool, 1953, pp. 25–49.

being Hellenized in language and culture, to be full citizens of Alexandria, stressing the fact that they were established in the city by its founder. This gave rise, from the beginning of the Christian era, to a debate in which each side was right and which as time went by became more and more embittered, since in their dealings with the Romans the Jews sought to separate their actions and destiny from those of the Alexandrians. At Rome, the delegations of the two sides followed one upon the other, irritating the emperors, who handed out remonstrances with exasperating impartiality, as Claudius did in his famous letter,[1] but yet sought no solution for a problem which they had no desire to examine. In Alexandria, meanwhile, the outcome was the massacre of the Jews of which Philo gives a powerful and gripping description in his *In Flaccum*. Anti-Semitism, with its religious and non-economic grievances, was born, and with it the 'pogroms', first of a long succession—for no one was pacified by Claudius' answer, 'Remain each of you in your own quarters and do not disturb the peace.' From the *Contra Apionem* of Josephus we get some idea of the bitter hatred of the anti-Semitic pamphlet to which it is an answer. This ever-mounting agitation reached its climax under Trajan in the terrible Jewish war which ravaged Cyrenaica and Egypt, decimating the Greek as well as the Jewish population of Alexandria, and affecting even the country districts.

Although the Delta sector of Alexandria was specifically assigned to them and Edfu seems to have had a Jewish quarter, one does not get the impression—in contrast to the position in the West in the Middle Ages—that Jews were under any obligation to live in a ghetto, or that there was economic discrimination. No doubt it was a very primitive feeling which led the Alexandrians to hate something which could not be assimilated, combined at the same

---

[1] The letter, dated in year 41, is preserved in a British Museum papyrus, Pap. London 1912, and published by H. I. Bell, *Jews and Christians in Egypt*, London, 1924, pp. 1–37 (also *Select Papyri*, ii, no. 212; *Corpus papyrorum judaicarum*, ii, no. 153, with full bibliography).

time with the desire, inherited from the Greek city state of the classical period, to restrict the privilege of citizenship. Pride in their independence, exacerbated in dealing with Rome, comes out in the insolent replies which the 'pagan martyrs' made, in the name of their city, to the emperors before whom they were accused. The massacre of the Jews was for the Alexandrians a form of substitute for the assertion of their independence.

Alexandrian Judaism has, however, left several positive legacies to our civilization. Before the growth of anti-Semitism at the beginning of the present era, this first, voluntary, diaspora succeeded, by coexistence rather than synthesis, in preserving for the Jewish community religious particularism in the midst of a foreign culture—more or less as is the case today in the countries of Western Europe and in America. What richness this participation in two cultures could confer on the personality is shown by Philo in the intellectual power of his work and the originality of his imagination and style.

Moreover, in becoming Hellenized, the Alexandrian Jews undoubtedly felt the need for a Greek translation of their sacred books, a need which must in the event have been regarded as sacrilegious by strict Jews. At the same time, the Library of Alexandria had, as we have seen, decided to commission translations of the great works embodying the traditions of non-Greek peoples, and the two objectives thus coincided. A book which mingles fantasy with truth and which flagrant anachronisms make it impossible to date, the 'Letter of Aristeas to Philocrates' (above, p. 326, n. 2), credits Ptolemy Philadelphus with the carrying out of a project proposed by Demetrius of Phalerum—which is chronologically impossible—namely, that of sending to Jerusalem for a commission of seventy-two translators to be chosen from among the most learned Jews. The divine inspiration attributed to the translation seems to have been designed to allay Jewish scruples about it. Whatever the facts behind this story, we know from a papyrus in the John Rylands Library, Manchester, that

Deuteronomy was translated into Greek as early as the second century B.C.

The translation, no matter who made it or for what purpose, provided, earlier than Josephus, an opportunity for the Greek world to get to know Jewry, an opportunity of which, admittedly, it took little advantage, while to the Jews it gave a Greek medium for expression of their religious feeling. Above all, it furnished Christianity with a Greek source for its references to the Old Testament, which non-Jews would not have been able to use had it not already been translated before Christ was preached. In this respect, the Greek version of the Bible is perhaps the most significant and influential legacy that Alexandria has given to the world. Written in ordinary Hellenistic Greek, the translation, despite its Hebraisms, is one of the principal monuments of the language. No poet or scholar, from Callimachus to Galen, has had so many readers as the Bible, and the language of the Greek Septuagint, mother of translations into every European language, has created a common heritage of metaphors which come so naturally that we are often forgetful of their origin. It is a whole world of imagination, full of poetic feeling, which Alexandria has handed down to us simply because the Jews were Hellenized there.

So far, it has been in relation to the king and the city, and to religion and culture, that the legacy of Hellenistic Egypt has been considered. There are other things, however, which in themselves bore no message and which no writer or artist handed down, but which, thanks to the Greek and demotic papyri discovered on Egyptian soil within the last century, we are able again to appreciate today.

First, there is the legal material. The legislation of the Ptolemies and the edicts of the Roman prefects, some examples of which have been found, provide evidence of the political and legal thinking of the Greeks and Romans.[1] Although we have very

[1] On Ptolemaic legislation, see M. T. Lenger, *Corpus des ordonnances des Ptolémées*, Bruxelles, 1964, and for the edicts of the prefects

few documents relating to private legal practice in classical Greece, the several thousand Greek contracts now published from Egypt enable us to trace the history of this branch of law, and a whole facet of life and thought is thereby added to our knowledge of Greek culture—for the few comparisons it has been possible to make show that in Egypt Greek law remained almost untouched by native influence. The reasoned combination of mutual agreements, promises, responsibilities, and sanctions shows how far the idea of obligation had developed in the conduct of Greek social life. It is the result, achieved through the democratic principles of the city states, of the attainment by the individual—or at least by men—of complete and independent legal competence.[1]

But this revelation from Hellenistic Egypt has certainly nothing peculiarly Egyptian about it. Greek law was there but a continuation of what it had been in the classical city state, and though it prolonged its career in Byzantium and still survives today in modern Greece, and though, moreover, certain elements passed into Roman law, this does not imply that either Alexandria or Egypt played any essential part in its transmission.

It is necessary to dwell at somewhat greater length upon the social structure imposed on Egypt through the efforts of the Greek administration to solve a problem of food supply—the methods used, that is, to ensure the subsistence of a city as great as Alexandria, and later the contribution of Egypt to the sustenance of those other great cities of Rome and Byzantium.

The relatively poor yield of the soil—in the case of cereals only ten or twelve times what was sown—and the limited effectiveness of methods of fertilization, which did not go beyond the burning of plant stems, the spreading of animal manure, the planting of

O. Reinmuth, *The Prefect of Egypt from Augustus to Diocletian*, Leipzig, 1935 (*Klio*, Beiheft 34); A. Stein, *Die Prefekten von Ägypten in römischer Zeit*, Berne, 1950.

[1] On law, see L. Mitteis, *Grundzüge und Chrestomathie der Papyruskunde. Juristischer Teil*, 2 vols., Leipzig, 1912; R. Taubenschlag, *The Law of Graeco-Roman Egypt*, 2nd ed., Warszawa, 1955.

vegetables, and, in Egypt, the depositing of Nile alluvium, made it necessary to leave ground lying fallow for long periods. Moreover, in the Mediterranean regions inhabited by the Greeks and Romans, the steep and rocky slopes, parched by the heat of the summer, denuded of trees and deprived of humus by the effects of erosion, were not particularly productive ground even in antiquity, and as a result development of very large cities was difficult.

In order to exist, the great cities of antiquity had to draw upon a vast countryside to support them. They needed to command the labour of a 'primary' sector (workers on the land) roughly five times as large as the 'secondary' and 'tertiary' sectors (artisans and non-producers) of which they were made up. It is this which, even in a city as highly urbanized as Athens, perpetuated the prestige of the landowner. In default of a countryside close at hand, any city which aspired to greatness had to organize the importation of foodstuffs, which was both costly and full of risk. Athens attempted to solve these problems of subsistence by building up a fleet and controlling the trade routes, which necessitated imperial power, while other Greek cities of smaller size sought a solution in colonization.

Although situated on the edge of the great supporting plain of the delta, of which the Faiyûm and the Nile valley are as it were extensions, Alexandria did not, for all that, find it easy to solve the problem of subsistence. From the model of Athens, by which so many of her institutions were inspired, Alexandria inherited an ideal of urban life which, while maintaining the prestige of landownership, yet sought to be free from the fetters of the land, and Aristotle, in his *Politics*, 1330a, had in a way foreseen the situation that was to develop—that of living at the expense of barbarian peasants. Moreover, it was necessary to impose upon these peasants—in this case Egyptians—a quantitative and qualitative programme of cultivation corresponding to the needs not only of Alexandria but of other Egyptian towns, and also capable of supplying the export surplus of agricultural produce needed for the purchase abroad of all the luxuries and comforts which the inhabitants of a great city required.

Within an economic structure based on the presumption of self-sufficiency, a great city's claim to existence represents a challenge, and a dangerous one. The ancient world was not able to support many great cities, and any disproportionate growth on the part of one urban community impoverished and ruralized its neighbours. The growth of Alexandria inevitably wrought changes in the social balance in Egypt, changes which the growth of Rome, itself partially fed by Egypt, was to accentuate. The great Egyptian cities of Thebes and Memphis declined, but there was still room for a fair density of urban life at Arsinoë, Hermopolis, Oxyrhynchus, Antinoë, and perhaps Ptolemaïs, all in fertile Middle Egypt.

This changing pattern is also apparent in the competition between towns and temples, the latter in themselves constituting a 'tertiary' sector which needed to tie down large areas of land and many peasants in order to feed the priesthood of the cults. The first Greek kings—as later the Romans—attempted to integrate them into a unified system by instituting control of temple revenues,[1] but this control does not appear to have meant any limitation. On the contrary, the temples were encouraged to manufacture fine textiles, which could then be exported. And, as we have seen, the political weakness of the kings led to the restoration of the temples' immunity and to the revival, through valuable gifts and new cult foundations, of the power of this 'tertiary' sector—so restricting the possibility of access to urban life for the peasants who served it.

Now since the arable area of Egypt and its yield did not increase

[1] For the royal control of temple revenues, see W. Otto, *Priester und Tempel im hellenistischen Ägypten*, 2 vols., Leipzig–Berlin, 1905–8 (i, pp. 262–82; ii, pp. 81–111), and, for control by the Romans, S. L. Wallace, *Taxation in Egypt from Augustus to Diocletian*, Princeton, 1934, pp. 238–54.

appreciably—apart, that is, from a few attempts at intensive cultivation on the great estates created in the third century B.C.— the country could hardly support more than some 7,000,000 inhabitants. Any urbanization such as that of Alexandria or any move to export corn was thus achieved at the expense of the food supplies reserved for the peasant population, and was therefore bound to lead to undernourishment or a drop in the birth-rate. Yet a state of equilibrium would seem to have been reached, for, as regards its rate of expansion, the population of Egypt in the second century A.D. is of a consistent pattern.[1] But such equilibrium was possible only at the cost of restraints imposed on the peasants—the obligation to fulfil a programme of sowing which, despite the collaboration of the farming community in its inception as well as certain agreed adjustments, seems often to have left an inadequate margin for unforeseen contingencies.

Officials, answerable for revenues and taxes on their patrimony, discovered various ways of exerting pressure on peasants to get them to take out leases on royal land. Intimidation, threats, and torture did not stop the withdrawal of labour or the flight from the land, which once deserted was valueless. It was therefore necessary to bind the peasants to the soil, to create for them a statute of enforced residence, and this in fact was what was done. There then remained private property, upon which there also had to be imposed an obligation to cultivate. Under cover of an economic crisis coinciding with the Syrian invasion of Egypt in 168 B.C., and caused by the confusion which hung over the Graeco-Oriental world as a result of Roman threats and demands, there appeared the practice of the *epibole* (*UPZ*, no. 110), a requirement that wealthy landowners should lease a part of the deserted royal lands proportionate to the size of their own patrimony. This obligation to undertake the cultivation of crown lands is found

[1] Cf. my article 'Papyrologie et sociologie', *Annales Universitatis Saraviensis*, 1959, 5–20, and M. Hombert and C. Préaux, *Recherches sur le recensement dans l'Égypte romaine*, Leiden, 1952, pp. 157–8.

again in Byzantium, and, though the Egyptian origin of the Byzantine institution is not proved, we know from the rescripts, letters, and constitutions of the emperors that the social problems of Egypt did penetrate to them, and it may well be that the solutions which for several centuries had been applied there were their inspiration.[7]

The transfer of these parcels of public land caused it to diminish in favour of private estates, without, however, ensuring the return which the Ptolemies and then Rome, and later Byzantium, expected from Egypt. For in the last analysis the only thing that ensured production was the presence of the labourer on the land. Enforced leases, extension of leases, the communal responsibility of the village for supplying the corn demanded by the central administration in Alexandria, were all designed to tie the peasant to the soil and tended to create a situation of serfdom. The flight from the land continued nevertheless, and the petitions found in papyri of the third century A.D. describe the distress of the last remaining inhabitants of abandoned villages, still held responsible for delivering the corn accounted due from them.

State serfdom then broke down, and the wealthy landowner came on the scene, attracting the fleeing peasants, establishing them on his land, and protecting them from the exactions of the state. The papyri enable us to trace the development of a system of serfdom biased in favour of the employers, as well as of the official Imperial attitude as expressed in a series of constitutions which at first prohibited and then, abandoning the struggle, acknowledged the patronage of the landowners. The medieval social structure in which the peasant was bound to the land for the benefit of the owners of great estates was thus in existence in Egypt from the end of the fifth century A.D. Indeed, the conditions

---

[1] Cf. my article 'Les Modalités de l'attache à la glèbe dans l'Égypte grecque et romaine', in *Recueils de la Société Jean Bodin*, ii: *Le Servage*, 2nd ed., Bruxelles, 1959, pp. 33–65 (particularly pp. 53–65 for constitutions with a broad effect on the whole Empire or the Orient).

obtaining in Egypt in the matter of landownership are specifically mentioned in constitutions applicable to the whole of the Eastern Empire in the fifth century,[1] and, while one cannot be certain that these were based on the Egyptian model, one may at least note that the situation in Egypt, in being from the end of the Ptolemaic period, preceded the development of similar conditions in the rest of the Roman Empire. The massive use of slaves on the great estates, particularly in Africa, made it unnecessary to bind a free labour force to the land, and so institute serfdom, and there was thus no reason for it to evolve elsewhere, as it did in Egypt. Moreover, the prefects sent by the emperors to Egypt remained there but a short time and continued their careers elsewhere, and it is not improbable that on their return to Rome they brought with them the fruits of their Egyptian experience.

In concluding this short inventory of the principal legacies of Hellenistic Egypt, it may perhaps be appropriate to indicate the negative as well as the positive aspect. Although there are a number of survivals from Graeco-Roman Egypt, it has nevertheless bequeathed to us but a small part of its heritage. Its poetry and drama, in both Greek and Egyptian, have almost completely disappeared, and the works of the majority of its scholars are known to us only through summaries in manuals and from occasional quotations. Of the Alexandrian corpus of classical works no more than a minute fraction has survived.

In fact, the items preserved are what had become an integral part of education: Euclid, but almost nothing of Aristarchus of Samos (enough, however, of his heliocentric doctrine—through the *Arenarius* of Archimedes—to serve as an inspiration to

---

[1] M. Rostovtzeff, *Studien zur Geschichte des römischen Kolonates*, Berlin, 1910, p. 393, thinks it is possible to establish a connection between the Egyptian evidence and the institutions of the late Empire concerning attachment to the land. For the resemblances between Egyptian institutions and those of the Byzantine Empire, see also G. Rouillard, *L'Administration civile de l'Égypte byzantine*, 2nd ed., Paris, 1928, pp. 90–1, 224; *La Vie rurale dans l'empire byzantin*, Paris, 1953, pp. 83–4.

Copernicus); Strabo, who compiled a systematic encyclopedia of geography, but not Eratosthenes, whom he used; Homer and Plato, but not the epic poets of the Cycle, nor the innumerable philosophers of the Academy and the Lyceum; none of the works of the Alexandrian philologists of the Museum, but the pale reflection of them which we read in the scholia. In this process of survival, Rome was a staging post, especially in the person of Pliny the Elder.

What survives is, in fact, that which was in keeping with the spirit of a system of education to which anything original and daring was repugnant, a system that did not include science in the instruction of a gentleman, who, in conformity with the curriculum laid down by Aristotle (*Politics*, 1337b), was meant to shun any technical or specialist training. If the work of the Museum of Alexandria did not reach more than a limited circle of initiates, it was because science had no part to play in society. It had, moreover, very few applications relevant to the pursuit of power and prestige, by which the survival of discoveries might have been ensured, and others stimulated, so carrying the knowledge down through the centuries. To the little that was salvaged the Renaissance gave a tremendous impetus both by pursuing practical applications and because, thanks to printing, it had the means of dissemination which Hellenistic civilization lacked—developed though its book industry was.

In the absence of such practical applications and the means of dissemination, the scientific discoveries elaborated at Alexandria made no impression on the mass of the people. Nor in any case was this mass sufficiently Hellenized to appreciate Alexandrian work, none of which seems to have been translated into Egyptian—save for the Greek Bible put into Coptic. It was thus left to the Arabs, through their translations, to ensure the transmission of works which native Egypt had not received.

That there was no Hellenization of the masses was the result of a policy which, by admitting only town-dwellers to the benefits of Greek culture, restricted the peasants to the countryside in their role as food-producers. This suppression of the native population, arising out of the prejudices and economic needs of the classical city, this form of rusticity imposed upon it through its being tied to the land, kept it imprisoned within the mental framework of its past. The medicine of Herophilus raised no doubts in the minds of the peasantry of Egypt (or anywhere else) as to the virtues of irrational remedies, and having no social foundation it has left only the smallest mark upon our heritage— a precious trace indeed, but how very fragile! By contrast, the survival of the tangible products of industrial art, the embroidered textiles, glassware, jewellery, and ivories that were scattered abroad in abundance, has been less hazardous.

The legacy of a civilization can be handed down only if it is offered generously to all.

CLAIRE PRÉAUX

BIBLIOGRAPHY

For the historical background see the relevant chapters of *The Cambridge Ancient History*, together with:

E. BEVAN, *A history of Egypt under the Ptolemaic dynasty*, London, 1927.
A. BOUCHÉ-LECLERCQ, *Histoire des Lagides*, 4 vols., Paris, 1903–7.

For the social and economic background:

C. PRÉAUX, *L'Économie royale des Lagides*, Bruxelles, 1939.
M. ROSTOVTZEFF, *The social and economic history of the hellenistic world*, 3 vols., Oxford, 1941.
W. W. TARN, *Hellenistic civilisation*, 3rd ed., London, 1952.

And for a selection of sources:

W. DITTENBERGER, *Orientis Graeci Inscriptiones Selectae* (*OGIS*), 2 vols., Leipzig, 1903–5.
A. S. HUNT and C. C. EDGAR, *Select papyri*, 2 vols., Loeb Classical Library, 1932–4.
U. WILCKEN, *Urkunden der Ptolemäerzeit* (*UPZ*), 2 vols., Berlin–Leipzig, 1927–57.

13

THE GREEK PAPYRI

PAPYRA, *throned upon the banks of Nile,*
Spread her smooth leaf, and waved her silver style.
—The storied pyramid, the laurel'd bust,
The trophied arch had crumbled into dust;
The sacred symbol, and the epic song,
(*Unknown the character, forgot the tongue*),
With each unconquer'd chief or sainted maid,
Sunk undistinguished in oblivion's shade.
Sad o'er the scatter'd ruins Genius sigh'd,
And infant Arts but learned to lisp and died.
Till to astonish'd realms PAPYRA *taught*
To paint in mystic colours Sound and Thought,
With Wisdom's voice to print the page sublime,
And mark in adamant the steps of Time.
      ERASMUS DARWIN, *The Loves of the Plants* (1789).

IN the year 1778 a commercial traveller in Egypt was offered by
the fellahîn some forty or fifty rolls of papyrus; one of them he
bought as a curiosity for a small sum and left the rest to be burnt
by the natives, whose noses were tickled (so the story goes) by the
aroma of burning papyrus. The survivor found its way into the
hands of an Italian and was by him presented to Cardinal Stefano
Borgia. The hopes cherished by many savants, Winckelmann
among them, that here was one of the lost treasures of Greek
literature were soon disappointed. The roll was found to contain
nothing more than a list of peasants who had performed in the
village of Ptolemais Hormou in the Faiyûm their quota of com-
pulsory labour on the neighbouring canals and dykes, and, as the
age of social history was still far in the future, it is no matter for
surprise that the roll and the circumstances of its discovery were
soon forgotten. And yet the incident is significant, for the Charta

Borgiana, apart perhaps from some scraps of 'Turkish paper'[1] of dubious origin presented by the theologian J. J. Grynaeus to the University Library at Basel in 1591, was the first papyrus to reach Europe since the trade in what had been the primary writing material of the ancient world flickered out in the Dark Ages.

Though more than a hundred years were still to pass before excavations were undertaken for the specific purpose of discovering Greek papyri,[2] the number of texts which were found by natives and, passing through the hands of travellers and private collectors, eventually found their way to the museums of Europe steadily increased throughout the nineteenth century. That the first literary papyrus to be found should be a manuscript of part of the *Iliad* was symbolic of the enormous, indeed unwelcome, preponderance of Homeric texts; of more promise for the future was the discovery in 1847 of fragments of six speeches, hitherto unknown, of the orator Hypereides. Not long after the plundering of the Greek rubbish-heaps of Arsinoë (Medinet el-Faiyûm) had flooded the market with thousands of papyri (often very fragmentary)[3] the age of scientific excavation began, and though it is not yet over it seems certain that no site will rival the riches of Oxyrhynchus which rewarded the pioneers in this field, B. P. Grenfell and A. S. Hunt. With it began that minor renaissance which has affected nearly every department of classical studies; today, when social and economic conditions are the recognized material of history, even the Charta Borgiana has come into its own.

[1] Now Papyrus Basel 1, an astrological text in looking-glass writing, together with some late Latin fragments.

[2] The term 'papyrology' is commonly used to describe the study of all written material from Egypt, except inscriptions on stone, i.e. parchment, ostraca, or potsherds, and tablets of wood or lead, as well as papyri, and is so used in this essay. The great majority of the texts are on papyrus.

[3] It is so rare for a literary text to be found entire (though documents often are) that it must be assumed that the literary texts mentioned, unless the contrary is stated, are, in very varying measure, incomplete.

For the legacy of the papyri is in its nature indirect, a legacy to civilization's knowledge of its own past rather than directly to the world of today, except in so far as modern institutions—the Church is an obvious example—are modified by increased knowledge of and insight into their own origins. Nor are papyri *objets d'art*, or only very rarely (we may think of the one or two illuminated papyri, such as that of the jockeys of Antinoë,[1] or of a few superb examples of calligraphy); though they have added a new chapter to the history of Greek palaeography, it is their contents that concern us here. This legacy is a novel one in that the information we derive from the papyri is often not merely new but of a new kind; in what this novelty consists it is the purpose of this essay to discuss.

By way of introduction, a little may be said of the material. Centuries before Alexander's conquest had made the Greeks the masters of the country, Egypt had manufactured papyrus out of the pith of the marsh plant of that name which once grew plentifully in the Delta swamps, and the Egyptians by their carefully guarded processes had made of it the finest writing material known; at no time in the ancient world was the preparation of papyrus for writing purposes carried on outside Egypt. Throughout the classical age of Greece it was commonly used; indeed, without such a relatively cheap and convenient material, literature and the sciences could scarcely have developed as they did, or at least their diffusion and survival would have been rendered much more difficult. Egypt supplied the whole Roman Empire, from Hadrian's Wall to the Euphrates and from the Danube to the First Cataract, and papyrus was used as naturally by Irenaeus in Gaul as by Origen in Alexandria. Its last recorded use is in the Chancery of Pope Victor II in 1057, but whether the papyrus was Egyptian, and, if so, whether it was recently imported, we do not know. Just as papyrus was of immense service in the creation and transmission of classical culture, so in the last hundred years it

[1] See S. J. Gąsiorowski, *JEA* xvii (1931), 1–9.

has been the means of renewing and increasing the legacy of Greece and Rome. The account is not yet closed; every year brings with it the publication of new texts, and their range is no less surprising than their number.

Until the Egyptian discoveries our knowledge of this material, and consequently of the form and methods by which literature was transmitted, was limited to a few papyrus codices of the sixth century, the small and late group of Papal and Ravenna documents, and the damaged rolls of Herculaneum. Today we have specimens of writing, both literary and documentary, in a series which, if not unbroken, has few serious gaps from the later fourth century B.C. down to the eighth century A.D.; we have some fragments of a roll of the *Phaedo* written less than a century after Plato's death, a papyrus of Cicero probably anterior to the Christian era, and what may even be the relics of a contemporary roll of Polybius.

At this point we should note what may well be called a direct legacy from Egypt to the West, whose character has been more clearly defined by the discoveries of papyri. It was only to be expected that the country which produced the material should also exercise a marked influence on the form and organization of the ancient book; for example, it is probable that the elevation of the parchment notebook, itself an Italian derivative of the wooden tablet of Greece, into a regular vehicle for literature in the form of the papyrus codex took place in Egypt. So to Greek Egypt we owe not only the first great general library, but a vital stage in the development of the modern book. In these matters Egypt means Alexandria, and it is to Alexandria that we owe the illuminated manuscript of the Middle Ages; but here the actual evidence of the papyri, valuable though it is, is scant.

This apart, to term this gift of Egypt a legacy is, in a sense, a misnomer and a paradoxical one; for never was a testator less conscious of what he was doing or a bequest more fortuitous. The great mass of our Greek papyri have been salvaged from ruined towns and villages of Upper Egypt and the adjacent rubbish-dumps abandoned to the desert when, in Byzantine and Arab periods, the irrigation system broke down. Occasionally the digger is fortunate enough to find some family or official archive, carefully stored in a jar or a box (Dioscorus of Aphrodito has earned our double thanks for choosing to wrap up his papers in the leaves of a codex of Menander); a few of our literary papyri have been found in tombs, as for example the Hawara Homer found resting under the head of a mummy of a young girl. To place grave goods with the dead was a widespread practice and for the Greeks a book could be as appropriate a companion as any other object. There has recently been found in a tomb at Derveni near Salonica the charred remains of a papyrus roll of the late fourth century B.C., a unique case of the discovery of a Greek papyrus on the soil of metropolitan Greece. The text is an allegorical commentary on Orphic poetry, and its owner was no doubt an adherent of the sect. The presence of such a text in a grave needs no explanation, nor perhaps does that of the Homer; but could Isocrates' sermon on the duties of a monarch addressed to Nicocles (found lying between the legs of a mummy of the fourth century A.D.) be anyone's first choice for the next world? We may surmise that this and some other discoveries (for example, the Timotheus roll, incomplete when it was buried) were placed in the grave not because of any appropriateness to the individual, but in imitation of the half-understood Egyptian practice whereby the native dead were almost invariably accompanied by excerpts from the 'Book of the Dead'.

Until recently such discoveries were very much the exception; in the past thirty years there has been a series of striking discoveries of texts not casually thrown away but carefully deposited in jars. With very few exceptions these texts are Christian, or at any rate religious, in character;[1] if not complete, they are much

---

[1] If the roll of *Iliad* v–vi and the *Dyscolus*, both now in the Bodmer Library, were discovered with the Christian Greek and Coptic codices in

more substantial than the average discovery. We can hardly be wrong if we associate these finds with the Jewish practice of burying outworn or unwanted sacred manuscripts or depositing them in a kind of ecclesiastical lumber-room known as a Geniza. The survival of some of the Qumran Scrolls is to be explained in this way; in Egypt we may think of the Chester Beatty papyri— all extensive, none complete—of the imposing texts in the possession of M. Bodmer in Geneva, and of the Gnostic library of Chenoboskion (Nag Hammadi), consisting of thirteen codices of the fourth or fifth century, eleven complete in their original leather bindings, two fragmentary. However, the great mass of our papyri (for example those from Oxyrhynchus and Arsinoë) were thrown away as so much waste paper; this is why they are so often broken and torn. The oddest transformation has been suffered by those papyri which were converted into a kind of papier mâché, and used to form the covering or stuffing of mummies, whether of men or crocodiles; from one such emerged the earliest fragments of any manuscript of the Bible, the Manchester papyrus of Deuteronomy, which were found covered with glue and wrapped in some pieces of the first book of the *Iliad*—as nice an example of cultural fusion in the second century B.C. as could be wished. We should note that the survival of papyri is determined, generally speaking, as well by the absence of rainfall as by height above inundation level, and that consequently almost all our papyri come from Egypt south of the modern Cairo. Since then, as now, the delta was economically the most important part of the country, while Alexandria was the fountain-head of its intellectual and artistic life, as far as this was Greek, we must be prepared to allow for a certain provincial bias in our texts, literary as well as documentary.

So, while from one point of view papyri are so much waste product, miscellaneous contents of a gigantic waste-paper basket

the library, this explanation might not apply; but the facts are far from clear.

steadily filled up in the millennium between Alexander and the Arab conquest, from another they are the raw material from which a civilization can be reconstructed. Indeed, it is only because they are the first that the second is possible; it is just because the material was not consciously selected (if we except for the moment the literary texts), was not intended to survive, that they are of unique value to the historian. Our knowledge of the ancient world rests primarily, and must always do so, on our literary authorities; but it is not their function to give us the raw material of history, nor can we always tell what are their principles of selection, nor, when we do know them, can we always share them. So if we wish to free ourselves from the aristocratic and political bias common to most of the ancient historians and to study the economic and social factors commonly of little interest to them, to catch the inhabitants of this part of the ancient world not posing in public attitudes but off their guard in their ordinary business and in their private correspondence, to look at government from the point of view of the governed, these ephemeral and humdrum, sometimes tedious, documents are invaluable. To select two out of the many themes that the documentary papyri illustrate: we can observe in a way impossible before what Greek colonization meant, how far the settler adapted himself to his surroundings and what were the effects of this invasion in social and political life, and we can watch what was the actual practice of Roman administration in Egypt, its methods and its spirit.

Before attempting to outline the kind of contribution that the papyri have made to historical studies, something must be said of what is certainly the most startling result of the excavations—the additions to Greek literature. When, after Alexander's conquest, there flooded into Egypt from every corner of the Greek world soldiers, businessmen, farmers, and administrators, they brought their literature with them. The Greeks were already a literary people in the sense that the literature of their own past had become a vital part of their own existence; when all else that had been characteristic of the classical civilization disappeared or changed almost out of recognition in the new empires of Alexander's successors, their education—literature and the gymnasium—remained. In provincial Egypt, at any rate, no attempt was made to keep the race pure; to be a Greek soon meant to speak Greek and to have had a Greek education. Hence it is no accident that so many literary papyri have been recovered from Egypt. The oldest papyrus yet found in Egypt is that of the *Persae* of Timotheus, and that a work so exotic and sophisticated should have come from the earliest period of the Greek occupation is significant of the endless variety of the literary texts. Not only is every branch of Greek literature from Homer and Hesiod down past the lyric poets and satirists, the Old and the New Comedy to the novelists and the Christian Fathers, represented by fragments however small, but there is scarcely an author of whom we can assuredly say that he was not read in Egypt. The greatest of these discoveries have now taken their place in the ranks of Greek literature, and are no more the preserve of the papyrologist. Menander has gained most; not only is there the great Cairo codex (owned by that Dioscorus of whose own attempts upon the Muse his editor wrote 'At no moment has he any real control of thought, diction, grammar, metre, or meaning'), but recently an all but complete play, the *Dyscolus* or 'Curmudgeon' has come to light in a manuscript of the late third century A.D. Thanks to these and smaller papyri Menander is no longer seen through the distorting mirror of Roman comedy but can be recognized as a playwright capable of dramatic power and delicate characterization; but it must be admitted that 'The Curmudgeon', an early play, with little elegance of style and little scope for the delineation of feminine character in which Menander later excelled, is a disappointment to many of his admirers.

Among the other discoveries notable in extent and in intrinsic merit are those of the odes and dithyrambs of Bacchylides, a poet all but unknown before, the 'Athenian Constitution' of Aristotle, the *Ichneutae* of Sophocles (the only satyric drama which we have from his hand), the *Hellenica Oxyrhynchia*, probably from the hand of Ephorus, poems by Sappho and Alcaeus, by Corinna and other lyric writers, and last but not least by Callimachus. The latter, as is proper for a poet whose home was Alexandria, has come into his own with the discovery of considerable parts of the *Iambi* and *Aitia*, types of his work of which no specimens were extant; no one would have appreciated better than he the irony of such a casual resurrection. But of the writers of Hellenistic Alexandria none has emerged more startlingly or to more effect than Herondas, whose mimes are vignettes of city life drawn with vigour, realism, and a marked preference for the seamy side; they unite vivid powers of characterization with a highly sophisticated attitude and great technical ability. One of his most successful mimes, 'The Schoolmaster', affords a good commentary on the school texts which are also found among the papyri. A roughly contemporary textbook found in the Faiyûm (probably one from which the master dictated to his class) provides interesting parallels; just as the boy in the mime is made by his father to spell out a proper name (and makes a hash of it), so the school-book contains lists of proper names, some of them selected as tongue-twisters. When he is asked to recite a piece of poetry for the edification of the family, he cannot get beyond the first two words and stammers at that—even his illiterate old grandmother, says his mother, could do better than that; sure enough in the school-book are two pieces of Euripides, doubtless to be copied and learnt by heart. The mime ends with the school-boy receiving a sound flogging; this is not specified in the book, but the motto, 'Work hard, boy, or you'll be beaten', copied out on a piece of papyrus six times as an imposition, tells its own tale.

To the grudging work of Egyptian schoolboys we owe not a few texts, though we may wish that Homer had not been quite such a staple article of diet. Ostraca were frequently used in schools—they were the cheapest material, since to the supply of broken potsherds there was no end—and so it may well be to this source that we owe a hitherto unknown ode of Sappho's; the uncertain hand and the mistakes in spelling which indicate that the copyist had only an imperfect grasp of what he was writing lend colour to this view. The poem is an invitation to the poet's friends to attend a solemn and joyous rite to which Aphrodite is invoked—

Where is a lovely grove of apple-trees and altars therein smoking with frankincense; there too cool water plashes through the apple boughs, with rose trees all the place is shaded and from the dancing leaves deep sleep steals down; there a meadow where horses graze is rich with the flowers of spring and sweet is the scent of the dill. Hither come, O sovran Aphrodite, and at the dainty feast pour out the nectar mixed in cups of gold.

From this scene to the parched land of Egypt is a far cry and many a reader by the waters of the Nile must have remembered Zion; but the presence of such a text in Egypt in so humble a form is at once a measure of the strength of Hellenism and an explanation of it.

These are a few of the more important accessions that we owe to the papyri; to give any but the most cursory description of them would take us far beyond the limits of this essay.[1] The majority of the finds are small and, as papyri were torn down rather than across, more often yield a row of broken lines than a few complete ones; but even a small fragment may have a contribution to make. So a small and nearly contemporary fragment of the grammarian Harpocration supports an emendation of Sauppe's in a speech of Lysias, confirms a quotation of some anthropological interest from the comic poet Theopompus which had been needlessly emended, and, for the first time, puts a

---

[1] An alphabetical list with select bibliography of texts published to date will be found in R. A. Pack, *The Greek and Latin Literary Texts from Greco-Roman Egypt*, 2nd ed., Ann Arbor, Michigan, 1965; for subsequent publications recourse may be had to the lists in *Aegyptus* and *Chronique d'Égypte*.

citation from the historian Ephorus in its proper place in his work; and all this in some twenty-five incomplete lines. To take two instances of dramatic texts somewhat more substantial but small enough: a single parchment sheet at Berlin from the *Cretans* of Euripides has restored to us Pasiphae's sophistic but spirited apologia for her crimes, while from an Oxyrhynchus papyrus we learn the plot of Cratinus' comedy *Dionysalexandros*, with the added explanation that the play was a hit against Pericles; it was a parody of the Trojan War with Dionysus playing the part of Paris and included a Falstaffian scene in which Dionysus, hearing of the approach of the Greeks, hides Helen in a basket and metamorphoses himself into a ram. It is not that the drama has been particularly favoured; there is scarcely a branch of Greek literature that has not gained similar unexpected additions. At times, indeed, the scraps are so small that they merely tantalize; such, for example, are the few 'sillyboi' or tags which were attached to the top of the roll as titles. One of these bears the complacent inscription 'The Complete Works of Pindar', another 'The Female Mimes of Sophron'. Yet even these are an assurance that the books from which they have strayed still circulated in Roman Egypt and therefore may have left some *disiecta membra* in the sand still to be discovered.

The art or science of textual criticism is another study that has benefited from the discoveries of papyri;[1] not far short of half the literary texts from Egypt belong to works already extant. With very few exceptions these papyri are much older than the oldest of our medieval manuscripts (for the greater part of Xenophon's *Cyropaedia*, for example, we have no manuscript earlier than the twelfth century, while our earliest papyrus fragments are of the second), and as a rule were copied before the families into which our manuscripts divide were formed; in consequence their evidence, as it stands outside the common tradition of the

[1] The best discussion of this subject, to which I am indebted here, is still that by B. P. Grenfell, *Journ. Hellenic Studies*, xxxix (1919), 16–36.

manuscripts, is often of particular value. To generalize on the relation of the papyri to the medieval texts is possible only within wide limits, as the text of each author has its own history and its own problems, but with this qualification some comments are justifiable. On the whole the papyri, at any rate from the second century B.C. onwards, support the general *consensus codicum* to a surprising extent; that our tradition is generally sound cannot be doubted unless far-reaching changes were made or corruptions occurred at a date earlier even than the papyri, and the very fact that some of the cruces in the medieval manuscripts were already recognized as such by the editors of the papyri supports the soundness of the tradition as a whole. The corollary to this is that the wilder flights of fancy in emendation on the part of modern scholars receive singularly little encouragement; the palmary emendation dreamed of by scholars has only very rarely obtained confirmation. (A classic exception is Wilamowitz's correction of the senseless καρπὸν εἰς ἀθάνατον in Diogenes Laertius v. 7 to καρπὸν ἰσαθάνατον which was later confirmed by the Didymus papyrus.) On the whole, the influence of the papyri has been towards a soberer and more cautious handling of texts. Again, we have learnt, rather paradoxically, that in assessing the value of a manuscript too much stress should not be laid on its antiquity: firstly because some of the early Ptolemaic papyri are conspicuously careless and sometimes worse than careless; secondly, and more important, because it is by no means uncommon for a papyrus to agree with a reading in one of the so-called *deteriores* against an earlier manuscript. That they support the earlier and better manuscripts more often than the *deteriores* is true; what is important is that they should support the latter at all. So, although the text provided by the papyri may not always be as sound throughout as that of the best medieval manuscripts, this eclecticism they display has had a marked effect on textual criticism.

The view that the function of the critic was to find, where possible, the best (and generally this was the oldest) manuscript of his author, and adhere to that as far as possible at the risk of dismissing attractive readings of other manuscripts as due to the ingenuity of scholars or the ignorance of scribes, has received a severe setback. In as far as the eclectic principle implies that the critic must rely more on his knowledge of the language and of the author and on his common sense and less on external criteria, the change has been wholly beneficial.

That some of our earliest texts are both slovenly and eccentric might seem a reason for doubting the general soundness of our tradition; but we should note that these texts are relatively few in number, that they mostly come from one or two village sites and so may be regarded as 'provincial' texts not necessarily representative of the best then in existence; further, that several of them are anthologies and in all ages anthologies are notorious corrupters of texts, and finally that (except in the case of Homer) their eccentricity has been exaggerated—there are several quite 'normal' texts of this age. But, when all this is said, a real difference remains between the early and the late texts, and the explanation of the change is to be found in Alexandria. It is worth noting that many of the most scholarly among the literary papyri were found at Oxyrhynchus, a provincial city that can be shown to have had at various times in its history close ties with Alexandria. The deep influence exercised by the scholars of the Museum and Library at Alexandria in establishing the texts and often the authenticity of classical works has always been recognized; now the papyri, and above all the papyri of Homer, allow us to observe this influence at work.

In the earlier papyri we find marked divagations from the received text and not merely in single words; whole lines are omitted or more commonly added (though these new lines are as a rule 'repeats' from other parts of the poems and make little or no difference to the context); in one *Odyssey* papyrus there are as many as nine additional lines out of seventy. That this 'eccentric' text is inferior to the received tradition is clear; it is equally clear that in the third century B.C. the text of Homer was in a confused and fluid state, at any rate in Egypt. But after about the middle of the second century B.C. these eccentric texts tend to disappear and in the several hundred papyri of Homer later than this the text is in all essentials that of the medieval manuscripts, is in fact far closer to them than in the case of any other author; indeed, the Homeric papyrus of the Roman period is rarely more than a witness to the poet's popularity. There can be little doubt that this is due to the skill and thoroughness with which the Alexandrian scholars did their work.

We can watch, too, to a limited extent in the papyri the process by which a classical tradition was formed, a result partly of the work of the critics and scholars of Alexandria, though originally they had no such object in mind (to the pre-Alexandrine age the idea was entirely alien), in part of the schools and the conservatism of the school tradition. In the Ptolemaic period we find that the new literary fragments greatly exceed in number those of known authors; in the Roman period the balance is fairly equally held between the two, while in the Byzantine age the known and standard texts predominate. But this was no single or even a deliberate process, at least in the early stages; that the Byzantines were not limited to the standard authors that survived in medieval times is clear from the discovery of the texts of Eupolis and Sappho to mention two names alone. Nor could any discovery offer clearer proof of the survival of Hellenism or suggest more markedly the continuity between the ancient and medieval worlds than does that of a treatise on Aristotelian physics, written after the Arab conquest of the country, and forming as it does a visible link between the philosophy of Greece and that of Averroes and Aquinas.

Christian literature has been enriched no less than pagan by the Egyptian discoveries. Here again we find the same variety in kind, in age, and in condition; side by side with the canonical books of the Bible have been discovered non-canonical and apocryphal works, stories and sayings of the saints, homilies, liturgies, prayers, and hymns. Taken together they present us with a fair picture of the reading and culture of the Christian community in Upper Egypt, at least in the later centuries; the impartial spade will turn up now a few verses of the Psalms scrawled on papyrus and carried round the owner's neck as an amulet, now a primitive hymn with musical notation, now part of a treatise by Origen or the letters of St. Basil. The additions to Christian literature need a chapter to themselves; all we can do is to note in passing that they include such famous texts as the so-called 'Sayings of Jesus' (now identified as part of the Greek original of the 'Gospel of Thomas') and the Unknown Gospel in the British Museum, a work whose sober and narrative character as well as its early date distinguish it alike from the theosophical fantasies of the Gnostics (the earliest representative of which is a leaf of the 'Gospel of Mary', now in Manchester) and from such romantic hagiographies as the *Acta Pauli*, which provided the faithful with a satisfactory substitute for the pagan novel. The recovery of the 'Homily on the Passion' of Melito, Bishop of Sardis towards the end of the second century, and of Origen's 'Discourse with Heracleides'—a *procès-verbal* of a case of heresy in which the great theologian was called in as expert assessor—if less celebrated is hardly less important to scholars.

But in Christian studies the history of the Bible text occupies a place of unique importance, and their debt to the papyri would still be great even if no new works had been found at all. As it is, we have witnesses to the text of the Bible from Egypt far earlier than those from any other source; recent discoveries enable us to follow the history of the text back to the second century A.D. The oldest fragment of the New Testament is the small fragment of St. John's Gospel in the Rylands Library, of importance not merely because we can infer that the Gospel was read in Upper Egypt in the first half of the second century, but because the text

B b

of this fragment, small as it is, is in essence that of our later manuscripts. But incomparably the most important event in recent Biblical scholarship has been the publication of eleven codices of the Old and New Testaments ranging from the second to the fourth century, the majority of them being the property of the late Sir Chester Beatty; to these must be added yet another collection of Christian manuscripts, now in the possession of M. Bodmer, including, among other works in Greek and Coptic, two early manuscripts of the fourth Gospel and one of the third. It will be some time before the new material is thoroughly assimilated and the full effect on textual criticism seen, but that they support the general integrity of the text of the Bible is certain. As Sir Harold Bell pointed out, whatever doubts may surround the historicity and origins of the New Testament books, 'it is probably true to say broadly that no vital Christian doctrine, no basic saying of Christ, no central incident in His life, depends on a reading about which there is any serious textual doubt'.

The relevance of these documents, those vast masses of official, business, and private papers, to New Testament studies is less obvious and the help they give certainly less spectacular; but the connection is there and is a striking instance of the relationship between vastly different types of material. We might hope to find among the documents direct evidence of the expansion of Christianity and of the way of life of the early communities; but here the papyri fail us, probably for the obvious reason that as long as Christianity stood in danger of persecution its adherents would be careful not to leave in writing evidence that might always be used against them. Even so, the distinctively Christian formula 'in the Lord' is found in several letters of the third century; one of these, from a boy to his mother, carries an unusually elaborate preamble to a simple message:

To my most precious mother Mary, Besas, very many greetings in God. Before all things, I pray to our Father, the God of truth, and to the Spirit of Intercession, that they may preserve you in soul and body and spirit, giving to your body health, to your spirit cheerfulness, to your soul life eternal. Whenever you find anyone coming my way, do be sure to write to me of your health, that I may hear and rejoice. Don't forget to send me the coat against the Easter holiday, and send my brother to me. I salute my father and my brothers. I pray for your lasting health.

And the so-called Decian *libelli*, certificates issued by local officials of the government at the time of the Decian persecution as evidence that their holders had duly sacrificed to the pagan deities, are an eloquent reminder of the dangers to which the ordinary Christian in the remotest village might be exposed, although there is nothing to prove that those we have were issued to recanting Christians. Later, as we should expect, the evidence is more plentiful and more detailed; here we can only refer to the archive of Meletian letters preserved in the British Museum.[1]

Of more importance is the indirect contribution made by the documents. From no other country of the ancient world have we such a wealth of varied material relating to all the complex forms of social and economic life. Although the bulk of this evidence is strictly relevant to Egypt only, it is fair to recall that at the time when the books of the New Testament were written the neighbouring lands of Egypt and Palestine were both provinces of the Roman Empire, that both were partially Hellenized with a large non-Hellenic population, that contact between the two was easy, and that the official and business language of both countries was Greek. This Koine Greek, derived from Attic, but influenced by other dialects, was the lingua franca of the Roman East and though different parts of the Empire produced their local variations, though within one country the spoken language differed from the written, and that of the educated from that of the half-educated, yet it was unmistakably a single language and the degree of uniformity in the written Koine was high. The publication of numerous contemporary documents, both papyri

[1] See H. I. Bell, *Jews and Christians in Egypt*, London, 1924.

and inscriptions, has radically altered the views formerly held about the Greek of the New Testament; in particular, the idea that its language was something peculiar and divinely unrelated to other forms of Greek has disappeared for good.

It is true that the Semitic element is strong in parts of the New Testament, that no letter remotely like the Epistles of St. Paul has been found in Egypt, and that the characteristic words of New Testament religion cannot be paralleled from the papyri; not only are few of our documents directly concerned with religion, but a new religion will commonly create its own vocabulary and Christianity deliberately avoided the usages of pagan cults. Yet these books were designed to be intelligible to, and to appeal to, the ordinary Greek-speaking public, and were not all intended for Jewish or Judaized audiences. Hence the resemblances between the language of the papyri and that of the New Testament books have given a new direction to the study of New Testament Greek and, particularly in the case of the Gospels, have brought it more into touch with the world from which it sprang; even St. Paul, whose style and thought is most his own, had to make concessions to the reader of the day. Such words as παρουσία (used of the Second Advent) or συνείδησις (conscience) can be placed in their contemporary setting, and we can form some idea of the overtones and associations they carried with them; while others, such as ἀρχιποίμην (chief shepherd) or ὀρθοποδεῖν (to walk uprightly), are seen to be not eccentric neologisms but normal, if infrequently used, expressions.

More difficult and more elusive is the question how far the conditions of life as the papyri represent them provide an appropriate background for the events described in the New Testament. Here, though we must guard against the tendency to press every chance parallelism into the service of exegesis, we must remember that even such specifically religious works as the Gospels, which have their own canons to obey, yet had to fit into the framework of the society of their day. A single example must suffice. When in a report of legal proceedings of A.D. 88 we find the prefect C. Septimius Vegetus admonishing the plaintiff for imprisoning on his own initiative a man probably his debtor (a practice to which there are plenty of references in the papyri), it is legitimate to recall the parable of the unmerciful servant; and when the prefect summing up observes 'you deserve scourging (for this action) . . . but I make a present of you to the crowd and will show myself more merciful than you', the parallel with the story of Pilate and Barabbas is inescapable.

Just as the Christian letters and the Christian literary texts supplement each other in that they combine to give a picture of the Church in Egypt, so a similar relation may be asserted between the Greek literary papyri and some of the documents. Even in isolation the former have their value for the historian. A phrase such as 'Hellenization of the Near East' takes on a more definite meaning when we reflect that on the site of the small Egyptian village of Socnopaiou Nesus, perched up on a rock above Lake Moeris and separated by miles of desert or water from the next village, centring on and dominated by the temple of the crocodile god Sobk, were found fragments of the *Hector* of Astydamas and Plato's *Apology*, while among the authors whom we know were read at the neighbouring Karanis are Chariton, Isocrates, and a Latin grammarian (? Palaemon). Taken together, the literary texts give us a fair idea of the extent and variety of the literature available to the Greeks of Egypt and constitute a kind of barometer of Hellenic culture in Egypt which steadily sinks from the third century A.D. onwards.

Of the subjects and methods of education we learn far less from the documents than we could wish or might expect. It was privately organized (if we except the foundation of the Museum and Library of Alexandria by the first Ptolemy and the official recognition of the gymnasia in the Roman period), but it seems likely that the Ptolemies were interested in the establishment of the gymnasia both in towns and villages. Among the numerous papers of Zenon, who was agent to Apollonius, Chancellor of Egypt under the second Ptolemy, and in close touch with him, are several references to the gymnasia; he is consulted about the building of one at Philadelphia, where Apollonius had his country estate, and on another occasion he writes to the trainer Hierocles to ask whether a young protégé of his is really worth his keep and whether his athletic achievements justify Zenon in taking him away from his books. The trainer's answer is that the boy is making excellent progress in his sport and in his other studies—only he would like Zenon to send him some more equipment. In another letter Zenon is informed that another protégé of his has been successful at the Ptolemaic games in the little village of Holy Island; the trainer who writes the letter improves the occasion by asking for a cloak 'thicker and of softer wool' for the boy to use at the Arsinoeia (games in honour of the late Queen Arsinoë). Here, though Zenon's interest is no doubt financial, we see that the institution of these games (which would be organized by the local gymnasia) was closely bound up with the cult of the royal house and was obviously not a matter to which government circles were indifferent. Just as the gymnasia had served the purpose of the Ptolemies, so in later times we hear of the city of Oxyrhynchus celebrating the *Ludus Capitolinus*, originally founded by Domitian; there is extant a letter from the gymnasiarch to the head of the athletic organization requesting him to round up as many competitors as possible; no doubt for these games to prove a failure would savour of disloyalty. Less political in its motivation and more disinterested was the action of the same city in the dark days of the later third century in exempting from taxation a long list of heralds, trumpeters, and poets who had distinguished themselves in the local festivals.

It was typical of Rome to substitute for the informal and perhaps casual encouragement of Greek education a defined and organized system; so Augustus, wishing on the principle of *divide et impera* to encourage the Hellenized elements in Egypt against the Egyptian influence which had grown in power under the later Ptolemies, gave official recognition to the office of gymnasiarch, and by abolishing the village gymnasia and granting financial privileges to the metropolites, made the towns strongholds of Hellenism to a greater degree than they had been before. Education was the road to a career for a Graeco-Egyptian; so Apion writes back from Misenum, where he has joined the Roman fleet, to his father in the Faiyûm:

On reaching Misenum I received three gold pieces for my travelling expenses from Caesar and all is going well. I beg of you, my Lord father, write me a letter, first that I may learn how you are, secondly how my brother is, thirdly that I may kiss your hand (the Greek word has the double sense of hand and handwriting), for you have given me a good education and with the gods' favour I hope to get on fast . . . I have sent you my picture (presumably in uniform) by Euctemon.

In another letter, discovered at Karanis in the same province, Apollinarius writes to his mother from Bostra in Arabia in terms of warmest affection ('whenever I think of you, I don't eat or drink, but just weep . . .') and tells her how, while the ordinary soldiers are sweating at stone-cutting, he as an officer of the legion (perhaps the Sixth *Ferrata*) moves around doing nothing at all.

Most of the letters relating to education which have reached us insist on the industry and application of the boys; one boy goes so far as to rebuke his parent for not coming to see whether his tutor is paying sufficient attention to him, but the inner meaning of this may be elucidated from another letter in which the lady of the house gives instructions for some pigeons and chickens, which she doesn't eat herself, to be sent to her daughter's tutor, 'that he may work hard with her'. This attitude is natural; but it is not surprising to see the other side of the picture in a letter of a Byzantine parent withdrawing his son who had proved an unsatisfactory pupil (it is possible, but I think less likely, that the boy was not at school, but apprenticed).

You have written to me about little Anastasius, and as I am in your debt, be sure you will be paid in full. Nothing of what has been told you is true except that he is stupid and a child and foolish. He wrote me a letter himself quite in keeping with his looks and empty wits. And since he is a child and stupid, I will fetch him home. I am keeping his letter to show you when I come. Chastise him; for ever since he left his father, he has had no other beatings and he likes getting a few—his back has got accustomed to them and needs its daily dose.

So few are the allusions to higher education among the papyri that the following letter deserves quotation. The writer, who was probably at Alexandria to complete his education, after relating how he has had an accident with the family chariot (which may be connected with some discreditable incident in the theatre to which he makes several references), expatiates to his father on the difficulty of finding good tutors:

He has also persuaded the sons of Apollonius to attend Didymus' school. For they and he since the death of Philologus have been looking for an abler tutor right up till now. For my part, I'd pray never to see Didymus, even from a distance, again, if only I had found tutors worth the name. What really depresses me is that this fellow, who was a mere provincial schoolmaster, has seen fit to compete with the rest. So as I know that apart from paying more and more fees all to no purpose there's no good to be had from a tutor, I've other resources of my own. Write and tell me soon what you think about it. . . . By attending the lectures of the professors— Posidonius is one of them—with the gods' favour I shall do well for myself. The worry over these matters is such as to compel me to neglect my health—I have the feeling that those who are still unsuccessful ought not to concern themselves with it, particularly when there is no one bringing in any money.

He then dwells on the enormities of a certain Heraclas, probably his *paedagogus* or attendant slave, and suggests that he might be set to earning some money, and after saying that when a young brother joins him they will move into more spacious lodgings, he ends by thanking his father for the usual supplies from home.

But, as we have seen, the idea of the gymnasium included education of the body no less than education of the mind. We have already mentioned the village games of the Ptolemaic period; in the Roman age, though towns such as Oxyrhynchus and Hermopolis ran their own games with considerable display and expense, the emphasis had changed and the really important events were the great international contests. The standardization of culture under the Roman Empire has its counterpart in the highly professionalized and international sport of the age. The documents from Egypt show us these professional athletes (they describe themselves as members of 'the sacred athletic international union, under imperial patronage') touring the world to take part in games at Sardis, at Sidon, or at Naples, and returning home to receive the grateful thanks of their fellow citizens and, more important, exemption from taxes, a monthly pension, and, in some cases, freedom from public burdens for themselves and their descendants. Not quite in the class of the world champions, but no less mercenary, was a certain Dius whose letter to his wife Sophrone has been preserved. He had gone to Alexandria with some friends to look for someone (probably a debtor) who had disappeared: 'we did not find the fellow,' he writes, 'instead we found our lord the king'. Games were held at royal command and Dius contrived to get himself admitted 'by an act of favour' (probably he was not qualified); he was, however, badly beaten in the *pancratium* by the professionals. Nothing daunted, he hit on the plan of challenging his own companions (with whose abilities he was doubtless acquainted) to a kind of all-in wrestling match, was victorious, and received a money prize from the emperor while the others were awarded clothes for consolation prizes. He repeated his success on a day when the emperor led the procession to the Lagaion (it is interesting to find a Roman emperor honouring the memory of the father of the first Ptolemy) and concludes his letter: 'so don't be vexed; though we haven't found the fellow, fortune has given us something else'.

But the great mass of the documents, whether public or private, have no direct connection with education or the history of Graeco-Roman culture. Although these may be reflected in the description of people as illiterate, or in the style, the syntax, and the orthography of the documents (for example, the stilted and repetitive language of Byzantine documents is proof enough that Greek was a dying tongue, kept alive by artificial stimulants), the documents are primarily sources for the economic, social, and administrative history of the country. These documents are now counted in their thousands; and, embarrassing though their number sometimes is, in it lies no small part of their value. One tax-receipt or a single account may not be very informative (though it is to a single papyrus of A.D. 359 that we owe the knowledge that the government was taking steps at that time to revive the trade between Egypt and India); its value is greatly enhanced when it can be treated as one of a series in which normal can be distinguished from abnormal practice, the incidence of the tax and its local variations calculated, or, in the case of accounts, the price-level of an article observed over a number of years. The same holds good of contracts which form one of the largest classes of documents; we have enough leases, for example, to follow the development of the system of land-tenure from Ptolemaic times down to the end of the Byzantine period, though evidence may be more plentiful for one period than for another, and as a lesson in social history few things are more instructive than to read through a series of deeds of marriage or divorce and to observe in the former the varying obligations assigned at different periods to husband and wife, in the latter the purely business-like character of the earlier documents and the somewhat longwinded pretexts of the later ones. Or we may compare an ordinary will of the Roman period with, for example, the *donatio mortis causa* of the fourth century in which Flavius Abraham, an ex-*praepositus* in the Roman army, binds himself to bequeath half his property to the holy Church, his wife to have the use of the other half until her death when it reverts to the Church, and gives instructions for all his slaves, male and female, to be freed (this, however, is not uncommon in pagan wills). Such dispositions of a man of high rank are an epitome of a whole social revolution.

Among the documents, contracts are of particular value to the social historian; if we take a representative selection,[1] we shall find that each gives a vignette of life in the ancient world. In one, a deed of adoption, the adoptive parents promise the real parents that the child shall inherit their estate and not be reduced to slavery; in another, two brothers set free 'under sanction of Zeus, Earth, and Sun' the third part of a female slave which they hold jointly, the other two-thirds being already emancipated; in a third, a father apprentices his son to a weaver, the latter to feed and clothe him and the father to pay a drachma for every day that the boy plays truant, while under the terms of another such agreement the boy is 'to sit at his teacher's feet from sunrise to sundown', but to enjoy twenty days' holiday with pay. Somewhat similar is the contract by which a man places his slave with a certain Apollonius to learn shorthand, two years being allowed the slave to learn to read and write it perfectly. Many, as we should expect, relate to agriculture; in one, for example, two men undertake to lease for one year all the operations connected with a vineyard and we have a detailed description of what this entails. They even provide some evidence about the lighter side of life, as when Onnophris and some friends of his at Oxyrhynchus hire a whole company of flute-players and musicians (the word used is συμφωνία) for the five feast-days, donkey transport to be provided, and part of the substantial fee to be paid in advance. From the darker side of ancient life we may quote a Berlin papyrus in which a widow contracts with her prospective mother-in-law to expose the child of her previous marriage; what is surprising to us is not that the exposure (which we know was common) should

---

[1] Each of those cited below with the exception of the last will be found in vol. i of the *Select Papyri* in the Loeb Library.

take place, but that it should be provided for by a legal document.

Much of the material that the papyri have provided for the historian is of this indirect character, though a date attached to a contract may effect a vital change in chronology, just as the geographical particulars in a deed of sale or lease may inform us of the existence of some unsuspected temple or cult; direct evidence, that is reference to persons or events of historical importance in contemporary documents, is rarer than we might expect. But examples of this are to be found; in the Zenon papyri, for example, historical personages occasionally figure. In one letter a garrulous and unknown correspondent reports to Zenon that he has called in an expert to 'cure' some dice made of gazelle bone; the expert thinks poorly of them and to confirm his judgement refers to his practice at the court, where he has 'cured' dice for Alexander the Etesian—a man who had once been King of Macedon for forty-five days (hence his nickname) and who some twenty years later appears as a pensioner playing knuckle-bone at the court of Ptolemy Philadelphus. Again, a scrap of a decree of no more than three lines is sufficient to show that Antiochus Epiphanes of Syria, when he invaded Egypt in 170 B.C., did, as our ancient authorities say, dethrone the reigning Ptolemy, while the fact that the Faiyûm is not called the Arsinoite but the Crocodilopolite nome may indicate that Antiochus wished to suppress a name that honoured the Ptolemaic house; the chronology of this crucial incident in Ptolemaic history has been startlingly elucidated by the dating clauses of a lease of a vineyard.

From the Roman period we have the two edicts of Germanicus of A.D. 19, in one of which he rebukes the Alexandrines for paying him the semi-divine honours proper to the emperor alone (his threat that, if they continued in this course, he would be obliged to show himself less frequently to them, may have seemed inadequate to his uncle Tiberius): the famous letter of the Emperor Claudius to the Alexandrines: a copy, though incomplete, of the revolutionary *Constitutio Antoniniana* of Caracalla, conferring the

Roman citizenship on all the inhabitants of the Empire, apart perhaps from the *dediticii*: the text of the proclamation issued by the prefect of Egypt introducing Diocletian's changes in the method of assessment for taxation, and so fundamentally changing the economy of the Empire, which proves conclusively that the *capitatio humana* was extended to Egypt. One result of Diocletian's monetary reforms can be seen in a letter in which an official who has inside information of a measure to reduce the face value of an imperial coin writes to his agent 'to make haste to spend all the Italian silver that you have on purchases, on my behalf, of goods of every description at whatever price you find them'. From the same period comes a copy of a circular letter, probably from the chancery of the Bishop of Alexandria, denouncing the tenets, and above all the practices, of the new sect of the Manichees—the earliest witness that we have to the spread of the religion of Mani; that the danger to the Church in Egypt remained is shown by the discovery in the Faiyûm of a number of Manichaean codices in Coptic.

But these, after all, are the exceptions; the subject of the documentary papyri is the ordinary rather than the extraordinary, government seen not with the eyes of the statesman or the political historian, but as it affected the masses of the people. To describe the intricacies of the administrative system as applied by the Ptolemies and adopted from them and made more rigorous by their Roman successors is beyond the scope of this essay; it has been justly described from the evidence of the papyri as *l'exploitation pratiquée sous le signe de l'absolutisme*. Countless papyri show how the principle that the subject existed for the benefit of the state was ruthlessly applied in every department of life; the position of the king in the Ptolemaic age as in theory the sole owner of all land in the country is but one instance of a principle of almost universal application. Individual kings or prefects might profess, and sincerely, their desire to see the taxpayer meet with fair treatment, but the system was too strong for them, nor did any remedy, such as, for example, setting one official to watch another, materially change the situation. A Tebtunis papyrus has preserved for us a memorandum with detailed instructions on the management of certain departments of the royal revenue; it was probably intended for the *oeconomi*, treasury officials stationed in each nome, and had we not the evidence of petitions, letters, and legal reports we might take it that the following quotation was typical of the administration:

> In your tours of inspection try in going from place to place to cheer everybody up and to put them in better heart; and not only should you do this by words but also, if any of them complain of the village scribes or the comarchs about any matter touching agricultural work, you should make enquiry and put a stop to such doings as far as possible.

Such handbooks of official instructions appear in the Greek world for the first time in the Hellenistic kingdoms, and the editors of this text point out that they were the model for the Roman *mandata principis*; in this, as in other matters, Rome built up the structure of her empire on Hellenistic foundations. A similar document of the Roman period is the Gnomon of the Idios Logos, regulations for the department of the Special Account originally drawn up by Augustus and preserved in an abbreviated form by a Berlin papyrus. No document gives a better picture of the spirit and practice of Roman administration than this, with its detailed instructions how this or that breach of the regulations (if, for example, a priest wears his hair long or wears a woollen garment, thus infringing the priestly law) might be turned to the financial advantage of the government.

The principles of administration were clearly recognized by the people; it is significant that petitions and complaints of robbery, injustice, or maltreatment commonly conclude by imploring the competent authority to take action 'lest any harm accrue to the state (or treasury)'; even where the dispute is purely private and no official is involved, the petitioner asks for assistance on the ground that if it is not forthcoming he will be unable to pay his taxes. A petition of A.D. 280, alleging abuse of his powers by a financial official, has been endorsed by the prefect of Egypt to this effect: 'With a view to what is expedient for the revenues . . . his Excellency the epistrategus shall sift the matter with the utmost equity.' Such petitions might be addressed to a variety of authorities from the king or emperor down to the local police commandant and deal with a great variety of topics; but when they are used for evidence of the state of the administration it is necessary to remember that no petitions are written to express satisfaction with the government. The incidental information they contain is varied and often valuable, particularly that circumstantial detail which a petitioner trusts will give verisimilitude to his claims. To take two from a group of Ptolemaic petitions addressed nominally to the king, though in fact decided by subordinate officials; from one, in which a widow of a soldier complains that her neighbour is interfering with her building of a wall, we learn that her husband had erected a shrine to the Syrian goddess and Aphrodite Berenice, and, as the lady's name is Asia, we may suspect that his predilection for a foreign deity was due to his wife's influence and that the neighbour perhaps objected to these foreign ways, just as we hear of Egyptians attacking Greeks because they were Greeks and vice versa. The second, in which a man complains that now he is old and suffering from a disease of the eye (still today one of the plagues of Egypt) his daughter, in spite of all he has done for her, will not support him, lets us see that education for women was not unknown in Ptolemaic Egypt.

One of the difficulties of the study of documentary papyri is that of finding a unifying principle by which to treat them. This may be done by considering together a group of documents such as petitions or leases, and, though temporal and local variations may be considerable, yet the results gained, particularly from the diplomatic and legal standpoint, will be valuable; as an alternative to this vertical view we can occasionally take a horizontal cross-section of miscellaneous documents. Such archives—large groups of documents from the same place and approximately of the same date, and relating in the main to one group of persons—are not very numerous; the largest and richest is that of the papers of Zenon, and second to it, at least among the earlier papyri, the large collection relating to the affairs of some inmates of the Serapeum at Memphis in the second century B.C. Among the smaller archives none is more homogeneous or more attractive than that of Apollonius, strategus of the nome of Apollonopolis Heptakomia at the end of Trajan's reign and the beginning of Hadrian's.

The papyri of this archive number nearly 150 and all fall within a period of seven years; they are a part, if only a small part, of the collected papers which Apollonius took with him when he laid down his office and retired to his property at Hermopolis. It is very rarely that we get such a clear view of anyone as we do of Apollonius both in his private and in his public life. It so happens that he held his office—in spite of its title, the office of strategus was a civil one whose holder was responsible for the general administration of his nome and in particular for the proper functioning of the taxation system—at the time of the great Jewish revolt in the eastern provinces which almost assumed the proportions of a civil war and caused widespread damage and loss of life. The position grew so desperate in Egypt that the strategus had to call out a levy *en masse* of the peasants and place himself at its head to hold the rebels till reinforcements of Roman legionaries could arrive—an incident which has no parallel in the history of the office. We find him writing to the prefect requesting sixty days' furlough to set his own affairs in order after his long absence (his tenure of his office was unusually long) and the havoc caused by the revolt of the 'godless Jews'. His immediate superior was the epistrategus of the Thebaid, who sends him instructions about the inspection of lands and adds a hint that the 'natives' are not to be subjected to extortion or false accusation. It is another epistrategus, Flavius Philoxenus, who writes, in a letter which is that of a man whose mother tongue is Latin rather than Greek, to introduce to Apollonius a friend of his: he concludes 'Treat him as you would myself. Need I say more? You know my disposition. Farewell.' Hadrian's accession to the throne was celebrated in the nome with speeches and dramatic performances, and among Apollonius' papers is a draft of the libretto of the pageant in which Demus and Phoebus announced the good news to the people and which hints that the festivities were also to include a fountain flowing with wine.

The routine business of his office is represented by long reports from the land surveyors on the state of the irrigation, by sworn attestations from village officials or peasants that so much land will be cultivated, by a report from the city clerk on men suitable to act as city police in which the names of the streets—Isis Crescent, Street of the Women's Bath—are of interest. Public baths, for both men and women, were a Greek innovation; to the Egyptian peasant, then as now content with the Nile, the idea was as alien as was that of the gymnasium; to the Greek these things meant civilization. The metropolis of the nome was small in comparison with a town such as Arsinoë; but though it had only 1,173 houses we know that sometimes quite small fractions of houses were leased, so that the population may well have been larger than at first sight would appear. To him, too, came the returns of the fourteen-yearly census in which every householder had to return all members of his household, their ages, sex, and status; for this purpose, as St. Luke tells us and the papyri confirm him, every man had to go to his place of origin. As strategus, he held a court of first instance, and consequently complaints and petitions figure among his papers; among them is one accusing the royal secretary (the next highest official in the nome) of illicit exactions, and another from a group of peasants who, suspected of implication in the murder of a Roman centurion, attempt to involve others in the charge; the case itself would be heard at the *conventus* of the prefect. It is no wonder that he was, as he himself says in a letter to the inspectors of the nome, 'distracted by the collection of the corn dues and all the other unfinished business of his office'.

Of his family circle we have in the private letters an unusually intimate picture. He and his sister Aline were deeply attached to each other; she was also his wife, a practice which, after it had received the sanction of the Ptolemies, had become quite common among the Hellenized population of Egypt. No concession by Hellenism to oriental manners is more striking than this; it is noteworthy that in the Gnomon of the Idios Logos it was found necessary specifically to forbid such marriages to Romans. Such a marriage carried no social stigma with it and did not prevent Apollonius from having many Roman friends. During the Jewish war Aline writes to him begging him to put the burden of the work on to his subordinates as other strategi did and not to run into unnecessary danger; when he went away, she says, she could taste neither food nor drink, nor could she sleep. Equally moving and sincere is the following letter from Taus, a woman who was perhaps a family servant:

Taus to Apollonius her lord very many greetings. Before everything I salute you, master, and I pray always for your health. I was distressed, my lord, not a little to hear that you had been ill, but thanks be to all the gods that they keep you safe from harm. I beg you, my lord, if it please you, to send for me; else I die because I do not behold you daily. Would that I were able to fly and come to you and make obeisance to you; for it distresses me not to behold you. So be friends with me and send for me. Goodbye, my lord.

We may mention too among his private papers some letters from Herodes, the architect of his new house; in one of them he explains that owing to a death in the foreman's family they can't work for a few days and so he asks leave to go and visit his brother. Herodes' references to his work and the details of the house are reminiscent of another letter, not of the same archive but not far distant in date, in which Capito writes to his friend Teres about the decoration of the latter's house which he is superintending; he discusses the problem of the colonnade which needs repair, and suggests that some mural paintings—scenes from the *Iliad*, or whatever his friend would like—would be very suitable; it is, he says, just what the place demands (ὁ γὰρ τόπος ἀπαιτεῖ).

One other letter from the Apollonius archive may be quoted, of interest both for the reference to home weaving (the most primitive form of an industry which was highly organized in Egypt) and labour troubles, and for the vivid picture it gives of the writer herself. It is from the hand of Eudaemonis, mother of Aline and Apollonius, and was probably written during the Jewish troubles:

Eudaemonis to her daughter Aline, greeting. Before all else I pray that you may be safely delivered and that I get news of a male child. . . . It was only with difficulty that I got the wool from the dyer's on Epeiph 10th. I am working together with your slave-girls as best I can. I can't find any able to come and work with me, they are all working for their own mistresses. For our people are marching round the whole city demanding higher wages. Your sister Souerous has given birth. Teeus wrote and told me how grateful she was to you; so I realize, my lady, that my commands are still good, for she has left all her own people and has travelled in your company. The small one (Aline's daughter, Heraidous) sends her love and is working hard at her lessons. I tell you that I shall have no time for God, unless I get my son back first. What did you send me the 20 drachmas for, when I'm so badly off? I've already the prospect before my eyes of spending the winter without a rag. Good-bye. P.S. The wife of Eudemus is inseparable from me and I'm most grateful to her.

In another letter she refers to some difficulty that she is having with a relative named Discas, probably about some family property, and writes as follows:

I have already performed my part, and I have neither bathed nor worshipped the gods because of my fear about your unsettled case, lest I too be driven to the lawcourts.

Her postscript is revealing:

At your wedding the wife of my brother Discas brought me 100 drachmas; and now that her son Nilus is about to marry, it is right that we should make a return gift, even if we have got grievances against them.

This attitude to religion, though it finds clearer expression here than is usual, was no idiosyncrasy on Eudaemonis' part; it is an attitude which goes far to explain the widespread use of magical practices in Egypt for all the purposes of life, trivial and serious alike. The papyri have brought us a large number of magical texts, actual amulets and incantations or magician's handbooks such as the great London or Oslo papyri, the premiss of all of them being that the appropriate acts can bend the heavenly powers to the service of the agent. Some of the spells recommended in these handbooks have a touch of the modern advertisement and their psychological appeal is not so different: for example—

A magic formula that restrains anger, secures goodwill, success in the lawcourts, works even with kings; there is absolutely nothing better. Take a silver plate, inscribe on it with a bronze pencil the figure drawn below and the names, carry it in the folds of your dress and you will win. (Then follow the names and actual formula.)

Among all varieties of public religion which we find in the papyri, magic and the attitude it expresses remain constant.

Not many of the private letters are so full of character and life as Eudaemonis'; they are excellent examples of the type of material for ancient history with which only the papyri can supply us. More typical of the ordinary letter, both in its concern with Egypt's abiding interest, agriculture, and in its unpretentiousness, is this:

Ammonius to his dearest Aphrodisius, greeting. I wrote a letter to the herdsman Heracleus that he should supply you with a donkey, and I bade Ophelion to supply you with another and to send me the loaves. You have sent me three artabae; I ask you therefore to do your utmost to send the remaining three artabae immediately and the relish, as I am on board a boat. As to the pigs' fodder and the rest of the price for the hay, make provision until I come; for I expect to make up an account with you. I have given you every allowance. Urge your wife from me to look after the pigs and do you also take care of the calf. Be sure, Aphrodisius, to send me the loaves and the relish . . .

No exact classification of documents, except by their formal character and not always then, is possible; they have the variety, the confusion, the irrational complexity of life itself. If, as the Elder Pliny thought, written records are of the essence of civilization, then to form a picture of an age, however imperfect and biased it needs must be, documents of all kinds are welcome; 'cum chartae usu maxime humanitas vitae constet et memoria'. If we think of *humanitas* in the sense which Pliny gave it, we may claim that the literary papyri have added some pages in the history of Greek literature and so enriched our perception of it; but there is a different sense too, in which we may assert a real relation between *humanitas* and the study of the papyri. Our view of life in the eastern Mediterranean in the millennium that separates Alexander from Mohammed has indeed been rendered more 'humane' by the concreteness and the vividness which papyri have brought to almost every branch of ancient studies, and with them our idea of what *humanitas* as applied to history can mean has developed. If a sense of the continuity of history, of the fundamental resemblances between civilizations, among their more obvious and very real differences, is an attribute of a civilized society, then we can claim that this is a legacy for which we may own a proper gratitude.

C. H. ROBERTS

14

CHRISTIAN AND COPTIC EGYPT

On the early development of the Christian Church Egypt exercised an important and, at times, decisive influence; at no other period of its history is the legacy of Egypt to the modern world so direct and so demonstrable. Greek culture, which had been an important factor in the intellectual and political life of Egypt since the foundation of Alexandria in 332 B.C., had a distinctive theological contribution to make. Different in kind, but no less fruitful, was the bequest of the Egyptian-speaking Christians, the Copts, as they have been known among European writers since the sixteenth century. The word itself is a transliteration of the Arabic corruption of the Greek *Aigyptios*, applied by the Muslim invaders of A.D. 641 to the indigenous Christian inhabitants who still used the ancient tongue of Egypt. It is now currently extended beyond its original religious denotation to describe also the latest stage of the ancient Egyptian language, its script, grammar, and literature, as well as a specific art style; in this broader sense the word need not necessarily imply a Christian content, form, or purpose.

At the beginning of the Christian era Alexandria, founded some three centuries earlier, still retained more than a semblance of the grandeur which it had enjoyed as the capital of the Ptolemaic empire. It was described by Strabo, no inexperienced traveller, as the greatest emporium of the inhabited world. From it the plentiful harvest of the fertile land of Egypt was exported to Rome; through it the luxury goods of the Eastern world which, reached Egypt on the newly discovered trade winds, were channelled into the Mediterranean.

Even in the ancient world Alexandria was recognized as being next to, rather than of, Egypt. Yet without the hinterland to support it, the city could not have fulfilled its destiny. Inevitably Roman domination of Egypt curtailed the political privileges of Alexandria. Its cosmopolitan citizen body, which comprised a strong organized Jewish community but no official native Egyptian element, resented the new order. Their stubborn individualism, intolerance, and internecine factions were a constant embarrassment to successive Roman emperors. The attitude to Roman management is revealed in the pagan 'Acts of the Alexandrines' which circulated in the second and third centuries. The Roman authorities were depicted as villainous tyrants, to whom these pagan martyrs replied with audacious, boorish freedom of speech. The emperors were impaled on the horns of an inescapable dilemma. They were haunted by the memory of the threat to the security of the Roman Empire created by the ambitions of Mark Antony and Cleopatra. Alexandria was a natural base from which usurpers might launch their claim to the imperial purple. The emperors could not, on the other hand, afford to treat the city with the harshness which, for instance, Titus meted out to Jerusalem. The part that Alexandria played in the economy of the Empire was too great and too necessary. In spite of its turbulent history the city continued to enjoy commercial prosperity. It remained rich enough to provide for the maintenance of academic institutions which made the city one of the leading centres of research and learning in the ancient world. Its lighthouse and its libraries are indelibly imprinted upon popular imagination as the symbols of Alexandria.

Eusebius of Caesarea, writing his 'Ecclesiastical History' at the beginning of the fourth century, is the earliest witness to the tradition that the Evangelist Mark was the first to be sent to preach the Gospel in Egypt and the first to establish churches in Alexandria (II. xvi). The traditional list of the Patriarchs of Alexandria is headed by his name, but its reliability for the first two centuries is rightly suspect because of the evenness of the length of reigns of the first eleven patriarchs. There is no inherent implausibility in the tradition. It was the policy of the primitive Church to concentrate its missionary activity in the major centres. Jews from Egypt were among those who heard the Pentecost sermon of Peter (Acts 2: 10) and at Jerusalem the synagogue attended, amongst others, by Alexandrine Jews opposed the appointment of Stephen to the diaconate (Acts 6: 9). No trace of the early Church has survived. In the official Roman mind Christians were classified as a sect of the Jews and the primitive Church could scarcely have survived unimpaired the pogroms carried out against the Jewish community of Alexandria in the first century.

Not until the end of the second century does Christianity emerge as an established force in the intellectual life of Alexandria. A catechetical school was in existence; about the year 180 its head was a certain Pantaenus, some say a converted Stoic. He was certainly conversant with current Greek speculative thought. The emergence of the school coincides with the first of the reasoned attacks on Christianity, the 'True Account' of Celsus, an Alexandrine writing in Greek, who clearly had knowledge of the Gospel narrative and of the historical Jesus. The catechetical school of Alexandria produced some of the first and some of the ablest of the Christian apologists.

The two great names are Clement and Origen, both of whom wrote in Greek. Clement (*c.* A.D. 160–215), according to tradition born in Athens and a convert to Christianity at Alexandria after a scholarly peregrination around the centres of learning in the Eastern Mediterranean, was the successor of Pantaenus as head of the catechetical school. His principal works were the *Protreptikos* or 'Exhortations to the Greeks', an attack on pagan religion and philosophy addressed to the intelligentsia of his age; the *Paidagogos* or 'The Tutor', an urbane manual of religious instruction which treated of manners as well as morals; and the *Stromateis* or

'Miscellanies', the theme of which was the superiority of Christian to Greek philosophy. In these works Clement revealed a diverse knowledge of Greek pagan literature, referring to over 300 minor authors whose works are otherwise unknown. He was thoroughly conversant with Greek mystery cults and, to judge from his statements on the nature of the native Egyptian scripts, he also made some attempt to inform himself concerning the native beliefs of the old Egyptian religion.

The influence of Alexandrine scholarship is particularly obvious in Clement's work in the emphasis which he places upon intellectual comprehension; progress in the Christian way of life is achieved by a deepening understanding of the Christian faith. The importance of knowledge as the means of entry into the band of the select is a characteristic tenet of Alexandrine philosophies, to which the term Gnostic is applied. Traditionally associated by Church historians with heretical philosophical systems of the second and subsequent centuries, Gnosticism has now been given a wider definition to embrace practically all semi-mystical speculation springing in its ultimate analysis from the irrational element in Plato's dialogues. In its narrower sense of distinct heretical sects it was particularly prevalent in Egypt. Two of its chief exponents in the second century were Valentinus, who was educated at Alexandria, and Basilides, who taught there. Clement is the representative of Gnosticism in a Christian context. In view of his Gnosticism and his manifest Hellenistic background, it is not altogether surprising that, in the West at least, his reputation has been subjected to some fluctuation. His name appears in official calendars for 4 December but was expunged from the Roman calendar in 1748 by Pope Benedict XIV.

The greatest of all these early Christian apologists is, by common consent, Clement's successor as the head of the catechetical school, Origen. He was born about A.D. 185, the son of a certain Leonides, martyred at the time of the persecution of Septimius Severus in 202. After his father's death he became a teacher but continued also to apply himself to study, attending courses at the catechetical school. Out of genuine desire for knowledge of philosophical systems, and not from doubt of the correctness of Christian truth, he became also the pupil of Ammonius Saccas, an early exponent of Neoplatonist philosophy, later developed and systematized by his pupil Plotinus. After the retirement of Clement from Alexandria, Origen became in name the head of the catechetical school and later, though still a layman, was officially recognized as such by the Patriarch Demetrius. He remained in this position until 215, when the massacre of Alexandrines ordered by Caracalla occasioned his withdrawal to Caesarea in Palestine. He returned to Alexandria with an increased reputation among the Eastern Churches, but relations with the Patriarch Demetrius became strained, partly as a result of the irregularity of his ordination in Greece by Palestinian bishops and partly as a result of suspicions concerning his orthodoxy both in his writings and in his private life. (He had, we are told, in an excess of zeal literally applied to himself the precept of Matthew 19: 12 and undergone castration.) Deprived of his priesthood and banished from Alexandria, he retired in 231 to Caesarea, where he continued his work until his death as a result of torture suffered during the Decian persecution (A.D. 250–1). Before he left Alexandria he had published the most important of his doctrinal treatises, 'On the Principal Doctrines' (*Peri Archōn*), a systematic exposition of Christian dogma, in the light of the revealed truths of Scripture and the deductions of reason. Much of our knowledge of his work comes not from original manuscripts but from such of his thought as has survived in passages in the writings of Basil of Cappadocia and Gregory Nazianzus in Greek, Hilary of Poitiers, Ambrose of Milan, Jerome, and Rufinus in Latin. In spite of the suspicion of unorthodoxy which has clung to his name, he has always commanded the respect of theologians.

No less monumental was Origen's work in a different discipline, that of textual criticism, one of the notable original contributions of Alexandria to scholarship. Controversy between Jew and Christian was bedevilled by conflicting texts of the Old Testament. A Greek version of the Hebrew Bible was first produced for the Jewish community of Alexandria in the third century B.C., according to a contemporary tradition under the patronage of Ptolemy II Philadelphus (285–246 B.C.)—the so-called Septuagint, since it was said to be the work of seventy scholars in seventy days. Origen's edition of the Old Testament, the *Hexapla*, was probably completed in his final years at Caesarea. Its title is derived from its six parallel columns, reading from left to right: Hebrew, a transliteration of the Hebrew characters into Greek letters, the versions of Aquila and Symmachus, the revised Septuagint text, and the translation of Theodotion. So great was the influence of Origen's text that the recovery of pre-Origen versions remains the most difficult unresolved problem of Septuagint studies.

The significance of the Alexandrine school lies in the fact that it represents the earliest attempt of the Church to provide a rational basis for its faith and ethics and to explain the mysteries of the revealed truth contained in its theology in the light of the current intellectual terms of the philosophers. Since Alexandria was the place where this attempt was first made, Christian thought was inevitably influenced by the scholarly environment of that city where mysticism was grafted on to the stock of philosophy, where Philo, Plotinus, and Valentinus were educated. Clement and Origen are their Christian counterparts. The measure of their stature may be gauged by a comparison of their works with other early Christian writing, pseudo-prophetic, concerned with the second coming, some of which, like the 'Epistle of Barnabas', probably had an Alexandrine origin.

That the school received ecclesiastical approbation was of particular importance in the history of Christianity. The period of its greatest fame and influence coincided with the episcopate of Demetrius (*c.* A.D. 188/9–231). Its influence sensibly declined after the quarrel between Demetrius and Origen; there were other heads but their contribution was of less account than that of the great theologian-bishops of the fourth century, notably Athanasius and Cyril. The school itself was finally destroyed in the struggle between the Patriarch Theophilus (A.D. 385–412) and the monks.

Its Christian apologists are Alexandria's legacy. No hymns evoke religious sentiment for its past, like the great medieval hymns to Rome; there is no architectural glory, like the great church of Hagia Sophia at Constantinople, to draw the modern pilgrim. Virtually nothing has survived of the art and architecture of its great days as a Christian centre. Only to the west of the city, about forty miles away in the heart of the once fertile region of Mareotis (Maryût) are the remains of the basilica, built by the Emperor Arcadius (A.D. 395–408) over the supposed burial place of St. Menas among the catacombs which date back at least to the Ptolemaic period. It was subsequently enlarged by the Patriarch Theophilus and his successor Timothy, to accommodate the flood of pilgrims visiting the great healing shrine. From here the devout from all parts of the Christian world took home oil from the lamp that burnt before the tomb of the saint in clay ampoules stamped with his figure between two camels. After the Muslim invasion of Egypt the shrine lost its international importance and slowly declined until it was finally abandoned, perhaps in the fourteenth century.

The diffusion of Christianity to the hinterland, to Egypt proper, is as obscure a story as its advent and development at Alexandria itself. Between the city and the predominantly Greek settlements in the Faiyûm and in the Nile valley there was free communication, and finds of Biblical and Apocryphal Christian writings, at Oxyrhynchus, Antinoopolis, and Karara, show the existence of Christian converts in the second century in Middle and Upper Egypt. It is unlikely that the Christian communities were numerically very strong; at Oxyrhynchus, for instance, one of the most important provincial centres, in the papyri of the second and third centuries A.D., only two Christian churches are mentioned, in contrast with about twenty pagan shrines or cults. By the fourth century no less than forty churches or chapels are known. Doubtless the example of the martyrs of the Decian persecution of 250 impressed the Greek-speaking element of the populace. The course of political events outside Egypt was, however, the decisive factor: in 313 Constantine, following his great victory at the Milvian Bridge in October of the previous year, granted freedom to the individual to follow what religion he would; in 341 Constantine ordered the cessation of superstitious practices and the abolition of the insanity of sacrifices: in 392 under Theodosius all forms of pagan cult were completely forbidden and the disobedient were to be charged with treason, an edict repeated in the subsequent century by the Emperors Honorius, Theodosius II, Marcian, and Anastasius.

Henceforth it might be said that the Greek-speaking Egyptians were, in the majority, Christians, though there remained a hard core of pagan intellectuals; Hypatia, the female philosopher, the subject of a novel by Charles Kingsley, was murdered in Alexandria in 415. Horapollo, who gave mystical explanations for the hieroglyphs, was one of a small group of Greek writers who flourished in the fifth century.

Archaeological evidence supports the belief that the diffusion of Christianity from Alexandria was slow. Excavation of the cemeteries of such predominantly Greek-speaking centres as the Faiyûm, Antinoopolis, and Panopolis (Akhmim) show that there is no radical break in burial customs before the fourth century. In the third century and later people were still buried in the Egyptian style, the mummies decorated with scenes drawn from the Osiris myth. Shrouds and *cartonnage* are painted with incidents drawn from the myth or with figures of gods intimately connected with the pagan funerary cult. The series of painted portrait panels of the deceased inserted in the bandages over the face of the mummy, which begin in the first half of the first century, persist until the fourth century. The realistic plaster masks typical of, but not confined to, Middle Egypt, with a representation of Osiris on the embalming table attended by the jackal-headed Anubis painted on the back of the neck, continue to at least the middle of the third century. The great number of wooden mummy labels, mostly from Akhmim, bearing a conventional prayer to 'Osiris-Sokar, the great lord of Abydos' in the demotic script, date mainly from the second and third centuries A.D. The practice is one almost unknown for Christian burial. The stone stele, with mixed Greek and Egyptian pagan motifs in their carving, characteristic of Terenuthis (Kom Abu Billo) in the Delta, date from the same period. Terracotta statuettes, particularly of the saviour and healing gods, are also common.

In the fourth century a dramatic change occurs. The body was wrapped in the garments of daily life or in old tapestries, with no indication of any belief in the efficacy of the Osiris myth for the future well-being of the dead. Surviving patterned textiles, coming chiefly from Panopolis and Antinoopolis, are usually called 'Coptic', a term which is correct only if it is remembered that it is used to describe an artistic style and not the religion or the language of those whom the cloths enshrouded. The decoration consists of geometric designs, of figure subjects drawn largely from the late Hellenistic romantic tales of gods, heroes, and heroines, and of the usual range of late antique decorative figures and patterns, mounted huntsmen, boy warriors, desert animals, baskets of flowers and fruits, dancing and pastoral figures. There is no indication in the subject-matter of the religious beliefs of the deceased; clearly, however, this radical change in burial customs marks the disappearance of the belief in the efficacy of the old ritual of mummification and reflects the spread of Christianity.

Among the Egyptian-speaking population propagation of the Christian faith was late in coming. There were, no doubt, individual cases of conversion, but it is not until about the middle of the third century that any marked success can be observed. Among the traditional names of the martyrs of the Decian persecution there are few who can be considered as Egyptian-speaking natives. As early as the beginning of the second century, the spread of Christianity outside the towns to the countryside had caused Pliny the Younger concern in his governorship of the province of Bithynia; in Egypt there does not in fact seem to have been any definite attempt to preach the message of Christianity in the native tongue of Egypt. The earliest occurrences of the use of the native language in a Christian context are forty-seven glosses in a fragmentary Greek codex of the Book of Isaiah (Chester Beatty Papyrus vii, no. 965), which on palaeographical grounds may be dated to the first half of the third century. From about the same time there survives a fragmentary glossary containing passages from the Greek text of Hosea and Amos with a rendering into Egyptian arranged in two columns, written on the back of a land register, dated perhaps a century earlier. The script used for the native language is Greek, supplemented by a small group of signs, derived from demotic, to represent sounds not present in Greek. Both this script and the vernacular language which it records are known as Coptic.

The earliest surviving Biblical codices or fragments thereof in Coptic date to the fourth century, when clearly a substantial number of the population who understood Egyptian only were Christian and required sacred books in their own tongue. From this time the Coptic Church, as distinct from the essentially Greek Church of Alexandria, may be said to have come into existence. In the Coptic calendar the number of the year is calculated from the date of the accession of Diocletian at the end of the third century in 284, in memory of the many martyrs, among them Egyptian-speaking Christians, who died in the great persecution which fell with particular severity upon Egypt during his reign.

Contemporaneously with the spread of orthodox Christianity to the Egyptians, heretical sects were also flourishing in the Nile valley. Papyri of the fourth and early fifth centuries reveal the presence of communities possessing translations into the native language of the esoteric and complex philosophical speculation of the Manichaeans and Gnostics, the understanding of which one might have supposed to have been beyond the comprehension of the indigenous Egyptians.

Once the movement had really begun, the spread of Christianity in the Nile valley was remarkably rapid and diffuse. Its success should probably be attributed to a deliberate and determined missionary effort inspired by the recognition of the need to preach in the native language (prompted perhaps by the success of the heretical sects in this direction). The use of native languages marks a new preoccupation of Eastern Christianity. It restored them to vigour. In Egypt its legacy was Coptic, in Syria Syriac, in Turkey Armenian. If in the case of Egypt the policy is to be attributed to any single patriarch, then it is probably to be associated with Dionysius (A.D. 247–64), the first patriarch, so we learned from Eusebius, who was interested in converting the Egyptian-speaking element of the population.

The conversion of the native Egyptians manifested itself in the monastic movements.[1] Attempts to trace the origin of monasticism in Egypt back to pagan institutions like the recluses who haunted the shrine of the Serapeum at Memphis, or to the encratic communal life mentioned by philosophers like the Jewish Philo, are misplaced. The movement is of native Egyptian origin and represents the greatest single contribution which the Coptic Church made to Christianity. Why monasticism took such deep root in Egypt cannot be explained satisfactorily. Three factors

[1] K. Heussi, *Der Ursprung des Mönchtums*, Tübingen, 1936; O. F. A. Meinardus, *Monks and Monasteries of the Egyptian Deserts*, Cairo, 1961; H. E. Winlock and W. E. Crum, *The Monastery of Epiphanius at Thebes* (Metropolitan Museum of Art Egyptian Expedition Publications, vols. 3–4), New York, 1926; H. G. Evelyn White, *The Monasteries of Wâdi 'n Natrûn* (Metropolitan Museum of Art Egyptian Expedition Publications, vols. 2, 7, 8), New York, 1926–33.

substantially favoured its development. The persecutions encouraged individuals to seek refuge along the edge of the empty desert which confines the inhabitable parts of the Nile valley. This happened, Eusebius tells us, at the time of the Decian persecution. The climate of Middle and Upper Egypt, with its even temperature and its absence of rainfall, is such that it is possible to live out of doors, in the shelter of an old tomb, quarry, or rock cave, without undue hardship. Economic conditions and the burden of taxation in the third century were inducements to the withdrawal of labour and the abandonment of marginal land. But none of these factors entirely accounts for the origin and rapid spread of the monastic movement. Persecution was not confined to Egypt. Economic recession and onerous taxation were general throughout the Roman world in the third century and again not peculiar to Egypt. Nor were the rigours of the northern European climate any discouragement to monastic withdrawal in imitation of the Egyptian model.

Monasticism appeared in different forms in Egypt. The way of life of the true solitary, the eremite, though probably in practice followed by a few only, represented the true ideal. The name applied to such a one more often than not in Coptic texts is 'anchorite', a term already used in pre-Christian papyri to denote one who withdrew his labour as a protest against the conditions of work. The eremite withdrew completely from habitation to the solitude of the desert, where a contemplative life of penance and prayer could be led without the distractions of this world. Who the first anchorite was is unknown; in Western tradition the credit was given to Paul (of whom little is heard in early Coptic sources) as a result of a 'Life' written in Latin by Jerome. Its authenticity as a historical document is suspect; it may perhaps be no more than a essay by Jerome in a popular field of hagiography, presenting his ideal of a hermit, and resting on a dubious historical person. Paul is said to have retired to the desert at the age of 16 to escape the Decian persecution, settling finally in the eastern desert, near the monastery dedicated to his name (Deir Abu Bolos), founded perhaps in the fifth or sixth century, abandoned after the revolt of the monastic slaves at the end of the fifteenth century, and recolonized in the seventeenth century.

From Coptic sources we learn the names of a number of solitaries, particularly in Middle and Upper Egypt. Their lives are given in accounts of journeys into the desert, often attributed to the monk Papnutius, undertaken with the aim of recording their names and deeds for the edification of posterity. The narrative is centred around certain questions which the traveller put to the hermit. In a unique Coptic codex, now in the British Museum (Or. 7029), which alone preserves the traditions of the advent of Christianity at the southern boundary of Egypt around Aswan, the narrator describes how he met four youths in the desert and asked them: 'How come you to this place? What do you eat? What are your names? Of what places are you natives and how do you partake of the Sacrament while you are in this place?' The plot is found in its simplest form in the collection of stories concerning the desert monks, the *Apophthegmata* or 'Sayings of the Fathers'. The great Macarius himself, at a commemoration mass in honour of Apa Pambo, disclaims to his audience that he is a true monk, explaining how he sat one day in his cell and the thought came to him to go out into the heart of the desert to see what there was to be seen.

I remained (says Macarius) fighting my thought for five years, saying, 'Perhaps it comes from the demons.' But, as the thought remained, I set out into the desert. I found there a lake of water with an island in its middle. The beasts of the desert came drinking from it. I saw in the middle of them two naked men. My body froze through fear, for I thought that they were spirits. But when they saw that I was afraid they said to me, 'Fear not, for we also are men.' And I said to them, 'Where are you from and how came you into this desert?' They said to me, 'We are from a monastery and having made an agreement we came to this desert forty years ago. One of us is an Egyptian, the other a Libyan.' And they asked me, 'How is it in the world? Does the inundation still come at its right season, does the world have abundance as of old?' I said to them, 'Yes.' And I asked them, 'How shall I be able to become a monk?' And they said to me, 'Unless a man renounce all the things of the world, he cannot become a monk.' Then I said, 'I am weak and have not your strength.' They said to me, 'If you have not strength as we have, then go, sit in your cell and weep for your sins.' I asked them, 'When it is summer are not your bodies burned? When it is winter are you not cold?' They answered, 'God has so ordained it for us that in summer the heat does us no hurt and in winter we feel no cold.' (Zoega, *Catalogus*, 347).

The tradition of the naked monks passed into medieval Western hagiography. The best-known of them was Onnuphrius, whose feast is celebrated in the West on 12 June. A church in Rome is dedicated in his honour. His naked figure, clothed in an enormous long beard, occurs in Western Christian art (Pl. 23).

In these accounts the eremitical life is ideally portrayed as a vocation, sanctified by the example of Elijah the Tishbite or John the Baptist; it was not altogether a selfish concern for personal salvation, a turning of one's back upon fellow Christians. There was a literal popular belief (not confined to Christians) in the physical presence of evil spirits who were thought to take the form of the monstrous animals of the desert; the athletes of God, as the monks were described, sought out the enemy and engaged him in battle away from the inhabited area of the Nile valley and so preserved it from the incursions of the demons. In the hagiographical literature their vocation is blessed by divine providence in the miraculous way in which their spiritual and simple physical needs were satisfied. Food was supplied by a date-palm bearing twelve clusters of dates, one for each month of the year. A spring provided one cupful of water daily. The Eucharistic host was miraculously brought down from heaven at the hands of an angel or by Christ himself.

Crude ink daubs, short graffiti, and disfigurement of the scenes in the ancient tombs by the Copts who found shelter in them are a familiar sight in Egypt. At Thebes true eremitical communities seem to have survived until about the middle of the seventh century. Further south, at Faras, a certain Theophilus converted an unfinished and undecorated tomb, probably of New Kingdom date, about two miles inland from the present course of the Nile, into a cell, covering the walls with passages in Coptic from the *Apophthegmata* in an elaborate book hand, against a yellow background in imitation of the actual leaves of a codex, completing the task in A.D. 739.

The title of founder of Egyptian monasticism rightly belongs to Antony, whose traditional 'Life' is attributed to the Patriarch Athanasius, his friend and his spiritual patron. Antony was born about the year 251 in Middle Egypt in the village of Koma, near Ehnasya (Heracleopolis), of moderately well-to-do Egyptian-speaking parents, who died when he was about 18 or 20 years old, leaving him to care for a younger sister. He himself spoke no Greek and, although not illiterate, had received no education after the Greek model. About six months after the death of his parents Antony heard read in church the saying of Jesus to the young man, 'If thou wilt be perfect, go and sell that thou hast, and give to the poor and thou shalt have treasure in heaven: and come and follow me' (Matt. 19: 21). Interpreting these words in a literal sense, he disposed of his goods except for a small sum for his sister's maintenance, and practised an ascetic life, at first in the neighbourhood of his village, receiving instruction from an old recluse. Later he retired further from the village to an empty tomb, a disciple bringing him bread from time to time. About 285 he withdrew to a still more secluded spot, to a deserted fort across the river called in the 'Life' Pispir, local tradition preserving the memory of it at Deir el-Maimoun. Here, immured in a living tomb, bread brought to him only twice a year, the seeping moisture providing his drinking water, he fought his battles with the evil one, a favourite theme of the Western medieval artist. His fame spread, but he remained deaf to the entreaties of those

who came to seek his spiritual advice until eventually they forced
their way into his retreat. For these disciples a common way
of life was established. After a sojourn of twenty years at el-
Maimoun, weary of the frequent interruption of his solitude which
his fame brought, he set out for the inner desert, finding seclusion
on Mount Kolzoun, three days' journey along the Wadi el-Araba,
the caravan route leading from the Nile at Beni Suef to the Red
Sea. Once more he was importuned by disciples and founded a
second community, still a monastery today, Deir Mar Antonios,
looking out across the Gulf of Suez towards the mountains of
Sinai. From here came many of the Alexandrine patriarchs of the
Middle Ages: it provided the representative of the Coptic Church
to the Council of Reunion at Florence in 1439. Like the nearby
Monastery of St. Paul, it has not been continuously occupied,
remaining abandoned after a revolt of the Muslim serfs until its
recolonization in the seventeenth century. Its great walls enclose
seven churches, and the modern pilgrims are shown the cell of
Antony high above the convent, where he is reputed to have died
at the age of 105.

The legacy of Antony was the establishment of some degree of
formal organization into the monastic movement. In this work he
received the powerful backing of the great Patriarch Athanasius,
who stamped an essentially lay movement with official ecclesiastical
approval. No written rule or constitution was formulated. No
vow of obedience to a superior was imposed. The pattern of
religious life allowed individual monks freedom to determine their
own course to salvation, leading a life of prayer and penance in
their own cells, often at some distance from their fellows. They
might tend a small vegetable garden, or acquire the bare necessi-
ties of life from sale in the cities of the mats and baskets which they
plaited from halfa grass or palm fibre, a mechanical manual task
which occupied the fingers but allowed the mind to meditate
upon spiritual matters. At the same time there was a loose informal association, a grouping of cells to form a *laura*, the monks

meeting on Saturdays and Sundays to celebrate together the liturgy, the officiant being one of their number who might be a presbyter. Custom and the example and exhortation of the seniors were the substitutes for written rules. Visits were exchanged, usually undertaken to ask advice of an elder. There was an accepted code of behaviour to be followed by guest and host. This relaxation of the principle of strict solitude in favour of some measure of communal life promoted a sense of mutual purpose and discouraged fanatical excess.

The system of *laura*, evolved largely under the spiritual direction of Antony, was that which flourished to the south-west of Alexandria in the various settlements in and around the Wadi Natrûn, a desolate area of dried natron lakes and desert, lying half-way along the present desert road between Alexandria and Cairo. The great names associated with the settlements there, at Scetis, Nitria, and the more remote Cellia, from the beginning of the fourth century, are Amoun, Macarius the Great, and Pambo. Situated as they were close to Alexandria and the Mediterranean litoral, these settlements were much frequented by those who came to Egypt to see the holy men. Already by the end of the fourth century a guest-house existed for these pilgrims. We know of the way of life chiefly from literary sources, in particular from the great anonymous collection of anecdotes and spiritual aphorisms, originally written down in the fifth century in Greek under the title of the 'Sayings of the Fathers' (*Apophthegmata Patrum*) and translated into every tongue used by the ancient Church. The Latin versions of Pelagius the Deacon and John the Subdeacon (*Verba Seniorum*), made in the sixth century, passed into the traditions of medieval Europe. Here there is little of the extravagant austerities commonly associated with the story of early monasticism, which found their worst manifestation in the unhealthy excesses of Syrian monks.

In the fifth century nomadic raids on the settlements of the Wadi Natrûn were already taking their toll, and forcing the anchorites into a closer communal organization behind walled enclosures. Four inhabited monasteries, each containing a score of monks or less, still survive. Monasticism in this sense, as a communal life regulated by rule, originated in Upper Egypt, under Pachomius, honoured in Coptic texts with Antony as one of the great pillars of the Eastern Church.

Pachomius was born shortly before the beginning of the fourth century, in the neighbourhood of Esna; like Antony he knew no Greek, learning the language late in life in order to instruct the strangers who sought to join him. He first came into contact with Christians while serving as a recruit in the army, when his unit received hospitality from them during a short stay at Thebes. After obtaining an early discharge, he was baptized at Chenoboskion and became the disciple of the hermit Palaemon. About 320, as the result of a vision, he established a community at a deserted village called Tabennesi, near Akhmim. In contrast with the independence of the *laura*, under Pachomius the monks' daily life was regulated in every detail by a formal rule which was written down. The inmates were grouped in 'houses', according to some accounts by trades, each with its own superior, responsible under the head of the monastery for instruction and discipline. The applicant for admission was required to spend a period of probation in the guest-house, learning by heart certain prayers and receiving instruction in the rule, before he was admitted to the community and clothed in the formal habit of a monk. The rule insisted on work, including work on the land, for the community was to be self-sufficient. There was to be no excess in fasting, no showing off in ascetic practices or length of prayers which might impair the physical strength of the individual.

The success of Pachomius' rule was immediate. Within a short time a second foundation was necessary at Pbow, also at that time deserted, and when Pachomius died, about 350, there were in all eleven foundations following the same rule, including two for women. The communities brought prosperity to abandoned land. Each year, in the month of August, the Coptic New Year, there was a meeting to appoint officers and to settle accounts.

The cenobitic rule became the normal form of monasticism in Middle and Upper Egypt. Dissension within the Pachomian communities immediately following the death of the founder, and their adherence to the Melkite faction in the fifth century, resulted in some check to their further expansion; but other monasteries established in Middle and Upper Egypt followed the spirit of the Pachomian rule, though modifying or altering its disciplinary aspects. The most famous of these was the White Monastery near Sohag, founded by Pgol in the fourth century, and reformed by his successor and nephew Shenoute, whose letters and those of his successor Besa represent (with the rule of Pachomius) the only original Coptic writing.

The cenobitic movement was truly Egyptian; with its establishment there was a sudden reappearance of business and legal documents and of private letters, on ostraca and papyri, in the Coptic language, reflecting the social and economic life of the communities and their relations with the secular world. They owned property; they farmed and manufactured; they sold and traded. Their prosperity was not diminished until after the Muslim invasion of A.D. 641.

Directly or indirectly, all Christian monasticism stems from the Egyptian example. Basil the Great, organizer of monasticism in Asia Minor, whose rule is still followed by Eastern Churches, visited Egypt about 357. The rule of Pachomius was early made known in the West through a Latin version by Jerome. In general in the West the cenobitic ideal was most imitated, but the example of the true solitaries and the traditions of the *laura* were passed on in the literary accounts of visits and sojourns left by some of the many pilgrims who were attracted to Egypt. They came partly because the land of Egypt had played a major role in the story of the Old and the New Testament; the pyramids in one popular belief were identified with the granaries of Joseph;

Matariya, by Heliopolis, was one of the places claiming to possess a sacred tree beneath which the Virgin and Child had rested on their flight to Egypt. But more especially it was the fame of the holy men which drew the pilgrims to Egypt. Jerome himself visited Egypt, or at least Alexandria, and has left some account of his experiences scattered through his letters. The pilgrims included women, like Melania and Paula, pious Roman ladies of high birth, who visited Scetis with their entourages in the last quarter of the fourth century, when Egyptian monasticism was exerting its greatest influence. With Melania was Rufinus, an Italian presbyter of Aquileia, who had already spent some years in Egypt; later he founded a monastery on the Mount of Olives where he translated into Latin the story of a pilgrimage of brothers from his monastery, drawing upon his own experiences of twenty years previously (*Historia Monarchorum in Aegypto*). Another in the company of Melania was Palladius, later Bishop of Helenopolis in Bithynia, author of the *Lausiac History*, so called after its dedication to Lausus, the chief chamberlain of the Imperial household, probably under Theodosius II. John Cassian of Marseilles, whose two works, the *Collationes Patrum* and the *De Institutis Renovitantium*, are the classical exposition of the ideals of Western monasticism, spent ten years in Egypt at the end of the fourth century. Visits to the monks continued to be made up to the eve of the Muslim invasion, one of the latest being that of John of Moschus, whose *Pratum Spirituale* was written at the beginning of the seventh century. Latin versions of these books were among the well-read works of the Middle Ages. The first printed compilation, the *Vitae Patrum* of Rosweyde, was made at Antwerp in 1615, a fine folio volume of more than a thousand pages of Latin in double column.

It is easy to criticize, as the rational historians of the nineteenth century did, the monastic movement and the simple, pious, ethical content of the hagiography which it inspired. In Egypt the monastic life failed to mature. It lacked the social and educational force which developed in the West under different historical circumstances, and which became implicit in the aims of the still later mendicant and teaching orders of the medieval friars. Even in its own particular sphere, that of the contemplative life, Egyptian monasticism produced no great mystical writers, no profound analysis of the Christian way of prayer and penance. The following extract concerning distractions from the *Apophtheg-mata* is as intellectual a lesson as one might expect to find:

> One asked an old man, saying: 'Why, when I sit in my dwelling, does my heart turn in every direction?' The old man answered him, saying: 'Because the other senses which are outside are ill, that is seeing, hearing, smelling, speaking. If now you produce their energies purely, then will the other organs of sense which are inside be at rest and in health.' (Zoega, *Catalogus*, 290).

Even in the fourth century monks were accused of turning their backs on the world, of degrading human dignity, and of insulting human intelligence. But, however commonplace their simple pious exhortations may now seem, the fact that men lived by them, as they did in Egypt, wrought a profound psychological effect upon the declining world of the Hellenic spirit. Let one example suffice: Augustine of Hippo, ranked as one of the greatest of the Church doctors, admitted that he was first stirred to the defence of wisdom by reading the *Hortensius* of Cicero, yet still he prayed that his concupiscence be glutted rather than quenched, and owed his final conversion to a mystical experience at Milan, following upon his hearing a friend tell of the life of Antony (*Confessions*, viii. 6–8).

The number of monks in Egypt and their proportion to the total population at the height of the monastic movement can only be guessed. The *Historia Monarchorum* refers, as an exceptional example, to 10,000 monks at Oxyrhynchus. Palladius' account would suggest a total of 7,500 in and around Alexandria, and perhaps as many in the parts of the valley which he visited. Ancient estimates of numbers are notoriously unreliable and too much credence should not be placed upon such totals, still less upon the impression that Egypt had more cells than houses, as the exuberant exaggeration of the literary accounts suggests. It is, however, clear that the number of persons in the religious life represented a significant percentage of the whole population, unparalleled in the Christian world and reminiscent of certain Buddhist countries at different periods of their history. Merely as a physical force the Egyptian monks were a potentially power-ful body and played thereby a significant part in the great doctrinal controversies which rent the Christian world, and particularly the Eastern Churches, during the third and fourth centuries A.D.

These controversies sprang from the need of the Church, as it attracted men of all conditions, to define and to determine its dogma. In the first two centuries, the early Christians, closer in time to the historical Christ, fervently believing in the imminence of a second coming, eager to prove their faith by a second baptism of fire (that is martyrdom), were not primarily concerned with abstract theological speculation. Differences which arose were largely matters of discipline, notably, for instance, the treatment of Christians whose human courage had failed them in the hour of persecution, which gave rise to the Melitian controversy, schism rather than heresy. In the third and fourth centuries the history of the Church is dominated by the problem of heresy, as the attempts to formulate dogma within the categories of accepted philosophical terms, in which the Alexandrine Church played a leading part, led to divergent views. Controversy was no academic exercise conducted in an atmosphere remote from real life. Throughout the story runs an undercurrent of personal ambition, lack of charity, and jealousy. The issues aroused passion and provoked civil disorder. To protect public order, to maintain the cohesion of the provinces, the emperors were drawn into these religious affairs.

The two great controversies both centred upon the person and nature of Christ, and the dogma of the incarnation, one of the fundamental differences between Christianity and paganism. The earlier of the two heresies was advanced by Arius, who denied the divinity of Christ. Arianism was finally condemned in 325 at the Council of Nicaea, and prompted the definition incorporated in the Nicene Creed, 'being of one substance with the father' (*consubstantialem Patri*). The other of the great heresies takes its name from Nestorius, at one time Patriarch of Constantinople, who held that in Christ there were two persons as well as two natures. Nestorianism was condemned at the Council of Ephesus in 431.

The contribution of the Coptic Church, and in particular of the monks, was not on the intellectual level. The argument in all its metaphysical subtlety was conducted in Greek; the intellectual defenders and apologists from Egypt came from the Hellenic, and not the Coptic, milieu. The Coptic legacy to the Christian world lay in the solid support which they gave to the protagonists of orthodoxy, Athanasius at Nicaea and Cyril at Ephesus. The dominant characteristic of the monks is their loyalty to the Alexandrian patriarch. In the protracted and bitter struggles, which divided the Christian world and provoked the intervention of the civil arm, there developed among the Copts a political feeling. Within the frontiers of Egypt, the temporal power of the Alexandrine patriarchs was formidable; their enemies taunted them with jibes about their pharaonic ambitions. They could and did act in defiance of the state when it was represented by emperors who favoured or actively promoted the heretical factions. During the patriarchate of Athanasius the Alexandrine and Coptic Churches were welded into a single, united force. Early in his office Athanasius made pastoral visits throughout the Nile valley: later when the clash came, during the great Arian controversy, for the six years following 356 Athanasius remained concealed in the Egyptian hinterland as a fugitive from the wrath of Constantius, the Arian emperor of the East, and of his successor, the apostate Julian.

A story told in the official 'Life' of the archimandrite Shenoute, attributed to his disciple Besa, illustrates something of the effect of the monks in the ecumenical councils summoned to define the Christian dogma. Shenoute was present, according to this account, in the great phalanx of monks who accompanied Cyril to the Council of Ephesus, when the condemnation of Nestorius was secured as much by pressure and intimidation as by superior theological argument.

Now our holy fathers gathered together at a council to ex-communicate that vile heretic Nestorius. Our holy father and prophet, Apa Shenoute, was present with the holy Cyril, Arch-bishop of Rakote (Alexandria). When they entered within the church and had arranged chairs and had sat themselves down, one chair was arranged in the midst of the throng and on it were placed the four gospels. The vile heretic Nestorius entered with great pride and insolence, picked up the four holy books of the Gospel, put them on the ground, and sat on the chair. Now when my father Apa Shenoute saw what Nestorius had done, rightly incensed, he jostled a way through the throng of the holy fathers; he picked up the Gospels from the floor, and struck the chest of Nestorius a blow. 'Do you want', he said, 'the Son of God to be on the floor while you sit upon a chair?' The impious Nestorius replied, saying to my father Shenoute, 'What business have you at this council? You are not bishop or archi-mandrite or priest. You are a monk.' And our father replied to him, 'I am one whom God has willed to come here, that I may reprove you for your sins and lay open your errors, seeing that you have rejected the passion of the only begotten Son of God, which he endured for our sakes, that he might deliver us from our sins.' Thereupon the holy Cyril arose and laid his hands upon the head of our father Apa Shenoute and kissed him. He put the mantle which was upon his own shoulders upon the shoulders of Apa Shenoute, gave his own staff into his hand, and made him archi-mandrite. And all who had come to the council cried out, saying, 'Worthy, worthy, worthy archimandrite.' (*Vita*, § 128).

What credence should be placed on this account of how Shenoute was elevated to the rank of archimandrite is question-able. There is sufficient of the miraculous in Besa's life of his spiritual father to arouse doubt concerning its historical value. Whether the story is true or not, clearly this rough, uncouth clerical behaviour is recorded for our approval. It is the correct measure of the Coptic contribution in these theological disputes. The aftermath is scarcely surprising. Within twenty years of the Council of Ephesus, so undisciplined was the conduct of the monks at a second council held there that it has been dubbed, in the immortal phrase of Leo the Great of Rome, the Council of Thieves or Robber Council (*latrocinium*). The leading bishop opposing Dioscurus of Alexandria was so badly frightened that he died within a few days of the rowdy end of the meeting. On this occasion the point at issue was again on the problem of the nature of Christ, the great monophysite heresy, one more durable than Arianism, more widespread than Nestorianism, more terrible than both for its effect, shattering the unity of the Eastern Churches, and dividing Greek, Syrian, and Egyptians to this day.[1]

Monophysitism is scarcely capable of precise definition. So far as it had any single heresiarch, the title might be claimed by an obscure priest, by name Eutychius, excommunicated by the Patriarch of Constantinople in 448 for heretical teaching on the nature of Christ which was based on an ill-chosen expression of Cyril of Alexandria. It has been said that the heresy was no more than a quibble over a single Greek letter, whether Christ should be defined, as in the Nicene creed, as *homoousios*, literally 'of the same essence', or *homoiousios* 'of like essence'. The heresy itself split into different sects. At the Council of Chalcedon in 451 the Alexandrine Patriarch Dioscorus took his stand on some words of his venerated predecessor, Cyril, and was condemned. But the council was by no means the end of the heresy. All attempts of the secular power to impose the decision of the

[1] J. Maspero, *Histoire des patriarches d'Alexandrie depuis la mort de l'empereur Anastase jusqu'à la réconciliation des églises jacobites 518–616* (Bibliothèque, École des Hautes Études, 237), Paris, 1923.

council were resisted; subsequent conciliatory moves to find a formula of words acceptable to all failed, backed though they were by the authority of emperors. The persistence of the heresy can be explained only as an expression of political dissatisfaction and of nationalistic sentiments on the part of the provinces, fanned in Egypt by the memory of the loss of precedence by the Alexandrine See to the See of Constantinople in 381, a canon ratified at Chalcedon. Monophysitism was at the beginning no more than an excuse, founded on a theological ambiguity, to justify a pre-existent schism. In the course of time the views of the different monophysite Churches became more rigid and their dogma hardened: Christ was declared to have a single nature. The Copts can scarcely have appreciated the subtleties of the theologians, expressed as they were in Greek terms; but their temper was such that they followed their patriarch Dioscorus with fanatical loyalty. Successive emperors were unable to impose the orthodox faith of Chalcedon upon Egypt. Patriarchs, enthroned in their cathedral with the help of the civil arm, remained for the most part ineffectual possessors of the see, dubbed 'Melkites' or 'Emperor's men', unable to exercise authority over, or command respect from, the Copts. Proterius, thrust upon the Alexandrians in place of Dioscorus, was murdered by the mob. The intervention of the secular power in the affairs of the Syrian Church caused the inevitable motley band of refugees to gather at Alexandria; refreshed by the presence of the exiled Severus of Antioch between 518 and 538 the monophysite Church was securely established as the national Church of Egypt, with its own buildings, and its own liturgical language, still in use to this day. While the Church of the country remained stable, sects and sub-sects flourished in Alexandria, and for one brief moment, on the eve of the Muslim invasion, the monophysite Damian was faced with three rival claimants to the title of Patriarch of Alexandria. From this time on, the influence of Alexandria and of the Coptic Church declines. Its leading figures can no longer claim like Athanasius, Antony, Pachomius, and Macarius to be pillars of the Eastern Church. It is ranked by Church historians as one of the lesser Eastern rites, of antiquarian interest for the extent to which, cut off from the main stream of Christian history, it may have preserved fossilized elements of the belief and practice of the early Church in its literature, art, and liturgy.

When in the seventh century the invading army of 'Amr reached the frontier of Egypt, it walked into a country in which the bulk of the population received it without overt hostility and the Imperial troops, aliens in a foreign country, surrendered the still great city of Alexandria virtually without fight, one of the most disgraceful episodes of Byzantine military history. At first, for some 200 years under the viceroys appointed by the Ummayad Caliphs, the native Church flourished. Under the succeeding Abbasid Caliphs the great persecutions began and civil penalties were imposed. There was a revival of the Coptic Church under the Fatimids (969–1171); Christian art flourished (most strikingly observed in the blind-stamped leather bindings and carved woodwork). Under the influence of the patriarch, now residing at Wadi Natrûn, much of the Church's literature was translated into the northern Bohairic dialect. But, when Saladin founded the Ayyubid dynasty, conflict between the Muslim and European worlds came to a head in the Crusades, persecution recommenced, and the Christian community shrank to a minority of the population.

Thanks to the pilgrimages of Copts to Jerusalem, two Coptic churches still exist in that city. It is, however, rare to find Coptic Christians outside Egypt; in the light of its history, particularly after the Council of Chalcedon, it is hardly surprising that its missionary activity has been small. In the south, the Ethiopian Church retains contact with the Coptic Church. Ethiopia was converted in the fourth century and its first bishop, Frumentarius, was consecrated by Athanasius. As a result it is considered as a daughter Church, and the Abuna or Patriarch of Abyssinia, though no longer sent from Egypt, requires for the validity of his orders consecration by the Patriarch of Alexandria. Of the other Christian Church of the Nile valley, that of Nubia, there is virtually no trace of its greatness, save in the remarkable archaeological finds, notably at Faras and Qasr Ibrim. Missionaries were first sent under the Emperor Justinian; no sooner had they left Constantinople than a rival mission of monophysite persuasion was dispatched by the emperor's own wife Theodora. The direct link with Byzantium is reflected in the church architecture and decoration; the liturgical language remained Greek, but after the Muslim invasion, when contact with Constantinople was impeded, the Coptic Church exerted greater influence upon the affairs of the Nubian Church; in order to preserve the apostolic tradition its bishops had to turn to Alexandria for consecration and a number of tombstones, texts, and documents in Coptic have survived. Coptic, however, never displaced Greek in the liturgy, or Nubian as the language of the vernacular. As a Church its great days seem to have been from the seventh to the twelfth centuries, after which it became submerged in the tide of Muslim penetration. Unlike Egypt and Ethiopia, no Christian communities exist in Nubia with an unbroken link with its Christian past.

The decline in the fortune of the Coptic Church is mirrored in the later history of the language as a living tongue. In the eleventh century bilingual Coptic–Arabic liturgical manuscripts, grammars, and vocabularies (*scalae*) were appearing. By the thirteenth century literary activity between Copts was almost entirely conducted through the medium of Arabic. According to the Arab historian al-Maqrīzī, Coptic was still spoken colloquially in the villages of Upper Egypt in the fifteenth century. But by the sixteenth it is generally considered virtually a dead language. Reports of Coptic being heard after this time in isolated villages of Upper Egypt outside the liturgy, if in fact true, can mean no more than an exchange of conventional phrases in church or school circles. All that remains of the speech of the Pharaohs, apart from

the passages of the liturgy read but unintelligible to the congrega-
tion, are the limited number of Coptic and Greek words which
have passed into the colloquial Arabic of modern Egypt. Omitting
place-names and words proper to Coptic worship, there are perhaps little more than fifty in common use, mainly names of fish,
foodstuffs, agricultural implements, and cooking-utensils, and
some vulgar expressions.[1]

It is paradoxical that at the moment when the Coptic language
was becoming obsolete in Egypt it attracted the attention of
Western orientalists, stimulated by the collection of manuscripts
by educated travellers of the day who were now being drawn
to oriental travel in increasing numbers. One of the first, the
Roman nobleman Pietro della Valle (1586–1652), brought back
to Europe a number of Coptic manuscripts, among them five
grammars and two vocabularies. In the seventeenth century
special agents were sent to build up European libraries; Vansleb
(Wansleben) was in Egypt in 1672–3, when he acquired the vellum
leaves from the White Monastery of Shenoute near Atripe which
form part of the 'old collection' of the Bibliothèque Nationale in
Paris, subsequently enriched from the same source by the discoveries of Gaston Maspero in 1883. The Assemani brothers
obtained in the first decade of the eighteenth century the rich
collection of Bohairic codices which are now mostly in the
Vatican Library, as well as the important Syriac manuscripts
from Deir es Suryani.

The first step to the understanding of the Coptic language
in the West was taken by the Arabic scholar Thomas Obicini
(Thomaso di Novara), who was responsible for the first Coptic
font cast in 1628. His untimely death in 1632 delayed the publication of the grammatical works brought by della Valle. Four years
later in 1636 the study of Coptic in the West was firmly established
by the publication of a work by the Jesuit scholar Athanasius

[1] W. B. Bishai, 'Coptic Lexical Influence on Egyptian Arabic', *Journ.
Near Eastern Studies*, xxiii (1964), 39–47.

Kircher entitled *Prodromus Coptus sive Aegyptiacus*, in which it was recognized that the Coptic language was the direct lineal descendant of the speech of pharaonic times. His work included the first Coptic grammar in a European tongue. Dictionaries were published by Lacroze (1775), Peyron (1835), and Henry Tattam (1835). The grammars of Blumberg (1716), Christian Scholtz (1778), Raphael Tuki (1778), Tattam (1830), and Peyron (1841) are precursors of the first truly scientific grammar, that of Stern (1880). The first publications of texts date back to the beginning of the eighteenth century, with David Wilkins's edition of the Pentateuch (1731), Tuki's *Missale coptice et arabice* (1736), *Divinum alexandrinum copto–arabicum* (1750), *and Pontificale et Euchologium* (1761), and Woide's *Appendix ad editionem Novi Testamenti graeci* (1799). In 1810 appeared the first of the great catalogues of manuscript collections, Georg Zoega's *Catalogus codicum copticorum manuscriptorum qui in Museo Borgiano Velitris adservantur*.

One immediate effect of this heritage of Coptic among Western scholars was that when chance placed in their hands a bilingual text for the decipherment of the hieroglyphs, through the discovery of the Rosetta Stone in the early spring of 1799, rapid progress was made in the understanding of the language. The reason why Thomas Young's contribution to Egyptological studies is dwarfed by that of Jean François Champollion is that the latter was an able Coptic scholar, within the knowledge of his day—which is aptly summarized by E. M. Quatremère in his *Recherches critiques et historiques sur la langue et la littérature de l'Égypte* (Paris, 1808). Subsequent philological and lexographical studies have made Coptic the best understood phase of the Egyptian language. By using the Greek alphabet with the addition of seven signs derived from demotic writing (the last development of the native cursive script) for sounds not present in the Greek tongue, it is the only stage of the language which satisfactorily reflects its speech sounds by adopting a purely alphabetic writing of both consonants and vowels. Coptic lexicography and grammar are still essential aids in understanding the earlier stages of the native Egyptian language.

The original stimulus to write the Egyptian language alphabetically in the Greek characters did not come from Christian sources. An isolated and barbaric attempt was the inscription of a Nubian king at Abydos in the second century B.C. From the Roman period there is increasing evidence of the growing practice of using Greek letters, mixed with alphabetic signs derived from demotic, in cases where it was desirable to indicate more precisely than the Egyptian system allowed the correct pronunciation of words. A papyrus fragment now in Munich, part apparently of a school exercise, suggests that there existed lists of Egyptian personal names with a phonetic transcription into Greek letters. In Heidelberg a *cartonnage* fragment from Akhmim, dated to the third century A.D., contains a few Greek words with their demotic equivalents written in Greek letters. In the demotic London and Leiden magical text, written in the third century A.D., there are over 600 glosses in Greek letters. A number of magical texts have survived from the first three centuries A.D., characterized by the use of Greek letters and a large number of demotic signs (known as Old Coptic), in which no doubt the correct rendering of the names of demons and the magical words of power were necessary for the efficacy of the spell. This improvement in the system of writing—so obvious that one can only be surprised how slowly it gained ground in Egypt—was adopted by Christian writers, who promoted and standardized its use by the restriction of the signs derived from demotic to seven.

Coptic is the only stage of the Egyptian language in which dialects are distinguishable, each with its own vocalic and consonantal patterns and idiomatic expressions. The dialect still used in the liturgy of the modern Coptic Church is known as Bohairic (in earlier works also called Memphite), from the Arabic name for the Delta. It owes its present dominance to the fact that it was the dialect of the Wadi Natrûn, which, from the beginning of the eleventh century, was the official residence of the patriarch. In the last century it was the dialect most studied in the West. At that time, in comparison with other dialects, there were to hand many complete manuscripts, the reading of which presented no difficulty and permitted immediate publication. With the exception of one major manuscript and a few isolated fragments showing Bohairic affinities, of the fourth or fifth century, the Bohairic manuscripts date from about the eleventh century; and many passages of the Bohairic Old Testament have survived only in copies of the thirteenth century. In consequence Bohairic has now yielded pride of place, which it owed to its more ready accessibility and its official character, to the Sahidic dialect, so called from the Arabic term for Upper Egypt.

In early works Sahidic is also called the Theban dialect, in the belief that Thebes was its original home. Oxyrhynchus, Ashmunein, Thebes, and, tentatively, Alexandria have also been suggested.[1] Already by the Christian period Sahidic seems to have been the form of the language most widely used for literary purposes. As a result of the authority which the Pachomian writers and Shenoute conferred upon it, Sahidic was standardized in its orthography and acquired its dominant position as the literary idiom for Christian use until it was in turn displaced by Bohairic. Sahidic influenced and finally suppressed the other dialects, Achmimic, Subachmimic, Faiyumic, and the closely related 'Middle Egyptian'. Of all of them we possess early and important manuscripts. Achmimic, probably the dialect of Thebes, is relatively uniform and survived as a literary dialect into the sixth century. Subachmimic, so called because it was first thought that it was an intermediate stage between Achmimic and Sahidic, was possibly spoken around Akhmim. It forms a less homogeneous group of rare manuscripts dating from the fourth to the sixth

[1] P. E. Kahle, *Bala'izah*, Oxford, 1954, vol. i, Chapter ix: 'The Coptic Literary Dialects, their Origin, Development, and Interrelationship'.

centuries. Faiyumic, the dialect of the Faiyûm, had a longer literary history, particularly in a form modified by Sahidic influence, documents continuing to the tenth century. The so-called Middle Egyptian is represented by a number of early fragments and two fine vellum codices, probably of the late fifth or early sixth century.

Surviving literature has come mainly from monastic libraries, like those of the Wadi Natrûn and the White Monastery, already mentioned, dating from the eighth to the tenth centuries. The handsome appearance of these Coptic codices, with their intricate tooled leather bindings, may best be seen in the remarkable collection of fifty-eight Sahidic vellum manuscripts in the Pierpont Morgan Library, New York. Discovered in 1910, they originate from the monastery of St. Michael at Hamouli in the Faiyûm. The earliest volume is dated by a colophon to A.D. 832 and the latest to A.D. 914. A similar, but less well-preserved find, made about 1907 in the region of Esna in Upper Egypt, is now in the British Museum. It comprises volumes, on papyrus, vellum, and paper, ranging in date from the ninth to the eleventh centuries.

The contents of these and of other finds display little variety or originality. With the exception of the letters of Shenoute and his disciple Besa and of some of the Pachomian writings, Coptic literature is a translation from Greek, almost wholly religious in subject-matter. Secular literature is represented only by a fragment of the Alexander Romance and by part of a pseudo-historical story in which a king, alternatively named Cambyses and Nabuchodonosor, attacks the Pharaoh Apries. Compilations of medical recipes, calculation manuals, almanacs, and a fragment of a world chronology giving the reigns of the Ptolemies are also extant; they scarcely deserve the title of scientific literature.

Biblical manuscripts or fragments predominate. For the New Testament complete books have survived in late Bohairic manuscripts. In Sahidic they are rarer. The great edition of the Sahidic New Testament by Horner was built up from fragments, particularly in the case of the Epistles, of different date and worth. Since its publication a homogeneous text of the Pauline Epistles has been edited by Sir Herbert Thompson from a vellum codex, probably dating about A.D. 600, now in the Chester Beatty Library, Dublin. A companion volume contains Acts, which is also preserved in a fourth-century papyrus codex in the British Museum (Or. 7594). Still less is preserved in the minor dialects. The Gospel of John, which monks were required to learn by heart, is best represented. It is almost complete in a Subachmimic version, of the fourth century, discovered at Gau in Middle Egypt and now in the keeping of the British and Foreign Bible Society, London. Considerable fragments are also represented in the older form of Faiyumic (Michigan). In addition, one of the few codices written in an early form of Bohairic (now in the Bibliotheca Bodmeriana) contains the Gospel of John.

For the Old Testament and Apocrypha, with the exception of the Book of Pslams, manuscripts are comparatively rare. For certain books, for instance, Genesis, Chronicles, Ezra, Nehemiah, and Maccabees, no complete Sahidic version exists, though passages are known from leaves and fragments of varying length and different age. Ruth, Ezra, Nehemiah, Ecclesiastes, Song of Songs, Esther, Judith, and Tobit are wanting in Bohairic. Of Joshua, Judges, Kings, Chronicles, Wisdom of Solomon, and Ecclesiasticus we possess only those passages included in liturgical texts. In the minor dialects there is still less, the most complete and important manuscripts being the Achmimic Proverbs (Berlin), the Subachmimic Minor Prophets (Vienna and Paris), and the Old Faiyumic Song of Songs, Lamentations, and Ecclesiastes (Hamburg).

To what extent the versions in the different dialects are independent of one another is a matter still requiring investigation. A detailed comparison, for instance, of the early versions of John mentioned above with the standard Sahidic and Bohairic texts should prove illuminating. In general the New Testament is rendered as literally as possible. The books of the Old Testament are more free, the underlying Greek text being at times simplified, at times interpolated, to make the narrative clearer. On the whole the manuscript tradition shows remarkable consistency, once allowance has been made for scribal blunders, differences of orthography, and stylistic idiosyncrasies, reflecting the human urge of the copyist to improve upon the literary idiom of his exemplar. And, when all allowance had been made for the differences between the Greek and Coptic languages, it is clear (particularly in the light of the early manuscripts now edited) that the Coptic translators had access to and made use of Greek codices, certainly of the third century and probably of the second half of the second century, with eccentric readings that for the most part have not survived in Greek. (The Washington Papyrus Codex, fourth century, the Codex Bezae at Cambridge, fifth century, and the Chester Beatty Greek Papyrus Codex of the Gospels and Acts are exceptions.) The Coptic version, together with finds of early Greek Biblical papyri from the second century, offers one of the more fruitful sources for recovering readings of manuscripts prior to the persecution of Diocletian (A.D. 303), when special measures were taken to burn the Scriptures. For Old Testament studies in particular, the early Coptic manuscripts now in our possession, originally copied before the Coptic version itself seems to have been standardized in matters of rendering and revised in matters of reading, throw a revealing light on the state of the Greek text before the revision of Origen; they may well transmit in places the renderings of Aquila and Symmachus, or at least versions closely related. The legacy of the Coptic Bible for the textual critic was brilliantly summarized by Woide as early as 1799, before most of these early manuscripts had been recovered. A future editor of the Septuagint will, he says, consult the Coptic versions with profit (*cum fructu consulet*). He points out from his own experience (*experientia teste*) that the Coptic manuscripts have retained matters lost in Greek, and in places have clarified obscure passages or have corrected errors. They have also preserved forms of proper names now wanting in Greek texts. A fourth-century papyrus Book of Joshua provides some noteworthy examples; the name of Joshua's father is regularly given as Naues for Naue (Nun), the town of Gai (Ai) is spelt Gait, the tribe of Gad Gaad.

Apart from the Bible, Coptic Christian literature comprised mostly hagiographic lives of saints, martyrs, and monks, and sermons usually falsely ascribed to historical figures, in which homiletic passages, frequently with little regard for the declared title, are strung together with a loose connecting thread of scriptural quotation. It is rich in apocryphal and pseudepigraphical writing, infancy stories being of particular appeal. The importance of this literature lies in the light that it sheds upon the type of book popular with the normal mass of a provincial Eastern Church. Coptic is the medium in which much of its ancient reading has survived.

Ironically, the greatest legacy of Coptic in the transmission of works lost in their original form is the preservation, not of Christian works, but of the heretical teaching of the Gnostics and the Manichees. Some complete Gnostic treatises in Coptic had long been known before the chance find of a Gnostic library at Nag Hammadi (Chenoboskion) in 1947.[1] A fine vellum codex, written in two different hands, dating from the fourth or early fifth century, containing the text known as *Pistis Sophia*, had reached the British Museum in 1799 (Codex Askewianus). At Oxford the Bodleian had acquired the Bruce codex, of similar date, about the same time. It contains the 'Book of Yeu' as well as a large fragment of an untitled work. Three other treatises, the 'Gospel of Mariham' (Mary Magdalene), the 'Apocryphon of John', and the 'Sophia of Jesus', are found in a fifth-century papyrus volume acquired by the Berlin Museum at the end of

[1] R. McL. Wilson, *The Gnostic Problem*, London, 1954; R. M. Grant *Gnosticism and Early Christianity*, New York, 1959.

the nineteenth century. Three other recensions of the 'Apocryphon of John' exist in the Nag Hammadi find: this 'secret book' ascribed to the Evangelist John is perhaps the clearest and fullest statement of the doctrine of a Gnostic sect. It seeks to explain the presence and the problem of evil by a cosmological myth according to which there have been endless emanations (*aeons*) from the ultimate supreme being, who is immaterial, beyond the reach of human comprehension and incapable of definition, except by a series of negatives. The universe is created not by him but by an inferior and imperfect being called Yaldabaoth, son of Sophia. It is, therefore, an imperfect world, in which the forces of good clash with the forces of evil, light with darkness, spirit with matter. We of this world, having within us a spark of the supreme light which seeks return to its ultimate origin, are doomed to participate in this endless struggle of the elements, from which there is no release, except in the knowledge of the true nature of man. If Christ has a place in the system, it is as a teacher rather than as a redeemer in the orthodox sense. A favourite setting for the expounding of this esoteric knowledge is in a garden to the apostles and disciples, singly or in small groups, after the Resurrection.

Possession of these Gnostic texts gives a truer understanding of the Gnostic systems than the references to them in the Christian fathers, from the end of the second to the end of the fourth century A.D., particularly Irenaeus of Lyons, Hippolytus of Rome, and Epiphanius of Salamis. It scarcely explains the strong and persistent hold that Gnosticism gained in the East and in the West, among the non-Greek element in an obscure village of Upper Egypt and among the Gauls of North France. Cosmology represents ancient thought at its most barren; the scholars were enthralled by it, and in the insecurity of daily life such systems as the Gnostic easily degenerated into plain superstition and magical nonsense among the unlearned. The later books, like *Pistis Sophia* with its mumbo-jumbo repetitions of sacred words of power, illustrate its degeneration.

The complete Coptic texts have made possible the identification of Greek fragments: a papyrus fragment in the John Rylands Library is from the 'Gospel of Mariham', an Oxyrhynchus fragment (Pap. Oxy. 1081) from the 'Sophia of Jesus'. Three other Oxyrhynchus fragments, which for long have attracted considerable interest, can now be identified from the Nag Hammadi find as a version of the 'Gospel of Thomas'. The complete text with title is perhaps one of the most important, and certainly the most intelligible, of the Nag Hammadi find. It is not a gospel in the usual sense of the word; it contains no narrative, but is a simple compilation of sayings (*logia*) attributed to Jesus, allegedly written down by Thomas Didymus Judas, and probably composed originally in Syria. It contains many echos of the synoptic gospels, rarely of the Gospel of John, and gives versions of well-known parables like that of the Sower, of the Wedding Feast, and of the Mustard Seed. Its opening words, 'These are the secret words which the Living Jesus spoke and Didymus Judas Thomas wrote. And he said whoever finds the explanation of these words will not taste death', clearly place the text within the context of Gnostic writing. But certain of the sayings are unexceptional from the orthodox point of view. It is still uncertain to what extent the recension evidenced by the Coptic text, borrowed directly from canonical gospels, had independent access to oral traditions, or drew on a document, not necessarily Gnostic, similar to but different from the canonical gospels. The primary value of the text is the example which it affords of the way in which Gnostics distorted the Scriptures; but in the light of its early date (the original version going back to the second century) it has a secondary importance for the study of the transmission of the text of Christian scripture.

Gnosticism was one of the important formative elements of Manichaeism, which with some truth can claim consideration as one of the world's religious systems for the success which it had beyond its birth-place and for the persistence with which it survived in Central Asia. It takes its name from its founder, Mani, a Persian of high rank born at Babylon in A.D. 216. He saw himself as a teacher and apostle whose mission it was to examine religions and purge them of error. The syncretistic religion which he taught drew also on Zoroastrianism and Christianity. It accepted without explaining the cosmological conflict of the Gnostics between light and darkness; release from the ensuing conflict was to be obtained by the acquisition of knowledge and the practice of an ascetic life. In Persia itself Manichaeism spread rapidly thanks to the official support of the Sassanian king Schipur; from there it penetrated westwards as far as North Africa, where it was particularly strong at one time and was singled out for repressive measures in the reign of the Emperor Diocletian. Eastwards it spread to north India and to west China. On the death of Schipur the movement lost its official backing. Mani himself was imprisoned and died in circumstances which gave rise to a passion story.

Great importance was attached by Mani to the writing down of his doctrine to prevent later corruption. Six works are attributed to the master himself. Until the turn of the century no original works of the Manichees were known, and knowledge of their beliefs and practices was confined to statements in early Church fathers, notably Augustine of Hippo, himself a Manichee for nine years, Ephraim of Syria, and Epiphanius of Salamis. Since then, however, Manichaean works have come to light in Central Asia, mostly composed in Iranian dialects and written in the Syriac script; they are late in date and reflect the last stages of the Manichaean Church. As in the case of Gnosticism, the most important original compositions have been recovered in Egypt, preserved in Coptic translations.[1] In 1930, according to the report of the time, some fellahîn, searching among the ruined houses of Medinet

---

[1] C. R. C. Allberry, 'Manichaean Studies', *Journ. Theological Studies*, xxxix (1938), 337–49; C. Schmidt and H. J. Polotsky, *Ein Mani-Fund in Aegypten* (*Sitzungsberichte, preuss. Akad. Wissenschaften*, Berlin, 1933) pp. 4–90.

Madi in the Faiyûm, unearthed by chance a wooden chest containing seven large papyrus volumes, much affected by damp, written at the end of the fourth or the beginning of the fifth century, the contents of which were translations into Subachmimic of early Manichaean manuals. It is noteworthy that the dialect in which they have been preserved is one associated with Middle Egypt, around Asyût (Lycopolis), one of whose bishops, Alexander, writes of the activities of the Manichaean missionaries (doubtless Syrians) sent by Mani himself. The individual works which have been edited in part or completely cannot be identified as original compositions of Mani himself; they were composed by his immediate chosen disciples and doubtless were used to instruct the neophytes in Manichaean religious beliefs and practices. The 'Psalm Book', now in the Chester Beatty Library at Dublin, is a collection of actual hymns sung in services, including the great Festival of Judgement (Bema-Festival). They are more than songs of praise and were clearly intended to have a didactic purpose and reveal in particular the Manichaean attitude to Jesus. In the 'Homilies', now in Berlin, are to be found a series of compositions which contain the official version of Mani's imprisonment and death, and the subsequent persecution under Bahram I and his successor; there is a lament for the dead master, a eulogy of his triumphal entry into the realms of light, and an eschatological description of the end of things. The *Kephalaia*, so called from the short chapters into which the work is divided, now preserved partly in Dublin and partly in Berlin, is exegetical in form and sets out Manichaean teaching in a series of answers to questions put to Mani within the circle of his intimate disciples.

The legacy of Coptic writing is unique, preserving as it does so much that would otherwise be lost for the Church historian, theologian, and textual critic, and providing for the student of language the last stage of a continuous historical development back to the earliest appearance of writing at the end of the fourth millennium B.C. In art the legacy of Christian Egypt is less evident.

As a cultural force Coptic art is approximately coeval with its writing. Strictly speaking the term should be confined to the art and architecture of the monasteries from the fifth and sixth centuries onward. Common usage, however, sanctions its application to earlier manifestations, particularly in the third and fourth centuries, of stylistic mannerisms, discernible even in some second-century products, which became characteristic of Christian work in Egypt. In this sense the series of portraits of tetrarchs in imperial porphyry of the first quarter of the fourth century (Pl. 24), and the decorative architectural elements of fourth century date from Oxyrhynchus and Ahnas (Ehnasya) are usually included in a survey of Coptic art, though neither in purpose nor in theme are they Christian.

Unlike the language, the art has little continuous link with the Egypt of the Pharaohs. The mode of its execution and the choice of its decorative themes derive in the main from the repertoire of Late Roman art current throughout the Eastern Mediterranean and found in both sacred and profane contexts. It is no longer possible to see in every bird and beast a conscious Christianization of the sacred animals so popular in late Egyptian pagan cults. It is fallacious to suppose that every naked man and woman pictured on a Coptic textile represent Adam and Eve in their innocence in Paradise; they are merely the lustful hero and amorous heroine of some romantic fiction of late Greek mythology, the popular light reading matter of the day.

One certain survival in Christian iconography is the peculiar looped form of cross derived from the hieroglyphic writing of the Egyptian word for 'life' (*ankh*). It is less certain that the bronze and terracotta votive statues of Isis suckling the infant Horus on her lap (Pl. 19*b*) consciously inspired a similar representation of the Christian Madonna and Child. The two are separated by centuries, virtually undocumented. If in the presentation of so universal a theme it is necessary to postulate influence, doubtless the explanation lies in the reluctance, or inability, of the craftsmen to depart from the inherited conventions of his technique (just as the earliest European draughtsmen to sketch Egyptian statues were unable to avoid imparting to them a classical look).

Whether Egypt played a creative role in the evolution of a distinct Christian art and iconography is debatable. Alexandria may be thought to have continued, with other great Greek cities of the Eastern Empire like Antioch and Damascus, the Late Roman style, little influenced by the provincial modifications which are partly to be explained by the lack of patronage, to support flourishing schools of expert craftsmen, to afford the costlier materials, or to maintain a high standard of finish. The belief that Alexandria did in fact remain a truly creative international centre of art rests upon certain ivories, for example, the St. Menas pyxis in the British Museum, and upon certain illuminated manuscripts, like the Cotton Genesis, of unknown provenance, with no history to connect them with Egypt, which for stylistic reasons have been called Alexandrine, a word which in the absence of actual material remains from the city can mean virtually anything that its user requires. Book illustrations in volumes certainly from Egypt, for example, the Moscow Greek papyrus codex of the Alexandrine World Chronicle, dating to the beginning of the fifth century, hardly lend support to the theory of a continued existence of an unadulterated Roman style in Alexandria.

Though drawing upon the repertoire of Late Roman art, the provincial craftsman handled these themes in a different way. Coptic art displays a movement away from the naturalistic rendering of the human form and features, the realistic rendering of light and shade, towards a purely decorative handling of themes, to simplification of outline and detail, to an ever-increasing monotonous repetition of motifs. What happened is admirably illustrated by the change in style between the early painted portraits placed over the face of mummies in the second half of the first century A.D. and the examples from the fourth century. The suggestion of movement in the pose, and the impressionistic handling of colour with its gradations, shading, and highlights, are replaced by a formal balanced arrangement of features and hair, frontal pose, and flat application of colour. The same change can be observed in the patterned textiles and stone sculpture of the fourth and fifth centuries.

Coptic art was perhaps one of the more individual of the local provincial styles. There was no sudden break following the Muslim invasion of A.D. 641 and the Coptic craftsmen were instrumental in passing on to Islamic art certain traditions, notably in tapestry-weaving and leather-binding. In architecture the high pulpit of the mosque was derived from the *ambo* of the Coptic Church. In the creation of a specifically Islamic art, the debt to Egypt might have been even greater had the country been, as it was later to become, the residence of Caliphs. Beyond the frontiers of Egypt the legacy of Coptic art is controversial. South in Nubia its contribution is not large compared with the native Nubian element in the art of the Christian period. Like the art of Ethiopia, Nubian art is distinguishable from Coptic art, as evidenced in the frescoes of Faras, the carved stonework of the churches, and the native decorated pottery. In the West certain decorative themes in pre-Caroligian art, for instance, the interlace pattern found in manuscript illumination from Hiberno–Saxon scriptoria, have been assigned a Coptic origin. The possibility should perhaps not be dismissed out of hand but such subjective and speculative suppositions must be treated with the greatest caution until considerably more is learnt of the trade routes between Western Europe and the Eastern Mediterranean from the excavation of Dark Age sites. The natural capacity of Egypt for the preservation of its ancient remains ensures that its Coptic material will remain a rich and fruitful quarry. When detailed study of the available material leads to a closer knowledge of its dating and a clearer understanding of its originality, when excavation of Christian sites and levels provides fresh and compelling evidence, it may be found that the artistic legacy of Coptic Egypt is more significant, possibly more direct, than a sober interpretation of the material evidence and a reasonable assessment of the historical role of Egypt after the Council of Chalcedon now allows.

A. F. SHORE

SELECT BIBLIOGRAPHY

B. ALTANER, *Patrology*, London, 1960.

H. I. BELL, *Cults and creeds in Graeco-Roman Egypt*, Liverpool, 1953.

BROOKLYN MUSEUM, *Coptic Egypt: papers read at a symposium*, etc., Brooklyn Museum, 1944.

O. H. E. KHS-BURMESTER, *The Egyptian or Coptic church. A detailed description of her liturgical services, etc.* (Publications de la Société d'archéologie copte; textes et documents), Cairo, 1967.

A. J. BUTLER, *The ancient Coptic churches of Egypt*, Oxford, 1884.

M. CRAMER, *Das christlich-koptische Ägypten einst und heute*, Wiesbaden, 1959.

J. DORESSE, *Des hiéroglyphes à la croix: ce que le passé pharaonique a légué au christianisme* (Publications de l'Institut historique et archéologique néerlandais de Stamboul, vii), Istanbul, 1960.

ESSEN, VILLA HÜGEL, *Koptische Kunst: Christentum am Nil*, Essen, 1963.

E. R. HARDY, *Christian Egypt: church and people. Christianity and nationalism in the patriarchate of Alexandria*, New York, 1952.

DE LACEY O'LEARY, *The saints of Egypt*, London, 1937.

O. F. A. MEINARDUS, *Christian Egypt, ancient and modern*, Cairo, 1965.

P. D. SCOTT-MONCRIEFF, *Paganism and Christianity in Egypt*, Cambridge, 1913.

W. TILL, 'Coptic and its value', *Bulletin of the John Rylands Library*, xl (1957), 229–58.

W. H. WORRELL, *A short account of the Copts*, Ann Arbor, 1945.

15

THE LEGACY TO AFRICA

ANY attempt to describe the legacy of Egypt to Africa is faced with a difficulty of terminology. What is meant in this context by Africa? If used in its proper geographical sense of the continent of Africa it includes Egypt itself, and it is not our purpose here to describe the influences of ancient on modern Egypt.

Egypt certainly lies in Africa and is in that sense African, but it is at a vital world cross-roads close to Western Asia and open to many influences that scarcely penetrated further west or south, and therefore developed a distinctive civilization in many ways different from that of the rest of Africa. The northern littoral of the continent has always been in close contact with southern Europe and has formed part of a Mediterranean culture area, so it, too, is excluded, and the many and interesting traces of Egyptian influence in Carthage and Libya will not be treated here as they more properly form part of a study of the Egyptian legacy to the Mediterranean and the Near East.

The Africa considered here is that major part of the continent known clumsily as sub-Saharan Africa, or sometimes to French scholars as *Afrique noire*. Both these terms are themselves inadequate since there is no barrier along the southern edge of the Sahara, nor are all the peoples lying south of it black. But some definition is necessary, and rather than use some more complicated and inevitably inaccurate term, Africa and African will be used here to refer to that part of the continent that lies outside the frontiers of modern Egypt and south of the Sahara, an area that is largely, but not exclusively, inhabited by negroid peoples.

It is by no means a homogeneous area, either geographically, linguistically, or culturally, and as much variation can be found here as in any other of the great land masses of the world. But there is also some unity, and there are common features which, though hard to analyse or define, make it possible in general terms to speak of African culture, and to use the word African to describe the social and artistic elements found in ancient Egypt which are neither peculiar to Egypt itself, nor introduced from Asia or the Mediterranean—and to use it also to describe that geographical and cultural area whose debt to ancient Egypt we shall consider.

To define this legacy of Egypt to Africa is a matter of some difficulty and much uncertainty. The paucity of sources in a largely illiterate continent and the still early stage of research into its history make such gaps in knowledge that much of what is said must be speculative, and detailed study of the history of Africa and the influences on it must remain full of queries and guesses for many years to come.

It is desirable that an attempt should be made to analyse this legacy, since in recent years much attention has been devoted to the question, and a great deal of questionable material has been published, often with little attention to the claims of scholarship or accuracy. Attempts have been made to show that some modern African peoples are either directly descended from the Egyptians or were closely influenced by them. These range from suggestions that the brass and bronze sculptures of Nigeria were directly inspired from Egypt, to attempts to bring the Yoruba or the Wolof from Egypt by claiming direct descent—or, in the case of the Yoruba, suggesting a mass migration from the Nile to western Nigeria. Tendentious works have been written to prove linguistic and cultural connections, many of them having no more truth in them than the eighteenth-century histories that sought to bring the British from Troy.

An example of this type of approach is Archdeacon Lucas's book *The Religion of the Yorubas* in which the claim of strong cultural and linguistic connections between the Yoruba and the

Egyptians is made. The appendix to the book, called 'Egyptian Survivals', cites supposed analogies, and lists Yoruba gods whom the author identifies with Egyptian ones on the evidence of approximate resemblances in the names. He also gives the names of a number of West African peoples which he suggests are of Egyptian origin, for example, that of the Ga of the Accra region in Ghana, which name is supposed to be derived from Egyptian on the ground that it resembles the Egyptian word *ka*. The name of the Fanti, another people of Ghana, he derives from *fnd* 'nose', though he does not explain why a West African people should do anything so bizarre as to call themselves by such a word. The whole speculation is fanciful, and shows an ignorance of linguistics. Lucas also gives a list of Yoruba words which he claims have an Egyptian origin. The list cannot be taken seriously, and it is clear that the author, apart from being unaware of the linguistic position of Yoruba, is also unaware that the Egyptians did not write vowels and that our vocalization is conventional. His authority for Egyptian words throughout his book is the long outdated dictionary of Budge. One example of his arguments will suffice—that is the equation of the Yoruba word *a-pa* 'house', with Egyptian *pr* with the same meaning, where the only common element is the letter *p*. It is only worth refuting arguments of this sort because of the wide currency that they have obtained in Africa in recent times.

The Egyptian origins of the Yoruba have also been claimed, though in a much more sophisticated way, by Dr. Biobaku, who, in his Lugard Lectures, suggested that they came from the Nile. He uses a mixture of oral tradition and aesthetic judgements, and one of his main arguments is that the famous Ife heads, in particular the Olokun head, are of Egyptian origin. As evidence he states that Meek, formerly government anthropologist in Nigeria, referring to Ife sculpture dug up by Frobenius, claimed that Egyptologists had dated the pieces to the sixth century B.C., his implication being that they were Egyptian. This statement has been repeated time and time again without any further authority and until recently was accepted as fact, though no such claim would be made by any Egyptologist today. The date is quite impossible and it is certain that the bronzes of Ife are not of Egyptian manufacture, nor even of Egyptian inspiration, though the *cire perdue* method of casting by which they were made may well have come from the Nile valley.

Much has been written on this theme of Egyptian survivals in Africa since Bowdich, whose visit to Ashanti in 1817 was the first by an Englishman, was inspired by his West African experiences to write what is probably the first book on the subject.[1] Not all of this literature can be discussed here, but mention may be made of the book by Mrs. Meyerowitz,[2] who, looking for remote origins for the Akan peoples of Ghana, has, by a series of imaginative analogies, attempted to show that Akan religion and ancient-Egyptian religion are substantially the same. A recent article[3] suggests that much of the court ritual and culture of the present-day Mossi of the Volta Republic is of Egyptian origin but it is no more convincing than Delafosse's articles of more than sixty years ago[4] which claimed that the Baoulé, an Akan people, now living in the Ivory Coast, also derived their culture from Egypt. Apart from the inherent improbability of cultural and artistic traits surviving in recognizable form over such a period of time, it is difficult to see how any objective study could find anything distinctively Egyptian in the cultures of the people described. Only strong attachment to a diffusionist theory which demands that Egypt must be the centre of cultural dispersion can possibly explain the desperate attempt to see in the slightest of resemblances, or even in none, the imprint of pharaonic Egypt.

These works do little to help in the appreciation of Egypt's

---

[1] T. E. Bowdich, *An Essay on the Superstitions, Customs, and Arts Common to the Ancient Egyptians, Abyssinians and Ashantees*, Paris, 1821.

[2] E. L. R. Meyerowitz, *The Divine Kingship in Ghana and Ancient Egypt*, London, 1960.

[3] R. Pageard, *Genève-Afrique: Acta Africana*, ii (1963), 183–206.

[4] M. Delafosse, *L'Anthropologie*, xl (1900), 431–51, 677–90.

legacy to Africa, and it is not in this way that her contribution to the development of the African continent can be discerned. But, leaving such exaggerated claims aside, there are possibilities that the civilization of Egypt had some influence on other parts of Africa, and there are here and there faint hints of a common culture or of influence of the one on the other. Through the haze of centuries of separation there is the suggestion that there were exchanges, some in the realm of ideas and institutions, some in the realm of material objects. It must be made clear, though, that in many cases there is no certainty that in these common elements we may not be seeing Africa's legacy to Egypt as much as Egypt's legacy to Africa.[1] The resemblances which can be found in cultural, social, and religious spheres between Egypt and other parts of Africa cannot of themselves tell us which way these influences may have travelled. Only the finding of material objects can tell us this, and here there is a complete absence of factual evidence, for although some objects in use even in modern Africa are reminiscent of pharaonic Egypt, no properly attested ancient-Egyptian objects have ever been found south of the northern Sudan.

A bronze figure of Osiris, found in the Congo and published by the Abbé Breuil and others,[2] is one of a small number of objects of assumed Egyptian origin which have come to light unexpectedly far south, but they are so few and the circumstances of their finding always so vague and uncertain that they cannot be accepted with out question as genuine. The finding of Ptolemaic coins in South Africa, subsequently discovered to have come in recent times in the pockets of Greek traders from Alexandria, points a warning.

The only absolutely certain Egyptian influence in Africa is in the area immediately to its south. Here, in the territory of the

---

[1] Cf. H. W. Fairman, *African Affairs*, Special Issue, Spring 1965, pp. 69–75 (with discussion on pp. 96–8).

[2] For a full bibliography of this find, see J. Leclant, *Bulletin trimestriel de la societé française d'égyptologie*, no. 21 (June 1956), p. 31, n. 9.

present Republic of the Sudan, Meroitic civilization flourished from the sixth century B.C. to the end of the third century A.D. Meroe is of the utmost importance for Africa, for it seems possible that it was from here that important techniques such as iron-working, the *cire perdue* method of bronze-casting, perhaps the cultivation of cotton, and the use of the horse for transport, spread into Africa.

Meroe was heavily influenced by Egypt in all its cultural, and possibly its political, development. It was the first purely African state to use writing, and it developed forms of state organization which may have had influence further south. In considering Egyptian influences in Africa, Meroe is an obvious centre of the possible diffusion of Egyptian ideas, and it is with a study of its history and place in the continent that we should begin.

Meroe developed from the Egyptianized kingdom of Napata, whose early kings figure in Egyptian history as the Twenty-fifth Dynasty, at some time in the sixth century B.C. For reasons which are still not clear, but were presumably both political and economic, the kings moved their capital from Napata to Meroe, perhaps in the reign of Aspelta, *c.* 590 B.C. The culture of the rulers of Napata had been completely Egyptian, whatever the race and language of the kings and people may have been, and they had derived it from the Egyptians who had conquered and ruled along the Nile from the first to the fourth cataracts from the beginning of New Kingdom times. Kush, as it was known to the Egyptians, became an Egyptian colony under the rule of an Egyptian governor and clear signs of Egypt are to be seen in the ruins of towns and temples throughout Nubia.

With the withdrawal up the Nile to Meroe, this Egyptian influence, while remaining strong throughout the whole history of the Meroitic state, becomes tinged with new elements deriving from Africa. The art changes and, though showing marked Egyptian and Hellenistic elements, it has a sufficient character of its own to enable us to speak of a distinctively Meroitic art as shown in its statuary and temple reliefs. The pottery, though much of it, in later times at least, is akin to Roman pottery of the first three centuries A.D., has also characteristics of its own, and in the burnished black ware known from Faras to Sennar provides a purely African pot fabric of a type previously unknown. This pottery is similar to a wide range of African ceramic styles, many of which are still in use today. The designs are normally incised before firing, and the surface is burnished. Most of these pots seem to have been used for containing liquids, and they are frequently referred to as beer pots, this being the purpose for which their modern analogues are largely used.

Of the political history of the Meroitic state we know very little. A list of kings has been compiled, based on Reisner's excavations at the royal cemeteries of Kurru, Nuri, and Meroe, and approximate dates can be given, but in the whole period from the reign of Kashta to that of the last king of Meroe, a span of nearly 1,000 years, we have approximately fixed dates only for the first kings, the Twenty-fifth Dynasty of Egypt; and, after Tanwetamani, only for Aspelta (*c.* 593–568 B.C.), Ergamenes (*c.* 268–220 B.C.), and Teqerideamani (*c.* A.D. 246–66), and even for these kings the dates are open to question. The remainder have to be fitted in by using average lengths of reign and by weighting the averages by such indications as size of pyramid or richness of tomb content. By this method a reasonable chronological framework has been drawn up, though the dates for each king are only a statistical expression of probability, and should not be understood as having any validity beyond that.

There is also a possible source of error in the order of the kings. This order was originally established by Reisner on the assumption that the first king to raise his pyramid on a new site would choose the most commanding position and that his successors would, each in his turn, choose the next best site. Study of variations in pyramid styles as well as of the contents of the tombs provides some check on this, and it is now reasonably certain that the main groups of rulers are in the right order, though within any group the order may well be in error.

The picture that we have of Meroe, from at least the fourth century B.C. to the end of the third century A.D., is of a stable, well organized African state, ruling from its capital, on the banks of the Nile, a great stretch of country from Maharraqa to at least as far south as Sennar.

It was a power in the ancient world during the last three centuries B.C. and the first A.D., and possibly earlier, and was known and described by classical writers as well as being mentioned in the Bible. The Biblical reference (Acts 8: 27) is interesting additional information that the title Candace, though misunderstood as a name, was well known in foreign countries.

Even in the third century A.D., well on towards the end of the Meroitic kingdom, ambassadors were passing to and from the Mediterranean, and a graffito of one of them from the Dodeka-schoinos, in the reign of King Teqerideamani, gives us one of the very few fixed dates in Meroitic history by referring to the Roman Emperor Trebonianus Gallus. It is a remarkable phenomenon that in this part of Africa at this early date such a state should develop, and, although there may well have been other influences, parti-cularly from further east, at work, the main influence and legacy came from Egypt.

We know nothing of the internal administration of the state. It was certainly a monarchy and apparently a hereditary one, in which the queens, at some periods at least, played an important part. It is highly likely that, as in Egypt and in many African states, the main decisions were taken by the king, but what curbs were placed on his authority, or to what advisers he had to defer, we do not know. There must certainly have been some powerful control to spread a unified culture over such a wide area, and Netekamani (*c.* A.D. 1–25) at least was able to build at Naqa and Wad ben Naqa in the Butana and as far north as Amara, where a temple of his once stood, though it has now vanished without trace.

Our only glimpse of court affairs is in the story, recounted by Diodorus Siculus, of the killing of the priests by Ergamenes. Diodorus tells us that Ergamenes, who had been educated by Greek teachers and whom we find associated with Ptolemy IV in the building of the temple at Dakka, stopped the custom of king-killing practised by the priests, and instead massacred them first. This looks much like a version of the custom, not uncommon in Africa and elsewhere, of the ceremonial killing of the king when his usefulness was past, and must surely be part of the African rather than the Egyptian element in Meroitic civilization.

The buildings of Meroe, though now much ruined, were a considerable achievement. The standard of workmanship may on occasion have been crude, and walls may often have been only two outer skins of dressed stone filled with rubble, but many other countries of the ancient world also built in this way. There is no doubt that the temples of Netekamani and other rulers of Naqa, the great complex of Musawarat dating in part from the fourth century B.C., as well as the buildings of Meroe itself, with its temple to Amūn, its palace, and remarkable bath-house, were major achievements, and that the main inspiration came from Egypt.

It was a literate culture, and here again it owed much to Egypt for its two forms of writing. Meroitic hieroglyphic writing, used only occasionally and only for royal inscriptions, contains a small selection of Egyptian hieroglyphs used in a slightly different manner, the signs being alphabetic and without the ideographic element of Egyptian. The other, more common, writing, misleadingly described as cursive, may be derived from the hieroglyphs or perhaps from Egyptian demotic, but it is an interesting and distinctive type of writing in its own right. Although the phonetic values of its signs are known, it can still not be translated and there is no knowledge of the nature of the Meroitic language or of its relationship to other languages, though it is a reasonable assumption that, when more is known of it, it will be found to be related to one of the existing families of African languages. There is at present just a vague hint that it may be related to the little-studied group of languages known as Koman, spoken up the Blue Nile and round Jebel Gule and south of it to the frontier of Ethiopia, but the written language died with the end of Meroe at the very beginning of the fourth century A.D., or perhaps a little earlier, and no legacy of writing from Egypt continued in the rest of Africa after this date.

From a technological point of view Meroe had one outstanding contribution to make, and that was in iron-working. The Nile valley had always been backward in metallurgy and when the Assyrians invaded Egypt in 668/7 B.C., the Egyptians and their Kushite rulers could put into the field forces armed only with bronze weapons as against the formidable iron ones of the Assyrians. But the bitter experience of defeat was not wasted, and it was not long before, in their southern homeland, the people of Meroe were working iron to an unprecedented extent. Starting in a modest way in the reign of Harsiotef (*c.* 416–398 B.C.), in whose tomb for the first time models of iron tools were found, the use of iron became increasingly common and the existence of the great iron slag-heaps at Meroe is now well known to all historians of Africa—as is Sayce's remark that Meroe must have been the Birmingham of Africa.

Favoured with a plentiful local supply of iron-ore in the ferricrete capping of the nearby hills, as well as with adequate sources of timber for the smelting furnaces, Meroe was well suited for the development of this technique. We know nothing of the spread of this skill from Meroe and there is no factual evidence yet discovered to suggest that from here the knowledge of iron-working passed south and west. But in spite of this lack of proof the common assumption that at Meroe we see the beginning of the African Iron Age can be accepted, so long as it is realized that we have no information about the date or nature of the spread of this technique.

For Africa, the spread of iron-working is an essential element in the development of state organization, and, so far as present knowledge goes, it was the introduction of this new technique and the mastery over nature which it gave that made possible a whole series of important developments. One of the major unanswered questions of the archaeology of tropical Africa remains that of the date of the introduction of iron-working and the routes by which it came. So few excavations have been made that there are only isolated scraps of information from widely scattered areas, and even where there is evidence of the early use of iron, the dating is often uncertain, so that it is still not possible to fix the date of the introduction of iron-working over most of the African continent. Such information as there is would support the suggestion that the technique was diffused from Meroe during the first centuries A.D. Iron-working communities of medieval times are now known from various parts of Africa, though in many cases their dates are not defined with any degree of accuracy. In the northern parts of West Africa it is not unlikely that iron was known before A.D. 500 but in the forest areas along the Guinea Coast it may well have been much later. There is a suggestion that iron-working was known in Rhodesia in the first two or three centuries A.D. but this must at present be taken with some reserve; by the tenth century, however, if the Carbon-14 dates are to be trusted, there was considerable settlement by iron-using peoples in the Rhodesias and East Africa. The dates have a certain consistency and run from the mid tenth century at Kalomo to the fifteenth century at Lusitu.[1]

One of the main iron-using cultures of East Africa, that associated with 'dimple-based' pottery, has now provided a Carbon date of A.D. 1037 (plus or minus fifty years). It looks therefore as though the years from about A.D. 500 to 1000, in very round figures, are the crucial ones for the spread of iron-working, and this could

[1] G. A. Wainwright, *Uganda Journal*, xviii (1954), 113–36, suggests from a study of the distribution of a Bantu word for iron in East Africa and its use in Swahili, where all other metals are known by Arabic names, that Bunyoro was the centre from which the knowledge of iron-working in East Africa came. He speculates as to the routes by which it could have reached Bunyoro from Meroe.

well fit with the idea that the technique was slowly spread from Meroe. There certainly seems no other source for its introduction, but when we look for the routes by which the knowledge may have travelled evidence is still lacking. It can be assumed that the Nile was the route by which iron-workers entered Africa, although, until there has been some investigation of the southern Sudan, it is difficult to be sure; but, so far as West Africa is concerned, the Sahelian way, along the savanna country, through Kordofan and Darfur, and round the southern edge of Lake Chad, must have been the route by which all and any Nile influences travelled. This route has been in use for centuries and is still used in the reverse direction by West African Muslims going on the pilgrimage to Mecca. We can speculate on the routes by which iron-workers went south and south-east; the upper reaches of the Nile are not easy to traverse, though the area of the Sudd is not so much of an obstacle as it is often claimed to be. It causes great difficulty to river traffic, but it is not likely that the river was the main means of communication, and in the dry season the country on either side of the Nile can be travelled with reasonable facility. There is, however, an alternative route to East Africa by going along the western foot-hills of Abyssinia and this may also have been used.

The means as well as the routes of this transmission of iron-working also remain very obscure, but ideas of mass migrations of peoples carrying this skill with them have little to recommend them. The widespread existence throughout much of Africa of small groups of travelling smiths, often of different tribes and speaking different languages from those amongst whom they work, may well give a clue to the method of dissemination. We do not know whether such specialized groups operated in Meroe, but their prevalence in Africa suggests that this is highly likely. If this were so, it is easy to envisage that under conditions of disturbance, such as there were in the last years of the third century A.D., such small groups of skilled men with their families could have moved off to seek their fortunes elsewhere and spread the knowledge, not of their craft, which they would have kept to themselves, but of the use and superiority of iron tools and weapons, amongst the previously stone-using peoples to the west and south of the Meroitic kingdom.

Meroe came to an end probably somewhere about the end of the third century A.D. The conventional view has been that it was the invasion by Aezanes of Axum in about A.D. 350 that dealt the final blow, but there are suggestions that the Black Noba were the real destroyers of Meroe, and that Aezanes came into a land already conquered and ruled by these new people. It has been suggested[1] that, after the fall of Meroe, the Meroitic royal house moved westwards to Darfur, thus setting in train the dispersal of the knowledge of iron-working as well as of a number of other culture traits which can be traced back to Egypt.

The evidence adduced for this westward march is not very convincing, being largely derived from the existence of modern tribal names which, it is suggested, contain the element 'Kush' and must therefore have come from the ancient Kush. Traditions amongst one of these tribes, the Kagiddi of northern Darfur, of having come from the east are also quoted as evidence. Oral traditions are notoriously unreliable and difficult to control and need extremely careful and critical handling, and it would be dangerous to accept these accounts at their face value. All the evidence we now have from many different parts of Africa suggests that reasonably reliable oral traditions go back only a few centuries and it is in the highest degree improbable that a tradition of this type would have been maintained for some 1,600 years.

Another argument is based on the existence of pockets of peoples in the western part of the Republic of the Sudan speaking languages related to Nubian, as in the Nuba hills of Kordofan and in Jebel Meidob in Darfur. The main body of Nubian speakers now live along the Nile from north of Aswan in Egypt to Debba in the

[1] A. J. Arkell, *A History of the Sudan*, 2nd ed., London, 1961, pp. 174 f.

Sudan and it is suggested that the western groups are the result of a dispersal from the river after the collapse of Meroe. This argument also is not very convincing. The problem of the original home of the Nubian language is a very obscure one but it is quite certain that Meroitic is not Nubian.

There is a further possibility which must not be excluded, namely, that Meroitic was the language of a ruling group whilst Nubian was spoken by the bulk of the population, and the present distribution of languages of the Eastern Sudanic family, to which Nubian belongs, suggests that this may have been so. If it was the royal house of Meroe that moved west, then they should have taken their language with them, but on present evidence it is more reasonable to see the pockets of Nubian-speaking people remaining in the west as users of the remnants of a language once very widely spoken over the whole of the western and riverain Sudan.

Ruins of burnt brick have also been cited as marking the trail of the supposed westward trek of Meroites, notably those at Abu Sufyan and Zankor. They may be Meroitic, but we know far too little of them to base any rational argument on their presence, and it is just as likely that they are of medieval date, as are those of their nearer neighbours in Bornu. So it can be said that the theory of a movement westwards from Meroe is a very attractive hypothesis which, if it were true, would certainly go far in explaining some of the hints of Egyptian influence in West and Central Africa. But in our present state of knowledge there is no certainty and many of the elaborate arguments based on this assumed migration are flimsy in the extreme.

But, having said all this, it can be seen that, here and there, there are strong resemblances to Egyptian objects and to Egyptian culture scattered throughout Africa. In the realm of material culture a small number of objects have been found which might reasonably be supposed to have originated from Egypt. Amongst these are musical instruments such as the small harp used by the Azande and other peoples of the southern Sudan and Uganda, wooden head-rests in various parts of the continent, certain types of sandals, and many other similar objects. In West Africa attention has been drawn to the use of ostrich-feather fans, very similar to pharaonic ones, in Wadai and Bagirmi and other places in the neighbourhood of Lake Chad. Such fans were certainly in use in Nubia in the Second Intermediate Period and a number were found at Kerma, but none has been depicted in any Meroitic reliefs.

In other parts of West Africa, particularly Nigeria, there are resemblances in the regalia of chiefs to the pharaonic regalia— whips, crooks, and flails have all been reported and some have seen them as direct borrowings from Egypt.

The god Shango, of the Yoruba, whose sacred animal is the ram, has been derived by some from the god Amūn, and Wainwright has cited a ram-headed breastplate from Lagos which certainly very strongly suggests an Egyptian origin.[1]

Frankfort drew attention to the resemblance between ivory arm-clamps found in an early dynastic grave in Lower Nubia and those in use amongst the modern Masai of East Africa; but, in the absence of any firm evidence as to the antiquity of such objects, they must be viewed with some scepticism, and they are too few to be regarded as serious evidence.

Some authors have attempted to list all these resemblances and Petrie[2] gives sixty-one examples of similarities between Egyptian objects and customs and those of Africa. Some of these, including those given above, are genuine resemblances, and may be evidence of influence one way or the other; some, such as his No. 18, 'Man sacrificed at royal funeral', are customs found in many parts of the world and quite capable of arising independently, while others are so vague as to prove nothing. Many of Petrie's authorities for artistic resemblances are suspect, and his reliance on Frobenius causes him to date the Ife heads to the fifth century B.C. and to state firmly that they are derived from Egyptian Memphite art

[1] G. A. Wainwright, *JEA* xxxv (1949), 170–5.
[2] W. M. F. Petrie, *Ancient Egypt*, 1914, 115–27, 159–70.

of the Persian period. From what we know now of Ife, although the exact chronology remains obscure, it is quite impossible that these heads are earlier than the Middle Ages and any direct Egyptian influence is out of the question.

The other aspect of Africa where Egyptian inspiration has been largely assumed is that of state organization and in particular the institution of 'divine kingship'. The main protagonist of this idea was Seligman, who was largely concerned to show that the existence of 'divine kings' in parts of Africa was a symptom of the infiltration of Egyptian ideas.

Much of the argument is now outdated by Seligman's continual insistence on a Hamitic-race culture area in North-East Africa which he, in common with many other earlier anthropologists and historians, regarded as always and everywhere superior to that of the negroes. The result was that nearly all cultural and social developments, as well as technological advances, were attributed to these superior Hamitic peoples who were claimed to be responsible for Egyptian civilization as well as for many elements in the culture of other African peoples.

Even the existence of a Hamitic race would now be challenged, though peoples speaking languages of the group, now better called Afro-Asiatic since it includes the Semitic languages as well as those previously called Hamitic, are widespread in North-East Africa. Ancient Egyptian belongs to this language family, as do the Cushite languages of the Red Sea coast, but there is no necessary correlation between language and culture. Many of the Cushite-speaking peoples live a very simple semi-nomadic life with a strong emphasis on cattle-owning, and it is difficult to see why the earlier scholars regarded them as socially and culturally superior to the agricultural negroes whom they are alleged to have influenced.

The concept of a 'divine kingship' as a culture trait is itself unsatisfactory; in many parts of the world the ruler has been considered as divine in one sense or another. Without a more

G g

detailed study of the nature of 'divine kingship' in African society, the existence of a god-king need not be taken as evidence of Egyptian influence. Seligman, taking the existence of such a king, or for some peoples the custom of king-killing, as an indication, suggests Egyptian influence at work amongst such diverse peoples as the Dinka and Shilluk of the Upper Nile, the Banyoro and Baganda of the Great Lakes, the Jukun of Nigeria, and the Bambara of the Western Sudan.

The only one of these where the case for Egyptian influence looks at all convincing is amongst the Banyoro, where he draws attention to two significant features:

1. The male members of the royal family are related to the eagle, though there is no eagle clan. Seligman suggests this is a memory of the Egyptian Pharaoh's membership of the falcon clan.
2. The custom of the King of Bunyoro 'shooting the nations' by bow and arrow, which he claims resembles the Egyptian *sed* festival.

Personal investigations have also shown that there is a ceremonial digging-up of the ground by the king at his accession, a custom which also has its Egyptian counterpart.

The royal family of Bunyoro have strong traditions of having come from the north, and in the royal enclosure at Hoima maintain a carefully attended clump of papyrus as a reminder of their Nilotic origin.

All this does suggest, however remotely, Egyptian influences. Yet the Bunyoro royal line cannot have reached its present home more than a few hundred years ago and, as Seligman himself observed, this makes Egyptian influence unlikely, it being just as probable that these traditions are due to old and widespread African beliefs which affected Egypt as they have affected other parts of Africa.

This attempt to prove an Egyptian origin for any resemblance of objects or ideas to known Egyptian ones has been made many

times, and was the main argument of the now long-discredited
'Diffusionist School', who saw in Egypt the origins not only of
African culture but also of that of peoples in many other parts
of the world, even America. The idea that, wherever cultural
or technological developments can be seen in Africa, they must
have been brought in from elsewhere, dies very hard, and arises
in part from a deep-rooted feeling amongst non-African scholars
that it is somehow *impossible* for Africans to have made these
advances on their own. There is now plenty of evidence to show
that many parts of Africa had highly developed societies, well
adapted to their environments, from early times, and that, although in Africa, as throughout the world, no society is isolated
and there is a two-way traffic in ideas and techniques, it is not
necessary to assume that everything in Africa came from Egypt.

Yet still most are agreed that some elements in technology,
particularly in the development of metal-working, were probably
spread to Africa from the Nile valley through Meroe. If the
legacy is to be seen anywhere in Africa it is at Meroe, and Meroe
was ancient Egypt's African heir.

There is one part of Africa where Egyptian influence can certainly be seen, that is, in the rock paintings at Tassili el Ajjer in
the central Sahara. Here there have been found a great variety of
paintings of widely varying style and date, and amongst them are
a number which show unmistakable signs of their painters having
had some contact with the artistic traditions of Egypt. The paintings are certainly not the work of Egyptians, but that of artists
who have in some indirect way been subject to influences which
have led them to reproduce art forms showing marked Egyptian
characteristics.

At what date this happened is uncertain but the finder of the
paintings suggests that they are of Eighteenth Dynasty times.
Whatever journeys or movements of peoples lie behind the strange
appearance of such paintings in mid Sahara, there is no evidence
of other Egyptian influence there. We do not know what people

executed the paintings nor do we know their subsequent history, and it does not seem that this contact with Egypt had any further results.

The fall of Meroe did not cause a break in relations with Egypt along the Nile, and during the period of the people known to archaeologists as the X-Group, perhaps to be identified with the Nobatae, in the fifth and sixth centuries, there was a steady trade in luxury goods from Roman Egypt and other parts of the Mediterranean. No doubt Egyptian religious ideas were common, and it may well be that this was the time when some of the apparently Egyptian elements further south and west were diffused. The X-Group seem, on the basis of rather scanty anatomical studies, to have been a predominantly negroid people, and this was probably the first time that such a people were settled in those parts of the Nile valley.

They may have been the bringers of Nubian speech, and if so played an important part in the transmission of Egyptian cultural traits into later times. Some bronze, or brass, lamps from Ghana, said to have come from graves at Atebubu and of unknown date, have a resemblance to lamps from X-Group graves which are certainly of Mediterranean inspiration even if not manufacture.[1] But whatever the date of the Ghana examples they are unlikely to be very old, and the time interval is so great that they must be regarded as doubtful examples of Nile valley inspiration.

With the coming of Christianity from Coptic Egypt and Byzantium we see again powerful Egyptian influence in these parts of Africa, and one that can certainly be seen to spread away from the Nile valley.

The first Christian missionaries came to Nubia in the middle of the sixth century, and, though the Egyptian Copts were not the only element in the new cultural and religious activity, their influence was considerable. The relative importance in Nubia

[1] A. J. Arkell, *Antiquity*, xxiv (1950), 38–40.

of orthodox Christianity, supported by Byzantium, and monophysitism, supported by the Coptic Church of Egypt, has been much argued, and the evidence is inconclusive. The usually accepted view is that the whole of Christian Nubia came under monophysite control at some time during the eighth century, and, indeed, it is hard to see how any contact with orthodoxy could have been maintained after the Arab conquest of Egypt in A.D. 641, though, from the existence of tombstones written in Greek as late as the second half of the twelfth century, there must still have been some knowledge of that language. But Coptic was certainly known and used and a large number of Coptic tombstones are recorded, as well as graffiti and ostraca. The Copts also gave to the Nubians their alphabet, which, with a few modifications, was used to write the Nubian language, Nubian thus sharing with Meroitic the distinction of being the only purely African language to be written in ancient times.

In Christian Nubia the material culture was also heavily influenced by Coptic Egypt, though it contained a number of new features, some apparently drawn from further east, from Syria, and from Persia. Lasting for some 800 years Nubian Christianity was a profound influence in the Nile valley and evidence is now coming to light of its spread to regions of Africa at a considerable distance from the river.

The pottery was of exceptional quality, beauty, and interest, and is the most easily identifiable of the elements in this culture. The fine painted pottery in particular lends itself to ready identification. Perhaps deriving from the painted pottery of Meroitic times, it incorporated many other characteristics, some derived from Christian symbolism and some motifs being taken from the zoomorphic designs on the pottery of Fatimid Egypt.

The discovery of this pottery on sites stretching from the Red Sea Hills in the east to Darfur and Koro Toro in Wadai shows that Christian Nubian influence must have been widespread. There have been many other hints of influence from the Nile valley westwards in Christian times, and now these can be supported by material evidence. There are also such other indications as the widespread use of the symbol of the cross as a decoration amongst the Tuareg and some of the peoples of Darfur.

In addition to this spread of Nubian pottery to the west, there is a group of buildings of red brick stretching from the sites in Kordofan, already mentioned as being possibly of Meroitic origin. Red brick is a very rare building material in Africa outside the Nile valley and the existence of ruins in Darfur, particularly at Ain Fara, at which Christian pottery has been found, as well as further west in Wadai, and in Bornu, where the fifteenth-century palace buildings at Gambaru, Birni Gazargamo, and Nguru mark the most westerly extension of the use of this material, strongly suggests that it was from Christian Nubia that this technique came. The Bornu buildings are certainly too late for Meroitic influence, which would have had to remain in a state of suspension for hundreds of years before emerging once more, but if influences from the Nile valley were at work in medieval times there is no great difficulty in accepting Nubia as the source.

It seems far more likely that the widespread traditions of eastern origin amongst many peoples of Lake Chad and northern Nigeria are due rather to this westward influence in medieval times than to earlier pharaonic or Meroitic contacts. Monneret de Villard has collected much of this evidence,[1] largely from oral tradition, and it need not be repeated in detail here, but it is quite clear that there are memories of Christianity amongst the Tuareg and the Zaghawa, of whom the latter were once a far more formidable people than they are now. The traditions are, as so often, confused and unreliable, but they have some consistency, and with the new evidence from the ceramic finds it seems safe to assume that they have some factual basis. It may be that the state organization of

[1] U. Monneret de Villard, *Storia della Nubia cristiana*, Rome, 1938.

Bornu, as well as of other parts of Nigeria, owes something to the kingdom of Dongola.

When this happened, and whether it was due to gradual influence or to movements of peoples or families after the Islamization of the Nile valley, we cannot be sure. The pottery from Darfur would seem to belong to the ninth or tenth centuries; that from Koro Toro is somewhat later.

The Nigerian traditions frequently speak of a folk hero called Kisra as responsible for the foundation of states, and some have seen in him the Sassanian king Chosroes, who invaded Egypt in the early seventh century and whose armies certainly came to the frontiers of Nubia, even if they did not enter it. There is a Sassanian element in Nubian Christian art, but chronologically it seems unlikely that this Persian influence could have been directly responsible for developments far to the west. On present evidence it seems safer to assume that these developments took place during the troubled times of the thirteenth and fourteenth centuries when Arab invasions disrupted the life of Nubia, brought Christianity to an end, and set in train movements of peoples which brought the Shuwa Arabs as far west as Bornu and may well have had wider repercussions.

P. L. SHINNIE

16

THE CONTRIBUTION TO ISLAM

In December A.D. 639, according to tradition, the Arab general
'Amr ibn al-'Āṣ withdrew from the siege of Caesarea in Palestine
and, with a force of some 3,500 Yemenite cavalry, entered Egypt.
Advancing through the Wādī 'l-'Arīsh, he captured the Byzantine
outpost of Pelusium (Arabic al-Faramā') in January 640, and then,
turning south along the eastern arm of the Nile delta, blockaded
and captured Bilbeys, only thirty miles from Egyptian Babylon.
He now took up positions in the desert fringes east of the city,
where he was joined by reinforcements sent from Arabia. With
them, he was able to win a decisive victory at the battle of Heliopolis, in July 640. After this, the defeated Byzantines abandoned
all Egypt to the Arabs, except for the main fortified cities, which
held out for a little longer. The citadel of Babylon fell on Easter
Monday, 9 April 641; Niqyūs was abandoned and sacked on 13
May; Alexandria, after an unsuccessful siege lasting a year, was
surrendered to the Arabs by an armistice and occupied in September 642. A brief Byzantine reoccupation from the sea was finally
ended in the summer of 646.

The Caliph 'Umar, the Arab historians tell us, gave his consent
with reluctance for 'Amr's expedition to Egypt, and attempted,
too late, to withdraw it when 'Amr was already on his way.
Modern criticism has thrown doubt on his opposition to an enterprise so obviously to the advantage of the Arab conquerors. The
Byzantine bases in Egypt could threaten the new dominions of
the Arabs in Syria and Palestine, and even their homeland in
Arabia; the rich corn harvest of Egypt, on the other hand, could
supply their needs—and, indeed, regular shipments from Egypt

to the Hijaz were organized soon after the conquest. The religious and political dissensions of late Byzantine Egypt, the aftermath of the Persian conquest and Byzantine reoccupation, and the growing disaffection of the Copts all helped to prepare and ease the path of the conqueror.

For over two centuries Egypt was a province of the Islamic Empire. Its administrative centre was Fusṭāṭ, a garrison city founded by the Arabs near Babylon, and hard by the present site of Cairo. It was ruled by a series of Arab governors, appointed by the Caliphs who reigned, successively, in the Imperial capitals in Arabia, Syria, and Iraq. Nearly a millennium after the conquest of Alexander, the Hellenistic era in Egypt came to an end. The Greek language soon died out; so too, though more slowly, did Coptic, the last survival of the language of the ancient Egyptians. Coptic Christianity, already weakened by its isolation from both the Eastern and Western Churches, suffered a loss of power and vitality; its followers gradually dwindled into a minority in the land of Egypt, and even these adopted the language, though not the faith, of the conquerors. The processes began by which Egypt became predominantly a land of Muslim faith, overwhelmingly a land of Arabic speech, linked by religion and culture, by politics and commerce with the Asian heartlands of Islam.

Unlike Syria and Iraq, Egypt seems to have had no Arab inhabitants before the advent of Islam. Arab colonization began with the conquest, and was encouraged by the Umayyad Caliphs, notably by Hishām (reigned 724–43), who in 727 authorized the planned migration and settlement of several thousand Arabs of the Yemenite tribe of Qays in the Nile valley. During the eighth and ninth centuries large numbers of Arab tribesmen, mainly of Yemenite origin, migrated to Egypt, where many of them were settled on the land.

The settlement of Arabs, though the most important, was not the only instrument of Arabization. Another was the growing use of Arabic as the language of communication, culture, and government. The Arabization of government is usually said to have been initiated by 'Abd al-Malik (685–705), the pioneer of the Arab-Islamic imperial idea, and extended to Egypt by his successor al-Walīd (705–15), probably soon after his accession. The stages of the process can be traced in the many administrative papyri that have come down to us. The earliest papyri of the Islamic period are all in Greek; these decrease in numbers and disappear in the second half of the eighth century. The first known Greek–Arabic bilingual is of 643; the last of 719. The first purely Arabic papyrus is of 709, after which Arabic rapidly becomes the principal language used. Coptic papyri are relatively few, and do not deal with official business.

The use of Arabic in government offices involved the adoption of the Arabic language by the numerous Copts employed as officials. The Copts seem to have had no national feeling like that which enabled the Persians to retain their separate identity even after their conversion to Islam. Though there were several Coptic risings against the Arabs, they were for the most part spasmodic and unorganized, concerned with local grievances against oppressive tax-collectors. Conversion to Islam began during the conquest, and, though coercion was rare, proceeded rapidly during the early centuries of Islamic rule, especially after the unsuccessful risings of 829–31. In the last outbreak Arab and Copt made common cause, and suffered a common fate. In 832 the Caliph Ma'mūn visited Egypt in person—the first Caliph ever to do so. Stationing a Khurāsānī garrison in the country, he inaugurated a period of stricter and harsher rule for all the inhabitants of Egypt, under which the Arabs lost their dominant and privileged position. With the subjection of Arab and Copt alike to the hegemony of new, alien, ruling groups, the distinction between Egyptianized Arabs and Arabized Copts ceased to be significant, and the processes of assimilation were unimpeded by local rivalries or divisions. The Egyptians—even those who rejected Islam—forgot their ancient languages and adopted Arabic; the Arab settlers were absorbed into the age-old pattern and way of life of the Nile valley.

A new phase in the history of Islamic Egypt began with the arrival in Fusṭāṭ of a new governor, Aḥmad ibn Ṭūlūn, on 15 September 868. His authority was at first limited in both scope and extent; his appointment derived not from the Caliph but from his own stepfather, like himself a Central Asian Turk, to whom the Caliph had granted Egypt as an apanage. Within a few years Ibn Ṭūlūn had won effective control of all Egypt, attained full financial autonomy, created a strong army, added much of Syria to his dominions, and achieved a large measure of real political independence. On his death in 884, he was succeeded by his son Khumārawayh, in what had in effect became a hereditary and autonomous principality. Khumārawayh ruled until 895, when he was murdered, leaving a young boy as his successor. The period of weakness and struggle that followed opened the way to the reassertion of the imperial power with the entrance of Caliphal troops into Fusṭāṭ and the restoration of the direct authority of Baghdad in January 905.

It lasted for thirty years. In 935 Muḥammad ibn Tughj, the son of a Central Asian Turkish officer in the Tulunid service, came to Fusṭāṭ as governor. In 937 he received the title of Ikhshīd, by which he is usually known, from the Caliph, with virtual autonomy as ruler of Egypt. The Ikhshīd resumed and continued the policies of Ibn Ṭūlūn. By means of sound finances, a strong army, an efficient bureaucracy, and a careful foreign policy, he was able to maintain his independent authority in Egypt and even, like Ibn Ṭūlūn, to extend it to Palestine and parts of Syria. On his death in 946 he was nominally succeeded by his sons, in fact by their tutor, a brilliant and able eunuch of Nubian or Abyssinian origin, known as Abu 'l-Misk Kāfūr, 'Musky Camphor'. Much of his energy was devoted to defending Egypt from the new threat in the west—the Ismā'īlī Fatimid Caliphate established in Tunisia at the beginning of the tenth century. His death in 968 was the signal for the Fatimid armies to advance to the conquest of Egypt.

The establishment of the Tulunid state and its revival by the Ikhshidids mark a new era in Egyptian history, and the emergence of a new power in Islam. The aims of the founders of this power were limited, personal, and dynastic. They did not aim at complete separation from the Caliphate, like the Umayyad and ʿAlid dynasties that had appeared in the eighth century in Spain and Morocco. Ibn Ṭūlūn and his successors were good Sunnīs, loyal to the principles of Islamic unity; their objective was an autonomous principality under loose Caliphal suzerainty, rather than complete independence. They were not backed by any national or cultural revival, such as accompanied the parallel rise of autonomous dynasties in Iran. Ibn Ṭūlūn and the Ikhshīd were Central Asians, Kāfūr an African. Their armies consisted of Turkish, Sudanese, and Greek slaves; their art and architecture reveal the continued—indeed, growing—influence of the imperial culture of the East, of metropolitan Iraq and neighbouring Iran.

Yet, despite these limitations, the Tulunids and Ikhshidids inaugurate the separate history of Islamic Egypt. Until Aḥmad ibn Ṭūlūn, Egypt had been a subject province of a great empire, with its centre elsewhere; under him and his successors it became, for the first time since the Ptolemies, the seat of a separate military and political power, with independent policies and a growing role in the affairs of the Middle East as a whole.

The role was enormously increased with the coming of the Fatimids, who conquered Egypt in 969 and founded their new capital, Cairo, immediately after. The Fatimid Caliphs were more than rebellious or ambitious governors. They were the heads of a rival religious sect, the Ismāʿīlī Shīʿa; as such, they did not recognize even the titular supremacy of the Sunnī Abbasid Caliphs in Baghdad, but claimed themselves to be the sole rightful Caliphs of all Islam. Under the Fatimid anti-Caliphate, Egypt became not merely an independent state but the centre of a vast empire, which at its peak included North Africa, Sicily, Palestine, Syria, the African Red Sea coast, the Hijaz, and the Yemen.

The Fatimids of Cairo failed to win the final victory over their rivals in Baghdad, and from the late eleventh century the Fatimid state, subject to both internal and external pressures, fell into a decline from which it never recovered. The remoter provinces were lost, and even in Egypt the Caliphs relinquished real power to their Turkish and other alien soldiery. Finally, in 1171, a Kurdish soldier called Saladin brought the Fatimid Caliphate to an end and restored Egypt to Sunnī orthodoxy and Abbasid suzerainty. He himself created a united Syro-Egyptian kingdom and founded the Ayyubid dynasty who ruled in Egypt, as nominal vassals of the Caliph in Baghdad, until the middle of the thirteenth century.

Though Saladin was himself a Kurd, his regime was of Turkish type, and extended to Egypt the changes that had been taking place in the Seljuq dominions in South-West Asia. His successors fell under the domination of their Turkish pretorians, and in 1250, with the death of the last Ayyubid ruler of Egypt, a new regime emerged, known to scholarship, though not to contemporaries, as the Mamlūk Sultanate. The Mamlūks were bought slaves, at first predominantly of Kipchak Turkish, later of Circassian, origin, who formed a separate, privileged, yet not hereditary, ruling class. Recruitment was by purchase and importation alone. The Egyptian-born descendants of the Mamlūks were systematically excluded from this class, to which all posts of military and therefore political power were reserved—though some of them managed to achieve important positions in the related fields of administration and religion, and to make some contribution to Egyptian Islamic culture.

The Sultan who ruled in Cairo was one of the Mamlūks. In the first series of Mamlūk Sultans (1250–1382) a loose hereditary succession was followed, but under the second, Circassian, line of Sultans (1382–1517) even this limited recognition of the hereditary principle was abandoned, and the throne went to the strongest of the Mamlūk commanders. Each new Sultan was by origin an imported slave.

In the meantime great changes had been taking place. During the eleventh, twelfth, and thirteenth centuries the Islamic lands had suffered a series of shattering attacks and invasions—Crusaders from the West, Turks and Mongols from the East, Bedouin and Berbers from the unsubjugated interior—which had changed the whole pattern of life in the Middle East, and directed the development of Islamic civilization into new paths. The final catastrophe of the Mongol invasions swept away the last remnants of the Abbasid Caliphate, and made Iraq itself a province of an empire with its capital further east. In place of the older, decaying, states and societies of the Fertile Crescent, new and more vigorous states were arising among the Persians and Turks, who were taking over both the political and the cultural leadership of Islam.

Egypt now acquired a new leadership in the diminished but still important Arab world. Iraq had become a dependency of Persia, neglected and remote; Syria a disputed borderland. Egypt alone remained as a rich and populous country, unified and centralized. Her position at the south-eastern corner of the Mediterranean, athwart the land and sea routes between Europe and Asia, gave her rulers a unique opportunity and a special responsibility. It was Egypt which served as base for the wars of reconquest which in time ejected the Crusaders from the Middle East; Egypt again that provided the resources for the Mamlūks to halt the armies of the Mongol Il-Khans and to save most of the Arab world from Mongol invasion.

The Mamlūks, like other rulers of Egypt, sought to extend their sway into Arabia and Syria; unlike them, they were remarkably successful, and were able to create a powerful military empire, strong enough to withstand the double menace from East and West, and to survive for some two and a half centuries. This political longevity, unusual in Muslim history, owes much to the warlike prowess of the Turkish and Circassian Mamlūks who fought and defeated both Mongol and Crusader; it owes at least as much to the native Egyptian bureaucracy, whose skill and devotion helped to make good the political failings of their masters. A formal legitimation of the Mamlūk Sultanate as an Islamic monarchy was provided by a line of puppet Caliphs, descended from an Abbasid refugee from Baghdad, who lived in Cairo as powerless protégés of the Sultans.

The end came from the north. The invasions of Tamerlane, the misguided economic policies of the Cairo Sultans, the decay of Mamlūk society, and the discoveries of the Portuguese all helped, in different ways, to weaken the Mamlūk Empire and make it an easy victim for the Ottoman Sultan Selīm I, who in a swift campaign in 1516–17 finally destroyed the tottering Mamlūk state and brought all its territories under varying forms of Ottoman rule. Though the Mamlūk system of recruitment and training and, with it, the Mamlūk social and administrative order continued to function, Egypt now became the seat of an Ottoman pasha, with a garrison incorporating both Ottoman and Mamlūk elements. The role of Egypt as a bastion of Islam was, for the time being, finished. The rise of the new, militant, Turkish power in the north had reduced it; the incorporation of Egypt in a Turkish empire with its capital in Constantinople brought it to an end.

The eclipse of Egypt was neither as total nor as immediate as was at one time believed. Trade through the Red Sea continued during the sixteenth century, albeit in diminishing bulk, and Egypt served as the base for Ottoman naval and military expeditions to Africa and Asia, to counter the menace offered to the Islamic world by the Portuguese expansion. These expeditions, however, proved fruitless and were abandoned, and by the beginning of the seventeenth century most of the trade had been diverted elsewhere. Egypt had lost her strategic and commercial importance, as well as her independence; now an outlying province of the Ottoman Empire, she served these new champions of the Islamic cause chiefly as a source of money and supplies.

A new phase began in the eighteenth century. For some time past the rulers of Egypt had been winning increasing internal autonomy, at the expense of the decaying Ottoman imperial power. In 1760 an ambitious Mamlūk called ʿAlī Bey became effective ruler of Egypt, under Ottoman suzerainty. Consolidating his power in Egypt, he took the path trodden by so many of his predecessors, and tried to extend it, with the help of local allies and supporters, to Arabia, Palestine, and Syria. A new theme was introduced by his attempt to obtain Russian help, which was in fact provided by a Russian naval squadron operating off the Syrian coast.

The plans and ambitions of ʿAlī Bey—variously nicknamed by his contemporaries ʿAlī the Jinn and *Bulut Kapan*, 'the cloud-catcher'—came to nothing. There were others, however, to take them up, and try again. The attempts of his Mamlūk immediate successors in Egypt were cut short by the arrival in July 1798 of a French expedition commanded by General Napoleon Bonaparte. Their departure four years later opened the way to Muḥammad ʿAlī Pasha, an Ottoman soldier who was for long acclaimed as the founder of modern Egypt.

Muḥammad ʿAlī's adventures in Syria, Arabia, and elsewhere ended in failure. In Egypt, however, his political and economic policies and measures enabled him to create a stable monarchical regime, enjoying substantial independence under nominal Ottoman suzerainty. A new phase began with the British occupation of 1882, which made Egypt in effect a British dependency. Like the earlier imperial rule of the Arabs and the Turks, British power in Egypt was gradually attenuated and finally abolished, to give way to a vigorous new regime, this time of indigenous origin. The dynasty founded by Muḥammad ʿAlī ruled or reigned—as pashas, Khedives, Sultans, and finally kings—for a century and a half. Their reign ended in fact with the Egyptian revolution of 1952, in law with the proclamation of the Egyptian Republic in 1953.

Until the seventh century Egypt was an integral part of the classical Mediterranean world, joined by strong and ancient ties to Hellenism and Christendom, to Greece, Rome, and Constantinople. The Arab conquest severed these ties, swiftly and almost completely. Henceforth Egypt was part of the house of Islam, cut off by barriers of faith, language, and holy law from both Greek and Latin Christendom. Both as a province and as a power of the Muslim world, her chief ties, political, commercial, and cultural alike, were with her Muslim neighbours, and especially with the Islamic heartlands in South-West Asia. The dominant cultural influence was neither Western nor indigenous but Eastern; its directive impulses came from Mecca and Medina, from Damascus and Baghdad and other Arab and Persian cities—until in time Cairo itself became a great centre of Islamic civilization, and a source of guidance and instruction to other lands.

The external influences that helped to reshape Egypt in an Islamic mould came from various sources. In the earliest period they were purely Arab—indeed, Arabian; their contribution was fundamental—the Arabic language, the basis of the Islamic faith, the beginnings of Islamic theology and law. The transfer of the capital to Iraq initiated a phase of Eastern and more particularly of Persian influence. Individual Persians are encountered in Egypt under the patriarchal and Umayyad Caliphs. They appear for the first time in force in the Abbasid army which entered Egypt in A.D. 750, and still more in the Abbasid garrisons stationed in Egypt in the ninth century. Several governors and other high officials sent from Baghdad to Egypt also appear to have been Persians.

The influence of the imperial civilization of the Caliphate on Egypt was if anything increased, rather than decreased, by the rise of independent dynasties in the Nile valley. These were of Eastern origin, culturally if not politically dependent on the East, and anxious to emulate the style, taste, and institutions of the metropolis. Even the Fatimids, despite their Arab and North African origins and their rupture with Baghdad, did not interrupt this process. The Ismāʿīlī sect, at the head of which the Fatimids had come to power, was dominated by Persian leaders and thinkers, and retained, even after its triumph in Egypt, important links with the Persian East. The Fatimid Caliphs of Cairo may have drawn their armies from North Africa and the Sudan; they found their theologians, missionaries, and teachers among the Persian followers of the sect. The institutions of the Fatimid state as well as the teachings of the Ismāʿīlī sect reveal the continuing power of Iraqi and Persian influence and example in Egypt.

Individual Turks play an important and, indeed, dominant role in the government of Egypt from the mid ninth century onwards; Turkish contingents begin to predominate in the armed forces. The Fatimid conquest brought on a temporary interruption of the growth of Turkish power, which was resumed with the recruitment by the Fatimid Caliphs of Turkish Mamlūk troops, and the final victory of the latter over their African—Berber and negro—rivals. Turkish hegemony was carried a step further by Saladin and his Ayyubid successors, and the power of the Turkish Mamlūks increased to the point where they were able to take over the Sultanate itself. The great Mongol conquerors of the thirteenth century never entered Egypt. They were, however, held back by leaders and soldiers who had themselves come from the great northern steppes—a fact which did not escape contemporary comment. Turkish influences remained powerful through the period of the Mamlūk Sultanate; they were reinforced, albeit in a different form, by the Ottoman conquest.

The dominant and formative influences of Islamic Egypt came from the East. There were, however, some, not without importance, that came from the Islamic West—from North Africa. There were scholars and merchants as well as soldiers among the many North Africans who followed the Fatimids to Egypt, and they played, for a while, a significant though diminishing role.

Even after the fall of the Fatimids, men of North African origin continue to appear in Egypt, and occasionally achieve some celebrity.

The most potent Western influence, however, came, not from the Muslim Maghrib, but from Christian and post-Christian Europe. It began with the French expedition to Egypt in 1798; it has continued, from different sources, ever since. Egypt was the first Arab country—after Turkey the first Islamic country—to undergo the massive impact of the West, of Western power and civilization. The Egyptians were thus among the first to grapple with the immense problems of readjustment—economic and intellectual, political and social—which this impact was ultimately to pose to the Islamic world as a whole. Their ideas and actions, during the successive phases of response, reaction, and recoil, were a guide to Muslims in many lands, and gave Egypt a central position in the world of Islam, such as she had never had before.

Islam is first a religion, then a civilization and way of life; it is with religion that any examination of the role of Egypt in Islam must begin. It is no easy matter to distinguish what is specifically Egyptian in the international culture of Islam, nor to separate the 'authentic' Egyptians from those many others, from Asia and Africa, who were attracted by the opportunities and amenities of the Nile valley.

Although the main directives, during the early centuries, came from the great Islamic cultural centres in Asia, Egypt began, like every other region of Islam, to develop its own specific contribution. The first religious figure of major importance to appear in Egypt was the great jurist al-Shāfi'ī (767–820), founder of one of the four orthodox schools of Islamic law, and the pioneer of theoretical jurisprudence in Islam. Al-Shāfi'ī was born in Gaza, of Arab stock, and lived for some years in Arabia. He finally settled in Fusṭāṭ, where he spent the last years of his life, and is buried at the foot of the Muqaṭṭam hill. His tomb is still a place of pilgrimage. The distinctive Shāfiʿī school of law began in Lower Egypt, which remained one of its main centres. It soon spread to many other areas. At the present time it is followed by most Muslims in Lower Egypt, the Hijaz, East Africa, and South-East Asia, by important communities in the Fertile Crescent countries and southern Arabia, as well as minority groups in Daghistān, Central Asia, and southern India. For all of these, the Shāfiʿī schools of Egypt, and the long line of jurists who have taught in them, are a major source of guidance. Among the most famous of these were a father and son, Taqī al-Dīn (d. 1355) and Tāj al-Dīn (d. 1370) al-Subkī. The latter was the author of a standard work on the sources of law (*uṣūl al-fiqh*) and of a famous biographical dictionary of Shāfiʿī jurists from the beginnings of the school until his own day. This work, published in six volumes, is a uniquely precious source of information for the history of the religious sciences in Islam, as well as for the social history of scholarship.

While Lower Egypt followed al-Shāfiʿī, Upper Egypt adopted the school of Mālik b. Anas, another of the Arab founders of Islamic law. Though stories of Mālik's teaching in Egypt are probably apocryphal, some of his disciples seem to have established themselves there at an early date. From Egypt the Mālikī school spread to the Sudan, to almost the whole of Muslim North and West Africa, and to Muslim Sicily and Spain. Among the many great Mālikī jurists of Egyptian birth, mention may be made of Khalīl ibn Isḥāq, known as Ibn al-Jundī (d. 1374), the author of a manual of law which for centuries has been a standard textbook in all Mālikī communities.

The strict discipline of the Holy Law represents one aspect of Islam. Another is the mystical, intuitive religion of the Ṣūfīs, later modified and institutionalized in the brotherhoods known as *ṭarīqa*. One of the earliest and most famous of Muslim mystics was Dhu 'l-Nūn al-Miṣrī (*c.* 796–861). The son of a Nubian, according to some sources a freed slave, Dhu 'l-Nūn was among

the first to expound and systematize what became the characteristic Ṣūfī teachings on the mystic states and way. Ṣūfī tradition
credits him in particular with having been the first to explain the
true nature of the gnosis (*maʿrifa*). Apart from a few poems and
prayers, his mystical teachings survive only in the reports of
others.

The coming of the Fatimids opened a new era in the religious
history of Egypt. Instead of a province of Sunnī Islam, Egypt
was now the centre of an Ismāʿīlī Shīʿite Caliphate dedicated to
the overthrow of the Sunnī faith and state and the winning over
of the whole Muslim world to the Fatimid allegiance. For this
purpose the Fatimids maintained a great network of missionaries
and propagandists in all the lands of Islam from Spain to India.
At their head was the *dāʿī al duʿāt*, or chief missionary, in Cairo,
presiding over a hierarchy of religious teachers and officials. To
train them, the Fatimids established great colleges, the most
famous of which was the mosque-university of Al-Azhar, inaugurated in Cairo in 972, soon after the conquest, by the victorious
general Jawhar al-Siqillī. A series of distinguished jurists and
theologians formulated and expounded the law and doctrines of
the Ismāʿīlīs. Their works, which were lost in the Sunnī reaction
that followed the fall of the Fatimids, are only now coming to
light. Notable among them are the Tunisian Qāḍī Abū Ḥanīfa
Nuʿmān (d. 974) and the Persian theologians Ḥamīd al-Dīn al-
Kirmānī (d. *c.* 1021) and Al-Muʾayyad fi'l-Dīn al-Shīrāzī (d.
1077), all of whom lived and worked in Fatimid Cairo.

The fall of the Fatimids and the restoration of Sunnī orthodoxy
in Egypt ended all this. The Ismāʿīlī faith never seems to have
had much of a hold on the people of Egypt, and soon died out.
The Ismāʿīlī literature was lost or destroyed, notably through
the dispersion of the great Fatimid libraries ordered by Saladin
after the fall of the dynasty. The famous legend of the burning
of the Library of Alexandria by order of ʿUmar, which first appears
at about this time, was probably invented to provide a sacred

precedent for this act of vandalism. Isma'ilism survived in Persia, the Yemen, and India, where some of the classics of Fatimid religious literature were preserved by the sectaries; Egypt returned to orthodoxy, and Al-Azhar, made over to the Sunnīs, entered on its long career as a centre for the formulation and dissemination of orthodox doctrine, serving not only Egypt but a widening range of countries from which students came to sit at the feet of the Egyptian masters.

A new feature of post-Fatimid Egypt was the growth and multiplication of the dervish brotherhoods. Most of these were introduced from Asia and Africa; some, however, were founded or received their characteristic form in Egypt. One of the best known of these was the Aḥmadiyya or Badawiyya order, founded by Aḥmad al-Badawī (d. 1276). A native of Morocco, al-Badawī settled in Ṭanṭā, Egypt, in about 1236. His tomb there is still an object of veneration. Other Egyptian orders or sub-orders include the Burhāmiyya or Dasūqiyya, founded by Ibrāhīm al-Dasūqī (thirteenth century), the Bayyūmiyya, founded by 'Ali al-Bayyumī (1696–1769), and the Sha'rāwiyya, founded by the Ṣūfī polygraph Abu'l-Mawāhib 'Abd al-Wahhāb al-Sha'rāwī or Sha'rānī (1492–1565).

The Egyptian contribution to classical Arabic poetry and belles-lettres is relatively small. Though some of the great poets of South-West Asia visited or even settled in Egypt, few native Egyptians are reckoned among the first rank of Arabic writers. An outstanding exception is the Cairene 'Umar ibn al-Fāriḍ (1182–1235), 'universally acclaimed as the greatest Arabic mystic poet and the only one who can challenge the great Persian mystics'.[1] Another poet, Sharaf al-Dīn Muḥammad al-Buṣīrī (1213–c. 1296), of Berber origin and Egyptian birth, is known only for one poem, but that one is perhaps the most famous in all Arabic literature, if not in all Islam. Known as the 'Mantle-Ode', *qaṣīdat al-burda*, from a legend according to which the

[1] H. A. R. Gibb, *Arabic Literature*, 2nd ed., Oxford, 1963, p. 129.

Prophet cured the poet of a paralytic stroke by throwing his mantle over him, Buṣīrī's eulogy of the Prophet is revered as possessing miraculous powers; it has been translated into many languages, and has formed the subject of more than ninety commentaries, in Arabic, Persian, Turkish, and even in Berber. Among the mass of lesser poets mention may be made of Ibn Sanā' al-Mulk (d. 1211), who introduced the Spanish-Arab *muwashshaḥa*, a kind of strophic verse, to Egypt and the East, and composed an important treatise on the history and technique of this new poetic genre, and Bahā al-Dīn Zuhayr (1185–1258), a court poet of charm and simplicity whom E. H. Palmer, his English translator, compared to Herrick.

The Egyptian contribution in another field, that of narrative literature, is richer and more important. The Egyptian in all periods has loved a good story, and excelled in telling it. The development of the anecdote, the tale, the apologue, and the romance in medieval Arabic literature owes much to Egyptian authors, as do the novel and the short story in modern times. One of the first works of this kind was the *Kitāb al-Mukāfa'a*, the 'Book of Recompense', by Aḥmad ibn Yūsuf ibn al-Dāya (d. 951), a scribe in the service of the government. The book consists of seventy-one stories, designed to illustrate the principle that both good and bad deeds find their due recompense, and told with a simplicity, a realism, and a sensitiveness that can still appeal directly to modern readers. Among many later collections, the most famous is the *Mustaṭraf fi kull shay' mustaẓraf* of Muḥammad ibn Aḥmad al-Abshīhī (or Ibshayhī) (d. 1416), a collection of anecdotes selected and retold with great skill and grouped around a variety of themes.

Another kind of narrative is the anonymous popular romance, written for the most part in semi-colloquial language, and not ranked, by Arab taste and judgement, as serious literature. Such, for example, are the sagas of Arab chivalry and Muslim holy war, containing old Arabian material and gradually developed during the wars against the Byzantines and Crusaders. Many of these contain Egyptian as well as Asian-Arab material; some of them, such as the romances of Sultan Baybars and his wars against the Christians, and of Sayf ibn Dhī Yazan and his wars in Arabia and Ethiopia, are, in their present form, of unmistakable Egyptian authorship. This tradition continued after the Ottoman conquest, and elements of popular romance may be found in some of the more or less historical writings of the Ottoman period.

By far the best known of these works, in the Western world at least, is the famous collection of tales known as *Alf Layla wa Layla*, the 'Thousand and One Nights'. Of Persian and perhaps ultimately Indian origin, this collection was translated into Arabic at an early date, and enriched with many new tales of Arab and Islamic provenance. The final version of the work, on which all modern translations are based, is Egyptian; many of the individual stories too are obviously Egyptian, including some of the most famous—such as the stories of Maʿrūf the Cobbler, of Abū Sīr and Abū Kīr, of Jawdar, and of the immortal Aladdin ('Alā' al-Dīn) and the Wonderful Lamp.

In the field of scholarship—especially of philology and history—the contribution made by Egyptian authors to Arabic literature is of major importance. The beginnings of Arabic philology in Egypt are ascribed to Ibn Wallād (d. 910) and Ibn al-Naḥḥās (d. 948). They are the first of a long series of distinguished scholars, whose work is central in the development of classical Arabic philology. Among the best known are Ibn al-Ḥājib (1174–1249), the son of a Kurdish chamberlain in the Ayyubid service, who wrote a series of classical works on grammar, as well as on prosody and law; Ibn Hishām (1308–60), a Koranic exegetist and the author of several major works on Arabic syntax; al-Damīrī (1344–1405), author of the most important work of Arabic philology on animals; and the polymath Jalāl al-Dīn al-Suyūṭī (1445–1505), the author of several hundred books dealing with almost every branch of classical Islamic scholarship.

It is in the writing of history that Egyptian scholarship made its greatest and most characteristic contribution to the common culture of Islam. The first great historian of Muslim Egypt was Ibn ʿAbd al-Ḥakam (d. 871), son of an eminent Mālikī jurist, and one of a family of distinguished scholars. His pioneer work on the Muslim conquest of Egypt and its aftermath inaugurates the long and rich tradition of Arabic historiography in Egypt. Other early historians include al-Kindī (897–961), who wrote histories of the governors and of the judges of Egypt, and Ibn al-Dāya (d. 951) and al-Balawī (tenth century), the authors of works on the history of the Tulunid dynasty. The works of the historians of the Fatimid Caliphate—such as Ibn Zawlaq (d. 978), al-Muṣabbiḥī (d. 1029), and Ibn al-Ṣayrafī (d. 1147)—are for the most part lost, though some of their material survives in the form of quotations in works of later periods.

It is in the Mamlūk period that Egyptian historiography achieves its fullest development, in the long series of authors whose vast and numerous works make late-medieval Egypt, potentially, one of the best-known regions and periods of pre-modern Islamic history. Some of these—like the Tunisian Ibn Khaldūn (1332–1406) and the Turk al-ʿAynī (1361–1451)—were immigrants who settled in Egypt; most were of Egyptian birth. The fourteenth and fifteenth centuries are particularly rich in historical and related writings, such as the works of Ibn al-Furāt (1334–1405), al-Maqrīzī (1346–1442), Ibn Ḥajar al-ʿAskalānī (1372–1449), Ibn Taghrī-Berdī (d. 1474), and al-Sakhāwī (d. 1497). The last historian of the Mamlūk Sultanate, Ibn Iyās (1448–1524), himself witnessed and described the Ottoman conquest of Egypt. Under Ottoman rule, Egyptian historiography did not entirely die out. Several minor chronicles were written, and one major one—that of Jabartī (d. 1825), the last great Egyptian historian in the traditional style. Linked with the historical literature of Muslim Egypt is a vast body of writings of biographical, topographical, geographical, and administrative content which, though mainly concerned with medieval Egypt, also contain much that is relevant to other times and places. The vast universal chronicles and encyclopedias of Mamlūk Egypt are still among our major sources of information on medieval Islamic history, government, and society.

In science as in letters, Egypt exerted a powerful attraction. Among the many scientists from other countries who found a home and a career in Egypt, mention may be made of the Iraqi physicist and mathematician Ibn al-Haytham, known in the West as Alhazen (d. *c.* 1039), author of a famous work on optics; the Spanish-Jewish physician and philosopher Ibn Maymūn or Maimonides (1135–1204); and the Syrian physician Ibn al-Nafīs (*c.* 1210–88), who discovered the lesser circulation of the blood. Though the first impact of Greek science and medicine on the Islamic world and the first great response to them occurred in the East, natives or residents of Egypt played a not inconsiderable part in the further development and elaboration of Islamic science. Such were the physicians Isḥāq al-Isrā'īlī, known in the West as Isaac Judaeus (855–955), and Ibn Riḍwān (d. *c.* 1067); the engineer Qaysar ibn al-Musāfir (d. 1251); the pharmacologist al-Kohen b. al-'Aṭṭār (thirteenth century). The two major classical Arabic works on the history of science are both of Egyptian provenance; both are biographical dictionaries, the one of physicians, scientists, and philosophers, by Ibn al-Qiftī (d. 1248), the other of physicians only, by the Syrian-born Ibn Abī Uṣaybi'a (d. 1270). The latter work, containing more than 600 biographies, is our major source for the history of medicine in medieval Islam.

In the arts, as in religion and literature, it is difficult to set apart what is specifically Egyptian in the international culture of Islam. The earliest surviving mosque is that founded by the Arab conqueror 'Amr b. al-'Āṣ in 643, but numerous subsequent repairs and reconstructions have left little of the original structure, which seems to have been designed on the model of the Great Mosque of Damascus. The first independent Muslim ruler in Egypt, Aḥmad ibn Ṭūlūn, built a magnificent mosque which, despite the ravages of time, is still one of the finest monuments of the capital. The structure and decoration of this mosque, like other surviving specimens of Tulunid art, such as woodwork and pottery, suggest a conscious attempt to imitate the art of Samarra in Iraq—the seat, at that time, of the Caliphate and thus the home of what has been called the Imperial style.

The art of the Fatimids seems to have suffered, though to a lesser extent, the same fate as their literature, and regrettably little remains of what seems to have been a brilliant and creative period. The major Fatimid mosques are al-Azhar (972), al-Ḥākim (1003), al-Aqmar (1125), al-Ṣāliḥ Ṭalā'i' (1160), and the mosque, with tomb and sanctuary, of al-Juyūshī (1085). The Fatimids also built a number of domed mausolea, notable among them those of al-Ja'farī and of Sayyida 'Ātika, both of the twelfth century. The ornamentation of these buildings, in particular, marks an important step in the development of the decorative arts in Islam. Fatimid architects resumed the Tulunid tradition, with some innovations imported from North Africa and some new features, such as the so-called Persian arch and the stalactite pendentive which reveal direct Persian influence. These became permanent features of Egyptian mosque architecture. Persian and Mesopotamian influence is strong too in the minor arts, including woodwork, pottery, textiles, metalwork, and—a Fatimid speciality—objects carved in rock crystal now scattered in the treasuries of many European churches. An important contribution was also made by Coptic artists and craftsmen who helped to transmit the legacy of Hellenistic and Christian Egypt to Islam, and played a significant part in the development of the characteristic Fatimid style. This style, with its harmonious blending of Eastern, Western, and indigenous Egyptian elements, was to exercise a wide influence in the Islamic world, notably in North Africa and Spain.

An important Ayyubid innovation was in military architecture, where the replacement of Byzantine by West European models reflects the influence of the Crusaders' castles in Palestine and possibly the employment of crusading captives. Other Ayyubid changes were the replacement of Kūfī by Naskhī writing for decoration and the introduction from the East of the cruciform *madrasa*. This developed local variants in Egypt, including minarets, rare on these buildings in the East. Under the Mamlūks, from whose time most surviving Muslim monuments in Egypt come, the *madrasa* replaced the earlier pillared congregational mosque as the most usual religious construction, and was often combined with the domed tomb (*turba*). A superb example is the combined tomb–mosque–*madrasa* of Sultan Ḥasan (1356). Muslim architecture is most original in decoration rather than construction, and it is perhaps in this elaborate, intricate, and stylized ornamentation that Islamic art achieves its most characteristic expression.

Egypt was one of the first countries to be conquered by the advancing Muslim Arabs, and almost from the beginning played a vital part in the further expansion and development of Islam The corn of Egypt was sent across the Red Sea to feed the Hijaz and its holy cities; the ports of Egypt, with those of Syria, were the home of the new Muslim naval power in the Mediterranean; the Nile valley and delta were the base from which the armies and the faith of Islam drove westward and southward, far into Africa. At first an outlying province of the Empire in the East, Egypt soon became an independent centre of Muslim power and culture, with a role of increasing importance in the later Middle Ages.

Egypt was never the centre of the whole world of Islam, as Arabia, Syria, and Iraq had been in their successive days of greatness, nor did her writers and artists equal that brilliant flowering of creative genius, in Persia and Arab Asia, that marked the classical age of Islamic culture. Her role was rather one of retrenchment and conservation, in some ways analogous to that of Byzantium in the Roman and Christian world. When the Islamic Empire crumbled under the attack of barbarian invaders from East and

West, the rulers of Egypt, though themselves often of barbarian origin, stood firm, and saved the Nile valley from both Mongol and Crusader. In the East, the great conquests and migrations of the steppe peoples, continuing from the tenth to the fourteenth centuries, destroyed the old order, and prepared the way for a new political and social order and a new Islamic culture, expressed mainly in the Persian and Turkish languages. In Egypt, despite great and powerful influences from the East, the older order survived, and Islamic culture in the Arabic form entered on its long-drawn-out silver age. Mamlūk soldiers and Egyptian administrators enabled the state to survive until and in a sense even beyond the Ottoman conquest in 1517; Egyptian scholars preserved, elaborated, and explained the rich heritage of classical Arabic civilization. The Arab world was no longer the centre of Islam, but Egypt had become the centre of the Arab world.

BERNARD LEWIS

SELECT BIBLIOGRAPHY

The encyclopaedia of Islam, ed. by M. Th. Houtsma and others, 4 vols. Leiden and London, 1913–36. Supplement, 1938. 2nd ed., 1954 and following.

The legacy of Islam, ed. by T. W. Arnold and A. Guillaume, London, 1931.

A. J. BUTLER, *The Arab conquest of Egypt and the last thirty years of the Roman dominion*, Oxford, 1902.

K. A. C. CRESWELL, *The Muslim architecture of Egypt*, i, . . . *933–1171*, Oxford, 1952.

M. S. DIMAND, *A handbook of Muhammadan decorative arts*, 3rd ed., New York, 1958.

H. A. R. GIBB, *Arabic literature: an introduction*, 2nd ed., Oxford, 1963.
—— *Mohammedanism: an historical survey*, 2nd ed., London, 1953.

P. M. HOLT (ed.), *Political and social change in modern Egypt: historical studies from the Ottoman conquest to the United Arab Republic*, London, 1968.

S. LANE-POOLE, *A history of Egypt in the middle ages*, 4th ed., London, 1925.

B. LEWIS, *The Arabs in history*, 4th ed., London, 1966.

J. SCHACHT, *An introduction to Islamic law*, Oxford, 1964.

INDEXES

By W. J. Tait

1. GENERAL

Entries in inverted commas indicate discussions of etymologies.

2. EGYPTIAN

3. COPTIC

4. GREEK

PLATES

PLATE 1

The Egyptian Hall, Piccadilly (from a print of 1828)

PLATE 2

Canina's Egyptian portico in the gardens of the Villa Borghese

PLATE 3

The so-called metrological relief in the Ashmolean Museum, Oxford

PLATE 4

Dyad of Menkaurē (Mycerinus) illustrating the typical stance of a pharaonic figure, and *b* a statue of Antinous from Hadrian's villa at Tivoli

PLATE 5

a

b

An Egyptian lion of Nectanebo I from the *Iseum Campense*, and *b* a Cosmati adaptation in the portal of SS. Apostoli, Rome

PLATE 6

Pedestal in imperial porphyry in the form of a sistrum handle,
with a figure of Bes supporting a Hathor-head capital

PLATE 7

Mummy of a little Roman girl of the second century A.D., found on the outskirts of Rome

PLATE 8

Fresco from Herculaneum, depicting a ceremony before an Isiac shrine

PLATE 9

The front of the Metternich stela, with a figure of
Horus upon the crocodiles

PLATE 10

Magical figure of Djedhor 'the saviour', supporting a stela of Horus upon the crocodiles and set in a pedestal with basin

PLATE 11

a

b

c

d

Some examples of magical gems, including *a–b* two gynaecological amulets

PLATE 12

a

b

A Judaeo-Christian-Gnostic amulet, and *b* an example of a familiar
pagan type depicting a pantheistic deity

PLATE 13

Quattrocento representation of Hermes Trismegistus presenting laws to the Egyptians, on a pavement in Siena cathedral

PLATE 14

a   *b*

The obelisk of Sety I in the Piazza del Popolo, Rome, which formerly stood in
the *Circus Maximus*, and *b* that of Domitian in the Piazza Navona, set up originally in the *Iseum Campense*

PLATE 15

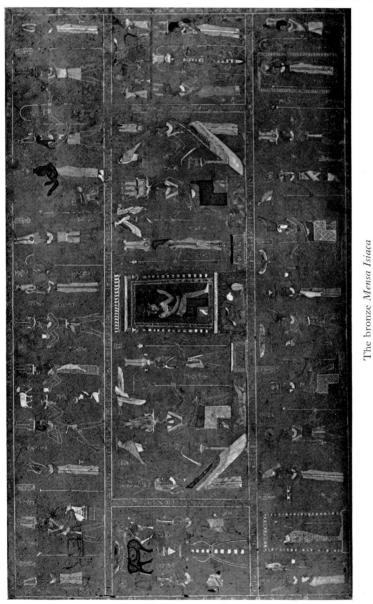

The bronze *Mensa Isiaca*

PLATE 16

AMSTELODAMI, *Sumptibus* ANDREÆ FRISII, MDCLXIX.

Frontispiece to the 1669 edition of Pignoria's work on the *Mensa Isiaca*

PLATE 17

Semitic tribesmen portrayed in a Middle Kingdom tomb (from a copy of Prisse d'Avennes)

PLATE 18

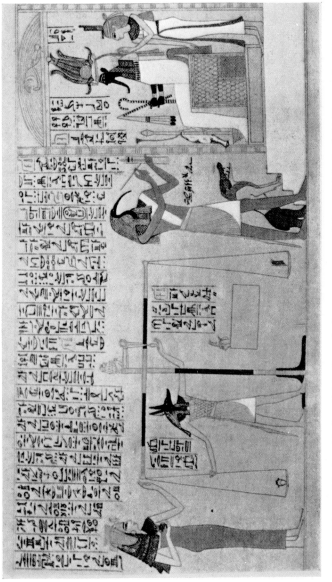

The weighing of the heart before Osiris, from the funerary papyrus of Queen Makarē of the Twenty-first Dynasty

PLATE 19

a   *b*

A Roman statue of Isis in *bigio* marble, and an Egyptian bronze of Isis with Horus

PLATE 20

Head of Serapis in imperial porphyry

PLATE 21

Ivory carving of the Alexandrian Isis, from the *ambo* of Henry II
at Aix-la-Chapelle

PLATE 22

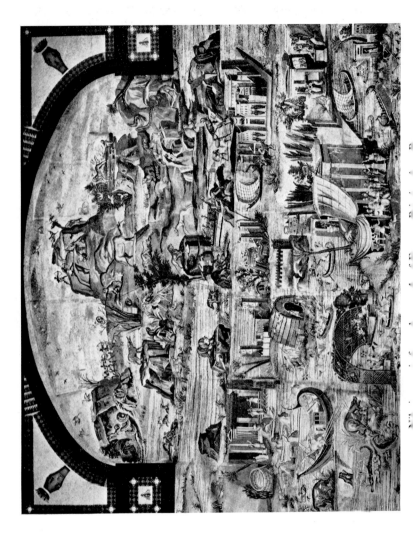

PLATE 23

Madonna and Child, with John the Baptist and St. Onnuphrius, by a follower of
Cristoforo Scaco, 1507

PLATE 24

Group of tetrarchs (*c.* A.D. 300) in imperial porphyry, formerly at Acre and
now in the façade of S. Marco, Venice